Trade Strategies for Development

Trade Strategies for Development

Papers of the Ninth Cambridge Conference on Development Problems, September 1972

Cambridge University
Overseas Studies Committee

Edited by
Paul Streeten

A HALSTED PRESS BOOK

John Wiley & Sons
New York — Toronto

382.09
C178

© Overseas Studies Committee 1973

First published in the United Kingdom 1973 by
THE MACMILLAN PRESS LTD

Published in the U.S.A.
by Halsted Press, a Division of
John Wiley & Sons, Inc., New York

Library of Congress Cataloging in Publication Data
Cambridge Conference on Development Problems, 9th,
   1972.
   Trade strategies for development.
   "A Halsted Press book."
      1. Commercial policy—Congresses. 2. Commerce—
Congresses. 3. Economic development—Congresses.
1. Streeten, Paul, ed. II. Cambridge. University.
Overseas Studies Committee. III. Title.
HF1410.C25   1972   382'.09172'4   73–8146
ISBN 0–470–83327–0

Printed in Great Britain

Contents

Foreword

Trade Strategies for Development is the most recent of a long series of conference topics in Cambridge, among them *Local Government in Africa* (1961), *Training for Development* (1962), *African Development Planning* (1963), *Industrialisation in Developing Countries* (1964), *Overcoming Obstacles to Development* (1965), *International Cooperation in Aid* (1966), *The Rural Base for National Devlopment* (1968), and *Prospects for Employment Opportunities in the Nineteen Seventies* (1970).[1]

Sponsored by the Cambridge University Overseas Studies Committee, all these earlier conferences were held under the stimulating chairmanship of Professor Ronald Robinson, formerly Smuts Reader in Cambridge University and Fellow of St John's College.

These conferences have been intended to provide an opportunity for those from both developed and less developed countries concerned with the intellectual exploration of common problems to meet in conference those involved with the more practical aspects of development policy and administration. Financial and administrative assistance has been generously provided by what is now the Overseas Development Administration of the Foreign and Commonwealth Office and in earlier days by the then Ministry of Overseas Development, largely on the initiative of the late Sir Andrew Cohen.

On this occasion the Overseas Studies Committee invited Paul Streeten, Warden of Queen Elizabeth House and Director of the Institute of Commonwealth Studies at Oxford, to take the chair at the conference and to edit the papers which are here presented

---

[1] Reports of these conferences have been published on behalf of the Overseas Studies Committee by Her Majesty's Stationery Office. Ronald Robinson, now Beit Professor of the History of the British Commonwealth at Oxford, subsequently edited the series as a book, *Developing the Third World: The Experience of the Nineteen-Sixties* (C.U.P., 1971).

in published form. That Paul Streeten responded to this invitation with characteristic enterprise and imagination will be apparent. The first duty of the Committee is to acknowledge with gratitude the magnitude of his contribution to the conference and the report.

Professor Edmund Leach, Provost of King's College, who had kindly accepted the invitation to act as Chairman of the Overseas Studies Committee during the absence on sabbatical leave of Mr B. H. Farmer, was much concerned with the organisation of the conference and was principal host during the proceedings. The Committee are deeply grateful for these services.

Once more the Overseas Development Administration gave generous financial support, and the Committee are also particularly grateful to those from the Ministry who provided such efficient and helpful services in the secretariat during the conference. Thanks are also due to Mr Bruce Wickham, who was appointed Conference Secretary, and his secretary Miss Yvonne Onsorge; on their shoulders lay the responsibility of all the burdensome administrative and organisational processes over the many months which preceded the conference. Special thanks are due to Jonathan Lewis and his team from the Zebra Trust who helped so much in the organisation of social events, tours, and entertainment for our visitors.

The Overseas Studies Committee are also grateful not only to those from among its own members who participated in the work of the Steering Committee, but also to those from outside the University: Mr R. A. Browning, Mr Hugh Corbet, Dr J. M. Healey and Mr P. H. Johnston, C.M.G.

The Committee wishes to thank the Vice-Chancellor of the University, Professor W. A. Deer, M.A., Ph.D., F.R.S., for receiving the conference members on arrival and opening the proceedings, and Baroness Tweedsmuir of Belhelvie, Minister of State at the Foreign and Commonwealth Office, for entertaining them at a reception on the final day and for her closing address that evening.

To the Master and Fellows of St John's College and all members of the College staff the Committee is very grateful for the use of the college facilities and the admirable services provided.

The success of the group discussions which preceded the various plenary sessions of the conference was due to those who kindly consented to act as group chairmen. These were His Excellency the Hon. H. B. Malmgren, Professor G. Ohlin, Dr Felipe Pazos, His Excellency the Hon. A. I. Phiri, Professor H. W. Singer, and Mr R. N. Wood.

Finally, the Committee wish to extend their thanks to the Secretary/Rapporteurs who so vigorously undertook the responsibility of recording the conclusions of the group discussions and whose contribution to the success of the conference as a whole was notable. These were: Mr G. A. Hughes, Mr M. G. Kuczinski, Mr D. M. G. Newbery, Mr N. R. Norman, Mrs S. E. Paine, and Mr M. J. Sharpston.

For the papers which follow our gratitude naturally is due to the contributors who responded to our invitation with such enthusiasm amid so many other preoccupations.[2] It should be noted that the views expressed in these papers are personal, and in the case of those who hold official or institutional positions should not be interpreted as necessarily expressing the views of the governments, international agencies, or other institutions they represented.

PAUL HOWELL
Secretary,
July 1973   *Cambridge University Overseas Studies Committee*

---

[2] Mr Mahbub ul Haq was unfortunately unable to attend the Conference owing to inescapable official commitments, but his paper is included among the others as it is particularly relevant and valuable.

Notes on the Contributors

OJETUNJI ABOYADE is Professor of Economics and Dean of the Faculty of Social Sciences at the University of Ibadan. He studied at Hull University and Cambridge, and joined the Economics Department at Ibadan in 1960. He has served the Nigerian government in various policy advisory roles, with particular reference to development planning, and has held visiting posts at the University of Michigan and the Economic Development Institute of the World Bank.

BELA BALASSA is Professor of Political Economy at the Johns Hopkins University, Baltimore, Md, and a Consultant to the International Bank for Reconstruction and Development. He studied at the University of Budapest and until 1956 was on the planning staff of the Hungarian Construction Trust. After emigrating to the United States he studied economics at Yale, where he taught from 1959 to 1967. He has acted as consultant to the United States government and various United Nations agencies, and lectured at universities in Europe, Japan and Latin America. His publications include *The Hungarian Experience in Economic Planning*, *The Theory of Economic Integration*, *Trade Prospects for Developing Countries*, *Trade Liberalisation among Industrial Countries: Objectives and Alternatives* and *The Structure of Protection in Developing Countries*, together with numerous articles in the fields of international economy, economic planning, economic theory, comparative economic systems and economic development.

GERARD CURZON is Professor of International Economics at the Graduate Institute of International Studies, University of Geneva. He is also on the staff of the Centre for Education in Industrial Management (CEI), Geneva, and editor of the *Journal of World Trade Law*. An engineer by training, he later studied economics at the London School of Economics and at Paris, Basle and Geneva. He has been visiting Professor of International Economics at the Graduate School of Business, University of Chicago, and the School of International Affairs, Carleton University, Ottawa. His main publication is *Multilateral Commercial Diplomacy*, and he has published other works on East–West trade and the institutional arrangements for monetary and commercial co-operation.

VICTORIA CURZON, his wife, is Lecturer in International Economics at the Institut Universitaire d'Études Européennes, Geneva. She is the co-author of *The European Free Trade Association and the Crisis of European Integration*, and with her husband has contributed to a number of essays on international trade policy issues. Her full-length study, *The Essentials of Integration: The EFTA Experience* (Macmillan), is to be published shortly.

The Curzons have published jointly: *After the Kennedy Round*, *Hidden Barriers to International Trade* and *Global Assault on Non-Tariff Barriers*.

SIDNEY DELL has since 1964 been Director of the New York Office of UNCTAD. He was educated at Oxford, and after service in the Second World War worked as an economist at the Board of Trade, London. Since 1947 he has held various posts at the United Nations, including that of Assistant Director in the Bureau of General Economic Research and Policies. His publications include *Trade Blocs and Common Markets*, *A Latin American Common Market?* and *The Inter-American Development Bank: A Study in Development Financing*.

JOHN H. DUNNING is Professor of Economics and Head of the Department of Economics at the University of Reading. He was educated at the City of London College, University College London, and the University of Southampton. He is a partner in the Economists' Advisory Group, has acted as economic adviser to the Board of Trade, the National Economic Development Office and UNCTAD, and has served on several government committees. He was visiting Professor of Economics at the University of Western Ontario and the University of California in 1968–9, and his publications include *Studies in International Investment, An Economic Study of the City of*

London (joint author) and various other books and articles on regional and urban economics and international investment.

MAHBUB UL HAQ is Director of the Policy Planning and Program Review Department of the World Bank. He studied economics at Government College, Lahore, King's College, Cambridge, and Yale. He has served on the Pakistan National Planning Commisssion as Chief of the Perspective Planning Division and Chief Economist, and acted as consultant to the Economic Commission for Asia and the Far East. He has held previous posts in the World Bank as Visiting Lecturer at the Economic Development Institute and Programming Adviser to the Programming and Budgeting Department. Among his publications are *Deficit Financing in Pakistan* (with Mrs Khadija Haq), *The Strategy of Economic Planning* and numerous articles on economic development.

SEEV HIRSCH is Dean of the Leon Recanati Graduate School of Business Administration, University of Tel-Aviv. He was educated at the Hebrew University, Jerusalem and at the Harvard University Graduate School of Business Administration. After completing his doctorate at Harvard in 1965, he joined Tel-Aviv University.

His publications include *Location of Industry and International Competitiveness* and *The Export Performance of Six Manufacturing Industries: A Comparative Study of Denmark, Holland and Israel.*

NURUL ISLAM is Deputy Chairman of the Bangladesh Planning Commission, Dacca. He obtained his doctorate in Economics at Harvard, and was thereafter Professor of Economics at Dacca University and from 1964 to 1971 Director of the Institute of Development Economics in pre-partition Pakistan. He has held visiting professorships at the Economic Development Institute of the World Bank and at Yale.

HARRY G. JOHNSON, a Canadian citizen, is currently Professor of Economics at both the London School of Economics and the University of Chicago, and recently Irving Fisher Visiting Professor at Yale University. Educated at Toronto, Cambridge and Harvard universities, he was Lecturer in Economics at

Notes on the Contributors

Cambridge and Fellow of King's College 1950–6, Professor of
Economic Theory at Manchester 1956–9, has been Professor of
Economics at Chicago since 1959 and Professor at the L.S.E.
since 1966. He is the author, among many other works, of
Economic Policies toward Less Developed Countries.

TIM JOSLING is a Reader in Economics, specialising in agricultural economics, at the London School of Economics. He
is a consultant to the Trade Policy Research Centre, and is also
engaged on work for the U.K. Home-Grown Cereals Authority
and the F.A.O. He studied at the University of London,
Guelph University (Canada) and Michigan State University,
where he was engaged on the recent study on the implications
for American agriculture of the enlargement of the E.E.C.
His publications include *Interdependence among Agricultural
and Other Sectors of the Canadian Economy, The United Kingdom
Grains Agreement: An Economic Analysis* and *Agriculture and
Britain's Trade Policy Dilemma*, together with contributions to
leading journals in the field of agricultural economics.

HARALD B. MALMGREN, presently Deputy Special Repre-
sentative for Trade Negotiations, Executive Office of the
President, Washington, D.C., has written widely on inter-
national economic problems. He has also been a Professorial
Lecturer at Cornell, Georgetown and the Johns Hopkins
School for Advanced International Studies, and his most
recent book is *International Economic Peacekeeping in Phase
II.*

GERALD M. MEIER is Professor of International Economics at
Stanford University. After studying at Reed College (Oregon),
Oxford (as a Rhodes Scholar) and Harvard, he taught at
Williams College (Mass.), Wesleyan University (Conn.) and as
Visiting Professor at Yale before taking up his present appoint-
ment in 1963. He is the author of *Economic Development,
International Trade and Development, Leading Issues in Develop-
ment Economics, International Economics of Development* and
Problems of Trade Policy.

I. G. PATEL is Secretary of the Department of Economic

Affairs in the Indian Ministry of Finance, and Deputy Administrator of the United Nations Development Programme. He was educated in India, Cambridge and Harvard, and was formerly Professor of Economics at the University of Baroda and Deputy (later Chief) Economic Adviser to the Ministry of Finance. He has both served with, and represented India at, the International Monetary Fund.

FELIPE PAZOS is Economic Adviser to the Inter-American Development Bank. After studying at the University of Havana, he was successively Commercial Attaché to the Cuban Embassy in Washington, Chief of the Latin American Division of the I.M.F., President of the National Bank of Cuba and a member of the Committee of Nine of the Organisation of American States. He is the author of *Inflation and Exchange Instability in Latin America*, *Economic Development and Financial Stability*, *Private versus Public Foreign Investment*, *The Role of International Movements of Private Capital in Promoting Development* and *Chronic Inflation in Latin America*.

IGNACY SACHS, born in Warsaw, is Director of Studies of the École Pratique des Hautes Études and Director of the Research Group on Development Strategies, Paris. His main books are *Foreign Trade and Economic Development of Underdeveloped Countries, Patterns of Public Sector in Underdeveloped Economies* and *La Découverte du Tiers Monde*.

FRANCES STEWART worked as an economist in the National Economic Development Office and the Department of Economic Affairs. From 1967 to 1969 she was a Lecturer in Economics at the University of Nairobi. She is now a Senior Research Officer at the Institute of Commonwealth Studies, Oxford, working on the questions of technology and development.

PAUL STREETEN is Warden of Queen Elizabeth House, Director of the Institute of Commonwealth Studies and a Fellow of Balliol College, Oxford. He was Professor of Economics at the University of Sussex, a Fellow of the Institute of Development Studies and Deputy Director-General of Economic Planning at the Ministry of Overseas Development. His publications include *Economic Integration, Value in Social Theory, Unfashionable Economics, Commonwealth Policy in a Global Context, Diversification and Development: The Case of Coffee, Aid to Africa* and *The Frontiers of Development Studies.*

JAN TUMLIR is Director of the Trade Intelligence Division of GATT and has been a member of the Secretariat since 1964. He was born in Czechoslovakia, studied economics at Yale and taught there as Instructor and Assistant Professor of Economics from 1958 to 1964.

1 Trade Strategies for Development: Some Themes for the Seventies[1]

Paul Streeten

DIRECTOR, INSTITUTE OF COMMONWEALTH
STUDIES, AND FELLOW, BALLIOL COLLEGE,
UNIVERSITY OF OXFORD

It would be difficult and unrewarding to attempt to summarise the discussions that took place at the Cambridge Conference on Development in September 1972. Nor would it be of any interest to distil a consensus, which would be vacuous and platitudinous. Instead I shall attempt to bring out a few themes that emerged at the Conference and, where appropriate, to define the *dissensus*, not the *consensus*, in order to highlight the issues.

I shall not attempt to bring out all the themes, important though many of them are. Thus we were all concerned with the question as to how the developing countries would be affected by the conflicts of the trade and payments relations between the large industrial countries. In particular, many saw the danger of the formation of new 'north–south' blocs for some developing countries. Protectionism on a national scale presents enough problems; but super-protectionism presents not only bigger but also different problems which are well analysed in Sidney Dell's paper. Regional zones of influence are not likely to have any of the advantages claimed for them. They do not make for good political relations, they do not guarantee markets, secure raw material supply or guarantee the sanctity of private foreign investment. A study of the history of the relations between the United States and Latin America, Britain and some Commonwealth countries, and France and

Algeria, shows clearly the difficulties and frustrations of regional north–south zones of influence.

Again, much of the discussion was concerned with commodity trade in primary products from which the developing countries still derive four-fifths of their export earnings. The fact that these issues, and particularly the question of trade in agricultural products, are not discussed in this chapter means neither that they were not fully discussed at the Conference, nor that they were not considered important.

If policy-makers and practical men reach agreement by blurring distinctions, avoiding clear language and defining terms in such a manner that they can be interpreted in different ways by different men, scholars resolve disagreement by clear formulations, drawing distinctions where there were none before, not permitting different interpretations, and outlining sharply the precise reasons for their disagreement.[2] It is not the purpose of this chapter to reach an agreed formula for action.

INWARD- AND OUTWARD-LOOKING POLICIES

At an early stage, many participants felt that these terms were not very helpful. In spite of this, they were used or kept at the back of our minds. One view that crystallised in the course of the discussion suggests that the distinction may be of some value. The static theory of comparative advantage is, of course, neutral between the two strategies: it bids us allocate resources between domestic activity and trade according to comparative advantage, so as to maximise the gains from trade.[3] Outward- and inward-looking must therefore refer to something other than the principle of comparative advantage.

One important difference is that the strategies embrace policies for factors of production, as well as commodity trade. Outward-looking policies encourage not only free trade but also the free movement of capital, workers, enterprises and students, a welcome to the multinational enterprise and an open system of communications. If it does not imply *laissez-faire*, it certainly implies *laissez-passer*.

But more fundamental than the effects on the allocation of resources resulting from the movement of goods and factors of production are the indirect, sociological, psychological and institutional effects to which 'outward-looking' policies refer. The early advocates of free trade, and most explicitly J. S. Mill, did not have a static theory of allocation in mind. They wished to bring out the educational effects of openness: the receptivity to new ideas and to new techniques; the stimulus to the creation of new wants, new incentives and new rewards; the growth of new forms of organisation. Adam Smith, Malthus, Ricardo and especially J. S. Mill[4] believed in the possibility of learning by trading. The outward-lookers then believe that free trade, free capital movements, openness to the multinational enterprise, free movement of people, especially managers and students, and open communications will achieve the dynamic growth of the economy and certain economic and social objectives.

When English (and Scottish) writers in the eighteenth and early nineteenth centuries advocated such policies, England was the first in the field of manufacturing and free trade was certainly in her interest. But since the gap in income and technology between the first-comer and the later-comer was then much smaller than it is today, it could plausibly be argued then that even late-coming competitors would benefit from 'looking outward' and that the prescription for others was not entirely ideologically disguised self-interest.

Inward-looking policies, on the other hand, bring out the educational effects of learning to do things for oneself, especially learning to manufacture instead of importing: a kind of learning by doing without. Of course, one can learn by manufacturing for world-wide exports, but high costs and risks are usually initial obstacles. Inward-looking policies emphasise the need for an indigenous technology, appropriate for the factors available in the country, and for an appropriate range of products. If you restrict trade, the movement of people and communications, if you keep out the multinational enterprise, with its wrong products and wrong want-stimulation and hence its wrong technology, you will evolve your own style of development and you will be stronger, more independent, master of your own fate.

Before examining the implications of this position, let us revert for a moment to the narrower meaning in which the reference is to trade and in which 'inward-looking' is identified with import-substitution and 'outward-looking' with export-promotion. It is then necessary to draw another distinction – that between primary and secondary or manufacturing production. This gives us a fourfold division: primary-outward and secondary-outward, primary-inward and secondary-inward. The colonial economy, with its foreign mines and plantations, was typically primary and outward-looking. It is partly as a reaction against the colonial economy that the newly independent states have put a good deal of weight on secondary production and import substitution. Primary-inward is typically the policy of some developed countries, especially the Common Agricultural Policy of the E.E.C., but, with the Green Revolution, substitution for imported food is a policy of many LDCs.

Secondary-outward has recently gained a good deal of support from carefully collected and analysed evidence, and a group of the participants that included the Curzons, Harry Johnson, Maurice Scott, Göran Ohlin, Jan Tumlir and Harald Malmgren strongly favoured it. It springs from the disenchantment with import-substituting industrialisation in developing countries, primarily but not exclusively in Latin America. Its advocates, while relying on the principle of comparative advantage, argue that developing countries have been more inward-looking than comparative advantage would warrant and should now become more outward-looking. The reasoning, somewhat over-simplified, runs like this. Protectionist measures raise costs and reduce international competitiveness of manufacturing industry. In addition, they differentiate between producers in the wrong way. The use of imported capital goods and other imported inputs is encouraged and agriculture and exports are discouraged. In extreme cases the excessive encouragement of imported inputs leads to the phenomenon of negative value added.

The tariff structure, while encouraging all import-substituting firms, whether large or small, domestic or foreign, is particularly advantageous to foreign (and domestic) companies that rely heavily on imported capital goods and intermediate products from their parent or sister companies. A substantial private profit of these companies is therefore consistent with a quite modest social benefit. If dividends are then remitted abroad, the national gain may be negligible or turn into a loss. Many of the complaints against foreign investment and foreign technology must therefore be laid at the door of misguided protectionist policies.

The argument is not only that protection, overvalued exchange rates and the resulting encouragement to excessive import substitution have penalised exports, but also that price elasticities for *manufactured* exports from developing countries are high and that *some* of these countries could have earned more foreign exchange by increasing *primary* exports.

Moreover, excessive import substitution thrives on a self-fulfilling prophecy. Import substitution is embarked upon because of elasticity pessimism and the strategy promptly leads to poor export performance, apparently justifying the initial pessimism. The proposed 'outward-looking' policies could achieve greater efficiency, higher employment and a fairer distribution of income.

A second and distinct theme of those advocating secondary-outward-looking policies is that administrative, central controls make for inefficiency and inequality, and that prices should be used much more as an instrument of policy-making and decentralised planning.

The advocates of this view were not simply 'growthmen', in opposition to another group more concerned with equality and other social objectives. It is part of the argument of the trade optimists that it is not the international trading system, the foreign companies or the capital-intensive foreign technology that are responsible for growing inequalities, but faulty, protectionist government policies. Less protection and a stronger orientation towards exports would not only accelerate growth but would also create more employment and reduce economic inequality. The countries that have adopted such policies have succeeded in closing the international and the domestic income gaps.

The fourfold division by sectors and trade policies – manufacturing *v.* agriculture, and outward- *v.* inward-looking – is important if we envisage changes in comparative advantages and if we bear in mind the typology of countries relevant for the choice of strategies discussed below (see pp. 15–21). While it is now widely agreed that much of manufacturing import substitution (secondary-inward) was wasteful and high-cost, this is not necessarily an indictment of the strategy as such but possibly the result of highly unequal income, wealth and power distributions, of an inefficient administrative apparatus or of initially high costs due to small markets and absence of learning effects, obstacles which could be overcome after a time. With the exception of Hong Kong and Singapore, cities without a rural hinterland, all developing countries that faced competition in world markets started to manufacture for exports only after a period of protection and production for the domestic market, though not necessarily in the same industries or products. There is neither an analytical nor a historical basis for general advocacy of free(ish) trade in manufactures, irrespective of the stage of development, the size of the industry, the level of skills and the resource endowment, though there is a (tautological) case against *excessive* import substitution.

OUTWARD-LOOKING POLICIES AND INEQUALITY

On many occasions during the Conference we were called back to the basic objectives of development. They are not statistical abstractions like growth of G.N.P. As Joan Robinson said, growth is the result, not the objective, of rational economic policy. The purpose of development is to raise the level of living of the masses of the people in the poor countries as rapidly as is feasible – to provide secure jobs, adequate nutrition and health, clean water at hand, cheap transport, education for the children. The test of any strategy is the extent to which it helps or hinders in meeting these basic needs of the majority of the people.

Another group of participants (among them Ignacy Sachs, Éprime Eshag and Frances Stewart) believed that strategies that look outwards towards the much richer, industrial societies will often tend to prevent the achievement of this objective because they will, though possibly promoting aggregate economic growth, reinforce international and internal inequalities. It might be said that growing inequalities do not matter if everyone is becoming better off, only at different rates. But poverty in a country depends upon what is regarded as an acceptable minimum, and this rises with rising average income. In addition, the process of growth and its accompanying changes impoverish the least skilled and poorest members of a community, so that absolute, as well as relative, poverty increases.

According to this view of the connection between openness, growth, and international and internal inequality, the personification of a country is misleading. There will be groups within developing countries which will benefit from the 'openness' because their interests coincide with those of the larger enterprises in the developed countries. Since they are often also the articulate groups wielding power, the false identification of their interests and those of the country is tempting. But a concern for the basic objective – the welfare of the mass of the people – will show up a conflict. However, the type of import-substitution strategy adopted in the past by many countries has also been responsible for major income inequalities and has created powerful vested interests in its continuation. Here again there is a false identification of partial interests with those of the country as a whole.

A curious paradox came out in the discussion. It seemed that both inward-looking, import-substituting, protectionist, interventionist policies and outward-looking, market-orientated, non-interventionist policies tend to increase inequalities: the former because they strengthen domestic market imperfections and monopolies and reduce the demand for labour-intensive processes, the latter because the market rewards most those factors that are relatively scarce (capital, management, professional skills) and penalises those in abundant supply, and because the market strengthens the ability to accumulate of those who have against those who have not. But though it is paradoxical that *both* a protectionist 'distorted' system of prices, interest rates, wages and exchange rates *and* a market-determined one should increase inequalities, there is no contradiction. It is plausible, that, within a certain social and political framework, both export-orientated market policies and import-substitution-orientated, interventionist, 'distorting' policies should aggravate inequalities, though it may take different forms: a small group of high-wage earners accompanied by unemployment in one case, a large group of low-wage earners in the other.

For many reasons besides those sketched out briefly above, one would expect 'outward-looking' policies to aggravate inequalities. But there are more specifically four sets of forces that make for inequality – international and internal: one well

known from conventional economics, one not normally
included in economic analysis, and the remaining two rather
more novel. The well-known one is the presence of increasing
returns. Much of conventional economics assumes, as Nicholas
Kaldor pointed out, a 'linear' world, in which processes can be
duplicated and multiplied without making much difference to
the outcome.

Where increasing returns prevail, on the other hand, equilibrium will be unstable. Freeing trade between two regions or
countries in which one sector is operating under conditions of
increasing returns will mean that the more advanced region will
expand this sector and establish a comparative advantage in
these exports, and the less advanced region will contract this
sector and confine itself to production and exports of the
products of the non-increasing-returns sector. Advantages will
accrue cumulatively to him who already has, and from him who
has less the little will be taken away. We know of these powerful
processes of polarisation and accumulation from our experience
of regions within countries, but here the authority of a central
government is exercised in order to attempt to remedy the
situation and to correct the inequalities. Even so, policies often
fail and regional inequalities are one of the most recalcitrant and
persistent problems of national policy.

Internationally, these forces are much more powerfully at
work, without any constraints from an international authority.
It is this that constitutes the so-called infant-industry argument,
which is sometimes applied to the whole manufacturing sector.
The precise method of protection is a secondary issue. Some
would say, do it by subsidies to labour or to industries rather
than through tariff protection. Others would point out that
externalities to the firm must be assumed, which, however,
must remain internal to the country, if government intervention is to be justified. But the fact remains that an industry
or a group of industries will have to go through a period of
losses in a free market before they can establish themselves in
competition with another set of industries established further
down a decreasing cost curve. All this is well known.

The second set of forces are social and political. We do not
really know the sources of inequality of power and wealth. Are
they to be found in the educational system which reserves places

for those already privileged and promotes and certifies those with initial advantages, or in the distribution of land ownership and of other assets, or in the enactment and enforcement of government policies? But whatever the sources of inequality, the mechanism allocating economic resources will tend to reinforce the differential power structure. Many participants emphasised this at various points in the Conference and it was one area in which the limitations of using only conventional economic variables were brought out particularly clearly.

The remaining two sets of forces (or possibly two aspects of the same set) are of a rather different kind. They were illuminated in the paper by Frances Stewart. There was no unanimity on her analysis or her conclusions or her policies, but a number of participants found them sufficiently provocative and novel to warrant closer investigation. The two forces are technology and products.

Technology, transferred from the advanced, industrial countries, reflects their historically determined, relatively high levels of saving and therefore of capital per head. It is a capital-intensive technology, intended for large-scale production, and is therefore inappropriate for the much smaller and poorer markets and the dearth of capital and savings of the developing countries. The point about appropriate technology is that it involves lower costs of capital equipment per worker, without raising the costs of capital per unit of output, more in line with available savings per head. It thus makes it possible to provide productive equipment for the whole work-force, whereas use of developed-country technology in much poorer countries means that only a minority of workers can be provided with equipment and that much equipment remains under-utilised. The equipment appropriate for poor countries should be capital-saving, and intended for small-scale production, not the labour-saving, large-scale equipment and plant appropriate to the factor availability and income levels of rich countries.

Mass-production methods and sophisticated equipment are linked with inappropriate products – products that cater for the average consumer in rich countries and the rich consumer in poor countries. They reinforce the unequal income distribution, partly by the distribution of income resulting from the production methods used, partly by the vested interests that

this creates. As Frances Stewart says, somewhat epigram-
matically, of many manufactured consumption goods, 'it is
inappropriate for developing countries to consume those goods
that developed countries produce, and inappropriate for
developing countries to produce those goods that developed
countries consume'. Free trade encourages the wrong pattern
of consumption and production.

Such an analysis is usually dismissed as arrogant and paternal-
istic. Its proponents are accused of wishing to ram down the
throats of poor countries second-rate products that they themselves would not look at. Such critics fail to see that the choice
of the so-called 'best' amounts to depriving the mass of the
people of the opportunity to satisfy their essential needs. They
are represented among the vocal elites, who have access to the
channels of communication, and who tend to identify their own
interests and tastes (acquired through foreign education or
imitation) with those of the country.

The distinction between inward- and outward-looking does
not quite fit the case. What matters is the direction of the
looking. While access to the markets of developed countries is
more profitable in the short run, trade between developing
countries at relatively similar income levels has much to offer in
the longer run. Developing countries can benefit from the
division of labour between themselves.[5] The danger arises from
looking too much at a world in which demand and production
patterns follow entirely different lines. The argument is for
trade among developing countries and the erection of limited
barriers to trade with the much richer countries. It is really an
extension and a reversal of J. S. Mill's argument quoted above
(Fn. 4). It uses the same, nowadays usually neglected, variables,
but suggests that the generation of tastes, wants and incentives
should be of a different nature and in a different direction.

Trade between low-income countries has in fact shrunk. The
share of developing countries' exports to other developing
countries fell from 21·5 per cent in 1961–5 to 19·5 per cent in
1969. There are many reasons for this. The large and expanding
markets were the industrial countries of Europe and Japan.
Transport and communications between developing countries
were poor. Until recently it was easier to ship goods from
Djakarta to the Netherlands than to Manila, and from Manila

to San Francisco than to Bangkok. Financial institutions, payments arrangements, tariff structures and marketing channels were also geared to the metropolitan market. It was easier to sell matches from Upper Volta to France than to neighbouring Dahomey. Aid-tying made it impossible to enter bids for contracts against the metropolitan donor country. For these and other reasons the trade pattern of the past is not necessarily a good guide to what a desirable regional trade pattern should be. The erection of barriers is not enough. What is needed is a set of institutions which facilitate the division of labour between a group of countries, sharing their poverty. Transport and communications, credit facilities and monetary arrangements would have to be adapted to such a pattern of exchange. A regional payments union, such as that suggested by Frances and Michael Stewart, or a joint large devaluation of all developing countries against the developed countries, suggested by Mahbub ul Haq, are contributions towards thinking out the institutional framework within which the new pattern can be evolved.

Moreover, trade between developing countries at different stages of development may raise the same issues of domination and inappropriateness as trade between rich and poor countries. True, income gaps will be smaller, but against this the least developed will have to pay more for imports from the more developed countries than for imports from the large industrial producers. Regional trade arrangements may therefore have to be accompanied by specific policies to assist the least developed.

Clarity about the objective and about the social and political power relations comes before the instruments chosen to achieve the objective. When it comes to a discussion of instruments, it is useful to distinguish between (1) free trade *v.* protection; (2) *laissez-faire v.* state intervention; and (3) direct, quantitative controls *v.* price policies. Sometimes there is a false identification of free trade with *laissez-faire* and of both with the use of prices. Prices can be used as instruments of policy and of planning or they can be left to the free play of market forces.

In principle, some of the objectives of protection (though not all) can be better achieved by domestic subsidies and taxes, permitting international trade to be guided by the prices thus set by policy-makers. Again, subsidies and taxes can in many cases be used to achieve the same results as direct controls. While these problems have attracted much attention in the recent literature and at the Conference, they are secondary issues. The primary problems are those of aims and of the structure of power and of the institutions within which controls or price policies function. So-called 'distortions' are much more a function of monopoly power, inequality, uncertainty and ignorance than of the choice between prices and direct controls. Within an unequal power and ownership structure both the use of prices and the use of controls will tend to reinforce the existing inequalities; within an egalitarian society, controls or prices can be used to allocate resources without destroying equality. Both 'distortions' and prices serve political purposes.

There is, of course, some overlap between these contrasts. In order to exclude the import of a luxury item that is wanted because *others* own and display it, total prohibition (including, of course, of domestic production) is more effective than an indirect tax. An indirect tax may simply stimulate the demand fed by the desire for imitation or ostentation or by habit. Where demand for a product derives from the *high price* itself, or from the fact that *others* consume it or that competitors buy it, or that it has been consumed *in the past*, though after having done without it for a while the consumer would not miss the product, prohibition will be more effective than indirect taxation, because *total* elimination of the product reduces consumers' satisfaction (or competitors' profits) by less than reduction through a higher price.[6] Reductions at the margin would impose a greater loss in these cases. Considerations affecting the burden on an often weak administrative system and the temptations to corruption or the need to collect revenue from tariffs will also be relevant to the choice of instruments and point in the opposite direction. But the main issue is the justification for a strategy that turns away from the rich countries and attempts to build up investment and trade between similar, low-income economies.

The type of argument against policies looking outward to the developed countries and for increased trade between developing countries put forward by Frances Stewart and by Mahbub ul Haq is of a different type from the more conventional arguments for protection or regional integration. It embraces variables not normally included in narrowly economic analysis.

Orthodox arguments for protection are based on the principle that, in order to protect one industry, we wish to pull resources *into* one type of activity. This implies – in conditions of full employment – that we wish to pull resources *out of* another type of activity. It would be nonsense to wish to protect *all* industries. When we argued above for protection of the whole manufacturing sector subject to increasing returns, this implied pulling resources out of agriculture or services.

But the Stewart–Haq argument points to some protection (though not autarky), at least in principle, of *all* activities. By opening up a society too widely, we reduce the incentives and opportunities to develop indigenous processes and products appropriate for the low-income groups in developing countries, for their small and low-income markets, for their scarcity of physical and human capital and for their desire for the wide spread of the benefits of development. The educational and institutional arguments against an outward-looking strategy point to the need to protect *all* activities from the eroding influences of the advanced world economy and, more important, they point to the need for constructive indigenous efforts, which indeed do not automatically result from looking towards like-minded countries, but which are hampered by an *excessively* outward-looking strategy and by emulation of the style of the rich.

Something like this also underlies the distinction drawn by some participants between self-reliance and dependence, between autonomy and domination. Countries that generate their own technological capability, their own social institutions and organisations (not only in technology and industry but also in land tenure and rural institutions) will be able to mobilise their efforts more effectively than those that always look at how they order these things abroad.

There are alternative styles of development, and one type of society may prefer to develop by adapting technologies and products from abroad, while another will find its identity by raising a curtain round its frontiers or round the frontiers of a group of like-minded countries with similar factor availabilities and similar income levels. It might even be that a judicious selection of features of an outward- and inward-looking strategy would give the best results, e.g. drawing on foreign research and developing indigenous research or drawing on and adapting foreign technology and products. The lessons of industrialising Germany, Japan and Soviet Russia, which used and adapted foreign ways, blending new institutions with old traditions, are not directly applicable because international gaps were narrower then and the dimensions of the demographic problem, which determine the scale of the need for jobs, were quite different. The main point is that there may be a choice of styles of development which can be understood only if we include institutional and educational variables in our scheme and transcend a narrowly defined static economic model.

Some participants, among them Ignacy Sachs and Éprime Eshag, preferred to put the contrast more starkly and simply in terms of planning *v. laissez-faire*. According to them, it is the need for centralised planning, according to social priorities, and the search for independence from the vagaries of the world market, that distinguishes the advocates of different trade policies. Others, while in sympathy with the planning approach, saw the differences in the area of learning, education and institutions. A third group saw them in the political power structure. Planning and controls in an inegalitarian society reinforce inequalities and encourage corruption; the use of prices in an egalitarian society need not conflict with equality.

THE HYDRA OF DEVELOPMENT

A second theme that emerged from the proceedings is the hydra-face of development. Scientists may have a solution to every problem, but the process of development has at least one problem to every solution. Second-generation problems are not peculiar to the Green Revolution. They also occur in international trade.

Freeing agricultural trade in the developed countries – an objective regarded as desirable by almost everyone at the Conference – generates such second-generation problems. If, as a result of reduced food surpluses, the terms of trade of food producers improve, poor food importers will suffer. A faster rate of industrial growth in developed countries, stimulated by their reduced agricultural protection, raises the comparative advantage of the developed countries in manufacturing industry and may, on this score, make industrialisation in developing countries more difficult. Of course, a two-sector model is too crude to deal with the complexity.

Two questions arise for developing countries' agricultural strategy. First, will the developing countries become more competitive in exports of agricultural products with a high income elasticity of demand – fruits, vegetables and livestock? Second, will they be able to produce enough food for domestic consumption to keep wage rates down and thus to keep exports of manufactured products competitive?

Freeing trade in manufactures between developed countries also raises problems for developing countries. Clearly, tariff-free trade between developed countries eliminates preferences for manufactures from developing countries. In order to break into the markets of the industrial countries and benefit from the economies of large-scale production, more is needed than just a move towards world-wide free trade.

The multinational enterprise is often cited as a useful agent for promoting exports from developing countries, penetrating new markets and overcoming the obstacles of initially high costs of an infant industry. But the multinational enterprise raises as many problems as it solves – political problems of foreign ownership and problems of the distribution of gains between host country and foreigners and between different groups, sectors and regions in the host country.

If there is to be a change in trade patterns, in the direction favoured by those who advocate that developing countries should export more manufactures, the structure of tariffs, quantitative restrictions and export incentives in developed countries requires radical reform. Much more attention must be devoted to adjustment assistance to industries hit by freer access for labour-intensive low-cost products. Not enough efforts are directed at these problems at the present time.

TYPOLOGIES FOR TRADE POLICIES

A proposition with which most participants at the Conference would agree is the generalisation that it is impossible to generalise about appropriate trade policies. I. G. Patel says that trade plays only a marginal role in the strategy of development. This

is a very Indian view. Trade may indeed play a small role but
be very important, like a link in a bicycle chain. If trade provides
crucial components without which whole sectors of the economy
cannot function, smallness must not be identified with unim-
portance. The nail of a horseshoe may make the difference
between victory and defeat of a kingdom. But for the majority
of countries (though not for the majority of individuals in
the world, because large countries contain many individuals
relatively unaffected by trade) trade is both large and important,
because most countries are small. Of 90 developing countries, 72
have fewer than 15 million people and 51 fewer than 5 million.

For this reason alone, and for others (to be discussed below),
it is necessary, for the purpose of formulating a trade strategy,
to evolve a typology of developing countries. Size and income
level are relevant for deciding on the economies of scale for
import substitution. Resource endowment will determine
whether primary products should be exported or processed, or
whether the country should rely on importing materials and
processing them. The level of skills and training will determine
the level of the technology.

But in addition to these obvious economic variables, so-called
non-economic variables will also play a part. The level of
administrative skills will determine the ability to change the
structure of production through public policies and the time
this is likely to take. The political structure and the interests
and allegiances of the ruling elites will determine what actions
are possible and where the political and sociological constraints
operate. The particular constellation of interests and power will
itself be the result of the economic, social and political history
of the country. A country which has industrialised through
import substitution behind high tariff walls will have to be
treated differently, in analysis and prescription, from one which
has neither started to industrialise nor departed from the
principles of free trade. All policies are bound to hurt some
interests. Régimes will differ according to their readiness to
violate the interests of urban industrialists or large landowners.
It would be naïve to assume that policies operate in a sovereign
sphere outside and above the arena of social conflict. Policies
often decried as stupid by the standards of economic textbooks
are the expression of powerful interests in a society.

Thus the limits to import substitution set by the size of the domestic market, the wealth of indigenous raw materials and foodstuffs, the level of human skills, the efficiency and honesty of the civil service and the interests reflected by the ruling elite are important determinants of the appropriate strategy. A typology along such lines will provide qualifications to an easy generalisation from the recent experience of successful exporters. If the heavy emphasis on manufacturing import substitution in the 1950s went too far in one direction, the new conventional wisdom of advocating universally 'outward-looking' policies of export promotion may have gone too far in the other.

Two questions may be asked: what are the limits to a policy of export expansion?; and within these limits, what is the distribution of gains?

LIMITS TO THE GROWTH OF EXPORTS OF
MANUFACTURED PRODUCTS AND THE DISTRIBUTION
OF GAINS

While the spectacular export performances of a few, but a growing number of, countries have shown that breakthroughs into the markets of developed countries are possible in spite of existing tariffs and non-tariff barriers, there was also evidence of growing restrictions against these exports whenever they began to be seriously felt. Annual growth rates in the 1960s of 10 to 15 per cent of exports from the developing countries are liable to run into obstacles on the side of importing countries. These would be more serious if the lesson were to be generalised and many more developing countries were to engage in exporting more, particularly if these exports were to be concentrated on a few 'sensitive' products.

Policy restrictions are liable to be supported by a form of 'adjustment assistance' which directs R. & D. and compensation expenditure at defensive investment to re-equip the industry hit by the low-cost imports or simply to subsidise it in order to remain competitive.

There are also well-known institutional limitations (lying between demand and supply) to increasing exports, such as export credits, marketing and sales organisation and knowledge of required designs. Calling in the multinational enterprise, which can overcome these obstacles, raises new problems to be discussed in a moment.

Some participants emphasised the supply limitations. These are said to lie not so much in shortage of capital as in a shortage of the entrepreneurial ability to spot the type of products for which world demand is expanding and which can be supplied at low cost; in organisational and administrative capacity both in the private and the public sector; in the ability of the economy to supply enough food for the workers engaged in manufacturing to keep industrial wages low and prices competitive; and in the ability to resist the power of the urban trade unions to extract ever-higher money wages.

While organisational and other supply obstacles clearly account partly for the export failure of some countries, such as India, it cannot be doubted that this failure contributed to the success of the successful exporters. Would their exports have done so well in the 1960s if all developing countries had adopted the Taiwan–Korea strategy?

This raises the question of the distribution of the gains from the rising volume and value of manufactured exports. When multinational enterprises are engaged in producing and selling exports, a part of the gain accrues to countries other than the exporting country. In conditions of oligopoly, low costs are not automatically passed on either to buyers in lower prices or to workers in higher wages, but may only swell profits.

As G. M. Meier and Felipe Pazos[7] have pointed out, what is often claimed as the peculiar virtue of private foreign enterprise, namely that it brings a 'package' of capital, enterprise, management and know-how, is also its peculiar defect: it means that monopoly rents and profits accruing to these factors go abroad, and that only the reward for unskilled or semi-skilled labour, in highly elastic supply and with little bargaining power, goes to the host country. If, on top of this, the country gives tax concessions to the foreign firm or subsidises it through trading estates or import privileges, the division of the gains is very uneven and the export figures give a misleading picture of the country's gain.

If we are interested in the limits to the growth of exports of manufactured products and the likely international and internal distribution of gains, another typology by product will be useful. We may then distinguish between the following.[8]

(1) *Processed local primary products.* These include products such as vegetable oils, foodstuffs, plywood and veneer, pulp and paper products and fabricated metal. The processing may be into semi-processed, refined or completely manufactured products. When these products are cheaper to transport in a processed form, rather than in their raw state, countries processing them enjoy an advantage over the countries in which they are sold. Cascading tariffs in developed countries discriminate against this type of export. Yet processing is clearly not appropriate in all cases. America exports wheat, not bread. Again, the processing may be too capital- or skill-intensive to be appropriate for a developing country.

(2) *Traditional labour-intensive goods.* These include garments, textiles, footwear and simple engineering goods. While low labour costs make developing countries' exports competitive in these products, they face particular obstacles in importing countries where the competing industries are often concentrated and politically well organised. Successful exporting here may have to be combined with the mobilisation of interests in importing countries. Independent retail chains, mail-order firms, trading houses or consumers' associations may organise pressures against the producers' organisations.

(3) *Newer labour-intensive goods.* Goods such as plastic and wooden items, rattan furniture, glassware, pottery and wigs have appeared in recent years. The fact that their impact on importing countries is more dispersed and less noticeable makes them better export prospects, as long as not too many countries compete in selling them.

(4) *Processes, components and assembly in a vertically integrated international firm.* G. K. Helleiner, in an interesting paper,[9] quotes a wide range of activities located in developing countries. Semiconductors, tubes and other electronic components are assembled in developing countries for the parent firm in developed countries. Garments, gloves, leather luggage and baseballs are sewn together in Taiwan, South Korea, Thailand and India; motor-car parts such as radio antennae, piston rings, cylinder linings, car lamps, braking equipment, batteries and springs are made in many countries. Data are

flown to South-east Asia and the West Indies for punching on tape by low-wage key-punch operators; watchmakers fly jewels to Mauritius for precision drilling. These industries are foot-loose, attracted by low wages, tax concessions, docile trade unions, relative absence of corruption and political stability. They also represent an organised interest in the importing country opposing import-competing interests and sometimes enjoy tariff advantages.

(5) *Import substitutes or local products turned exports.* These products, often goods such as motor-cars (Brazilian Volkswagen are an outstanding example), car parts, steel pipes and tubes, electric wires and cables, bicycles, electric motors and diesel engines, were set up initially to replace imports and, having become established, have entered the export market. They represent the last stage in the product cycle.[10] Marginal cost pricing for exports is common and exports may be subject to anti-dumping measures.

This classification is useful for identifying the problems of adjustment and the pressure groups in the importing countries, and hence the possible limits to growth in the exporting country and the division of gains between different factors of production and different countries. The classification also indicates that it would be rash to jump to the conclusion that the promotion of exports of manufactures through appropriate price incentives is always and necessarily the best strategy for all developing countries. We have heard a good deal recently about negative value-added in import-substituting manufacturing as a result of excessive protection. We should not forget, as G. M. Meier reminds us, that negative value added can also occur in exports and that a recipe of universal export promotion, extrapolated from the experiences of the 1960s, supported by multinational enterprises with a good many concessions, privileges and incentives, can have this result.

The conclusion of this section is that the 1970s will be a more difficult period, especially as more and more countries adopt export-promoting strategies; that over-expansion may turn the income terms of trade against the exporting countries; that import capacity and import willingness are not likely to keep in step with accelerated export expansion; that protectionism in developed countries may increase; and that even when exports are successful, the gains to the developing countries may be small or, in extreme cases, negative. This does not mean that developing countries should not devote considerable efforts to promoting exports. It *does* mean that 'getting prices right' is not everything; that institutional and political constraints will have to be overcome and that some co-ordination between developing countries is essential if they are not to erode the benefits through excessive competition.

OUTLOOK

A final theme that recurred was the scope for transferring resources from rich to poor countries under the cover of trade arrangements. Concealing transfers in this way has the advantage of the 'quiet style' for which I. G. Patel had pleaded,[11] but it has the drawback that political strings may be attached to general preferences or commodity agreements just as they are attached to open aid, and concessions may be withdrawn when political disagreement arises.

The picture that emerges for the trade outlook in the 1970s is not a cheerful one. A good deal was said at the Conference about the great difficulties in the way of adjustment assistance in the industrial countries in response to larger imports of manufactured or agricultural products from the developing countries. If agricultural protection continues and 'disruption' is invoked against more imports of low-cost, labour-intensive goods; if the major aid donors are weary of stepping up official development assistance; if migration and possibly capital flows are restricted and if commodity schemes are ruled out; then all routes to international co-operation are blocked.

It may be argued that such blocking assists the self-reliance and autonomy of the developing countries which was advocated by one group of participants. But it would be better for world prosperity and co-operation if their efforts for self-reliance were supported and encouraged by the developed countries – as U.S. Marshall Aid assisted Europe to recover – rather than if hostile confrontations were to occur and the few channels where mutual benefits are possible were to be blocked. In any case, the trade options should be left open to the developing countries and should not be restricted from outside, unless adequate compensation were to be offered for deprivation of trading opportunities.

I. G. Patel has warned against the use of monopoly and bargaining power by the developing countries because he fears that 'once you get into a mood of warfare in trade, it is going to be difficult to keep the firing within any prescribed limits'. But such moderation presupposes that world-wide co-operation is possible. It should be the task of the rich, industrial, developed countries to support the efforts of the poor, developing countries to evolve their own style of development. Dependence, from which these countries wish to free themselves, derives from the lack of an indigenous range of technological and organisational choices, from not having the know-how, the organisation and management, the social and cultural institutions, to respond in an appropriate way to investment and trade opportunities. It is in the complex links between technology, marketing, private investment, product range, bargaining, trade and trade policies that the contribution of foreign trade and investment to the remedy for poverty and underdevelopment has to be sought.

Notes

1. I am grateful to Peter Ady, Sidney Dell, Gerald Helleiner, Angus Hone, M. G. Mathur, Deepak Nayyar, Göran Ohlin, Ignacy Sachs, Maurice Scott and Jan Tumlir for helpful comments, some of which I have stubbornly resisted accepting. I am also grateful to the rapporteurs of the groups who skilfully summarised the discussions. They were Michael Kuczynski, Gordon Hughes, David Newbery, Neville Norman, Suzanne Paine and Michael Sharpston. This chapter does not attempt to be a fair summary but the impressions of a not entirely impartial chairman.

2. F. Machlup describes wittily this difference in approach, experienced by all scholars who have worked with policy-makers, in *Remaking the International Monetary System* (Baltimore: Johns Hopkins Univ. Press, 1968) p. 7.

3. On this and the importance of education and learning, see Hla Myint, 'International Trade and the Developing Countries', in Paul A. Samuelson (ed.), *International Economic Relations*, Proceedings of the Third Congress of the International Economic Association held at Montreal (London: Macmillan, 1969) pp. 16ff.

4. 'There is another consideration, principally applicable to an early stage of industrial advancement. A people may be in a quiescent, indolent,

uncultivated state, with all their tastes either fully satisfied or entirely undeveloped, and they may fail to put forth the whole of their productive energies for want of any sufficient object of desire. The opening of foreign trade, by making them acquainted with new objects, or tempting them by the easier acquisition of things which they had not previously thought attainable, sometimes works a sort of industrial revolution in a country whose resources were previously undeveloped for want of energy and ambition in the people: inducing those who were satisfied with scanty comforts and little work, to work harder for the gratification of their new tastes, and even to save, and accumulate capital, for the still more complete satisfaction of those tastes at a future time.

'But the economical advantages of commerce are surpassed in importance by those of its effects, which are intellectual and moral. It is hardly possible to overrate the value, in the present low state of human improvement, of placing human beings in contact with persons dissimilar to themselves, and with modes of thought and action unlike those with which they are familiar. Commerce is now, what war once was, the principal source of this contact. Commercial adventurers from more advanced countries have generally been the first civilizers of barbarians. And commerce is the purpose of the far greater part of the communication which takes place between civilized nations. Such communication has always been, and is peculiarly in the present age, one of the primary sources of progress. To human beings, who, as hitherto educated, can scarcely cultivate even a good quality without running it into a fault, it is indispensable to be perpetually comparing their own notions and customs with the experience and example of persons in different circumstances from themselves: and there is no nation which does not need to borrow from others, not merely particular arts or practices, but essential points of character in which its own type is inferior.' J. S. Mill, *Principles of Political Economy* (London: Longmans, Green, 1902) pp. 351–2.

5. Staffan Burenstam Linder, who was with us at the Conference, argues that trade in manufactured products will tend to be most intensive between countries with similar levels of income per head. This argument also applies to poor countries. Linder says that the expected pattern does not apply to underdeveloped countries, because 'trade may indeed be dominated by more aggressively marketed imports from industrialised countries and, to some extent, consist of products less suitable than those obtainable elsewhere. Although the potential scope for imports from industrialised countries is relatively small, actual imports may thus be greater than from countries with the same income level.' S. B. Linder, *An Essay on Trade and Transformation* (Stockholm: Almquist & Wiksell, 1961) p. 108. The task of policy would then be to transform *potential* trade into *actual*.

6. The demand for ties illustrates the point. Wearing ties is partly a matter of habit and partly dictated by the fact that others wear ties. In Israel even in five-star restaurants few men wear ties and everyone is better off as a result. Ties are also demanded because of their high price. Advertisements for Countess Mara ties in the *New Yorker* create a

demand for displaying $250 on one's neck. 'Each tie discreetly displays the CM coronet, befitting a design for "my man in a million".' *New Yorker*, 11 Nov. 1972, p. 26.

7. Felipe Pazos, 'The Role of International Movements of Private Capital in Promoting Development', in John H. Adler (ed.), *Capital Movements and Economic Development* (London: Macmillan, 1967) p. 196.

8. See Robert S. McNamara, *Address to the Board of Governors* (Sep. 1972) Appendix; and Gerald K. Helleiner, 'Manufactured Exports from Less Developed Countries and Multinational Firms', *Economic Journal* (Mar. 1973).

9. Loc. cit. Fn 8.

10. Seev Hirsch, *Location of Industry and International Competitiveness* (Oxford Univ. Press, 1967). Professor Hirsch participated in the Conference and contributes a chapter to this book. Also Raymond Vernon, 'International Investment and International Trade in the Product Cycle', *Quarterly Journal of Economics*, LXXX (1966) 190–207, and *Sovereignty at Bay: The Multinational Spread of U.S. Enterprises* (London: Longman, 1971).

11. I. G. Patel, 'Aid Relationship for the Seventies', in Barbara Ward, Lenore d'Anjou and J. D. Runnals, *The Widening Gap: Development in the 1970s* (New York and London: 1971) p. 308.

2 Opening Addresses

International Trade and Economic Development

Harry G. Johnson

PROFESSOR OF ECONOMICS, LONDON SCHOOL OF
ECONOMICS AND POLITICAL SCIENCE AND
UNIVERSITY OF CHICAGO

The purpose of this Conference is to consider the ways in which
different trade policies might help or hinder the development
efforts of what has come to be known as 'the Third World'. I do
not myself like that particular terminology, both because it
smacks of condescension unjustified by any innate or effort-
acquired superiority of the one over the other, and because I
prefer to think of the world as one world inhabited by one
human race, though a world in which people start life from
vastly different circumstances and with vastly different opportunities of bettering themselves by their own efforts. The
most important difference among individual starting-points,
from the viewpoint of this Conference, is that people are born
and brought up in different nation-states, some of which for
historical reasons afford rich opportunities for enjoying and
improving on a high standard of living, and in others of which
even the most desperate of hard effort can make the difference
only between tolerable and abject poverty.

This difference in starting-points would be of far less importance, perhaps even negligible, if people regardless of their
national origins were able to move freely over the face of the
earth. For then able people regardless of national origin would
be entitled to share equally on competitive terms in the affluence
that some nations of the world, or some sectors of the world
economy, have made possible through technological advance
and the development and education of human skills and talents.

And poverty would be a question, not of nationality irrespective of ability, but of inability to make a sufficient economic contribution to world output, irrespective of nationality. Hence the relief of poverty would be a question of making income transfers from the rich to the poor, according to conscience, religious belief, political philosophy and the human responsibility of one man to another, regardless of race, creed, religion and nationality. It would not be a question of transfers from the governments of rich countries to the governments of poor countries. And it would not raise the questions of power politics, national rivalries and resentment of the aid-donation obligation on both sides that characterise the contemporary process of aid-giving from rich countries (which may contain many poor citizens) to poor countries (which may contain some very rich citizens), each country by virtue of being a country having a voice in international politics that counts for something, even if not very much.

In fact, however, the world is divided into nation-states, and its most fundamental characteristics are, first, that each country is entitled by the rules of the game to prevent citizens of other countries from sharing in its affluence by immigration and competition for jobs with its own citizens – each country has the right to try to monopolise its affluence for its own citizens. Second, each country has the right – though this right is constrained by subscription to the General Agreement on Tariffs and Trade and the principle of non-discrimination among foreign countries in trade policy – to prevent or inhibit the citizens of foreign countries from participating indirectly in its affluence by producing in their own countries goods to be exported to its own affluent market.

There is a standard proposition in the theory of international trade, that if technological knowledge were freely available all over the world, and if countries were not too different in their relative availabilities of capital and labour, prohibition of international movements of capital and labour would not prevent the world economy from arriving at the same state of efficiency – and equalisation of the rewards to labour and to capital investment – as would occur under free international mobility of capital and labour. In other words, with free trade and free transmission of technical knowledge, plus if necessary free international investment, nationalistic discrimination between citizens of national states and foreigners would cost the world nothing, in terms either of a world output of goods and services below world potential productive capacity, or of differences in the earnings of capital and labour resident in different national states. If, for example, people in the United States were unwilling to live side by side with Indian, Chinese or African immigrants, but were able to buy Indian, Chinese or African products which competed freely with goods produced by American labour, and if race prejudice were not transferred from the absentee producers to the presently available products of their labour (which it rarely is), there would be no reason why Indians, Chinese or Africans could not enjoy as high a standard of living in their home countries as American workers do in the United States.

This proposition assumes, however, that there exists freedom of trade without subjection to tariffs, free communication of technical knowledge among countries (or at least equal access to such knowledge) and freedom of capital investment between rich and poor countries. In fact, all these requirements for eliminating the economic impact of discrimination among citizens of various nations with respect to freedom of migration are violated by the international commercial policies of both the developed and the less developed countries.

On the one hand, the developed countries place barriers in the way of imports from the less developed nations, and in particular barriers to imports of the labour-intensive, low-technology imports in which the less developed countries have a comparative advantage. A major reason for this is that the developed countries, in spite of their vaunted 'economic flexibility', have not really mastered the problem of moving labour out of low-skill labour-intensive industries into high-labour-skill capital-intensive industries; and this includes both agriculture, as a major sector of the economy, and labour-intensive products such as cotton textiles. In addition, the developed countries, particularly the United States, have become worried about the implications for domestic wages and employment of the transfer of capital and productive knowledge implicit in direct foreign investment by domestic corporations, and anxious to preserve by commercial policy measures the

monopoly of cheap capital and advanced technological knowledge enjoyed by domestic labour.

On the other hand, the less developed countries have tended
to be reluctant to accept, or even to refuse, the advantages of
the opportunities left open to them by the trade policies of the
developed countries, in two respects. First, they have pursued
policies of import substitution in disregard of the fact that the
relative cheapness of imports at world prices indicates a
comparative disadvantage for them at world market prices, and
a comparative advantage for them in the goods they export;
and where they have paid attention to exports, as many of them
have come to do in recent years, they have tended to choose
exports that demonstrate their competence as industrially
competitive economies, rather than those that are socially
profitable. Second, they have almost universally been hostile
to the direct inward investment of foreign capital, through
excessive concern about ownership rights over physical capital
and insufficient recognition of the association between physical
capital ownership and the transmission of technical knowledge.
Much of the contemporary concern about direct foreign
investment rests on the mistaken idea that productive knowledge
is a free good, costing nothing to produce, and that local
capitalists possessed of capital should by virtue of that fact be
entitled to the fruits of knowledge acquired by foreigners at
considerable expense as well.

The main theme of the foregoing argument is that, in a world
of national discrimination against citizens of other countries,
there are two alternative ways of promoting the economic
development of the less developed countries. One, which has
been the characteristic method of the post-war period, accepts
as axiomatic the unfairness between people born in different
parts of the world created by the existing division of the world
into nation-states, discriminating against each other by all the
available means of so doing, and seeks to compensate the losers
from this discrimination by transfers of resources from rich to
poor countries in the form of development assistance. The
trouble with this solution is that, being essentially a combination
of conscience money and bribery, the compensation is the
minimum acceptable to the conscience on the one side and not
sufficient consolation for needing a bribe on the other. The

alternative is to establish a world trading and investment system under which the less developed countries can obtain the economic advantages of membership in a single world economy; and this requires both freedom of international trade and freedom of international capital investment.

Unfortunately for the less developed countries, the evolution of world trading and investment arrangements since the second world war in this century has tended to deprive them of the advantages of what has been a general movement towards freer world trade, or at least to reduce their participation in the benefits of the general movement. Admittedly, this is a difficult problem to which to give a quantitative answer, since there has been a general movement towards the lowering of tariffs on industrial products; but this has been combined with an equally general movement in the advanced countries towards greater protection of agricultural production, and also with exceptions and new restrictive arrangements for manufactured products of special interest to the less developed countries, notably cotton textiles. But even taking account of the general trend towards trade liberalisation in manufactures, there is reason to believe that the overall trend has been substantially less favourable to the trade and development prospects of the less developed countries than it could (and should) have been. On the one hand, while protection for manufactured products has been steadily negotiated away on the average, exceptions have been maintained for the labour-intensive, low-technology goods in which less developed countries have a comparative advantage and to which they must look for stimulus to economic development. On the other hand, protectionism with respect to agricultural products has been definitely on the increase, with the United States agricultural policy initially setting the pace and the Common Agricultural Policy of the European Economic Community vastly compounding the felony. Since agriculture of one form or another constitutes the largest part by far of economic activity in the less developed countries, and an increase in incomes in their agricultural sectors could constitute an engine for their economic growth, this is a serious inhibiting factor on their development. In fact, economic history shows that economic development – contrary to many popular current theories – typically begins with an increase in agricultural productivity based on the existence of a thriving market for agricultural products. This was true of the origins of the industrial revolution in England, which started with technical improvements in agricultural production methods; it has also been true in the economic development of such countries as Canada, Australia and South Africa, which were originally populated (in a broad sense) by people who sought to exploit the fertility of the existing land, via exports to the mother country, England, gradually developed scientific methods of increasing output per acre and per man, and in the process generated a market for local production of manufactured goods. The process involved both the free movement of labour of a particular type and of capital out to the peripheral agricultural regions, as well as free trade in agricultural products. The agricultural protectionist policies of the advanced countries at present constitute an important obstacle to the utilisation by developing countries of this engine of economic growth. The most important obstacle lies in the chaos of trade in agricultural products in their raw state; but another obstacle is the tendency of the tariff policies of the developed countries to discriminate against the processing of raw materials in their country of origin, in order both to protect their own raw production and to protect their processing industries.

In brief, there are two important aspects of the commercial policies of the developed countries that tend to thwart the natural forces working for the economic development of the less developed countries. One is the policy of agricultural protectionism, which prevents the economically natural and rational transfer of the source of agricultural production from high-income to low-income countries. The other is the policy of protection of labour-intensive, low-technology industry from competition from low-wage countries, which inhibits the economically natural and rational gradual transfer of such industry from the higher-wage to the lower-wage countries. In both cases, efficiency in the development of the world economy, and as a corollary justice among citizens born in different nations, requires that the developed countries do two things. First, and probably most important, they should desist from efforts to support incomes in domestic agriculture by support-price and import-exclusion methods, and develop more efficient ways of relieving rural poverty. All the evidence collected by a large army of theoretical and empirical researchers indicates that these methods are an extremely inefficient means of attacking rural poverty, as well as being pernicious in their effects on international economic relationships. Second, the advanced countries should desist from trying to protect their inefficient, low-wage low-skill workers from the effects of economic development in the poor parts of the world by imposing tariffs and other trade restrictions to prevent workers in poor countries from competing through production with workers in rich countries. This policy also is demonstrably not very effective in securing its poverty-relieving objectives, despite the adverseness of its effects on the welfare of the poor countries. In place of both types of policy, the rich countries should concentrate their policy efforts on improving the mobility of labour out of low-wage into high-wage industries. This would be to the advantage both of their own labour – which from a long-run point of view has no vested interest in remaining relatively poor, and dependent on governmental support policies – and of labour in the less developed countries which has no vested interest in remaining really poor for the benefit of workers in developed countries who are relatively poor in those countries but absolutely rich by comparison with their fellow workers in the less developed countries.

These recommendations add a new dimension to the theory of free enterprise. That theory stresses the benefits of competition; but it pays no attention to the costs imposed by the competitive process on the victims of economic change. The victims react by using their political power to forestall or mitigate the force of competition; and in international relations this takes the form of securing tariff and other forms of governmental protection. This is inefficient from the point of view of all concerned; a better procedure would be compensation for the victims and assisted mobility into better-paid employment. To establish an international trading system more conducive to promoting the economic development of the less developed countries, it seems absolutely essential that the developed countries adopt more intelligent policies of adaptation to the effects of economic change than their present reliance on protectionism.

The general position adopted in this paper, which is in stark opposition to much that has been written about the problem of promoting the economic development of the less developed countries, is that there is nothing wrong with the classical principle of the beneficiality of freedom of trade, other than the fact that the rich and the poor countries are equally not prepared to live with and adapt themselves to that principle: the rich countries by using protectionist policies instead of assisted factor mobility, the poor countries by seeking to promote economic activities on the basis of emulation of rich countries rather than comparative advantage. The less developed countries would be better advised to insist, so far as they can, that the developed countries should accept and live by the principle of comparative advantage, than to tolerate rich-country violations of the principle and attempt to counteract these violations by violations of their own, coupled with demands for compensation in the form of foreign aid and trade preferences.

There is a natural and understandable, but still regrettable, tendency for the spokesmen of the less developed countries to accept the rules of the game of international economic relations as laid down by the developed countries, especially the declaration of the principles of competition combined with the practice in fact of monopoly power, and to try to bend the rules to serve their own purposes. It is a well-known fact that the poor man is always the loser at this kind of game, when he confronts a rich man. His objective should be not to outsmart the rich man in a game conducted by a crooked set of rules, but to get the rules changed into something constituting a closer approximation to honesty. Specifically, the less developed countries should have a strong concern with the promotion of freer world trade on a global basis, and especially with respect to agricultural products, and should not allow themselves to be diverted into pursuit of such gimmicks as special trade preferences, the linking of international reserve creation to development assistance, and the like. A world economy that is really neutral with respect to nations and their trade is in the long run much to be preferred to one that is in fact discriminatory among nations and for that reason makes special concessions from the rich to the poor seem to be advantageous to the latter even when they are not.

Some Reflections on Trade and Development

I. G. Patel

SECRETARY, DEPARTMENT OF ECONOMIC AFFAIRS,
MINISTRY OF FINANCE, GOVERNMENT OF INDIA,
NEW DELHI

I. INTRODUCTORY

When Mr Farmer first wrote to me to invite me to take part in this Conference on Trade and Development, he suggested that in my remarks I might 'consider whether the developing countries can go ahead successfully without having to appeal to and to depend upon the trade liberalisation of industrial countries'. Having been exhorted so often in recent years to consider whether the developing countries cannot dispense with aid and rely instead on trade, it was certainly a sobering reminder that liberal access to the markets of the richer countries may also not be a reliable route to rapid progress.

A little later, you, Mr Chairman, wrote to suggest that since I was to share this platform with Professor Johnson who might argue in favour of freedom in international trade, I could perhaps redress the balance and state the case for protection in developing countries. While I am happy to respond to the suggestion, I hope I should not disappoint anyone if in trying to redress the balance I end up, so to speak, on both sides of the controversy.

I should, however, confess that there is another – rather personal – reason why I welcome the opportunity of being here this afternoon. The subject for this Conference is exactly the same as the one which I chose some twenty-five years ago for my dissertation as a postgraduate student at this university. It is naturally tempting for me to wonder whether the questions that appeared to me to be important then are still relevant; and if not, whether this change over the past quarter of a century has some significance which might be worth noting.

I propose, therefore, to approach my task this afternoon from three different points of view. First, I shall consider the relationship between trade and development in a somewhat longer historical perspective. Next, I shall offer a few remarks on the controversies regarding trade policy that seem to have held the stage now for so many years in almost every discussion on development. And finally, I shall turn to Mr Farmer's question.

II. IN PERSPECTIVE

When I wrote my dissertation, the questions that were uppermost in my mind were the following:

(a) Can countries like India and Indonesia overcome their inherent disadvantage in growth potential by exploiting fully the opportunities offered by international trade? Can trade, in other words, be 'an engine for growth', to use the well-known expression of Professor Dennis Robertson, for overpopulated countries like India in the second half of the twentieth century in much the same way as it had been for the United Kingdom or Australia in the nineteenth century?

(b) To a certain extent, the question just posed was linked with another question, namely whether international trade itself had much of a future. Was world trade likely to grow at least in proportion to the growth in world production despite the spread of manufacturing capability, the growth of synthetic substitutes and other factors which tended to reduce, to use again Professor Robertson's formulation, 'the width of these gaps in the comparative advantages of different countries for the production of different goods'?

(c) Is there any advantage which a poor developing country might seek for itself in its quest for rapid progress which could legitimately be regarded as unfair by countries at a much higher stage of development? For an Indian student, studying in England with memories of Lancashire's onslaught on handlooms, of Imperial Preference and of the constant castigation of Japan as a country which sought 'unfair' advantages for itself by maintaining exchange rates and real wages unduly low, this was a question which was obviously relevant.

Do these questions appear really important now? There are many exponents today of the virtues of international trade in both the developing and the developed countries. But I have not seen one serious argument during the past two decades to suggest that international trade can once again be an engine for growth for countries like India and Indonesia in the same manner as it had been for countries like the United Kingdom or Australia in the nineteenth century. No one today seriously argues that the comparative abundance of labour in a large part of the developing world can be turned to an advantage through international trade to such an extent that it can enable most of the poorer countries to overcome shortage of capital or of natural resources to any significant extent.

Some of you perhaps would recall that in those early post-war years Professor Samuelson had caused quite a stir by arguing that international trade could bring about equality of factor prices in different countries and thus provide a perfect substitute for mobility of factors across national frontiers. But I think it is significant that, despite its analytical elegance, no one has really taken Professor Samuelson's argument seriously as a practical proposition.

Regarding the future of international trade, it is I think fair to say that to most students of economics this question appears rather unimportant today. The feeling still persists that when world trade is rising rapidly, there are likely to be fewer restrictions on trade all round; and the lack of concern with the future of international trade may merely reflect the fact that world trade has in fact increased faster over the past two decades than most people had anticipated. But there is, I think, also a recognition now that if there are natural causes for international trade to decline relatively to world production, this is not a matter of any great consequence in itself.

I recall all this because it has not always been recognised that trade has only a marginal role to play in the strategy of development in most poor countries. Neglect of the opportunities for trade that exist or could be created can be costly. But let us be clear also that the poorer countries cannot seek their salvation largely through a preoccupation with international specialisation. If I may quote from my dissertation: 'One can change the entire pattern of colour and design in a kaleidoscope by shifting only one or two bits of glass. But by shifting resources only on the fringe, a nation cannot infuse new richness or vitality into her economy.'

I wish I could say that questions regarding what might be fair or unfair in matters relating to trade policy or wage policy are also no longer relevant or important. In a sense, it is true that these questions have not aroused much excitement in the recent past, at any rate in relation to the developing countries. It is now generally recognised that there is nothing wrong if a labour-surplus poor country tries to keep wage rates low in the interest of capital accumulation and diffusion of employment opportunities. And as far as exchange rates are concerned, the current fashion is to advise the developing countries to devalue on each conceivable occasion. And yet one suspects that as more and more developing countries emerge as significant exporters of manufactured products, these attitudes will change and the old questions of what is fair or unfair in trade or wage policy will become troublesome once again. Indeed, Mr Farmer's question to which I referred at the outset would seem to suggest that the poor nations might as well be forewarned about this.

III. TRADE POLICY IN DEVELOPING COUNTRIES

While it is true that international trade is no longer offered as a panacea for economic growth, matters relating to trade and trade policy have continued to be highly controversial subjects in any discussion on economic development. Seemingly, much of the heat generated concerns the question of protection or import controls. But we are not likely to get much light thrown on this question unless we distinguish between at least two sets of propositions:

    (*a*) If the argument belongs to the realm of proper allocation of resources, do those who oppose protection or import restrictions merely wish to emphasise that import substitution and export promotion should receive the same attention? Or have they something else in mind?

(*b*) Similarly, if the argument shifts to another plane such as the effect on savings or investment, is it the contention that import restrictions increase the propensity to save or that they prevent a part of the savings potential already in existence from becoming infructuous?

I have a feeling that most people who argue against protection are really saying in effect that while developing countries might give special attention to import substitution, this should not be at the expense of export promotion. But if the proposition is merely that the investment decisions taken today should not result in the self-defeating process of reducing export potential tomorrow while increasing the potential for import substitution, no one, I am sure, would quarrel with it.

Or is there something more to it than that? Basically, those who argue in favour of import restrictions are trying to say that since development is a process of learning by doing, we cannot overlook the fact that, when a thing is produced at home, certain advantages in terms of development of skills, experience and the like occur which would be absent if the demand were met exclusively or even predominantly by imports. Even the most ardent free-traders have recognised the validity of the 'infant industry' argument. Only they have wondered whether this argument does not have a rather limited validity in practice (and some have questioned whether this argument leads to a case for tariffs or for taxes and subsidies on internal production). Advocates of protection, on the other hand, are prone to argue that the 'infant industry' argument is applicable so widely and generally that it takes on the character of an 'infant country' argument.

Here again, I think, we should be better able to keep the argument in focus if we were to ask whether, at any given time, it makes sense to talk of encouraging any particular activity without asking correspondingly for a definition of the activities which are not to be given encouragement. Clearly, if there is an advantage in doing things at home rather than abroad, this advantage cannot be claimed only for activities which compete with imports. Exports also require production at home so that they too result in the kind of learning while doing which is supposed to be the main rationale for protection to 'domestic' industry. Thus the case for protection boils down merely to saying that import substitution and export promotion should be preferred to other forms of activity.

If so, what is this activity over which they are to be preferred? In international trade theory a distinction is sometimes sought to be drawn between goods which enter into international trade and goods which do not. In a static sense, one could perhaps give meaning to such a distinction. Generation of electricity and transport, for example, would in this sense belong to the category of activities which are generally neither exported nor imported. But quite clearly it does not make sense to say that export promotion or import substitution should receive encouragement over generation of electricity or provision of transport facilities. In the ultimate analysis, everything is either exportable or importable or is necessary for the production of that which could be exported or imported. If this is the case, I really do not see what concrete meaning we can assign to the 'infant industry' or the 'infant country' argument in the context of trade policy when this policy is considered in the macro or the aggregative sense.

Having said this, I still feel that the 'infant industry' argument has one major practical implication. It implies, I think, that even at the expense of some gain in the immediate future, developing countries should try to concentrate their energies from time to time on some leading or limited sectors to realise in full 'economies of scale' in sector after sector and thus achieve over time as diversified a structure of production as possible. In this process they should not shun the use of special inducements or protection to the activities selected from time to time for a special growth push. In other words, instead of dissipating their energies somewhat ineffectively over a wide area, developing countries should choose from time to time certain leading sectors (in exports, import substitution as well as supporting activities) for special promotional efforts. This would enable them to acquire competence quickly and decisively in area after area and would give them a diversified capability over time, thus accelerating the tempo of growth as well as providing greater insurance against vicissitudes of change. I doubt if the traditional arguments for protection can be pressed any further. Perhaps the whole debate on this question will gain in clarity if it is conducted in terms of defining proper criteria for investment decisions rather than as an elaboration of the somewhat sterile propositions of the traditional theory of international trade.

So far we have considered the traditional or the classical case for protection based merely on considerations of allocative efficiency. There are, however, some other arguments for import restrictions which have also been urged, particularly in recent years. It has been said, for example – among others by the present writer himself – that the balance of payments barrier to development is reached before the savings barrier, so that anything which helps to overcome balance of payments difficulties makes it possible to step up investment beyond what would otherwise be possible.

Whether in fact the balance of payments barrier is reached before the savings barrier is difficult to prove statistically as, at any given time, it is not possible to distinguish between the savings gap and the gap in balance of payments. To harassed government officers or ministers in developing countries, who can get over the shortage of local resources at least in the short run by resort to the printing-press but cannot equally get around foreign exchange difficulties by drawing down reserves, the proposition that balance of payments difficulties arise in advance of difficulties regarding internal resources appears almost self-evident. It is also true that to a certain extent internal savings can be forced whereas one cannot force exports on unwilling buyers. In the short run there are also difficulties in converting local resources into exportable products. Nevertheless, I feel now that this particular argument for import restrictions is generally less valid than most people in the developing countries are inclined to think.

While savings can be forced in the short run, it is also the experience of country after country that those who are forced to save today will retaliate in one way or the other, so that over time the net savings which can be forced out of unwilling savers and taxpayers are not really all that great. Equally, local resources can be converted into export earnings at a price; and it is by no means self-evident that while local resources cannot be easily converted into exports, it is easier to convert them into something which can substitute for imports.

More often than not, the attempt to save on foreign exchange resources by restricting imports does not even succeed in the limited purpose of reducing foreign exchange outgo. This is so because the ban on the import of luxury commodites is very often followed by a permission to produce the same things at home with the help of foreign capital and a large import of components and the like.

On the other hand, there is a great deal to be said for so influencing the pattern of domestic demand that the consumption and import of luxuries is automatically reduced. It is certainly arguable that the fascination for imported products is so great in most poor societies that, unless the population is kept away from these products over a wide range, both the propensity to consume and the level of demand for imports would be so high as to cripple the growth potential of the economy. In other words, what seems more relevant to emphasise is not that the savings and the balance of payments barriers are two distinct phenomena, but that there is such a thing as a wasteful or meaningless preference for imported luxury articles which, unless it is successfully resisted, can and does come in the way of rapid economic development both by reducing the community's capacity to save and by increasing the pressure on the balance of payments.

But a plea for austerity of this sort can hardly be of any real significance unless the campaign for austerity is carried over to all forms of less essential consumption irrespective of whether they have a direct or an indirect foreign exchange component or not. In the ultimate analysis, austerity, like peace, is indivisible. And indeed, if it is to be properly enforced, it requires a more or less thorough overhaul of social and economic structures so as to achieve a much greater degree of equality in incomes and consumption than prevails in most developing countries today. To do nothing about these prevailing inequalities and to concentrate merely on banning the imports of a few luxury items of consumption would achieve hardly anything over a period.

In short, import controls have something to do with the saving and growth potential of the developing countries. But this beneficial effect flows not from the mechanical effect of import control but from a whole set of policies which are geared to reducing the demand for luxuries and of which import control is only one and a somewhat smaller part at that.

IV. IS TRADE LIBERALISATION VITAL?

Let me turn finally to the question which was specifically posed to me when I was invited to attend this Conference: Can the developing countries go ahead successfully without having to appeal to and to depend upon the trade liberalisation of industrial countries? Basically, this question in turn requires us to answer a series of other questions such as:

(a) Is it possible for the developing countries to grow by turning inwards so to speak, so that they do not have to import much and therefore do not need to export a great deal?

(b) Alternatively, to the extent that the developing countries have to depend on outside markets and outside sources of supply, can they do so by co-operating among themselves, whether on a regional or on a global basis, so that the dependence on countries already advanced is correspondingly reduced?

(c) Or, to the extent that the developing countries have to depend upon industrial countries for markets for their products, can they not secure on their own what they need without asking for any favours, e.g. by (i) aggressive action to undercut other industrially advanced countries; or (ii) by combining with other developing countries to secure better terms of trade for themselves as a group?

I have no doubt, as I have said earlier, that the developing countries must try to develop their economies on the basis of considerable diversification of their economic and industrial structure rather than rely on excessive specialisation in a few directions. In that sense, growing inwards is unavoidable for most of the poorer countries of the world today. At the same time, the logic of development and of resource availability in most developing countries today is such that they will have to export also on a diversified basis if they are to meet their minimum requirements of imports from time to time. And as long as you have to depend upon exports to a considerable extent, it is no use pretending that the absence or presence of liberal import policies in countries which after all would still provide the major part of the world market for many decades to come is of no significance or consequence. All one can say is that this factor is not all that crucial or decisive.

As for co-operation among themselves, it is not easy for the developing countries to co-operate effectively on a global basis in a manner which requires a certain artificial independence from the rest of the world, at least during the transitional period. It is difficult to visualise a situation, for example, in which India, Brazil and Ghana or Korea would exchange goods among themselves on a preferential basis so as to reduce their combined dependence on imports from the U.K., France and Germany. If we are talking only of regional or sub-regional co-operation among developing countries, there are perhaps better chances of success, particularly where political and cultural factors are favourable. But it is by no means clear that even when such a co-operative effort on the part of some developing countries does succeed, the success would be achieved essentially by increasing the independence of the group vis-à-vis the industrially advanced countries rather than in relation to other developing countries. It is at least possible that a series of common markets among developing countries would reduce their trade with other developing countries as much as – if not somewhat more than – it would with the advanced countries who, after all, will have a lot of bargaining power left to prevent discrimination against them.

As for selling aggressively by undercutting other exporters, this argument can apply primarily to the export of manufactured products from the developing countries to the industrially advanced countries. But as more and more developing countries become exporters of manufactured products, their exchange rate and wage policies will be subject to the same critical review as was exercised over Japan for many years with threats of countervailing duties or restrictions. The way in which restrictions against imports of cotton textiles continue to be maintained and enhanced as a protection against 'cheap' labour, and the concern which is beginning to be felt in the

United States and elsewhere regarding undervalued exchange rates, is proof enough that as long as the richer countries are unwilling to open their markets fully to exports of manufactured products from the poorer nations, the latter cannot, so to speak, sneak in through aggressive salesmanship.

When it comes to aggressive action to combine to secure better terms of trade for primary products one might feel that, judging from the recent success of the OPEC countries, there might be a greater chance of success in respect of other products also. But I am afraid it is too much of a simplification to think that the poorer countries are producers of primary products and the richer countries are consumers of the same. There is no doubt that in the years to come there is going to be much greater confrontation between the rich and the poor in regard to this question of terms of trade. But while confrontation there will be, it is by no means certain that it will lead to any concrete and significant advantage for the developing countries taken as a whole. The recent action of the OPEC countries, for example, has hurt a large number of developing countries. If India, Australia and Brazil were to combine to secure higher prices for iron ore, a part of the incidence at any rate will fall on some of the poorer countries. It is not my intention to suggest that the developing countries should not act in concert to improve their terms of trade wherever possible. But I have a feeling that such concerted action should stop short of unabashed monopolistic action. For once you get into a mood of warfare in trade, it is going to be difficult to keep the firing within any prescribed limits.

In considering this question of being able to do without liberal trade policies on the part of industrial countries, we may also consider some other possible courses of action. It could be argued, for example, that once again the world might return to four or five major trading blocs, each with its centre of industrial strength surrounded by a large number of developing countries and each having a preferential trading arrangement within itself. Unfortunately, the danger of a return to some such form of economic colonialism is all too real, as is clear from the attitude of the European Economic Community. In such a world the developing countries will not have to ask for liberal trade policies in general because they will be divided into spheres of influence and willingly given such liberal access (within their sphere) in return for corresponding preferences in trade and other matters. All one can say about such a possibility is that, however real it may be, it would still deserve the same condemnation which the policy of discrimination in favour of British goods in the colonial empire received from Professor Dennis Robertson when he described it as 'a policy which has been indifferent economics, bad morals and shocking diplomacy'.

There is, of course, another possibility which is also real and equally unfortunate. This is that the developing countries will progressively find that they get little justice, let alone preference, in matters of trade so that they will soon come to the conclusion that the only alternative for them to get what they need from the industrial countries is to extort capital one way or the other.

While so much is being said about the so-called need for giving preferential or liberal treatment to the exports of developing countries, in reality the developing countries are not able to enjoy even equal treatment in regard to opportunities for export. Thus, for example, the normal disadvantages that they naturally have in the export of manufactured products are often compounded by the fact that practically all bilateral aid today is tied. Time and again countries like India have lost export orders for capital goods because an industrially advanced competitor has been able to offer in the name of aid far more favourable terms and conditions of payment.

What is even more iniquitous is that, while aid is tied, the repayment of credits is not similarly tied to purchase of goods by the creditor country from the debtor country. The result is that debt payments require a degree of export effort which is out of proportion to the benefit secured earlier through the credits which are being repaid.

Even in regard to the so-called general scheme of preferences, it is now clear that when the industrial countries get organised into a vast common market such as that in Europe, the preference given to the exports of developing countries becomes virtually meaningless. Far from getting preference in the German market vis-à-vis the U.K. or in the French market vis-à-vis Germany, countries like India will remain at a permanent disadvantage when it comes to competing in Germany with the U.K. or in France with Germany.

Against this background, it is not at all unlikely that, faced with continuing balance of payments difficulties, the developing countries in future will react exactly by assuming that there is no point in trying to increase exports to industrial countries or to reduce imports from them. They may well be persuaded by now by Professor Johnson and others that by restricting imports they will only harm themselves; and while they cannot afford to give up the effort to increase exports, they may well feel with Mr Farmer that, beyond a point, they are bound to meet with resistance of one kind or another in increasing exports.

Can it not be, then, that the developing countries will seek to confront the industrial countries in other ways, e.g. by insisting that debts contracted through tied aid should also be payable only through tied exports? Once this is tried even on a modest scale by a few countries, we would, as the Americans say, be in an altogether different ball park in so far as trade relationships between the developed and developing countries are concerned. Are the industrial countries really so averse to throwing open their markets to the products of the developing world that, when faced with the dilemma of 'import or abandon your claims', they will really opt for the latter?

It is tempting to ask: if the developing countries cannot depend on liberal trade policies on the part of the industrial nations, can they seek their salvation through invisible earnings? Visions of millions of tourists and pensioners from the West basking in the Indian sun (in the winter months at least) have not been altogether absent from the minds of development planners; and a few visionaries have even dreamt of migration of labour from the poor to the rich nations on a scale which would, through remittances, make it redundant to worry too much about trade. Add to this the prospect that even large segments of industry might shift wholesale from the industrial to the developing countries in response, shall we say, to differential endowment of pollution. It is certainly nice to make Professor Samuelson's argument stand on its own head and say that if we cannot have free movement of goods, we can make do with a freer movement of factors of production. But this sounds too much like hoping that while bread may be in short supply, there would be plenty of cake to go round.

It seems, in conclusion, we are left with the following rather conflicting thoughts:

(*a*) whether the developing countries can go ahead successfully or not is not an issue which will be decided essentially by whether or not the industrial countries are prepared to pursue liberal import policies;

(*b*) at the same time, it is idle to pretend that liberal import policies on the part of the richer countries will not facilitate significantly the progress of the poorer nations;

(*c*) if liberal trade policies on the part of the richer countries become an exception rather than the rule, the developing countries are not likely to adjust to this situation by restricting imports unduly. Nor will they be able to meet their needs by keeping their wage rates or exchange rates low as this would invite retaliation in an essentially restrictive trade environment;

(*d*) since the rich can live with relative stagnation in their standard of living (and can even be lured into thinking that limiting growth improves the quality of life) while the poor cannot, the only way the problem can be resolved amicably in the absence of liberal trade policies is by periodically converting loans into grants or by continuing transfers of capital by one device or another; and – there is the rub –

(*e*) if we cannot accept the need for liberal import policy and are not prepared at the same time to accept the logical consequences such as a continuing transfer of capital or a phase of mutually agreed debt relief, there is every danger of our drifting into a world of rival trading blocs or of frequent but frustrating confrontations between the rich and the poor to improve their respective terms of trade.

One can only hope that after twenty-five years of sensible efforts to secure international economic co-operation, we should not, out of impatience with our limited success, lapse into a spell of madness before returning to a modicum of sanity.

3 Outward-Looking *v.* Inward-Looking Strategies: The Developing Countries

Outward-Looking Strategies: A Dangerous Illusion?

Ignacy Sachs

DIRECTOR OF STUDIES, ÉCOLE PRATIQUE DES
HAUTES ÉTUDES, PARIS

Trade as an engine of growth *redivivus*. Dismantle controls, devalue, forget about planning and land reform. Instead let middlemen and money-lenders perform their job, open the doors wide to foreign private investors by making attractive to them your natural endowments and cheap labour (for this purpose maintain wages low enough to please multinational corporations, and concentrate on infrastructural investment)[1] and keep smiling: thanks to Comparative Advantage, you will enter the road to prosperity by reviving the good old colonial division of labour. The industralised countries might graciously co-operate in this noble venture by accepting to buy some shirts, shoes, wigs (a buoyant market indeed for Chinese girls' hair in Hong Kong!), electrical appliances and transistor radio sets; furthermore, as they become alarmed by the level of industrial pollution in their territory, some of them (in particular Japan) might also envisage replacing imports of mineral ores by semi-processed metals, thus giving an opportunity to South Asian and Latin American countries to engage in 'export substitution'.[1]

This old vinegar in rather old bottles (don't plan, don't industrialise, rely on agriculture and primary exports, trust the world market) is being sold now under a new label. Political analysts have suggested that the disenchantment with import substitution might be conveniently explored by insisting on outward-looking strategies. A similar intellectual operation is at work now with respect to growth. Growth-mania is becoming unpopular, so people might buy non-growth and quality of life.

A full swing is so much simpler than asking about the misuses of growth, the uneven distribution of benefits and incomes derived from it, and searching for ways of harmonising growth with social justice and environmental concern.

The authors quoted above point with perspicacity to many severe shortcomings of import-substituting industrialisation in many less developed countries. Their views on the subject are widely shared.

Excessive protection has been granted to industries (in many cases subsidiaries of foreign companies) turning out inefficiently non-essential products and selling them at exceedingly high prices to a narrow, wealthy elite.

A mix of unselective fiscal, credit and exchange policies, added to availability of foreign assistance for imports of capital goods, made it both possible and advantageous to the entrepreneurs to rely on highly capital-intensive equipment manufactured abroad and technologies unsuited to the factor proportions prevailing at home. Industrialisation of this type created little new employment, the more so since it displaced the cottage industries. Excess capacity is endemic, as the imperfections of the market allow for shifting to the consumer the burden of over-investment. When profits are a mark-up over costs and the price elasticity of demand is low, the higher the costs, the more money the entrepreneurs earn.

Import substitution thus turned out to be self-defeating, as induced imports of equipment, components and material inputs run high, while royalties and expatriated profits constitute a severe drain on scarce foreign exchange receipts. Furthermore, the limits of import substitution in consumer goods have been quickly exhausted; easy import substitution has come to an end.

At this point two questions must be asked before recommending, as a remedy to the evils described above, a return to unrestricted free trade and an outward-looking strategy:

(1) Why did so many less developed countries opt for import substitution, in spite of the efforts of the former colonial powers and the United States to keep them on the opposite track?

(2) Is the blame for the poor results described above to be

put on import substitution as such or on the inability (and/or unwillingness) of the ruling elites to engage in a different and more efficient process of import substitution?

As far as the first problem is concerned, the situation has been aptly summarised in a recent paper [5]:

At the present time, the developing countries are being criticised for their approach to the process of import substitution, and emphasis is being placed on the negative aspects of this policy in that it distorts the factors of production and therefore leads to inefficiency in the use of resources.

Nevertheless, it is pertinent to ask whether conditions in the world market were such that it would have been possible for the less developed countries to apply a different policy at the time, in view of the internal and external pressures on them. It may be agreed that the import substitution policy could often have been carried out more efficiently and with greater foresight; however, it is sufficient to reflect on the situation in which the less developed countries would now find themselves if such action had not been taken to realise that this process was inevitable, socially, economically and politically.

If during the last twenty years different action had been taken on a world-wide basis – with the industrialised countries adjusting the conditions of access to their markets and the less advanced countries developing accordingly – a more rational international division of labour would doubtless have been achieved, which would have benefited the international community as a whole.

It is pointless to discuss whether an outward-looking strategy would have been better, if for most less developed countries the real choice was between an inward-looking strategy and sacrificing growth altogether. Import substitution became thus the proverbial virtue made out of necessity. We may add that an inward-looking strategy does not imply forgoing reasonable opportunities to increase exports.[2] It really amounts to maximising the rate of growth for a given capacity to import, i.e. treating the coefficient of imports as a strategic variable and not a parameter [9]. But no effort should be spared by the planners to explore all the means of maximising the capacity to import, both by fostering exports and by compressing all payments abroad that are not essential.

Let us turn now to alternative patterns of import substitution.

Most of the criticisms referred to above apply to the *shallow and extensive import substitution* in the realm of consumer goods that belongs to the syndrome of *perverse growth* [10]. Controls of foreign trade, imposed to save foreign exchange expenditure on imports of non-essentials, were not combined with income redistribution leading to a change in the consumption pattern, and investment allocation was left to the market mechanism. The stage was set in this way for the hypertrophy of the sector turning out luxuries and non-essentials, to the detriment of the remaining sectors of the economy: production of essentials could not progress for lack of a market, resulting from the skewed income distribution, and no serious incentives were provided to explore backward linkages towards intermediate and capital goods, i.e. to engage in the *deepening of the import-substitution process*. Concentration of scarce resources, including foreign exchange and skills, in the luxury-goods sector, the only one that does not participate in the process of enlarged reproduction,[3] must lead at some point to a blind alley: the opportunities for import substitution of non-essentials become exhausted (the more inefficient the local industry and the higher its unit prices, the sooner this limit is reached), but the ground is not prepared at all to go ahead with import substitution in the capital- and intermediate-goods industries. Technological dependence aggravates the situation.

In other words, what is to be blamed is *badly* conceived import substitution and not import substitution as such: the naïve idea that controls on foreign trade, together with an *indiscriminating* support of any industrial investment, would be a *sufficient* condition to promote the right type of industrialisation. Although unavoidable under prevailing conditions in the world market, and certainly necessary for planning, import controls could not work properly for lack of accompanying measures in the realm of income redistribution, choice of more adequate consumption patterns and resource allocation. While agreeing thus with the description of the actual distortions of the industrialisation process in developing countries contained in the sources quoted above, we reach the diametrically opposed conclusion with respect to the remedies. Controls must be revised and made more effective – not be dismantled. It makes no sense to speak of planning and to accept free trade as well as to give up any consumption planning, relying instead on the demonstration effect of Western patterns of consumption on a tiny elite. Foreign exchange is the joker of the planning game, as all the internal tensions of an economy can always be translated into additional demand for imports of goods and services. (In that sense, the U.N. Secretariat is right to emphasise the importance of the foreign exchange gap rather than the savings gap. The latter can, at least theoretically, be closed by adequate fiscal and income policies.[4]) To forego the opportunity of influencing the pattern of growth by intervening at the borderline between the national and the international economy is tantamount to letting the forces of the world market shape the destiny of one's country. Instead the less developed countries are discovering by experience that their only chance lies in more self-reliance, which is not tantamount to commercial autarky but consists in the capacity for autonomous decision-making and, above all, for setting development objectives distinct from the models followed by industrialised countries, be it at the level of consumption pattern or of technologies.

As for the argument that controls invite corruption, one should keep in mind the fact that corruption is, alas, also present in free-market economies. No doubt there is more scope for it when controls are in operation. But is this reason enough to change the whole approach to development, rather than postulating more social control on the public administration entrusted with controls?

Are the prospects for outward-looking strategies better now than in the past?

Professor Myint's optimistic study on South-east Asia foresees a tremendous increase in Japan's imports from the area. This may prove true, although one would have liked a more cautious assessment of the political implications of the Japanese expansion for the small countries of the region. Are we heading for the resurgence of a new imperial zone of influence? Some Japanese economists compare the future pattern of Japan's relation with South-east Asia to that of the United States with Latin America. This is quite a frightening perspective indeed,

left entirely outside the cost–benefit calculations advocated both
by the O.E.C.D. and Myint.[5]

Moreover, the situation of most countries in other parts of
the world does not warrant the same optimism, even on the most
narrow commercial grounds, with the exception perhaps of some
oil exporters.[6] All recent UNCTAD and U.N. studies ([13],
[14], [15], [16]) converge in pointing out the following lessons:
no progress was made in commodity trade with respect to
granting the less developed countries access to markets; the
United States, Britain, Japan and the E.E.C. spend from $21
to $24 billion per year on direct and indirect support of domestic
production of importable primary commodities; this figure is to
be compared with $7·7 billion of net official flow of financial
resources to less developed countries in 1970.

While the share of manufactures in less developed countries'
exports rose from 10 per cent in 1960 to 18 per cent in 1969,
six countries (Hong Kong, Taiwan, India, Yugoslavia, Mexico
and the Republic of Korea) account for three-fifths of the total.
The less developed countries' share in developed market
economy countries' imports is a bare 5·5 per cent, concentrated
on a few items: 20 per cent for food products, 26·2 per cent for
clothing, 15·7 per cent for leather and footwear, 13·5 per cent
for textiles, but only 0·8 per cent for pulp, paper and board,
2·4 per cent for iron and steel, 0·1 per cent for motor vehicles,
1·9 per cent for other engineering and metal products. One can
argue, of course, that such a low share leaves room for expansion, but this is not a very convincing argument.

The system of generalised preferences recently adopted could
lead on most generous assumptions to an increase of 3 per
cent in less developed countries' exports. But a more realistic
estimate, taking into account the prevailing restrictions unlikely
to be removed, points to an increase of no more than $500 to
$600 million per year, without allowance for the probable
adverse price effects of competition between less developed
countries [5]. If there is thus some room for satisfaction with
respect to the measures taken in principle in favour of less
developed countries, 'the most important thing remains to be
done: namely to apply the norms that have been proclaimed'
[15], both between developed and less developed countries and
among less developed countries.

Recent developments, analysed in the last U.N. *World Survey* [16], indicate that the basic premises of post-war trade liberalisation are being increasingly questioned, protectionism is on the rise and regional groupings are strengthened. In the same vein, a prospective study released by the French Planning Commission [2] envisages as one serious possibility the return to protectionism of Western countries and a fierce rivalry, if not a commercial war, between the United States, Japan and Europe.

At a moment when the non-protectionist interlude in world trade may be nearing its end, to advise less developed countries to shift towards more outward-looking strategies is, at best, indulging in the typical mistake of generals who prepare themselves for the last war they have won and, at worst, helping to reinforce the neo-colonial grip on their economies.

The above statement must be qualified with respect to genuine efforts for expansion of trade and the creation of regional groupings among developing countries, such as the Andean Pact. Their success depends, however, on the ability to promote a new industrial division of labour, while mere trade liberalisation is likely to serve only the interests of multinational enterprises operating from inside. Moreover, it should not be understood as an *a priori* preference for import substitution as against export promotion. The propositions between export promotion and import substitution can be established for a given country and period on a fairly pragmatic basis by using, as a sub-optimisation device, the criterion of net domestic cost per unit of foreign exchange earned or saved.

The case for an outward-looking strategy, based on a rational and equitable division of labour, may be argued on normative grounds as a chapter of welfare economics, quite apart from the assessment of its feasibility in present world conditions. The main proponent of this theory is Professor Jan Tinbergen [12]. In a nutshell, his proposal amounts to a return to the normative implications of the theory of comparative advantage, based upon different factor proportions prevailing in different countries. Less developed countries should accordingly be given an opportunity to expand labour-intensive industries, while the advanced countries should concentrate on capital- and skill-intensive products. This approach raises, however, several doubts briefly summarised below.

Maximisation of welfare is assumed to be tantamount to maximisation of total net output and its more equal distribution. This is, however, a narrow criterion characteristic of 'economic reductionism'; it leaves out of account many externalities and, in particular, the role of 'industrialising industries' in the process of structural economic, social and mental change. The proposed division of labour petrifies the differences between more developed and less developed countries and in this way amounts to a repetition of the old colonial pattern, the only difference being that the list of industries allocated to the less developed countries is expanded.[7] Pricing and wage determination are dealt with by means of the neo-classical theory of factor productivity. This makes Professor Tinbergen's proposal vulnerable to all the objections to neo-classical economics, too well known to be recalled here. At any rate, income inequalities are perpetuated. A more radical approach would consist in disconnecting wages from the productivity of labour and postulating equal incomes for all citizens of the world (related to average world productivity of labour). In this way, the economic case for Tinbergen's division of labour would be made more convincing. But the problem of externalities would still remain. In particular, people working with labour-intensive methods might consider their work more painful even though it yields the same income.[8]

It would seem thus that the criteria of labour intensity and natural factor endowments do not add up to a satisfactory theory of the international division of labour, even if one were to foresee a joint management of natural resources on a world-wide basis [1] and in this way take care of the difficult problem of unequal paths of depletion of non-renewable resources.

A different approach has been tried by Eastern European countries inside the C.M.E.A. Specialisation should result not only from natural endowments and factor proportions, but also from the recognised need of building complex industrial structures in each country as a policy objective; exchanges are to be promoted thus inside each branch of industry and specialisation carried out with respect to the products, models or components. This is, however, easier said than done and the record of the C.M.E.A. has been remarkably unsuccessful, judging by the number of competitive industries built in member countries. Part of the failure is to be attributed to political circumstances – the mistrust of the Soviet Union by its partners. One should point then to the doctrinaire attachment to heavy industries and to industrial exports as symbols of economic advancement, to the point of aiming at balanced exchanges in each major commodity group to the detriment of natural comparative advantage, e.g. in agriculture. But to a great extent the difficulties spring from a lack of an adequate measuring-rod for comparing costs, pricing new goods and distributing more evenly the investment burden. World prices (to the extent to which they can be identified) are a very poor indicator of economic rationality. There is no reason to give the world market more credit as resource allocator than the market as such, not to mention the distortions imposed by the operations of multinational corporations. But to invent a new price system and to agree on it is still more difficult. As to the calculations of effectiveness of investment, they are open to the same criticism as the cost–benefit analysis with respect to the arbitrariness involved in dealing with externalities (what do we do when externalities become all-pervasive?) and with the dynamisation of parameters that in a developing economy must be treated as variables. Finally, when it comes to participation in projects with a long gestation period and therefore a high capital–output ratio, all principles of solidarity vanish and the parties concerned engage in hard bargaining.

The experience of the C.M.E.A. suggests, however, an approach for developing countries wishing to foster exchange in new products. It should be possible for them to build up, step by step, a new division of labour, through patient negotiations of sets of long-term contracts of supply of selected commodities matched by guarantees of markets for other commodities. This would allow each investor to enjoy economies of scale, while avoiding the inconveniences of joint management of enterprises working for several national markets.

Such an approach may seem very pedestrian. But it has definite advantages. Benefits need not be equal, so long as all the partners will gain by building plants with economies of scale, made possible by the foreign market guarantee. Simultaneous negotiation of a set of contracts should allow the establishment of new industries in all countries participating in the exercise. Finally, the cumbersome administration of joint supranational enterprises would be avoided. The countries of the Andean Pact have just signed an agreement on the division of labour in metal and engineering industries which may be considered as a first modest step in the right direction. The next move might consist in engaging in a functional analysis of backward linkages of such resource-based industries as mining, forestry and fisheries, with a view to planning jointly the implantation of a regional capital-goods industry. If such efforts are paralleled by a drive towards more technological independence, they may result in building into the development strategy of the member countries a very valuable and lasting outward-looking element.

Notes

1. This is the gist of the recommendations contained in a study on South-east Asia, commissioned by the Asian Development Bank [8]. The same trend emerges from [6]; although the authors' approach is more balanced and qualified, Professor Johnson's article [4] has the immense advantage of being frank, as stressed by him in the sub-title.

2. Theoretically, exports can always be stepped up, but at the expense of a growing capital–output ratio of foreign trade-orientated investment. It is up to the planner, as M. Kalecki has shown, to decide at what point the advantages derived from increased earnings of foreign exchange are offset by the burden of additional investment.

3. The sector turning out essentials participates in the reproduction of the labour force.

4. The O.E.C.D. study quoted above criticises, however, the foreign exchange gap approach.

5. For a penetrating review of the limitations of the cost-benefit approach, see [11].

6. Addressing the UNCTAD in Santiago, the President of the World Bank quoted illuminating figures of oil-exporting countries (representing less than 4 per cent of the world population): over the last decade, their G.N.P. grew at an annual rate of 8·4 per cent, against an average of 5 per cent and 3·9 per cent for countries with a G.N.P. of less than $200 per capita (representing 67 per cent of population). Fuel exports grew at 10 per cent per year and represented one-third of total export earnings of the less developed countries, but three-quarters of those earnings accrued to six countries with less than 3 per cent of world population [7].

7. See [3] on this point. Furtado insists, however, on the petrification of the differences in labour productivity. This does not seem to us to be the central problem.

8. One might further complicate this exercise in Utopia by introducing differential degrees of alienation, working perhaps in reverse.

References

[1] BORGESE, Elisabeth Mann, 'An International Earth Resource Management Organisation: A New Development Strategy', *Bulletin of Peace Proposals*, no. 2 (1972).

[2] COMMISSARIAT GÉNÉRAL AU PLAN, *1985 – La France face au choc du futur* (Paris, 1972).

[3] FURTADO, Celso, 'Dépendance externe et théorie économique', *L'Homme et la Société*, no. 22 (1971).

[4] JOHNSON, Harry G., 'A Word to the Third World: A Western Economist's Frank Advice', *Encounter* (Oct. 1971).

[5] LACARTE, Julio A., *Aspects of International Trade and Assistance Relating to the Expansion of Employment in the Developing Countries*, United Nations (Committee for Development Planning), Doc. E/AC.54/L.45, 21 Jan. 1972.

[6] LITTLE, Ian, SCITOVSKY, Tibor, and SCOTT, Maurice (Development Centre of O.E.C.D.), *Industry and Trade in Some Developing Countries: A Comparative Study* (London, 1970).

[7] MCNAMARA, Robert S., *Address to the UNCTAD* (Santiago, Apr. 1972).

[8] MYINT, H., *South-east Asia's Economy: Development Policies in the 1970s*, a study sponsored by the Asian Development Bank (Harmondsworth, 1972).

[9] SACHS, Ignacy, *Foreign Trade and Economic Development of Underdeveloped Countries* (Bombay, 1965).

[10] ——, *La Découverte du Tiers Monde* (Paris, 1971).

[11] STREETEN, Paul, 'Cost–Benefit and Other Problems of Method', in I. Sachs (ed.), *Political Economy of Environment: Problems of Method* (Paris, 1972).

[12] TINBERGEN, J., 'The Optimal International Division of Labour', *Acta Oeconomica Academiae Scientiarum Hungaricae*, III (1968).

[13] UNCTAD Secretariat, *Commodity Problems and Policies: Access to Markets*, Doc. TD/115, 27 Jan. 1972.

[14] ——, *Review of Trade in Manufactures of the Developing Countries*, Doc. TD/111, 20 Dec. 1971.

[15] UNITED NATIONS (Committee for Development Planning), *Attack on Mass Poverty and Unemployment*, Doc. E/AC.54/L.50, 9 Mar. 1972.

[16] ——, *World Economic Survey, 1971* (New York, 1972).

Advancing Tropical African Development: A Defence of Inward-Looking Strategy

O. Aboyade

PROFESSOR OF ECONOMICS, UNIVERSITY OF
IBADAN, NIGERIA

The literature of economic analysis on the development of underdeveloped countries has witnessed significant changes in the last three decades in respect of prescriptions for general policy strategy. These changes may be viewed lightly, as fashions; and more seriously as movements. The rapidity of this seemingly endless process of analytical affirmation and reversal is probably most evident in the relationship between international trade and domestic development. The chorus of professional opinion has moved from primary export specialisation to protective import-substitution manufacturing, through industrial export promotion, back to gradual import substitution. In general policy terms, the bias is now often posited as a conflict between an inward-looking and an outward-looking development strategy.

This paper is based on the proposition that the assumed policy choice may not in fact be a real one at the level of operational decision-making. The contrasting policy prescriptions derive largely from a historical fact that different parts of the underdeveloped world with varying resources and conflicting objectives of social policy have dominated analytical thinking at particular periods in time, and especially so in the last three decades. This paper argues that in the specific world-historical context in which tropical Africa finds itself today, the real policy option for the 1970s is an inward-looking strategy first at the national level and later at the regional level. It is important to emphasise the dimension of time and place, because it is both wrong and unnecessary to prescribe a universally valid strategy of development for all countries over all periods.

If we recall that the central issue of development theorising remains today as it has been since Ricardo, namely to seek the rate of growth compatible with the changing resources, institutions and technology available to a given economy, then a clear case can be made for revamping the external economic relations of tropical African countries as a necessary condition for achieving more rapid and meaningful development. Its present pattern of international trade is essentially neo-colonial, resulting in superficial output growth rather than sustained development. Its exports are in general facing secular declining demand in the world market. Its economic distance from the rest of the world is so large that it cannot simply and uncritically take over strategies which may be currently in vogue in other regions of the world. The main thrust of this paper is to lay the ingredients for a defence of an inward-looking strategy for tropical Africa that goes beyond conventional import substitution.

I. GENERAL IMPORT-SUBSTITUTION EXPERIENCE

Since the Second World War, developing country after developing country has shown that the path to industrialisation (and hence generally to economic transformation) lies in import substitution with a protectionist policy. The notable exceptions which prove this rule are the city-state open economies of Hong Kong and Singapore. The concentration on industrialisation arises partly from the realisation that the nineteenth-century free-trade regime that benefited so much the primary-products specialisation of 'countries of recent settlement' (mainly the Anglo-Saxon extensions in North America and Australasia) is today far from being in evidence – at least, not to the primary-product exporting economies of tropical Africa. The industrialisation emphasis also arises partly from its multiple role in the development process: meeting growing domestic demand for manufactured consumer goods, providing employment opportunities for trained labour, easing the strain on the balance of payments and strengthening the long-run productive capacity of the economy.

Even countries which are relatively small in size have found the industrialisation path the most rewarding. The growth curve of small countries which have an industry orientation has been found to be consistently above that of small countries with a primary-product orientation over most income ranges. And if industrial exporting is regarded as the ultimate test of successful industrialisation, the small primary-orientated economies reach the threshold norm of industrial export status much later than the small manufactures-orientated economies.

The general process of industrialisation is for import-substitution activity to take place, following the erection of protectionist walls. Usually in a colonial-type external trading arrangement, high profit margins are made by an importing business sector controlled by metropolitan monopoly capital. With high protection, the old importer's market could be protected and his rate of surplus preserved without even having to raise domestic prices. At this stage the policy choice does not arise between creating industries which cater primarily for the domestic market and those which are domestic-resource based (whether they are for the home or the export market). Import substitution is the rule because it is a logical step from manufactures import with an established market, because the problems of production scale and plant size are not as serious, and because most of the simple resources needed are generally available in different countries.

As the domestic market for simple consumer goods becomes saturated by showing tendencies towards inefficient capacity utilisation, the choice between continuing import substitution to the higher stage of intermediate and capital goods and expanding industries which are essentially resource-based begins to arise. This critical stage is fraught with great risks of failure and the future of industrial development may be compromised according to the resource endowment of the economy and the skilfulness of its national economic management. Also important at this stage would be the efficiency of previous import-substitution activities, an efficiency related ultimately to prevailing levels of effective protection and the financial structure of industrial capital.

Because a number of underdeveloped countries have thus ended up with distorted high-cost industrial sectors, the impression is rapidly gaining ground that an import-substitution (or inward-looking) strategy is inimical to the long-run development of an underdeveloped economy: in other words, that industrial protection should be viewed strictly as a temporary deviation from the desired norm of free trade. Protection results in import restriction which causes distortion of both trade and prices. Government intervention with normal trade flows leads to economic inefficiency; and an import-substitution strategy often results in unhealthy bias against agricultural expansion and export. Through unviable turnkey projects, suppliers' credit and contractors' finance, a number of developing countries have ended up only with high-cost industries that use more foreign exchange than they save and that survive only through expensive fiscal incentives and relatively high domestic prices. Thus, import substitution can be, and has in cases been, counterproductive and anti-developmental.

All these have created a general atmosphere of professional disenchantment with import substitution as an industrial strategy of development. It connotes a retreat from the challenge of international competition, perhaps reflecting a nation's lack or loss of confidence in itself. It sounds myopic, based on crude nationalistic sentiment and charged with an emotive reaction to the economic superiority of foreigners. Developing countries are thus being enjoined to move out of the stultifying strait jacket of import substitution to the healthier open air of international competition. But whatever the empirical basis for this policy prescription from the experience of Asia and Latin America in the last three decades, it is not likely to promote the economic interest of tropical Africa in the 1970s.

II. TROPICAL AFRICA AS A SPECIAL CASE

It is probably necessary to first put in better perspective the real interpretation of the experience of developing countries with import substitution as an industrial strategy. There have certainly been many success stories of import substitution: Mexico, Iran and China, to mention three familiar cases. The policy issue is not whether or not there should be protection, but of how high the protection, on what goods and for how long. In this context it is perhaps necessary to recall that the infant-industry justification for early-stage import-substitution protectionism can be analytically extended to the long-run dynamics of a technological learning process, needed improvements in the quality of products and the achievement of cost efficiency to overcome initial international competitive disability.

It is generally agreed that import substitution with some protection is virtually inevitable for any developing country embarking on the transformation process. The question then becomes one of under what conditions such an inward-looking strategy could be sustained as a stimulus to development without net adverse consequences. The question becomes easier to resolve if we focus on the real essence of development as the process of mobilising *and* utilising the *total* resources (natural, human and financial) of an economy, by creating and exploiting market opportunities. It is in this totality of the development process that some developing countries may now not only succeed with import substitution but also considerably shorten the conventionally expected time-lag in moving from light consumer manufactures to the production of intermediate and capital goods.

Since resource endowments, market opportunities and the international environment thus all vary from one region to another and from one period to another, it follows that the question of what development strategy to adopt cannot be answered with the attribute of universal validity. Fundamental differences in the decision-making environment have led economists to question the applicability to the developing countries of some analytical apparatus designed in or for the advanced industrial economies. Because of the heterogeneity of the developing countries themselves, this limitation of the special case must be extended to a second order of applicability. It is clear from any look at the literature that the economics of underdeveloped countries over the last three decades have been dominated by the economic and social circumstances of Asia and Latin America. Africa has only been treated peripherally, and largely in a descriptive way; it has remained substantially outside the main analytical stream. To relate the issue of development-strategy bias to the African scene requires that the analytically essential differences between it and the rest of the underdeveloped world be recognised as a starting-point.

There is first the obvious fact that tropical Africa (south of the Sahara and north of the Zambezi) is the economic backyard of the contemporary world and is a late-comer in the modern version of world development. It is the world's last economic frontier. It consists essentially of enclave economies, dominated by foreign-controlled concessions and having a satellite status in external relations to the industrial economies of Europe and North America. In spite of the flurries of output growth since the Second World War, all tropical African countries still lie in the lowest fourth of the world's development hierarchy, and account for sixteen of the twenty-five national economies now listed by the United Nations as the least developed.

Not only is the economic distance from the rest of the world large, but the gap is getting wider. Per capita gross domestic product in tropical Africa has in recent decades been of the order of about 1·5 per cent per annum, compared with the 3 per cent for Europe and America. The gross national product is further lagging behind even this low performance in the gross domestic product as an increasing proportion of the wealth moves to the metropolitan countries as factor payments and colonial surplus. This still lower national product is furthermore characterised by considerable instability between one year and another. Industrialisation has neither gone deep nor gone far, representing still an insignificant share of gross domestic product. And even that is dominated by foreign direct investment and is run practically as extensions of the industrial plants in metropolitan countries.

It is true that when compared with Asia and Latin America, the average tropical African country is a small national economy. The median country is one with a surface area of 124,500 square miles, a population of 4 million growing at 2·5 per cent per annum and a population density of 40 persons per square mile. Statistically, it represents a cross-breed between Guinea and Ivory Coast. In economic organisation it is more of a hybrid than a mixed economy. Its most characteristic feature is economic and social alienation. Yet it often represents an exhaustible comparative advantage case as a development typology, that is, one with a depletable stock of natural resources or concentrated transfers of foreign exchange in a well-defined period, and one where value arises not from the *flow* of production activity but from the *stock* of non-reproducible assets. In terms of potential resources for development, tropical Africa is generally more favourably placed than Asia and Latin America. Even after allowing for deserts, mountains, swamps and the like, each tropical African still has at least 20 acres as potential farmland. The foreign exchange bottleneck is not as constraining on the development process. Although there is now a high rate of urbanisation, the rate of rural unemployment or underemployment is very low and sometimes zero.

At present there is a high degree of external-trade dependence on the part of most tropical African economies. This situation of high primary export does not necessarily arise from a rational allocation of total available resources, but is a result of a long legacy of colonial economic relations. To say that the engine of growth of tropical African economies comes from the external sector does not imply that that is the only or the best stimulus for an objective development process. Indeed, the contrary can be hypothesised, in the sense that the low performance of tropical African economies can be explained by the level and nature of its external-trade dependence as an engine of growth. To achieve a faster and more meaningful development will therefore involve on the one hand a destruction of the basis of economic alienation, and on the other hand the adoption of a positive self-reliant strategy within a general equilibrium framework.

III. CRITICAL POLICY ISSUES

The adoption and design of a self-reliant strategy is predicated on a proper appreciation and validation of the critical policy issues defined by the situation. It presumes that we are able to sort out the essentials from the inessentials, and thus focus on the strategic policy variables. There are three interrelated steps in the quest for such policy variables. Firstly, we must identify the distortions inherent in the existing situation. We must secondly postulate an objective function of social policy representing the goals of development. Thirdly, we must seek to define a feasible solution for removing the distortions identified in the first step and reaching the goals set in the second.

Most of our discussion in the preceding section is in fact taken up by the identification of various distortions in the development process. Most of these distortions have a common root in the colonial or neo-colonial nature of the economic relations in the tropical African countries: control over domestic resource allocation by foreign monopoly capital, instability of income growth, disparity between the growth of domestic and national products, prevalence of growth without development such as leads to a widening process of economic discontent and social alienation, the paradoxical existence of good development potential with poor development performance, absurd internal contradictions between resource availability and resource use, and the absence of the critical minimum size of public-sector power as a leverage for conscious social mobilisation and faster national development.

Setting the distortions in this way opens the discussion and leads directly to the second step in the quest for strategic policy variables. The primary objective becomes the need to gain firm and effective control by the nationals over the resources and behaviour of the domestic economy. This means not only that the discretionary powers exercised by foreigners in the allocation of domestic resources be eliminated, but also that in a structural sense the umbilical cord of primary export dependence as the main engine of national economic growth should be cut. The percolation effects of a leading export sector cannot provide sufficient motive force to satisfy legitimate and feasible social aspirations. In a neo-colonial situation, growth is an almost unconscious process – an incidental or accidental fact of a historical process originating elsewhere. When the system is replaced, it must be based on a development process that goes well beyond mere mechanistic growth by grappling with the questions of who shall, and in what proportions, receive the benefits that flow from the development process, and how shall the inherent costs or burdens be apportioned.

The ultimate policy issue then becomes the evolution of a national self-reliant strategy that can maximise the national value added in the production process and lay the basis for national social cohesion through a conscious concern with questions of internal distribution equity. The central problem of development is still one of national mobilisation of all resources for the satisfaction of social wants. The issue of external-trade bias is only incidental to that central objective. In the peculiar circumstances of tropical Africa in the contemporary world environment, it is clear that decolonisation is a necessary condition for such national mobilisation and that the external-trade bias which has served it so (relatively) poorly must be reversed. Looked at in the total perspective of total resource allocation, a self-reliant strategy does not necessarily mean a lower volume of or involvement in external trade. It only means a fundamental restructuring of such trade and its replacement (or at least supplementation) by other forces as engines of growth. Indeed, it can be argued that it is only such restructuring that can promote a greater and more meaningful international economic exchange. A system of neo-colonial control is the very opposite of the free-market conditions which are assumed to be necessary for a rational international division of labour. The trade policy question for tropical African countries is how to translate involvement in international economic transactions into real participation.

IV. MEASURES FOR STRUCTURAL BREAK

A more meaningful participation in world trade would require that tropical African countries undertake a structural break with their colonial legacies of trade dependence. Not only should they not rely on the single factor of export dependence as an engine of growth, but it is unnecessary for them to do so in the context of their resource endowments and market opportunities. Even if their national markets are on the average relatively small in size (and it is not evident that this is consistently a development disadvantage), this is really not a relevant or important factor in the early stages of the development process to which they mostly belong.

Their general stage of development against the background of their factor endowments makes the tropical African economies approximate the early stages of the classical transformation process as formulated by Malthus and Ricardo. The main reason why they fail to achieve the high rate of growth by the early-stage classical model lies precisely in their colonial structure of economic organisation which prevents a high rate of profit from being translated into high wages and a high rate of capital accumulation. The concentration of colonial capital in the enclaves of exhaustible resources (ores, petroleum, timber) also means very weak structural integration and sectoral interdependence.

The starting-point of a decolonisation process is the consolidation of the nation for social cohesion and the elimination of foreign discretionary powers in the economy. Through aggressive indigenisation, even at the expense of initial loss in the growth of output, the nationals must acquire full control over the mobilisation, allocation and utilisation of their natural, human, financial and other resources.

The next step is the reversal, or at least the weakening, of primary export dependence. This is the normal import-substitution process of domestic manufacturing with adequate (but no more than adequate) protection. The weakening of primary export dependence does not mean the weakening of export earnings by abandoning export activities. It could even mean increased export earnings by a combination of a variety of measures, especially in cases of exhaustible comparative advantage. What it does mean is that more engines of growth are developed and added as further impetus to rapid growth. Import substitution provides a second such stimulus to growth, as it involves an increasingly greater attention to domestic investment and policy incentives. A vigorous pursuit of import substitution does not imply an absolute discrimination against export activities, particularly in resource-rich situations when the two types of operation may not be competing for the same resources.

There is a third engine of growth available to such resource-rich countries, especially in the land-surplus cases which most tropical African economies typify. Such situations conform neither to the neo-classical assumptions of variable proportions nor to the classic underdevelopment model of unlimited labour supply. There is every possibility of achieving rural development in tropical African countries. Even without substantially changing the technology of farming, value productivity per man-acre or per man-year can be raised by merely changing the product mix in favour of commodities which are likely to command relatively high market prices. Increased production can be achieved by increasing both land and labour inputs and

operating with fixed proportions at constant returns to scale.
Furthermore, still greater output expansion can be brought
about by a combination of simple technological innovations,
improved-variety seeds and seedlings, better storage and
transportation, extension service and credit, organised marketing and more favourable internal terms of trade. This last factor
is, incidentally, one of the considerations in determining the
height and duration of protectionist measures for import-
substituting domestic manufactures.

A fourth possible engine of growth can be found by a re-
consideration of the long-held invalidity of the Keynesian
public investment expenditure prescriptions in the circumstances
of underdeveloped countries. It is true that, almost by definition,
the capital-goods industries in such economies are not in a
position to serve as an engine of growth as in the advanced
industrial countries. But looking at the urban sector of an
underdeveloped country, it is unmistakably becoming a storage
point for a growing floating labour force, exercising a disproportionate socio-political pressure but also available as a
potential catalyst for economic development, given a favourable
framework of economic organisation. Just as rural development
programmes are designed to attack the problem of poverty
directly at the roots, a sustained programme of public works
can also attack directly at the roots the problem of urban
unemployment and reduce the degree of under-utilised resources.
Both types of programme also have the additional advantage
that they can make available and redistribute certain essential
goods and services for mass consumption: food, housing,
education, health and culture. They also have the added merit
that in a society with a scanty administrative machine and
relatively small wage incomes, an incomes policy designed for
redistributive equity is best executed by such budgetary intervention from the supply side.

This kind of four-pronged approach to the problem of
structural break-away from neo-colonial dependence constitutes
the core of an inward-looking strategy of development. Rather
than concentrate on a narrow view of the development process
from the standpoint of external trade, it starts from the general
consideration of total resource availability and use. Although
virtually every known strategy of development has an external-

trade component (if only in terms of implications, consequences and social costs), the external-trade dimension of this approach comes out of the wider wash of total domestic activity and market potential. An inward-looking strategy indeed represents the most effective way of achieving a development-structural break, by asking the most relevant questions and seeking a wide range of solutions for making the most use of available resources.

V. FOREIGN TRADE AND THE DEVELOPMENT PROCESS

We have seen that there is always an external-trade element to every development strategy that has been devised. In a world that is becoming even more rapidly interdependent, it is clear that autarky is neither possible nor necessary. The real issue for tropical Africa is not whether it should be involved in external trade. It is historically over-involved: over-involved in terms of the alternative uses to which it could put its overall resources. The question is how to increase its effective participation by strengthening its economic international bargaining position. We have argued that the answer lies in a process of policy introspection, whereby inspiration for social organisation and the engines of structural change are sought in and designed around the domain of domestic resources.

This introspection is probably temporary; but it is certainly necessary. It may be temporary because experience has shown that in order to sustain a high rate of industrial growth, a developing economy should move to industrial export promotion (if only at first on the basis of regional and sub-regional economic integration) *before* it exhausts its market opportunities for domestic import-substituting manufactures. A gradual but decisive reduction in the level of effective protection is usually a necessary precondition for raising the level of cost efficiency required by the rigours of such international exposure. But we have argued that, for the 1970s at least, most of the tropical African economies are still far from such pressure for industrial export promotion, and that their relatively small size is not an effective deterrent against successful import substitution.

It is true that, by expanding the market horizon, external trade stimulates greater output and economic growth. But in a colonial or neo-colonial setting it sets a nation's economy on a secular growth path that distorts its objective or rational pattern of resource use and thus inhibits its process of transformation. An outward-looking strategy is based on a free-trade solution that derives from the neo-classical assumptions of perfect competition in both product and factor markets, international mobility and the absence of discretionary exercise of power. Obviously, such assumptions are the very antithesis of the tropical African scene. Whatever growth may have taken place there historically on the basis of external-trade dependence it would be difficult to sustain the view that the economic distance between tropical Africa and the rest of the world can be bridged by continued reliance on such a strategy. Even on the basis only of the empirically established long-term income elasticity of demand for tropical African export produce (estimated at below 0·7), it can be confidently predicted that the region would continue to receive a diminishing share of the world's income if it does not reverse its situation of primary export dependence.

Apart from this dimension of adverse international income distribution, the domestic consequences of external-trade dependence can be counter-productive for the development process. Theoretically, the growth of external trade operates indirectly to reduce the area of subsistence. But in practice, any such erosion of the subsistence sector is not only a long process but also weak and uneven. By concentrating on extractive activities and commercial agriculture, external-trade dependence leaves much of domestic activity untouched. Even where it touches some of this activity indirectly, it sometimes only suppresses rather than transforms the subsistence sector. The result is frustrated growth and stunted development. This is important when it is remembered that most of the specialised commodities involved (petroleum, cocoa, rubber) do not enter in any significant sense the domestic consumption streams; neither do most (copper, tin, vegetable oil) have any appreciable linkage effects on the rest of the economy.

If thus the policy challenge of the 1970s for tropical Africa is the mobilisation and utilisation of its total resources for rapid economic development and social change, the case for an inward-looking strategy that reverses the present pattern of external-trade dependence as the sole engine of growth would appear a strong one that is difficult to refute.

References

ABOYADE, O., 'A Note on External Trade, Capital Distortion and Planned Development', in I. G. Stewart and H. W. Ord (eds.), *African Primary Products and International Trade* (Edinburgh Univ. Press, 1965).

AVARAMOVIC, Dragoslav, 'Industrialisation of Iran: The Records, the Problems and the Prospects', *Tahqiqat-e Eqtesadi* (Quarterly Journal of Economic Research), VII 18 (Spring 1970).

BALDWIN, R. E., 'Export Technology and Development from a Subsistence Level', *Economic Journal* (Mar. 1963).

CHENERY, Hollis B., 'Growth and Structural Change', *Finance and Development*, VIII 3 (Sep. 1971).

—— and TAYLOR Lance, 'Development Patterns: Among Countries and over Time', *Review of Economics and Statistics* (Nov. 1968).

CURRIE, Lauchlin, 'The Exchange Constraint on Development: A Partial Solution to the Problem', *Economic Journal* (Dec. 1971).

FURTADO, Celso, *Development and Underdevelopment* (Berkeley: Univ. of California Press, 1964).

HOLLISTER, R. G., 'Problems of Strategy in Developing Countries with Exhaustible Comparative Advantage', Center for Development Economics, Williams College, Mass., Research Memorandum No. 39 (mimeographed, Nov. 1970).

MAIZELS, Alfred, *Exports and Economic Growth of Developing Countries* (Cambridge Univ. Press, 1968).

LITTLE, Ian, SCITOVSKY, Tibor, and SCOTT, Maurice, *Industry and Trade in Some Developing Countries: A Comparative Study* (Oxford Univ. Press, for O.E.C.D., 1970).

SEERS, Dudley, 'The Limitations of the Special Case', *Bulletin of the Oxford Institute of Economics and Statistics*, XXV (May 1963).

National Import Substitution and Inward-Looking Strategies: Policies of Less Developed Countries

Nurul Islam

DIRECTOR, BANGLADESH INSTITUTE OF DEVELOP-
MENT ECONOMICS, DACCA, AND DEPUTY
CHAIRMAN, BANGLADESH PLANNING COMMISSION

Import substitution has been and continues to be a major development strategy in the poor countries. This is in part a reaction to export pessimism which has been widespread among the developing countries in the last two decades. The slow growth of agricultural exports from the poor, developing countries, some of which are dependent on one or two major agricultural crops, and the limited progress in the diversification of the agricultural sector in these countries, have strengthened this trend. The growth of demand for major agricultural products has been slowed down by technological changes involving synthetic substitutes and increasing economy in the case of raw materials. The protectionist policies in the developed countries, combined sometimes with inappropriate export policies, including exchange-rate, internal pricing and production policies, have no doubt contributed their share.

In such an environment, both national and international, import-substitution strategy appeared an appropriate policy as a step towards diversifying the structure of a developing economy. Domestic production which relates to the replacement of imports is quite obviously based on easily identifiable investment opportunities. By shutting out or reducing imports, the domestic market is assured to the domestic producers.

The import-substitution strategy usually receives its impetus during periods of balance of payments crisis brought about either by internal or external policy or by a combination of both. An inflationary situation at home or a policy of export restriction for ensuring domestic consumption of exportables as well as collapse of the export markets, as happened after the Korean boom, are examples of internal and external factors which contribute to the balance of payments difficulties.

Import substitution can also be associated with the pursuit of a policy of 'autarky'. Usually, however, hardly any country pursues a policy of autarky in respect of all commodities. There are strategic items or essential items of mass consumption like food-grains in respect of which dependence on foreign sources of supply is frowned upon on the basis of non-economic considerations.

Import substitution in the sense of replacement of imports by domestic production has various connotations. It is undertaken in various degrees under different circumstances. What is important and interesting in the analysis of national import-substitution strategy is an examination of the activities, techniques and policies which are pursued in order to implement the strategy.

How does one measure import substitution?

If import substitution is merely to imply that a few items which were previously imported are now produced at home, this is an inevitable phenomenon associated with the diversification of an economy in the process of economic growth. Import substitution is, however, sought to be measured more precisely. One straightforward measurement is a decline in the share of imports in total supply (including imports and domestic production). Other measurements are variations of the same theme. Taking this straightforward measurement as a starting-point, it is worth noting that a decline in the ratio of imports to total supply is consistent with a constant, a decreasing or an increasing volume of imports. This is true in the case of one particular item of import or a large number of individual items of import, as well as in the case of aggregate volume of imports for the country as a whole. Import substitution is also measured in terms of the ratio of imports to G.N.P. Here again, a decline in this ratio is quite consistent with an increase in the aggregate absolute volume of imports.

The pattern of import substitution is critically related to the pattern of growth and changing structure of an economy. Since developing countries are overwhelmingly agricultural and their imports consist mainly of manufactured goods, any significant step towards diversification consists primarily of industrialisation based on import substitution. The evidence of the historical path of industrialisation indicates that in the developing countries import substitution initially takes place in the consumer-goods industries. This is partly because in the early stages of development most of the imports consist of consumer goods. Also, for many consumer-goods industries, technology is relatively simple, capital requirements are not large, and existing domestic demand is adequate relative to the economic size of an industry. A young, industrialising country with low per capita income, small savings and limited familiarity with advanced technology expects to find it easier to develop comparative advantage in the field of such consumer-goods industries.

The next step in the import-substitution process relates to the domestic production of consumer durables. This is facilitated by a highly unequal distribution of income which prevails in many a developing country. Such inequalities often get accentuated during the early stages of growth, owing to the initial pattern of capital ownership and government policies. In private-enterprise economies, a limited number of entrepreneurs, in view partly of scarcity of managerial and entrepreneurial skills, tend to own and control a disproportionate share of investment and productive activities. The government also frequently plays a significant role in providing financial and other incentives for the development of private entrepreneurs through direct controls over the distribution of scarce inputs such as capital and foreign exchange. The mechanism of control, by its very nature, favours a few rather than many.

However, import-substitution policy, directed primarily towards consumer-goods industries, quickly reaches its limit as set by the narrow domestic market. It then gradually extends in successive steps to intermediate and capital goods. By then the newly developed domestic consumer-goods industries tend to provide a market for intermediate goods and capital goods. The pattern of import substitution moves in this direction because these are the sectors which provide obvious opportunities for profitable investment. To be sure, the size of the domestic market is frequently inadequate for the production of the intermediate and capital goods on an efficient scale. However, there is no alternative if industrialisation is to proceed primarily for the domestic market and in substitution for imports.

As the experience of many developing countries demonstrates, the limits to the expansion of markets are set by two particular features of the development path followed by many developing countries. Firstly, since import-substitution strategy has been closely identified with industrialisation, agricultural development in the poor countries has not received adequate attention. Import substitution in the industrial sector proceeded apace in many overpopulated and poor countries, while at the same time imports of agricultural products, especially of food-grains, increased rapidly. Agricultural stagnation hampers the growth of primary exports and in some cases has turned a net exporter into a net importer of agricultural products, including food-grains. Since the large majority of people are employed in agriculture, which also contributes the major proportion of national income, stagnation in this sector limits the growth of demand for mass-consumption goods. In view of the inequality of incomes between the agricultural and non-agricultural sectors, agricultural growth contributes not only to the growth of aggregate demand but also to its more equitable distribution. Growth in agricultural income, especially where such growth is associated with a more equitable distribution of the benefits of agricultural progress, enlarges the market for mass-consumption goods. This in turn provides the basis for an expanding consumer-goods industry which can also reap substantial benefits from economies of scale. Moreover, many consumer-goods industries are based on the supply of domestically produced agricultural raw materials, which depends on agricultural growth. Therefore the success of and limits to the import-substitution strategy in the industrial sector are closely linked with agricultural growth.

The second factor which limits the progress of import substitution in the industrial sector is the slow growth of exports of manufactured goods. This in turn is related to (*a*) the choice of specific activities which are selected for import substitution, and (*b*) the techniques and instruments which are used to implement the import-substitution strategy. If import substitution is indiscriminate and without any regard for a country's comparative advantage, the exports of the industrial sector are unlikely to find export markets, not to speak of the barriers put up by the advanced countries in the way of expansion of manufactured exports from the developing countries. Moreover, the instruments which are used to regulate imports also discriminate against exports. The incentives provided to investment in import-substituting activities often exceed those afforded to the export-promoting activities. The nature and extent of discrimination against exports, which follows from the particular pattern of exchange rates, tariffs and quota restrictions adopted by the developing countries, have been the subject of considerable discussion in the literature. Briefly, the argument that a strategy of industrialisation, which is non-discriminatory between import substitution and export expansion, ensures a more efficient allocation of resources has not been properly appreciated. The participation by domestic industries in the export markets exposes them to forces of competition; it also provides access to and familiarity with the advanced methods of marketing and organisation. Furthermore, access to world markets provides scope for specialisation consistent with a country's endowment of resources. Above all, the domestic industries are no longer constricted by the limited size of the domestic market; instead they can reap the benefits of economies of scale.

This brings us to the examination of the instruments of policy used to implement a strategy of import substitution. Tariffs and import licensing are both used to implement this strategy. For the purpose of import control, tariffs are redundant if, under a regime of quantitative import restrictions, domestic prices of imported goods exceed the world price by more than the tariffs. However, in addition to being a major source of government revenue, tariffs also serve as a cushion to the import-substituting industries against sudden exposure to foreign competition in the event that fluctuations in the balance of payments cause corresponding changes in the intensity of such import restrictions. The structure of tariffs and that of import licensing are usually such that they impose higher restrictions on the imports of consumer goods than on those of raw materials and capital goods. As between intermediate imports and capital goods, the degree of restriction is usually lower on the latter than on the former.

The rationale of this approach appears to be an attempt to ensure that import-substituting consumer-goods industries are able to secure intermediate inputs and capital goods at a rate cheaper than that which a uniform degree of restrictions on all imports would imply. This reduces the cost of investment as well as the requirements of working capital: on the one hand, therefore, in financial resources required for investment; on the other hand, profitability of domestic production is enhanced through the imposition of a higher degree of restrictions on the competing output than on imported inputs used in the industry. This policy, then, results in increasing the effective rate of protection for the import-substituting consumer-goods sector, correspondingly reducing the degree of effective protection for the domestic intermediate- and capital-goods sectors. Thus the maintenance of a structure of import restrictions, which discriminates heavily in favour of consumer goods, militates against the establishment of intermediate- and capital-goods industries, even when these sectors may develop long-run comparative advantage. However, as import substitution extends to the intermediate- and capital-goods sectors, the intensity of import restrictions is increased on them and the relative degree of effective protection to them is thus increased.

Over time, the structure of effective protection, which results from the differential structure of high nominal protection, results in a range of effective rates of protection, often rising up to 500–1,000 per cent. Moreover, instances of value added in domestic activity, when measured in world prices, being negative are also not infrequent. Domestic production in such cases as these is rendered possible or found profitable only because of the very high rates of effective protection. Under a regime of import restrictions, there develops a structure of domestic prices for inputs and outputs and a range of techniques which, if evaluated at prevailing world prices, would have been found unprofitable. The cost of import-substituting activities, evaluated in terms of scarce domestic resources, thus turns out to be very high and, in the limiting case, extends to infinity.

The question may legitimately be asked why a regime of import restrictions with its attendant shortcomings is so popular in the developing countries. This is mainly because the reaction of the policy-makers to a situation of shortage is very strongly in the direction of price control and rationing. If the supply of foreign exchange falls short of demand, the predilection is towards controlling the price and rationing of foreign exchange. This suggests a confusion in thinking about the nature of shortage. It is somehow believed as a matter of habit that shortage is a short-term phenomenon which corrects itself, once the 'circumstances' improve. There is inadequate understanding that circumstances, in the sense of an improvement in the supply of foreign exchange, do not improve by themselves; it is not independent of policies which are pursued during the period of shortage. That the price of foreign exchange should be raised in order to adjust demand to the level of supply is not considered advisable, because supply and demand of exports from developing countries is somehow considered inelastic. The 'inelasticity' assumption and the assumption of the non-workability of market mechanisms are somehow believed to be the primary characteristics of developing countries. While there is a considerable degree of truth in the assumption of inelastic demand for many raw materials and foodstuffs provided by developing countries taken as a whole, this is not necessarily true for individual countries and their export performance in the world market. The experience of the Green Revolution has provided examples of supply functions of agricultural output which are responsive to improvement in income and profits of the agricultural sector, provided a proper price-support programme is adopted to cushion the fluctuations in agricultural prices. The developing countries themselves are beginning to question the assumption of universal inelasticity of supply and demand for agricultural products, although old habits of thinking die hard.

The 'elasticity' pessimism militates against adjustment of exchange rates for dealing with foreign exchange shortage through a straightforward devaluation. But then why is the effective rate of exchange for imports not allowed to rise for the purpose of allocation of foreign exchange, which could be done, for example, by auctioning of import licences? One version of the answer is that this will result in the foreign exchange being channelled to the highest bidders, who will be the richest groups in any society. In other words, it will be inequitably distributed. So long as income distribution is unequal, the argument runs, to let the price of foreign exchange reach the level warranted by scarcity and have it distributed to the highest bidder is to let the richest get the largest allocation of foreign exchange. This is sought to be mitigated by distributing import licences among the widest section of the population, with the stipulation that no one gets more than the maximum. The distribution of import licences necessarily has to be limited to the traders, i.e. those who are familiar with foreign trade or, at least, with domestic trade, with the hope that the latter will learn the techniques of foreign trade soon enough. However, given the aggregate shortage of foreign exchange and the limitation of a maximum value of licences which could be issued to one licensee, without sacrificing substantially economies of scale in the handling of imports, the potential number of import licences far exceeds the potential number of import licensees. Therefore there has to be some arbitrary method of rationing import licences, even if they are distributed in small amounts. In this exercise it is usually the small man, away from the seat of government, the small importers in the distant, small cities and the small or cottage industries dispersed all over the country who are left out. Special organisational and institutional arrangements are necessary in order for them to benefit from the import and financial facilities, be it under a system of import licensing or under a more realistic exchange rate and freer exchange market. The disadvantages which a small enterprise in trade or industry suffers are multifarious, including inadequate credit facilities and limited access to physical infrastructure, transportation and communication facilities, etc., to which a wide distribution of import licences provides no solution. In the absence of concomitant facilities, the small trader is more likely to sell the import licence at a premium rather than utilise it himself.

It is also said that if import licences are not specified in terms of commodities, only luxury goods required by the rich or raw materials which are used by industries making high profits would be imported, and the requirements of the poor or of the essential industries will go unsatisfied. The remedy of restricting luxury imports by direct financial measures for redistribution of income and by means of heavy consumption taxes is seldom resorted to. Instead, it is found easier to control distribution of income and consumption by controlling imports according to broad criteria of social priority. Import-control authorities decide not only the eligible importers but also the amount of licence for each importer and the commodity composition of his licence. The basic objection against restoring the price mechanism in the allocation of imports is the realisation that the existing income distribution is inequitable, but there is inability or unwillingness on the part of the political authorities to deal with the adverse effects of unequal income distribution by direct taxes or domestic income policy. It is felt that there is a time-lag in the adjustment of demand to higher price because of pent-up demand, so that any relaxation of controls will lead to speculative purchases, even at high prices. Stocks will be built up following the liberalisation of controls, the foreign exchange shortage will be aggravated and the import restrictions would have to be tightened again. In a situation of acute shortage of foreign exchange and considerable overvaluation implied in the prevailing rate of exchange, a sudden rise in the price of foreign exchange, up to the level which equilibrates present demand and supply, is neither desirable nor efficient. Supply takes time to respond to price changes and hence the present scarcity value of foreign exchange does not or may not reflect the long-run equilibrium rate. It is therefore widely held that the movement towards an equilibrium rate has to be a gradual one, with a progressive dismantling of controls.

As already mentioned, earlier import restrictions are not only often high but also discriminatory. It is not that import restrictions discriminate only between broad categories of imports; they also discriminate between individual commodities in each category. Frequently, imports are banned or high tariffs are imposed as soon as there is adequate domestic production capacity, irrespective of costs. Not infrequently, tariffs are imposed to equalise landed costs of imports with domestic costs, plus an adequate margin of profits for the domestic industry, independently of any yardstick by which the degree of protection granted to an industry is to be evaluated.

Duties are also imposed for revenue purposes, without any regard for the pattern and degree of protection which they generate. Faced with a deficit in the balance of payments, luxury imports are either banned or very heavy duties are imposed on them, affording, in the process, a very high rate of effective protection and thus a considerable degree of incentive for the indigenous production of such goods. The intensity of import restrictions is often determined with a view to domestic availability; in other words, the larger the domestic availability, the greater is the degree of restrictions. In fact there is almost an automaticity in higher rates of protection being awarded to the industry which provides a larger proportion of total supply (imports plus production) from domestic sources.

The relative degree of restrictions on various categories of consumer goods is also based on 'essentiality' criteria; imports of commodities which are somehow considered essential and whose domestic production is inadequate are usually more liberally licensed. These 'essentiality' criteria necessarily reflect, except in the case of mass-consumption goods, the preference pattern and value judgement of the ruling group and are sociologically and politically determined phenomena. The essential industries are given preferences over the non-essential industries for the purpose of raw material licensing. The raw materials for 'non-essential' industries thus tend to receive a higher degree of protection under this system than those for essential industries.

The brief outline of the structure of import restrictions given above is primarily based on the experience of South Asia. The differences from other parts of the developing world may not be so considerable as to cast doubt on the relevance of this kind of analysis. The intensity of import restrictions determines the relative profitability of output expansion and investment in the different economic activities. The profitability of industries is a function of the size of the market as well as of the magnitude of differentials between the c.i.f. and domestic prices of imports. However, it also depends on the availability of imported raw materials which determine the rate of output and therefore affect the level of costs. The relative profitability of domestic industries is also closely related to internal policies, most important among which are (*a*) financial and credit policies, and (*b*) domestic investment licensing policies and controls of various kinds. These domestic policies exercise considerable discrimination between alternative economic activities. Under these circumstances, the observed levels of effective protection, as indicators of relative profitability, are not necessarily determined by restrictions on imports. The domestic policies and controls also determine the level of domestic output and hence influence the relative activity levels of different industries and the levels of their prices.

One can reasonably postulate that industrialisation, in the context of an overwhelmingly primary-producing country, requires in general a certain degree of protection. This is necessary in order to accommodate external economies which follow industrialisation and which market prices do not adequately reflect. Industrialisation contributes to the formation of skills and the development of attitudes and habits of work and discipline which are relevant to urban, 'machine-paced' societies. It generates willingness to take risks and to experiment with new ways of doing things, not always associated with traditional and agrarian societies. These changes are brought about over time, and these external economies of industrialisation are seldom reflected in market costs and prices. In order for a country to reap these benefits of industrialisation, it is necessary for it to discount, by a certain factor, its high current costs in excess of international prices. That this requires protection for domestic industry against foreign imports is obvious and it is a necessary cost of industrialisation in so far as the society sacrifices cheaper imports in favour of higher-priced domestic output. It is therefore for the society to decide the margin of excess costs over international price which it must impose upon itself in its attempt to derive the benefits, both economic and otherwise, of modernisation and transformation of the traditional economy which industrialisation brings in its wake. However, it is not only the magnitude of the cost but also the time period for which this must be borne which should be decided by the society.

The rationale for tariff protection, discussed above, establishes the case for a generalised, uniform rate of protection for securing the general benefits of industrialisation. It does not provide a rationale for a discriminatory, differential protection. Over and above this general range of protection, providing – let us say – a 20 or 30 per cent uniform rate of protection, the basic rationale for discrimination as between individual import-substituting industries has to be sought elsewhere. The differentiation between industries can be justified on the basis of an 'infant industry' argument for protection or on the basis of an 'optimum tariff' argument used to exploit inelasticity of the foreign supply–demand situation. This would ideally require analysis of the time profile of progressive reduction in costs through learning by doing, and the determination of the appropriate rate of interest at which savings in costs in the future years are to be discounted. Ideally, the unit costs in the future must fall below the level of world price and the discounted value of future saving in costs should equal, if not exceed, the excess of current costs over the international level. This is a difficult exercise from the quantitative point of view, involving as it does not only a projection of future domestic costs but also, strictly speaking, the future movements in the world prices of competing products.

That in a developing economy there is a justification for providing protection to the domestic industry at a uniform rate over its entire range, and that, in addition, there are specific cases which deserve a higher rate of protection on the basis of an 'infant industry' argument, does not imply that import substitution must be associated with discrimination against exports. An industry that is protected in the home market must not get a lower return if it attempts to sell in the export market. But this is usually the consequence of an import-substitution policy by means of tariffs or quantitative restrictions which does not provide equivalent incentives for export expansion. Import restrictions, without corresponding and equivalent export incentives, cause the investment of domestic resources to yield a higher return in production for the home market than for the export market. The high costs of import-substituting industries, in so far as they sell inputs to the export industries, also raise the costs of the export industries and reduce their competitiveness in world market. Furthermore, the high profits, nurtured under import restrictions, in the import-substituting industries enable them to pay higher wages which spread to the rest of the economy, including the export sector, and thus raise their costs. The adverse consequences of import restrictions on export expansion can only be counterbalanced by corresponding incentives for export expansion. There may, indeed, be exceptional instances where discrimination in favour of exports against import substitution may be justified. This relates to circumstances when private evaluation of (*a*) uncertainties of selling in the export market, which is subject to interruptions due to factors beyond the control of the exporting country, and (*b*) the additional private costs of finding profitable export markets, exceed social costs.

Limits to and shortcomings in the import-substitution strategy, pursued via conventional techniques of import restrictions, have been referred to in the foregoing analysis. A few other important limitations of this approach are summarised below. The widespread prevalence of excess capacity in the manufacturing sector is one of the important features of the developing countries. Apart from overvalued exchange rates, this phenomenon is caused by the market assumptions of the import-substitution strategy. The degree of capacity utilisation, as permitted by the size of the domestic market, often falls short of the installed capacity in many industries because of technical indivisibilities of investment in such industries. If investment is to take place only in areas where the domestic market is adequate, while exports are discouraged, the total investment in industrialisation would be very limited indeed. The need for expanding industrialisation necessarily implies that instead of concentration in a few selected sectors, industrialisation is spread over the entire industrial sector. Since industrialisation in a few selected sectors cannot be carried far enough, for reasons explained above, the alternative to calling a halt to the process of industrialisation is to establish enterprises wherever there is room for one or two plants. This pattern of industrialisation prevents specialisation by product or processes and therefore stands in the way of realisation of economies of scale or benefits of specialisation.

As already stated, the prevalence of widespread excess capacity in the manufacturing sector is partly due to the underpricing of imported capital goods because of low effective rates of exchange for the import of capital goods. The system of licensing of industrial raw materials which is related to installed capacity implies that the manufacturing concerns, in order to obtain additional licences for raw materials, must install additional capacity. It thus pays to increase output by creating additional capacity while the existing capacity is unutilised. Again, it is not just the import-licensing system which favours a more liberal import of capital goods in relation to raw materials; the additional foreign exchange through external aid in most of the poor countries is supplied relatively more in the form of 'project aid' (i.e. assistance in the form of capital equipment and plant rather than intermediate inputs) than in the form of commodity assistance. Aid-giving countries and agencies demonstrate a distinct preference for project aid rather than for programme loans, since development or capital accumulation is mistakenly associated with the import of capital goods and consequent increase in investment rather than with a fuller utilisation of capital and consequent increase in output and income, domestic savings and employment. A more liberal licensing of capital goods is combined with a lower rate of tariffs to cheapen capital goods vis-à-vis imported raw materials. Quantitative restrictions on imports, which are coupled with the persistence of overvalued exchange rates make imported inputs cheaper than domestic inputs. Thus import-incentive techniques and projects are encouraged. This, combined with liberal licensing of capital goods to the users of capital goods, i.e. industrial enterprises, also leads to a preference for capital-intensive techniques and projects.

In most poor countries suffering from heavy pressure of population, the choice of capital-intensive techniques and projects militates against the growth of employment. The restrictions imposed by advanced countries on labour-intensive exports from the developing countries aggravate the difficulties in the development of labour-intensive industries. The factor-price distortions, i.e. provision of capital and imports to those with privileged access to imported capital and raw materials at prices below their scarcity levels, are aggravated by the domestic monetary and fiscal policies in the developing countries. The rate of interest is kept artificially low by the cheap money policy and capital is rationed by financial institutions, under governmental controls, to those who receive industrial licences to expand existing capacity or install new capital. Since licensed imports and rationed capital funds are available to a limited few, such a policy encourages, as a by-product, the concentration of income and wealth. Moreover, the limited size of the domestic market contributes in yet another way to the concentration of income and wealth. There are only a few firms in each industry, which limits the degree of competition. Thus the domestic enterprises are, on the one hand, immune from foreign competition owing to import restrictions and, on the other hand, face a very limited competition within the domestic economy. Because of the way in which import licensing for raw materials is related to already installed capacity, the more efficient firms in an industry cannot expand at the expense of the less efficient ones. Similarly, an industry which has adapted to the factor endowment of the economy cannot expand its output by having a more liberal access to the imported raw materials on the basis of its own appreciation of the cost and demand conditions.

Under a regime of import restrictions, the major source of capital accumulation is derived from the high profits which accrue to those who receive foreign exchange at a rate lower than its scarcity price in the domestic economy. They are mainly traders or importers, or industrial units, which may directly obtain import licences for raw materials and equipment. These profits accrue to a small section of the economy, whereas the export sector and the agricultural sector are correspondingly deprived of high profits. There is thus a shift in the distribution of income to the import-substituting sector, away from the rest of the economy. The concentration of high income and profits in a few hands also leads to a concentration of investments in a few hands. Reinvestment of profits provides the major source of accumulation of capital and of the financing of development activities. Growth through reinvestment of profits necessarily implies that the existing owners of capital or existing productive enterprises either expand along the lines they are already familiar with, or they themselves branch out into new enterprises, either horizontally or vertically. In this scheme of things, the financial intermediaries, which traditionally serve the function of mobilising savings and channelling funds for investment, are thwarted. The habits of saving and investment are not encour aged among a wider range of the population. The low interest-rate policy, aided by capital rationing through direct licensing, adds to the difficulties of mobilising savings from the larger segment of the population.

The strategy of mobilising savings and channelling investment through a limited number of high profit-earners, brought into being and nourished under a regime of import restrictions, is not conducive to growth. It inhibits the growth of entrepreneur-ship and the diversification of the economy. If the limited number of profit-earners are the only source of entrepreneurial and investment activities, then a limit is set to the extent and nature of investment by their ability to manage a large and more diversified range of investment projects. The limited reliance on professional management, which is often a pro-nounced characteristic of these economies, depending mainly as they do on family management, further inhibits the growth and diversification of investment activity. The foregoing analysis indicates that import-substitution strategy, as an aid to diversi-fication and identification of profitable lines of investment in a developing economy, has its merits. But it should not be implemented without regard to the need for an efficient allo-cation of resources. It has sometimes been argued that the allocative inefficiency of the import-substitution strategy, following from the use of inappropriate techniques, may be more than offset by the dynamic gains from modernisation, such as the rise of entrepreneurship and accelerated capital accumulation. The above analysis attempts to suggest that these dynamic advantages may also be secured without the use of inefficient policies.

The experience of the last two decades indicates that the basic ingredients of an import-substitution strategy should consist of (*a*) movement towards a greater uniformity of exchange rates, and (*b*) elimination of discrimination against exports, implied in the multiple exchange rates built up as a part of the regime of exchange control. The basis for detailed commodity-wise discrimination in terms of exchange rates, either for imports or exports, does not exist either in theory or in fact. It would be hard to suggest that the prevailing system of multiple exchange rates is based on a quantification of differential elasticities of demand and supply of exports and imports. For a developing

country, generally speaking, one can postulate that industrialisation would most probably require protection, for reasons
discussed earlier, and therefore the manufacturing industries
require a higher exchange rate. But the higher exchange rate
should be available to the manufacturing sector, irrespective of
whether it sells in the domestic or the export market. A system
of dual exchange rates, i.e. a higher rate for manufactures, both
for exports and imports, and a general rate for the rest of the
economy, seems to be a justifiable pattern in the circumstances
of developing countries. The general rate of exchange should
take cognizance of the new analysis, which questions the
universal justification of elasticity pessimism relating to
the demand and supply elasticity of the agricultural commodities. Any suggestion for considerable and detailed discrimination in exchange rates for accelerating the pace of
industrialisation, or of diversification of the economy in general,
must be based on a serious justification in terms of differential
elasticity, associated external economies and 'infancy' of the
particular industry or economic activity.

Industrialisation and Trade Policies in the 1970s: Developing Country Alternatives

Mahbub ul Haq

DIRECTOR OF THE POLICY PLANNING AND
PROGRAM REVIEW DEPARTMENT OF THE
WORLD BANK

Whatever else the developing countries may be suffering from, they certainly do not suffer from any lack of advice in the field of trade policy alternatives. These days they are being offered a liberal choice between outward-looking strategies, inward-looking strategies, regional and sub-regional co-operation and many shrewd combinations of all three alternatives.

Clearly, the front-runner is the outward-looking strategy. This is the favourite prescription of most economists from the academic community. They argue, with a good deal of righteousness, that the pursuit of an outward-looking strategy would be consistent with international comparative advantage and ensure an optimum allocation of resources. They dismiss, with a certain degree of irritation, some of the practical difficulties in persuading the international world to become more liberal in its actual trade practices, as they believe that the world should be more rationally organised along the lines of international division of labour – and if it is not so organised at present, it ought to be changed. On the whole, they represent the voice of economic liberalism and command considerable respect and support.

On the other hand, the policy-makers from the developing world generally throw up their hands in despair and frustration every time one mentions outward-looking strategies. They come out with a handful of statistics and a long litany of terrible experiences they have had in gaining access to the markets of the developed countries.

With considerable justification, they point to the agricultural protectionism in the developed countries. They contend that not only is the demand for their primary commodities growing slowly, but they have to suffer a further injury as the developed countries keep some of their primary exports out of their markets through deliberate action to protect their own farm lobbies. For instance, the United States, Britain, Japan and the E.E.C. spend about $21 to $24 billion a year on direct and indirect support of importable primary commodities, which contrasts rather sadly with the $7·7 billion of net official development assistance.

In the field of manufactures, the policy-makers from the developing countries are apt to raise an accusing finger at the high tariffs and restricted quotas in the developed countries for the import of manufactured goods from the developing countries. With considerable anger, they point to the fact that the average tariff on imports of manufactures into industrialised countries is 6·5 per cent for the developed countries but 11·8 per cent for the developing countries, despite the recent Kennedy Round cuts of early 1972. This is because most of the manufactured exports of developing countries are concentrated in certain groups such as textiles, leather and footwear and other cheap consumer goods which are subject to heavier than average tariffs in the developed countries, in addition to restricted quotas.

Many policy-makers in the developing countries would acknowledge that, despite all this, the manufactured exports from the L.D.C.s to the developed world increased at a healthy rate of about 14 per cent in the 1960s. But they are quick to point out that over half of this increase was accounted for by only four countries – Hong Kong, Taiwan, Korea, and Yugoslavia. Obviously, it pays to be small if you are pursuing an aggressive export policy. If India or any other large country were to try to unload, on a per capita basis, the same quantity of manufactured goods as Taiwan and Korea presently do, the world markets would surely become chaotic and it would severely test the economic liberalism of the most ardent advocates of outward-looking strategies.

As if this is not a sufficient list of grievances, the developing country policy-makers keep pointing out, from any forum of which they can get hold, a number of other complaints which restrict their freedom of action in international competition. One of the favourite complaints is that the developing world faces unfair competition from tied aid from the developed countries, which often ensures that high-priced imports available under the cover of aid from developed countries win over lower-priced imports available from developing countries without the benefit of the cover of suppliers' credits. The developing countries are also likely to point to the strength of the pressure lobbies and vested interests in the developed countries which normally assure that protectionism would triumph over liberalism when the chips are down and actual policy decisions are taken.

It is difficult to decide between the liberal academics and the complaining policy-makers in this case. Basically, outward-looking strategy, while attractive in principle, is still a very high-risk strategy. It assumes that developed countries are also likely to become outward-looking. But in the international field, as in any other walk of life, it takes two to tango. Since it is not quite under the control of the developing countries to make the developed world 'tango', except of its own accord, the developing countries take a tremendous risk in basing their entire future development strategy on the assumption that – to pursue the metaphor – the developed world will definitely tango. If they are denied a fair access to the markets of the developed countries, they are likely to be stuck with unwanted export capacity. On the other hand, import-substitution strategy carries fewer risks for the harassed policy-makers because high-cost goods produced under protective walls can still be shoved down the throats of the local populations by closing down any decent alternative. It is my feeling that, as far as the L.D.C. policy-makers are concerned, particularly in the large countries, this high element of risk is fairly decisive in their attitude towards outward-looking strategies.

The alternative strategy is what is described as inward-looking, though such a description is often resented by many of its advocates. This is generally the preferred operational strategy in many developing countries, even though it is attacked with considerable vehemence by the academic community. Its advocates use all possible arguments in its favour – from export pessimism to the infant-industry argument, and from balance of payments crises to the need for the development of capital-goods industries to sustain long-term development. If one looks around the developing world scene in the 1950s and 1960s, one would find that import substitution has generally been the basis for industrialisation strategy, particularly in simple consumer goods. It is being argued by many developing countries that the 1970s should be a decade for import substitution in capital goods, as possibilities for easier consumer-goods substitution are already being exhausted and as they are not likely to obtain the capital goods they require for their accelerated development through generous aid or expanding trade.

Import-substitution strategies have traditionally been the favourite target of the academic community. Many fair-minded analysts concede that import substitution is a necessary stage in the industrialisation process, but they accuse the developing countries of taking import substitution to an excess and managing it behind inefficiently high protective walls, resulting in serious misallocation of resources. Often the criticism here is directed to inefficient types of import substitution rather than to import-substitution strategy as such, but too often the attack is carried so far as to lose this important distinction.

It is sometimes forgotten in this debate that in most industries some part is meant for import substitution and some part becomes available for export expansion. It is clearly wrong to characterise certain industries as import-substituting or as export industries because, over a period of time, one characteristic can shade into the other. What is far more important, most of the debate on import substitution has unfortunately concentrated on the industrial sector, while policy-makers in the developing countries view this strategy as a fairly broad-based one. For instance, considerable import substitution is possible and desirable in agriculture and in services. The unconscious identification of import substitution with industrialisation has often meant that its critics have tended to overlook the possibilities of domestic agricultural development to replace food imports and manpower training to replace foreign consultants. However, I do not wish to say anything further about inward-looking strategies at this stage, as I shall have a good deal more to say about this aspect later, in a different context.

Some people, who have felt increasingly disillusioned with the debate on outward- and inward-looking strategies, have turned to regional co-operation among the developing countries as a viable alternative or, at least, a supplement. These people argue that if the developed world is not being accommodating and not opening up its markets to the developing countries, then these countries can gang up together and form regional groupings wherein they can exchange their simple consumer goods and equipment with greater assurance and at better prices. The idealists in this field think in terms of grand designs of regional markets covering large areas. The realists, however, stick to the possibility of sub-regional groupings among a limited number of countries, particularly small countries, sharing similar problems and having some natural complementarities.

Unfortunately, the developing countries, which display considerable keenness in ganging up against the developed world, have shown conspicuous unwillingness in co-operating with one another. The experience from the sub-regional groupings in Central America or in the East African Community, or in Regional Co-operation for Development (R.C.D.) between Turkey, Iran and Pakistan, has been fairly disappointing and has calmed down even some of the ardent supporters of the regional co-operation alternative. There is nothing wrong with the alternative as such, but it appears that the time for this idea has not arrived as yet. It is possible that the developing countries may sink their political differences and turn to one another if they feel sufficiently disturbed about their poor bargaining position in the international world and about the unfair treatment that they are getting in the markets of the developed countries. But so far at least, they have shown very little inclination to do so. And it is my own belief that regional co-operation on any worth-while scale is a matter still a decade or two away and not a practical possibility during the 1970s.

At the same time, I believe that it is possible for the developing countries to agree on one or two bold, audacious actions which may protect their interests in the international world vis-à-vis the developed countries. One such action can be a major and uniform depreciation of the exchange rates in all developing countries, which could help insulate them as a group and set up a natural advantage for trading among themselves. For instance, I believe that the developing countries should explore among themselves the possibility of a large devaluation, say 50 to 100 per cent, particularly for manufactured exports, which would leave their exchange rates vis-à-vis one another the same as before but would give them a major advantage in the markets of the developed countries. Such a bold action can succeed only if there is complete uniformity on it in the developing countries and if the developed countries do not retaliate. My own feeling is that at a time when the developing countries still cannot come to any agreement among themselves on a host of detailed measures which are necessary in forming regional markets, it is better to concentrate on some overall sweeping measure, preferably through the price system, which would give them collectively an edge over the developed countries and an incentive to trade among themselves.

The other fields where some collective action might be possible by the developing countries are the negotiation of prices of agricultural commodities or minerals and the exploitation of common-property resources of mankind, such as sea-bed resources. Many analysts are fond of pointing out that the recent action by the OPEC countries in negotiating higher prices for petroleum cannot set a precedent for other natural resources or for other developing countries as it was a fairly specialised case. I, for one, do not believe that. I believe that a number of situations are likely to arise during the 1970s where collective action on specific commodities or on specific situations may become feasible. For instance, the imposition of a uniform or varying tax on consumption of non-renewable resources in the developed countries and use of the proceeds for the benefit of the developing countries can become a serious possibility during the course of this decade. Again, the developing countries can argue, with considerable justification and probable success, that they should get a proportionate share from the exploitation of sea-bed resources by multinational corporations in the developed countries. I do not regard these entirely as areas of confrontation but as areas where the natural interests of the developing countries are likely to bring them together for collective action against the developed countries, who are better organised with a better bargaining power and who would otherwise dictate the outcome of these negotiations unless the developing countries get really organised.

After having said all this, I must also say that whenever I read or review the heated debate on outward-looking or inward-looking strategies or possibilities of regional co-operation, I often wonder whether these are really the relevant policy alternatives in the developing world. All these alternatives assume, implicitly or explicitly, that trade is the main engine of growth or can be the leading sector of development in the L.D.C.s. There seems to be a certain harking back here to the experience of the developed countries a century ago when expanding trade paced economic development. To my mind, however, such an approach to development strategy starts by asking the wrong question or – to repeat a trite phrase – puts the cart before the horse. I believe that these countries should define a viable development strategy first and regard trade merely as a derivative from such a strategy, not as a pace-setter.

There is a growing consensus today that the developing countries need a new development strategy, concentrating more on a direct attack on the problems of unemployment and mass poverty. Increasingly it is being realised that it is not enough to rely on a rapid rate of growth in the G.N.P., hoping that it would eventually filter down to the masses. What is required is specific and direct attention to the poorest sections of society through programmes, projects and public services which would reach these sections. If this strategy is taken to its logical conclusion, planners in these countries will have to start with an identification of the minimum basic human needs for survival and a production programme geared to satisfying these basic needs in the field of nutrition, clothing, shelter, education and health. This will require either a deliberate turning away from the signals given by the market, which are weighted by the current income distribution, or sweeping institutional reforms to get the income distribution right first before defining the development strategy for the country.

Whichever way it comes out, such a development strategy

would inevitably mean a greater emphasis on the production of essential commodities such as food, clothing and housing, a much simpler, second-best standard of living geared to the poverty of the country, and an all-out effort to create some kind of employment for everyone participating in the labour force. An inward-looking strategy becomes, as such, part and parcel of a revamped development strategy on these lines. But this is not inward-looking in the same sense of the word as import-substitution strategies so far. If there is substitution involved here, it is substitution for the life-styles of the developed countries which the developing countries cannot afford on a nation-wide basis at the present stage of their development. The developing countries would have to define for themselves the living standards or life-styles that they can afford on a nation-wide scale and which are consistent with their present state of overall poverty. It is inevitable that this would mean not only a much simpler standard of living, but a much greater concentration on public services which can be distributed more equitably – public buses, public hospitals, public education, even communal housing. If the developing countries really undertake such a sweeping change in their development strategies, the prestigious symbols of private ownership may also change – the familiar example being a bicycle economy instead of an automobile economy.

How important is trade in the context of such a new strategy of development? Frankly, I cannot think of many consumer goods from the developed countries which would still be imported by the developing countries if they were to accept and manage such a comprehensive change in their economic and social systems. Probably they could import some essential medicines or books, but beyond that the consumer goods from the developed countries would only end up by catering to the needs of the privileged few and not to the majority of the population. Again, I can think of few practical illustrations of intermediate technology which could become available to the L.D.C.s from the Western world. While machinery and raw materials would still figure prominently in the import budgets of the developing countries embracing the new developing strategy, such imports would naturally be more limited when these countries increasingly improvise domestically and use whatever local resources and talent they have to look after their own problems. In other words, a 'poverty curtain' would descend across the developing world, isolating its development and trade from the traditional pattern.

So where do I come out after this rather rushed and sweeping survey of developing country alternatives? Let me recapitulate briefly, for I do not wish to be misunderstood.

First, I believe that we should deliberately reverse the presumed relationship between trade and development. Trade should not be regarded as a pace-setter in any relevant development strategy for the developing world but merely as a derivative. The developing countries should first define a viable strategy for attacking their problems of unemployment and mass poverty. Trade possibilities should be geared to meeting the objectives of such a strategy.

Second, I am convinced that if this approach is followed, trade sectors will change in character in most developing countries. The privileged minorities, which are often one of the largest consumers of imported goods, will lose their foothold. These systems will also turn to a good deal of improvisation with domestic raw materials, local skills and indigenous technology. Probably some new trade possibilities may emerge in pots and pans, bicycles or simple consumer goods among developing countries themselves as these countries evolve a new and indigenous life-style more consistent with their poverty.

Third, the developing countries should attempt to build themselves into a viable trading bloc by fashioning a new institutional framework for promoting intra-L.D.C. trade. Most of the present institutional framework – shipping, banking, suppliers' credits, exchange rates, etc. – is geared to stimulating trade between L.D.C.s and the developed world. The UNCTAD can play a constructive role here by concentrating its energies on the evolution of an entirely different pattern of institutions which are more suited to the promotion of intra-L.D.C. trade. It is in this perspective that the proposal for a uniform devaluation on manufactured exports, or the recent Bank of Israel proposal regarding export refinancing for capital goods, or the demands for a review of the current pattern of shipping rates, should be viewed. All these measures will help establish the 'poverty curtain' which is needed to encourage the adoption of a relevant development strategy and a sensible trading pattern in the developing world.

Finally, while I strongly believe that any trade strategy should be clearly subordinated to a new development strategy, I am also convinced that the developing countries should take advantage of the trade sector in meeting their genuine needs and not turn towards autarky. It is in this context that the current debate over outward, inward and regional strategies in the field of trade policy is both helpful and necessary. Such a debate illuminates the areas of efficient international resource allocation, brings out the legitimate grievances of the developing countries in gaining access to the markets of the developed world, points out some genuine possibilities for regional cooperation and collective action, keeps a pressure on the developed world not to turn increasingly protectionist and on the developing world not to become completely autarkic. But it should also be frankly acknowledged that such a debate barely touches a fringe of the policy alternatives that developing countries must consider in fashioning their development strategy, primarily because it is traditionally conceived in a framework of accelerated growth and resource efficiency rather than within a broader framework embracing unemployment and mass poverty. It is necessary – indeed inescapable – that the present debate on development strategies should also be used to redefine the framework for the debate on trade policy alternatives.

4 The Impact of the Developed Countries

The Impact of the Developed Countries

G. M. Meier

PROFESSOR OF INTERNATIONAL ECONOMICS,
STANFORD UNIVERSITY, U.S.A.

The richest country behaves as if it were poor: it cuts aid, imposes quotas and restricts imports. In affluent nations there is worry that growth will impair 'amenity rights', but moral attitudes do not extend beyond national boundaries to a concern about the culture of poverty – wherever it exists – even though it is said that the world is becoming a 'global village'. Despite a rise in investment and G.N.P., many a less developed country experiences more unemployment; and although development supposedly occurs, inequality persists. In many L.D.C.s a strategy of industrialisation via import substitution actually intensifies the foreign exchange constraint, and private foreign investment earns a high rate of return in activities where the value added may be negative. It is known that the amount of agricultural output sets the upper limit to the growth of the non-agricultural sector, but agricultural output is neglected in development plans and aid programmes. Government policies create easy profits for the few, and former adherents of development planning urge more reliance on the price mechanism. It is all a little confusing.

So development economists are now at sea. But while the development practitioner in government must perforce live with the roughness of the waves, the academic development economist should not lose sight of the tides underneath.

A quarter-century after Bretton Woods the developed and less developed countries alike are seeking a new international economic order. As part of the new order, there must be attention to the 'second-generation' problems of development. These relate to: (i) realising the potential of the Green Revolution and rural development; (ii) promoting industrialisation via export substitution; (iii) reducing unemployment and making low-skilled surplus labour economically relevant in a world economy that ranges from pre-industrial to post-industrial societies.

Outward-looking policies are normally advocated to secure the gains from trade, the intertemporal gains of export-led development, and relaxation of the savings and foreign exchange constraints through the inflow of foreign capital and diffusion of non-monetary resources (ideas, institutions, technology). Although these objectives are certainly worthy in themselves, it is even more important that outward-looking policies now contribute to the solution of the second-generation problems of development. This is the major concern of this paper.[1]

At the outset, we should recall the fundamental principles of the usual gains from trade and the possibilities for development through trade. As Samuelson reminds us, if there is one proposition in all the social sciences which is both true and non-trivial, it is that of comparative advantage.[2] On an intertemporal basis, the theory of comparative cost merges into export-led growth models.[3] These models emphasise an export base for development and indicate that the indirect effects from international specialisation can be more substantial than the static gains from trade.

We should also note empirical evidence that the greatest increases in real G.N.P. in the L.D.C.s are correlated better with rising exports than with any other variable. Moreover, the higher-income L.D.C.s grew more rapidly in the 1960s, and they also had a higher ratio of exports to G.N.P. and a faster rate of export growth. And those countries which increased the diversification of their exports made better progress than those which held to traditional commodities.[4]

On both theoretical and empirical grounds, we could make out at length a positive case for outward-looking policies. Yet the case is not fully persuasive: the theory at one and the same time proves too much and too little. Unsettling questions remain to be answered.

Comparative advantage is not given once and for all; it can be acquired, and it is continually evolving. The sources of dynamic change in the structure of comparative cost need illumination. The export-growth models also need to be related more deeply to the domestic development process. They have to be disaggregated, and functional relations specified more exactly if causal relations between exports and development are to be established empirically. It is not sufficient to judge export 'performance' merely by export earnings.[5] From the standpoint of supporting development, export performance is much more a matter of 'carry-over' and the social yield on the export investment – that is, the total contribution to development per unit value of exports. It is therefore necessary to proceed beyond export-led models and relate 'performance' of different exports more specifically to differences in their production functions, production externalities, connectivity with other sectors, effects on patterns of income distribution – and, not least, social and political change. This is just to say again that outward-looking policies have to be relevant for the solution of domestic problems of development.

When examined more closely, experience is also disappointing. First, if the findings published by the United Nations and other international agencies on growth rates are questioned, as Kuznets has recently done, the growth rates in per capita product in the L.D.C.s turn out to be significantly less than the official calculations.[6] Moreover, Kuznets's procedure suggests there has been widening in the inequality of the size distribution of income and the regional income differentials in the L.D.C.s.[7] In welfare terms, this would mean a further sizeable reduction in the properly weighted rate of growth of per capita product for the L.D.C.s.

The evidence is also disappointing in showing that exports have not risen significantly for the least developed of the L.D.C.s. In several countries the unemployment problem continued to intensify despite respectable growth rates in exports and G.N.P. For these reasons, we must consider the second-generation problems confronting the L.D.C.s, and emphasise policies that will secure not only the gains from trade through an exchange of resources, but also a transfer of additional resources, and a more appropriate diffusion of non-monetary resources.

Although the L.D.C.s remain pessimistic about exporting primary products, it is still possible that the contribution of agriculture to development can be strengthened by the policies of the developed countries (D.C.s). As the Green Revolution allows a shift from a natural resource-based agriculture to a science-based agriculture, it is essential that this potential be used to ameliorate the unemployment problem, support the industrialisation process and promote export-substitution industrialisation (X.S.I.). If directed properly, the Green Revolution can give much impetus to industrialisation – both for the domestic market and the export market.

Rural development has a crucial role to play in ameliorating not only the unemployment problem but also in supporting the industrial sector. On the supply side, gains in agricultural productivity are necessary to supply 'cheap' labour, raw materials and foodstuffs to the industrial sector so that the consumption component of industrial output will be restrained. When export-substitution industrialisation involves the export of manufactures and semi-manufactures, the development of the export-substitution industrial sector must be protected from a shortage of saving, which comes down to this assurance of a supply of cheap labour and food to the exporting sector. The agricultural sector may also contribute directly to an expanded export-substitution programme by supplying minerals, timber or agricultural products to be exported as semi-processed or processed materials.

From the demand side, agricultural development gives rise to a greater demand from the industrial sector for inputs into the agricultural sector and a rising home demand for simpler and cheaper consumer goods (in contrast with import-substitution industrialisation or I.S.I.), thereby supporting a less artificial and broader-based pattern of industrialisation for the home market.

What can the developed countries do to support those outward-looking policies that have been made possible by the potentialities of the Green Revolution? Policies of the developed countries may be most effective in two areas: greater concentration of aid on agriculture, and the revision of the developed countries' own national agricultural policies. Aid must spread the new technology as widely and as rapidly as possible so that the adopters of the new technology will not be in only the more advanced regions. Aid should now try to ensure small-farmer participation in the Green Revolution – by providing trans-portation, communication and irrigation investments to bring under-utilised land into expansion of peasant export production; supplying agricultural inputs to raise the productivity of agriculture; concentrating research on developing technologies appropriate to local conditions; disseminating technical infor-mation; extending rural credit institutions; and widening the market network and supporting processing facilities. Rural employment must also be expanded through crop diversification, multiple cropping, small-scale rural industries and rural public works.

In sum, aid should be directed to strengthening the entire set of complementary policies that must be undertaken in an integrated fashion to ensure a successful outcome of the Green Revolution with respect to exports, employment and income distribution.

If inward-looking policies have led to distortions in the development process, so too have the agricultural policies of the D.C.s led to distortions in their own economies and on inter-national markets. While agricultural products have been generally undervalued in L.D.C.s, they have been overvalued in D.C.s. Through protectionist policies and the dumping of surplus agricultural commodities on to international markets (through both commercial and concessional channels), the D.C.s have aggravated a widening disequilibrium in agricul-ture.[8] Structural changes in agricultural trade as a result of the new production possibilities in L.D.C.s may also dislocate trade in the future, especially the world cereals trade. The need for adjustments in the developed countries is intensified by the possibilities for reducing import requirements and actually generating exportable surpluses of cereals and feed-grains within a few years in a number of L.D.C.s.[9]

It may be too idealistic to say that 'what is needed, basically, is an international agreement among the developed countries to share the burdens of overproduction in grains in ways that permit expanding world trade and expanding production in the poor countries'.[10] It may also be idealistic to hope for another round of trade negotiations that would lower tariffs on agricul-tural commodities, increase quotas, lessen the incidence of excise taxes and remove the escalation in the tariff structures of developed countries so as not to impede the processing of raw materials. And yet if the current agricultural and trade policies of the major industrial countries are continued throughout this decade, the following undesirable consequences are highly probable: (i) the level of costs of the farm programmes in the industrial countries to taxpayers and consumers will continue to increase; (ii) a substantial and increasing fraction of the world's agricultural output will be produced under high-cost conditions; (iii) the percentage of the world's trade in agricultural products that is managed and manipulated through export subsidies will increase from its current level; (iv) the developing countries will face increasing difficulties in obtaining markets for any farm product that is directly competitive with farm products grown in temperate zones; (v) the degree of effective protection provided to agriculture will gradually increase in several industrial countries.[11]

If a full-scale round of negotiations to reduce agricultural protectionism on a broad scale is not politically feasible, it may none the less be possible to limit at least the competition with exports from the L.D.C.s. Food aid from the United States (under P.L. 480) should not compete with exports from developing countries and should not artificially depress grain prices in countries that are beginning to realise the benefits of new production possibilities. The E.E.C. system of export subsidies financed by variable import levies is also competitive with exports from L.D.C.s. And Japan's high price-support level of domestic rice production has not only limited imports of rice into Japan, but has also led to surpluses that will compete on export markets. Whatever can be accomplished through international trade negotiations to lessen the adverse effect on the developing countries' primary export earnings is to the good. It is, however, more relevant to recognise that the major impediments are national agricultural policies. Trade restrictions follow from the domestic agricultural policies, not the other way around. What is needed are internal adjustments in agricultural resource use and changes in domestic policies.[12] A change to direct income payments (so as not to restrict consumption) instead of protection through high price supports without production controls may help limit high-cost production. Even more to the point is a proposal for negotiations to limit the level of effective protection for agriculture. Purchased inputs are becoming of greater importance in agriculture, and most of these purchased inputs have a much lower degree of protection than does agricultural output. This means that, with a constant differential between domestic farm prices and world prices of farm products, the effective protection of agricultural production is increasing over time in most D.C.s.[13] It would therefore clearly stimulate an expansion of more efficient agricultural trade if a code of acceptable trade-restrictive devices could be devised to maintain, after a certain transition period, an agreed-upon degree of effective protection (say, a 25 per cent rate of average effective protection).

In addition to promoting exports of processed materials, a strategy of X.S.I. must rely heavily on exports of labour-intensive manufactures. As with the Green Revolution, the potentialities of technological change, new forms of international enterprise and the changing international division of labour are making this possible. Indeed, the technical elements for a new international industrial revolution are discernible. It is essential that policies of the developed countries help nurture the course of this new industrial revolution to the advantage of the developing countries.

The real (non-monetary) forces of the international economy are forever tending to change the international division of labour and to integrate the international economy more closely.[14] If the pattern of international trade is interpreted in terms of technological lead and the product cycle, it can be readily recognised that an evolving pattern of international division of labour stems from the diffusion of technology and skills and from the age and differentiation of products.[15] In the future these changes can be expected to be even more rapid. The increasing rate of diffusion of technology, transportation and communication developments, new forms of transnational enterprise – all these are the technical elements of a new international industrial revolution. There may be some science fiction in Norman MacRae's forecast of international trends over the next generation or two, but there is surely also much to be taken seriously when he concludes that 'in the next forty years the rich one-third of the world should concentrate more on the knowledge-creating and knowledge-processing industries, while more and more of the old manufacturing industries should move to any parts of the poor two-thirds of the world which are politically stable'.[16] MacRae's specific forecasts of technology, labour training and transnational managerial control are not in themselves significant, but their major implication is: it is out of date to analyse development in terms of separate national industrial revolutions. The relevant system is already that of an international industrial and post-industrial revolution.

The policy elements of the new international industrial revolution must encourage the beneficial effects of the technical elements and limit their detrimental effects on the developing countries. To do this, priority must be given to the granting of trade preferences by D.C.s, coupled with the low-cost transfer of appropriate knowledge, and supported by domestic measures of adjustment assistance in the importing D.C.s.

It would be desirable to have a general preference system (G.P.S.) covering as many L.D.C.s and exports as possible. Even though the average nominal tariff on imports into the D.C.s may be relatively low, there is *de facto* discrimination against L.D.C.s because of higher tariffs on commodities that matter to L.D.C.s. Specific, instead of *ad valorem*, duties also tend to be levied on lower-quality and cheaper-manufactured imports of interest to L.D.C.s. It is also desirable now to introduce a G.P.S. that might forestall the proliferation of mutually exclusive regional preferential arrangements. Contrary to GATT, the present trading system is not non-discriminatory, and there is a *de facto* discriminatory bias that may be an nth-best solution compared with a G.P.S.

The efficacy of preferences depends on certain conditions. A system has to be devised that will benefit those L.D.C.s that are on the margin of becoming exporters of manufactures – not only the more competitive countries such as India, Singapore, Brazil and Mexico. If preferences are to act as aid, then the most competitive countries should be equally eligible; but if preferential policies are to stimulate industrialisation, special concessions should go to the least competitive of the L.D.C.s. After preferences are granted, 'market disruption' safeguards should not be allowed simply to substitute for the prior protection. Market access must be given to commodities now subject to quantitative restrictions, and tariff escalation must be reduced. The opportunity cost in policy-making should also be minimised: preferences should not be an excuse for a reduction in open aid or for less trade liberalisation in other directions.

Aid may support preferences, but even more significant is the provision of 'private technical assistance' through foreign direct investment. The components of managerial and technical knowledge – the 'private technical assistance' – that come with the equity capital are essential for the production and marketing of manufactured exports. The multinational enterprise (M.N.E.) has considerable potential for fulfilling this role. Its multi-country operations and its prominence in fast-growing industries tend to make the M.N.E. less of a risk-averter in an individual L.D.C. Its multi-product, multinational production process makes the enterprise willing to undertake a single production activity or the manufacture of a component or intermediate product within the L.D.C.[17] For this type of export trade it is not necessary to have a prior home-market demand, and Linder's restrictive conditions for exports can be by-passed.[18] The M.N.E. also has the marketing knowledge essential for export of manufactures and semi-manufactures. In essence, the Japanese model of capital stretching by farming out and subcontracting to small-sized labour-intensive industry can now be reproduced on an international scale. The point may have even more immediate relevance in the context of regional economic integration.

The virtues of the M.N.E. may also be its vices – if it exploits its proprietary knowledge by receiving an excessive return, inhibits the development of more appropriate knowledge, or is the source of external diseconomies in the host country. The dangers of 'technological imperialism' and 'false decolonisation' cannot be ignored. Moreover, because of the high mobility of this type of 'component' investment, the L.D.C.s may compete unduly among themselves and over-concede to the foreign investor. It is therefore not mere rhetoric to fear that a country which under the nineteenth-century system of foreign investment was a 'plantation society' might become under the latter twentieth-century system of investment by multinational enterprises simply a 'branch plant society'.[19]

World trade in manufactures stopped growing in the inter-war period, but it is presently the most dynamic sector of the world economy. If the unskilled surplus labour of the L.D.C.s is now to become economically relevant in the world economy (as it once was, but unfortunately in the plantation society), the most opportune way is through the export of labour-intensive manufactures. To do this, the redundant labour must be combined with higher skills, technology and managerial knowledge that can be derived (at least initially) only from the developed countries. The L.D.C. must therefore weigh the different benefit–cost ratios in this combination of factors, as achieved by various institutional means. Even if a 100 per cent equity participation is initially allowed in the new manufacturing enterprise, there may be a time limit after which some local participation is required. Once the benefit–cost ratio becomes less than one, because the costs of the 'foreignness' in the investment mount up over time while the benefit of the 'foreignness' may level off or diminish, complete divestment is in order.[20] It is also possible to require a joint venture from the very beginning. Or the 'package' of direct foreign investment may be decomposed through contractual arrangements in the form of management contracts, technical collaboration agreements, co-production agreements, licensing agreements or management consultant services. These contractual arrangements avoid the high cost of the return on foreign equity, while obtaining the necessary foreign knowledge in technology or management.[21]

The encouragement of these new institutional arrangements depends mainly on the policies of the L.D.C.s. The D.C.s should, however, support R. & D. efforts for more appropriate technology; should not provide tax shelters to the disadvantage of the L.D.C.s; and should not institute tax policies or investment guarantees that bias the flow of foreign investment. Legislation to prevent the outflow of capital or the importation of products from run-away plants must also be avoided. Finally, foreign aid conditions or other political considerations should not be used to dominate the host countries' policies with respect to foreign investment.

Assuming that a preference system with 'bite' can be adopted and that the foreign knowledge needed to take advantage of the opportunities provided by preferences can be obtained in 'appropriate' form at a 'reasonable' cost, it will then be necessary for the D.C.s to underwrite their import of labour-intensive manufactures with a domestic adjustment assistance programme. This is necessary to avoid invocation of a 'market disruption' clause or the negotiation of 'voluntary quotas'.[22]

Solution of the market-access problem is a necessary prior condition for the efficacy of preferences. When the imports injure an already depressed domestic industry, or complicate the maintenance of full employment, or affect disadvantaged minority workers, then the plea of market disruption will strike a receptive note in the developed country. Today this is true of textiles; but tomorrow it may apply to typewriters, transistors, TV sets, toys or Toyotas. Contrary to the present situation,[23] adjustment assistance should therefore not be granted grudgingly – as only an *ex post hoc* ameliorative measure according to a very narrow standard of serious injury 'as a result in major part of concessions granted under trade agreements'. The substantive and procedural standards used in the determination of eligibility for adjustment assistance should be changed so as to make relief from the dislocation of imports more easily obtainable. An early warning system and an easier causation standard are needed. The objective of adjustment assistance measures should be conversion aid, i.e. remedial measures to move resources out of the injured industry, not to subsidise their retention. If adjustment assistance measures encourage the retention of resources in the affected industry, they will be as trade-distorting as tariffs or quantitative restrictions. Special measures must therefore be adopted to promote an outflow of resources to other industries: relocation allowances and manpower training, for example, may facilitate the needed reallocation of labour. It may also be possible, in some regions, to attract new industries to the displaced labour supply. In either event, governmental assistance will be necessary to effect the resource transfer, and this will amount in essence to aid to domestic workers or concessional finance to firms. While the basic case for preferences is that it is tantamount to 'aid through trade policy', the aid received by the exporting L.D.C. will depend on the willingness of the importing D.C. to give aid also to domestic industries in the form of adjustment assistance.

So far our discussion of outward-looking policies has centred on promoting the real forces that lie behind changes in the comparative cost structure. But if the real forces of trade are to be liberated and allowed to operate with full force in an ever more integrated world economy, they must be permitted to do so by the international monetary system. Most often national politics confront internationalist economics over the balance of payments. As every country seeks a surplus in its balance of payments, neo-mercantilism thrives – to the especial detriment of those L.D.C.s that are more dependent upon foreign trade and capital inflow. Restrictions on trade, retardation in growth rates and inward-looking regional blocs are associated with balance of payments problems. Unless there is a more effective adjustment mechanism or additional international liquidity, the protection of the balance of payments – through restrictionism, retardation and regionalism – will limit the rate and impair the quality of development in L.D.C.s. Just as it was necessary in the 1930s to free domestic full-employment policies from the balance of payments constraint, so too in the 1970s is it essential to relax the balance of payments constraint if there is now to be international full employment. The problem of international development is very much a problem of international investment and international savings – a problem of transferring savings from the D.C.s to investment in the L.D.C.s. Until 15 August 1971, when the United States government decided it could no longer afford a balance of payments 'deficit' (just as an earlier government in the 1930s had decided it could not afford a fiscal deficit) the United States was playing a major role as an international financial intermediary in accordance with its comparative advantage in trade in financial assets. But while the United States was an investment banker it was also a deposit banker – lending long through private investment and government loans and borrowing short through short-term capital inflow. In the latter capacity it had a banker's problem – not a balance of payments problem.[24] But 15 August 1971 occurred, and the U.S. government has chosen to submit to balance of payments discipline, even though it means less provision of international liquidity, trade restrictions, limits on private capital outflow and foreign aid cuts.

The best that can now be done is to make the U.S. action at least a wrong step in the right direction. The action has opened the possibilities for international monetary reform – providing both more liquidity and a more effective adjustment mechanism. The L.D.C.s clearly have an interest in seizing the opportunity to remove the drag that the gold exchange standard has exercised on the world economy. The par value system and adjustable peg of the Bretton Woods agreement may have been designed to achieve the best of both worlds – fixity in the short run and flexibility in the longer run. But actually the result has been the worst of both worlds, and, in addition, the problems of the Third World have been superimposed on the Bretton Woods system. It would be to the advantage of the L.D.C.s if the demonetisation of gold could now be made complete, and new international reserve assets, such as the S.D.R.s, created so as to provide additional international liquidity. As often advocated, a strong case can be made for providing an 'organic' or institutional link between S.D.R.s and development finance. S.D.R.s can initially be allocated directly to the L.D.C.s (instead of giving the major share to the rich countries as under the Rio agreement), or a percentage of the additional S.D.R.s could be retained by the I.M.F. to finance expanded I.D.A. development assistance.[25] Profits from gold demonetisation might also be used for aid to L.D.C.s.[26]

A slow rate of development has also meant unstable development. Instability remains a major problem for an L.D.C. and stabilisation measures could be supported strongly by external financing. Extension of the short-run compensatory financing facilities by the I.M.F., plus the longer-term supplementary financial measures as advocated by a World Bank group, could help cushion the effects on a country's development programme of an unexpected shortfall in export receipts. It would also be helpful if the creation of S.D.R.s could be used in a counter-cyclical fashion.

While movement away from the limited liquidity of the gold exchange standard, and a more favourable distribution of reserve assets, would undoubtedly benefit the L.D.C.s, it is not so clear that a system of fluctuating exchange rates would also do so. The most likely alternative to the I.M.F. system of rigid rates with an adjustable peg is a widening of the band with a gliding peg (or a trotting peg as in the case of Brazil). In the context of development problems, more analysis is needed of the implications for the L.D.C.s of flexible rates (whether limited or unlimited); and if limited, whether the support points are to be defined in relation to gold, or dollars, or S.D.R.s. Against greater rate flexibility, it might be argued that the effects of an undesirable redistribution of income, impartation of an inflationary bias, inhibition of regional integration, creation of uncertainty for private foreign investment and increase in the burden of servicing external debt would all be detrimental to an L.D.C. with a depreciating currency. Opposed to this, however, has to be weighed the alternative of *ad hoc* discriminatory import restrictions to control the chronic excess demand for foreign exchange, and the build-up of a speculative mass attack on the overvalued currency with all the attendant distortions of the development process.

Perhaps the most illuminating empirical research relevant to the issue of rate flexibility is Cooper's study of the effects of most of the major devaluations by developing countries in the 1960s. Although several of the more important economic effects of devaluation were found to be favourable,[27] the political fate of those responsible for the devaluation was not nearly so encouraging. Governments lost power in 30 per cent of the cases examined, and ministers of finance fared much worse, losing office in nearly 60 per cent of the cases.

A major argument for greater flexibility can be that it would make exchange-rate movements less traumatic for both officials and the public by depoliticising the whole question of devaluation. We have thus reached the stage where, if a previous Cambridge Conference dethroned G.N.P., this one might choose to demonetise gold and depoliticise devaluation. (In the cause of accelerating development, economic regicide is often politically and morally imperative.)

It remains to say a word about 'aid'. But only a word – because economists have written themselves out on the subject, and because donor and recipient countries alike have become disenchanted with the process. The real amount of aid is *de minimus:* even this amount is not related to need; and political and military complications take the aid process out of the realm of economic calculations.

The challenge is not to say something new about aid, but to devise new policies that will transfer resources from richer to poorer countries. First, it is necessary to relieve the inherited problem of debt servicing by some funding operation to meet the burden of short-run debt and some debt rescheduling. After that, we must look to new means of aid as suggested above: aid through trade policy in the form of preferences; increasing the amount of development finance through international monetary reform; attempts to secure private technical assistance at lower cost; and domestic aid through adjustment assistance programmes so that surplus labour might move in the guise of commodities from the L.D.C.s.

In lieu of a more positive summary, we conclude with a cautionary list of what must be avoided if the outward-looking policies proposed above are to succeed.

The richest country in the world must cease acting as if it were poor. Textile quotas are symbolic of a range of commodities that indicate the U.S. is too rich to produce cheaply what can be more efficiently produced under freer trade in developing countries. Retardation of domestic growth, restrictions on imports and limitations on capital outflow are indicative that every country cannot have a surplus in its balance of payments; the U.S. should live with a capital outflow in excess of its surplus on current account; and West Germany and Japan should also encourage more imports and capital outflow instead of accumulating reserves.

In a more subtle sense, the cause of development will also be handicapped if rich countries become inward-looking with respect to problems of the domestic environment. No form of pollution is more offensive than the poverty of man. And this is a world problem – from which attention should not be diverted by excessive concentration on the comparatively minor problems of environmental pollution within affluent countries.

It is also necessary to avoid in the strategy of export-substitution industrialisation the very weaknesses of the strategy of import-substitution industrialisation. Just as I.S.I. has been over-subsidised, it would now be possible to over-subsidise X.S.I.; this would be equally wrong. And just as many an import-substitution industry has remained an enclave, it is also possible for export-substitution industries to remain enclaves unless complementary policies are taken to increase the carry-over effects from exports. The export-led model is only the beginning of the story; and export performance – in terms of developmental impact – means more than export receipts.

Finally, international policies, such as a general preference system or measures of international monetary reform, must avoid conferring benefits on only the more developed of the L.D.C.s. The policies must also avoid zero-sum aspects, with a gain to one L.D.C. being at the expense of another L.D.C.

If these strictures do not remain only pious hopes, a more optimistic view may then be taken of the underlying tides during the next generation of development.

Notes

1. I have deliberately made this paper broad and general – not only because of the nature of the assigned subject, but also to provide as wide a context as possible for the more detailed discussions within the working groups of this Conference. I have also tried to focus on policies that may be politically feasible, not simply in the realm of the ideal.

2. P. A. Samuelson, Presidential Address, in *International Economic Relations*, Proceedings of the Third Congress of the International Economic Association (1969) p. 9.

3. M. H. Watkins, 'A Staple Theory of Economic Growth', *Canadian Journal of Economics and Political Science* (May 1963); H. Myint, *The Economics of the Developing Countries* (1964) chaps. 3–4; R. E. Caves, ' "Vent for Surplus" Models of Trade and Growth', in R. E. Baldwin *et al.*, *Trade, Growth and the Balance of Payments: Essays in Honor of Gottfried Haberler* (1965); I. B. Kravis, 'Trade as a Handmaiden of Growth', *Economic Journal* (Dec. 1970).

4. Barend A. DeVries, *The Export Experience of Developing Countries* (1967); B. I. Cohen and D. G. Sisler, 'Exports of Developing Countries in the 1960s', *Review of Economics and Statistics* (Nov. 1971); C. G. F. Simkin, 'Asia's Trade in the First Development Decade' (mimeographed, 1972).

5. As is done unfortunately by Kravis, op. cit., pp. 865–9.

6. Simon Kuznets, 'Problems in Comparing Recent Growth Rates for Developed and Less Developed Countries', *Economic Development and Cultural Change* (Jan. 1972) pp. 195–6. Kuznets corrected the conventional calculations of the combined totals for gross domestic product to allow the growth rate of per capita product of a region or country with lower per capita product to be given a larger weight than that for one with a higher per capita product.

Unlike the official calculations, Kuznets permits a given percentage rise in per capita product to be assigned more than the population weight when the initial per capita product is low. Unlike the conventional procedure, Kuznets's calculations weight growth rates by constant population, and he makes other adjustments for weighting the sectoral growth rates of output within countries. Ibid., pp. 192–5, 199–209.

Kuznets's calculations with alternative weighting methods indicate that the growth rate in per capita product for the less developed regions has been only about half the rate shown in the U.N. estimates (1·06 per cent per year for 1954–8 to 1964–8, compared with 2·2 per cent in the U.N. calculations). Ibid., p. 208.

7. Ibid., p. 199.

8. Y. Hayami and V. W. Ruttan, *Agricultural Development* (1971) pp. 242–3.

9. For details of trend-orientated projections on agricultural products, see F.A.O., *Agricultural Commodity Projections, 1970–1980;* Eric M. Ojala, 'Impact of the New Production Possibilities on the Structure of International Trade in Agricultural Products', paper presented at Conference on Strategies for Agricultural Development in 1970s, 13–16 Dec. 1971, Food Research Institute, Stanford University (mimeographed).

10. Lester R. Brown, *Seeds of Change* (1970) p. 171.

11. D. Gale Johnson, 'Agricultural Trade – A Look Ahead – Policy Recommendations', in *United States International Economic Policy in an Interdependent World* (July 1971) pp. 881–2.

12. Ibid., p. 879.

13. Ibid., pp. 882–3.

14. For some theoretical underpinnings of a dynamic approach to the explanation of international trade, see H. G. Johnson, *Comparative Cost and Commercial Policy Theory for a Developing World Economy* (Wicksell Lectures, 1968).

15. See R. Vernon, 'International Investment and International Trade in the Product Cycle', *Quarterly Journal of Economics* (May 1966); Seev Hirsch, *Location of Industry and International Competitiveness* (1967); G. C. Hufbauer, *Synthetic Materials and Theory of International Trade* (1966).

16. Norman MacRae, 'The Future of International Business', *The Economist*, 22 Jan. 1972, pp. xii–xiii.

17. For an illuminating study of component industries, see Jack Baranson, 'Bridging the Technological Gap between Rich and Poor Countries', in G. Ranis (ed.), *The Gap between Rich and Poor Countries* (1970); Helen Hughes and Yoh Poh Seng, *Foreign Investment and Industrialisation in Singapore* (1969).

18. Staffan Burenstam Linder, *An Essay on Trade and Transformation* (1961) pp. 87–90.

19. L. Best, 'A Model of Pure Plantation Economy', *Social and Economic Studies* (Sep. 1968); G. Beckford, *Persistent Poverty* (1972); Norman Girvan, 'Bauxite: The Need to Nationalise', *Review of Black Political Economy* (fall 1971); S. Hymer, 'The Multinational Corporation and the Problem of Uneven Development', in J. Bhagwati (ed.), *Economics and World Order* (1971) p. 114.

20. There may be various degrees and means of divestment. See A. O. Hirschman, *How to Divest in Latin America, and Why*, Princeton Essays in International Finance, no. 76 (Nov. 1969).

21. For some elucidation of the specific benefits and costs to be considered in comparing the alternatives of foreign ownership or national

ownership or hired management, see Daniel Schydlowsky, 'Benefit–Cost Analysis of Foreign Investment Proposals', Harvard Economic Development Report, no. 170.

For a discussion of various modes of diffusing technology, see W. A. Chudson, 'The International Transfer of Commercial Technology to Developing Countries', UNITAR Research Report, no. 13 (1971); Jack Baranson, *Industrial Techniques for Developing Economies* (1969); Terutomo Ozawa, 'Transfer of Technology from Japan to Developing Countries', UNITAR Research Report, no. 7 (1971).

22. The meaning of 'market disruption' is defined in the Contracting Parties of GATT, decision of 19 Nov. 1960, *Basic Instruments and Select Documents*, 9th supp., p. 26.

23. More precisely for the United States, the situation as presented by the provisions of the Trade Expansion Act of 1962 which expired in 1967 and has not yet been replaced with new trade legislation. The strict construction of the Trade Expansion Act of 1962 is discussed in 'The Tradect A of 1971: A Fundamental Change in U.S. Foreign Trade Policy', *Yale Law Review* (June 1971) pp. 1427–45.

24. *International Economic Reform: Collected Papers of Emile Despres* (Oxford Univ. Press, 1973) Papers 15, 16.

25. Cf. Paul Streeten, 'Linking Money and Development', *International Affairs* (Jan. 1970).

26. Countries could sell their official gold holdings to the I.M.F. at the official monetary price in exchange for an issue of S.D.R.s; the Fund could then sell the gold to the I.B.R.D. at the same official monetary price; and the I.B.R.D. in turn could sell the gold on the private market, earning whatever premium was then offered, and use the profits to make soft loans or grants to L.D.C.s. L. Krause, *Sequel to Bretton Woods* (1971) p. 37.

27. R. N. Cooper, *Currency Devaluation in Developing Countries*, Princeton Essays in International Finance, no. 80 (June 1971).

The Impact of the Developed Countries

Harald B. Malmgren[1]

DEPUTY SPECIAL REPRESENTATIVE FOR TRADE
NEGOTIATIONS, EXECUTIVE OFFICE OF THE
PRESIDENT, WASHINGTON, D.C.

There has emerged in recent years a consensus that trade is crucial to economic development. Increasing emphasis on trade is in part due to frustrations in the foreign aid field; in part to the 'trade not aid' sentiment; in part to fundamental beliefs in efficiency of resource use; and in part to simple recognition that exports provide some 80 per cent of the foreign exchange acquired by developing nations.

The special trade problems facing developing nations have been discussed in other papers for this Conference, and have been catalogued in a wide variety of journal articles and books. Some analysts conclude that the key problem lies in elasticities of demand for primary commodities (other than energy resources) and the substitution possibilities, together with the heavy reliance of some developing countries on primary products for their export earnings. Some would argue that exports of manufactures offer hope, but these are frustrated by policies of the developed countries and by the infant-industry and structural disequilibrium positions of the developing countries. There are views expressed that the exploitation of the poor by the rich, and of the technically unsophisticated by the scientifically advanced people of the world, is at the heart of the matter. But more recently there has been a growing view that the policies of the developing countries themselves lead to such mismanagement or misallocation of resources that trade and growth both suffer.

While there is much agreement on the importance of trade,

there is much less agreement on what to do about it. Thus the Pearson Commission considered expanded trade 'by far the most important of the external conditions for growth',[2] but then noted the enormous political difficulties implicit in efforts to change the trade environment. 'Indeed,' they said, 'aid has sometimes been termed a "soft option" compared to the measures which are indicated in the field of trade.'[3] The difficulty of introducing more liberal trade policies lies in the politics of trade. In the monetary field, a relatively small number of central bank and finance ministry officials can negotiate new arrangements between countries without much political disturbance. In the aid field, there can be greater problems, particularly in years of budget-cutting or domestic frustrations over foreign policy, when the typically small political constituency which supports foreign assistance is insufficient to move an increase in development assistance flows. But in trade, the politics are far more complex. A government trade decision affects particular economic sectors at home. These sectors are often situated in particular regions, so that consequent adjustments are perceived to be highly concentrated on certain plants or certain towns or regions.

In relation to products imported from developing countries, there may be particularly great sensitivity because of the nature of the imports. In manufactures, the exports most likely to penetrate developed country markets are those for which the labour content is high. These products are consequently likely to displace, or put pressure on, similar high-labour-content products in the importing country. From an economic efficiency point of view, that is as it should be. But from the point of view of specific workers, such imports are seen as a force of disruption and displacement. Moreover, these workers are probably low-wage, low-skilled workers in labour-surplus regions in the developed countries – which is why the labour content is high. The problem can easily become perceived as a job here for my people *v.* a job there for citizens of another nation. The same problem applies in temperate agricultural products, or substitutes for them. Most of the developed countries have great difficulties in forcing a continued rationalisation of the agricultural sector, and have policies designed to distort trade flows to favour home production and protect domestic farm incomes.

The general rural–urban political balance is an element of this political sensitivity to domestic agriculture. Thus, very basic political questions are raised by the need for rapid adjustment to new sources of imports, especially from developing countries.

There is now a pattern, limited but perceptible, that successful exporters among the developing countries do tend to generate restrictive reactions in the trade policies of the developed countries. Consequently, the developing countries face two sets of problems: first, they are confronted with the traditional impediments (tariffs and tariff escalation, taxes on tropical products, and various non-tariff barriers); and second, they increasingly find that if their exports are particularly rapid or enter particularly sensitive world markets, there may be a reaction in the form of requests for export restraint.

In the latter case, Japan has tended to bear the weight of requests for export moderation first, with other Eastern Asian countries following. But as Japan's labour supply becomes more of a constraint, as services rise relatively to manufacturing in G.N.P., and as Japan's industrial space becomes more limited, it will be the countries around Japan which will become the main alternative source of high-labour-content manufactures. There are already indications that even Japanese textile manufacturers are now concerned about imports into Japan from surrounding countries. Thus, in the long run, if present tendencies are an indication of what can be expected, the developing countries will face an increasing number of actions to moderate or control the volume and direction of their exports of manufactures.

On the agricultural side, the gross distortions throughout the world are well known. But the problem is not only one of import protection. In a number of cases the high price supports maintained by certain countries tend to generate significant production surpluses, which are then pushed onto world markets through export subsidies. This results in a highly distorted international market, subject to more highly concentrated competition from major exporters and subject to substantial governmental financial intervention. The developing countries themselves have not been averse to following similar policies, and in a number of them high price supports are also used as instruments of agricultural policy, particularly in cereals.

The problem of agriculture is a problem of long-term adjustment to changing world economic conditions. It is a problem of moving farmers to other occupations, but not so rapidly as to create excessive social disturbances and unemployment conditions in urban areas.

We could continue to discuss the trade policies of developed countries in traditional terms, listing the impediments to trade, criticising especially the new requests for 'voluntary' export restraint, and suggesting removal of all these impediments. The effort to bring about implementation of the general preference scheme was carried out in this spirit, but going further by introducing an element of preference for the manufactured products of the developing countries. Because of the political difficulties and the fear of excessively rapid adjustment in certain sectors, however, most of the discussion leading to the establishment in some countries of preferential schemes centred on the exceptions and on the 'safeguard' mechanisms which might be employed in the event of too rapid growth of imports. The upshot was hesitation on the part of the United States government to seek Congressional approval for its preference scheme, because of the clear possibility that Congress would on its own initiative append to the preference authority new safeguard mechanisms to control the flow of imports quantitatively. In Europe and Japan the upshot was the implementation of a scheme with semi-automatic safeguards, set at levels of import growth which offer very little genuine opportunity for new export activity.[4]

Again, at the heart of the general preference scheme is the issue of how to prevent too rapid change in importing countries as a consequence of import stimulation through tariff preferences. It is an adjustment problem.

In this light, it might be worth some effort to turn the discussion of the trade policies of the developed countries away from simplistic arguments about one-time liberalisation of the impediments to trade and talk instead about the long-term international economic adjustment problems which are likely to be faced with the emergence of developing countries in the world market system.

At the present time, preparations are under way for significant changes in the international economic system. The decisions to reform the monetary system and embark upon new trade negotiations were taken at the Smithsonian and in certain subsequent inter-governmental declarations. They were decisions forced by events, not the least of which was the American programme of economic measures implemented on 15 August 1971. From the American side, the argument was made that the international mechanisms – the rules, procedures, institutions and methods of balance of payments adjustment – were outmoded, their efficiency decreasing over time with changes in the basic world economic structure.

While there is now a negotiating debate under way concerning the causes of some of the difficulties in the present international mechanisms, there is a growing consensus internationally that the adjustment mechanisms must be adapted or modernised.

What is the adjustment problem? There is the macro-economic adjustment problem of balance of payments adjustment, in which reserves, exchange-rate policies and national fiscal and monetary policies all play a role. Reform of the world monetary system is likely to be directed towards improving the mechanisms of adjustment to ease the difficulties presently generated between countries by differences in productivity growth, inflation rates, pattern and volume of money flows, capital investment, and so on. But there are other levels at which adjustments take place, and at which difficulties are encountered. Between the various major sectors of the balance of payments there can be adjustment problems, as for example when the trade account turns adversely while other elements of the balance of payments maintain a reasonable course. Finally, on the micro-economic level, individual industries or regions may be forced to adjust relatively to the rest of the economy. Even when the system as a whole adjusts with reasonable flexibility, there can be sectoral variations in the rates and nature of adjustment.

This is obvious enough once said. But this conception of the international economic adjustment process has certain implications. It implies the need for reform of the world trading system as well as the monetary system, with a view to facilitating efficient transition on the micro-economic as well as the macro-economic level.

Yet at the same time, in seeking reforms on both fronts, we

have to bear in mind the highly political character of the micro-economic trade-adjustment problems. If we want to facilitate change in the trade field, it is not realistic to assume that this can be accomplished solely by opening markets fully to free trade all at once. Internal adjustment policies and objectives would then tend to conflict with external pressures. The adjustments in particular sectors, as well as the social disruption, would almost certainly generate new measures of intervention to restrict the cause of the adjustment difficulties (imports) as well as to assist domestic industries through other means.

The question then becomes one of finding a means by which nations might moderate the rate or form of micro-economic adjustment, but within a framework which facilitates long-term structural change along the lines of an efficient international division of labour.

Trade liberalisation, in other words, should be pursued in the context of an overall effort to improve the international economic adjustment mechanisms. Without more flexible macro-economic adjustment opportunities than exist today, governments will resist meaningful liberalisation; or, whenever faced with market disturbances, or balance of payments difficulties, they will seek to nullify the concessions made in negotiations by imposition of new forms of protection. But even more than this is required. Even if there were a responsive, flexible system at work on the macro-economic level, there will have to be opportunities made available at the micro-economic level to assist orderly adjustment.

One of the most popular suggestions for dealing with the micro-economic adjustment problems is the provision of official aids to structural adjustment, or 'adjustment assistance'. It can, of course, be argued that special aids for import-induced dislocations should be subsumed in a broader approach to rationalisation of industries in the face of domestic as well as foreign stresses on the economy. It can even be argued that there would be no adjustment problems if an appropriate domestic full-employment policy were carried out. But these arguments assume a far more rational political world than exists today. They assume that governments will make no distinction in policy decisions between problems induced internally and problems arising from causes outside the country and therefore outside the control of the government concerned.

Adjustment assistance may be helpful in engaging the co-operation of business and labour to accept structural change brought about by changes in the competitive position of foreign producers. But there will be cases when industries and workers will still resist change. Arguments are made that the import pressures come too rapidly to allow orderly internal adjustment, or that the magnitude of change required would be too large to be effectively assisted within reasonable levels of governmental expenditure. These arguments have, for example, been used in the United States in defending the desirability of quantitative controls on imports of textiles. The imposition of some form of restraint on imports may be irresistible when the pace and scale of adjustment would otherwise dictate very substantial budget costs for domestic remedial action. If political pressures from special interest groups are added to these considerations, it should not be surprising that governments often choose to restrain imports over the alternative of absorbing adjustments internally.

The difference between agriculture and industry in this regard is one of degree rather than kind. It is often said by negotiators and by agricultural technicians that the problems in agriculture are inherently different. If, however, one examines the arguments in favour of special forms of protection for agriculture, they are almost all couched in terms of the structural adjustment problems, especially the relations between rate of labour movement away from farming, rate of increase in productivity, capitalisation of land values and rural income levels. In other words, the problems of transition are bound to be drawn out over longer periods, but the difference lies mainly in the length of the time-frame for effective solutions. The problems in agriculture could be solved more quickly if greater public expenditures were made for structural adjustment, but the level of expenditures could be so high as to distort the rest of the budget, tax structure and general conditions of the economy. So governments make trade-offs, in agriculture and in industry, between measures of intervention to assist structural change and measures to control external pressures, in some cases taking a short-range view of the situation and in other cases making decisions within a very long-range framework.

The problem the developing countries face is that the developed countries make such decisions in an *ad hoc* manner. The criteria for action and the form of action vary from country to country and from product to product. The international rules are often overlooked, even where they exist. The environment for export promotion is therefore unstable. The conditions of market access in developed country markets are unpredictable. This clearly acts as a disincentive to invest in capacity for export when selling in the highly protected home markets is far less risky.

The problem is not yet so great that the more efficient exporters, such as Korea and Taiwan, cannot achieve high growth rates for exports of manufactures in general. But as the number of developing countries capable of exportation of high-quality manufactures grows, the problems of adjustment in the developed countries may well multiply. This has certainly been the experience in international trade in textiles. The United States, for example, started with a bilateral export restraint agreement with Japan for cotton textiles, and within a decade found itself in need of bilateral agreements with twenty-five or so countries, and seeking wider product coverage and agreement of more countries so as to bring all textile trade under control.

As for trade between developing countries, the conditions of access to many developing countries are highly unfavourable. In addition to high tariffs, many of the developing countries employ a wide variety of non-tariff barriers (N.T.B.s). Often there is wide discretion in the hands of those who control customs clearance or foreign exchange or other documentation. These non-tariff impediments to trade in the developing countries themselves figure largely in the GATT inventory of N.T.B.s.

This, then, is the context in which trade relations between developed and developing nations, and the trade prospects of the developing nations, should be seen. Both the macro-economic and the micro-economic adjustment mechanisms are inadequate. Smooth adjustment in the face of growing economic interdependence and changing patterns in the international division of labour does not seem achievable. Governments do intervene, to retard change as well as to stimulate it. The interventions are usually tailored to the particular economic circumstances and to the particular political considerations with which a government must cope at a given time. Moreover, under present conditions the pressure to make changes in policy varies from country to country, depending not only upon bargaining strength but also upon such broader considerations as whether the country is in surplus or deficit position, and upon the size and form of its official reserves, its capacity to control financial flows, the height of its unemployment, the composition of its budget and other such constraints.

If the developing countries are to succeed in improving their export performance, they shall need a better international economic system which facilitates orderly adjustment. It is most important that they participate constructively in the coming multilateral negotiations on the monetary and trading systems, to help ensure that negotiated changes will lead towards a more efficient, flexible and responsive set of adjustment mechanisms.

In the field of trade, some imaginative thinking will be required. It has been suggested, for example, that the *ad hoc* actions by developed countries to moderate the rate of import growth into their markets should be replaced by a 'multilateral safeguard system'. As matters stand now, a given country can be pressured into implementation of 'voluntary' export restraint on particular products. Then other countries are asked to do the same on the basis of equity for the country first agreeing to restrain its exports. One country's disruptive exports can readily become the reason for controls on several other nations' exports. Or there may already exist import restrictions imposed unilaterally, which may or may not be consistent with the importing nation's GATT obligations.

GATT was originally designed to avoid such circumstances. Quantitative limitations on imports were deemed to be illegal, except under very limited circumstances relating to national security, public health, certain types of farm programmes and serious balance of payments difficulties. Problems of domestic injury due to imports were to be handled under Article XIX, which allowed withdrawal of concessions where material injury could be demonstrated; but in such cases specific procedural consequences followed. In practice, Article XIX is

rarely used as the basis for unilateral actions or for forcing
exporting nations to agree to a bilateral understanding to
restrain exports.

The concept of market disruption was introduced in the Long-
Term Agreement (L.T.A.) on Cotton Textiles, setting aside for
cotton textiles the applicability of Article XIX. In practice,
some countries were then restrained under the market disruption
formula, and others subsequently under the formula that
certain countries should not be favoured over others. Today
the pressures from industries for special forms of protection
are usually articulated in relation to market disruption rather
than the traditional concept of injury. The arguments for
protection in agriculture are not very different, although the
concept of market disruption is not normally referred to
explicitly. The difference between market disruption and injury
is considerable. Injury suggests some perceptible decline in the
circumstances of an industry (including decline in the absolute
level of employment). Market disruption suggests only some
form of disturbance to the market which might have long-term
consequences, at least as the term has been used thus far.

Nations thus have considerable freedom to impose special
restraints. The use of bilateral agreements to accomplish these
ends means that the bargaining position of the two parties
concerned is the only meaningful consideration – and developing
countries have very little bargaining power normally.

Since governments do revert to various 'safeguards' of this
type, it has been suggested that practices be regularised by
establishing new procedures in GATT. Multilateral rules and
procedures would at least harmonise the practices of various
governments and subject them to multilateral discussion in
relation to common conceptions of reasonable and unreasonable
action. In the recent report of the O.E.C.D. High Level Trade
Group, for example, it is suggested that a multilateral safeguard
formula be negotiated in GATT which would, among other
things:

   (i) provide for mediation procedures when a country
      concerned requested them;
  (ii) provide a time limit for special restraint action; and
 (iii) require that import ceilings not result in roll-back to

lower levels of exports than recent experience, and that reasonable growth in annual ceilings be allowed.

Setting up a new multilateral safeguard procedure could also involve new criteria and rules, depending upon their negotiability.

The developing countries may resist opening such a new avenue through the various rules and obligations of GATT. However, the present situation provides almost no protection for the rights of developing countries in day-to-day practice. A multilateral procedure that involved international publicity to the economic arguments of both sides, and which set limits to the form and duration of action, and even possibly the conditions under which action might be taken, would provide far more protection to the export interests of developing countries than exists now. Most important of all, it would provide some stability of expectations – some greater degree of predictability about market-access conditions over the long run. It would, on the other hand, recognise the inevitable, that developed countries will from time to time intervene to moderate or distort trade patterns in relation to domestic economic, political and social objectives.

It would be desirable to go even further with this concept, and require that governments implementing special restraint measures report annually to GATT such supplemental economic programmes as have been undertaken to assist structural transformation of the industry. In other words, the purpose of temporary restrictions should be explicitly related to structural change, or transition, and not be allowed to be considered in terms of protection as an end in itself. It might even be desirable to require that governments wishing to restrain imports introduce a government-financed adjustment programme at the same time, whether or not the industry concerned wishes it. This would have several advantages. It would make governments hesitant to restrict imports because of the budgetary implications for them. It would ensure that structural change did indeed take place during the period of protection.[5]

In agriculture too, there is need for some type of procedure for encouraging structural transformation and liberalisation of trade. The problems are more complex, however, because governments have already intervened so heavily that the world market has become the net result of a variety of conflicting governmental policies. In most cases, import protection devices are integrally related to domestic farm programmes, and cannot simply be discarded without significant changes in domestic practices and policies. There are exceptions to this generalisation, of course. For example, the taxes on tropical products imposed by some European countries for revenue reasons affect no products actually raised in Europe. They could be dropped tomorrow without damage to European agriculture.

Most protective measures are not so easily removable. Tariffs, quotas, variable levies, health standards used to restrict trade, and other such devices are all used for the same ends – to ensure that domestic programmes are not undercut. The problem is that the GATT countries in many years of negotiation have not liberalised the conditions of trade in agriculture in any significant way. Restrictions even seem to multiply and become more restrictive instead.

Governments often follow policies which encourage domestic production at levels above what might otherwise materialise. This gives rise to the need for protection of the home market and to a need for special handling of any surpluses generated. The surpluses can be stored, and some governments do this. Others, however, find this expensive in budget terms, or in terms of the political appearance of vast stockpiles in a world of hungry people, and so they utilise export subsidies extensively to clear their markets. In the case of the European Community, the export subsidies are financed from revenues derived from the import levies, so that the question of national budget cost does not arise.

The upshot is a kind of chain-reaction process at work internationally. Country A protects its home production and subsidises exports. Country B, an export competitor, then subsidises its exports. Country C, which not only imports some of the product in question but also produces it at home, finds the import price structure disruptive to its own domestic programmes, and introduces new protection. A and B then find themselves competing even more intensively in the remaining open markets, which tend to become few in number. Country C in the meantime tends to increase production and may even shift to an exporter role as a result of the artificially stimulated home production.

Rationalisation of agriculture world-wide is badly needed. The remedy cannot be found in all-at-once liberalisation of trade, because the government policies concerned would immediately generate the same kinds of problems all over again. It is the internal policies and practices which have to be brought into some kind of harmony.

Progress can be achieved in a variety of ways. It is not the purpose of this paper to catalogue the alternatives. Some general points that relate to the logic of international adjustment should, however, be made. First, the programmes maintained by governments are usually not well tailored to the very objectives the governments themselves set. Use of price supports to aid farmer incomes, for example, tends to give substantial windfall benefits to large-scale, efficient farmers while providing little to the low-income, small-scale farmer whose volume of production is insufficient to provide much benefit from price supports. Yet price supports do generate increasing levels of production and rising land values, which simply compound the difficulties. Second, the built-in conflicts between the policies of the various nations in their interaction with one another through world markets tend to multiply the difficulties and the costs.

There is need to reach agreements in agriculture on two levels: there is need for some internationally agreed objectives towards which governments should aim in the long run, and there is need for short-run agreements on actions which might be undertaken to relieve some of the distortions and move countries towards the longer-term objectives. Negotiations towards these ends would be of great importance to developing nations, not only to improve the conditions of access for them in the short run, but to relieve them of the artificial, heavy pressures of the highly distorted market forces now at work, and to allow long-term development of production for home consumption as well as export at levels of cost reflective of an efficient international division of labour.

Unfortunately much less thought is given to these longer-run questions of structural change in agriculture than to short-run actions to ease the pains of the symptoms of all the underlying distortions. For example, special efforts to liberalise conditions of access on particular commodities, without regard to government policies, are often recommended, especially by developing countries, or recommendations are made for negotiation of commodity arrangements to stabilise prices.

Commodity arrangements which aim solely to stabilise prices in a world of conflicting national policies are not workable. The incentive to cheat on the agreed price structure through shipping rates, terms of sale and classification of qualities of the product is so great as to be irresistible, or at least in past experience this has been so. The substitutes are often sufficient to undercut efforts to stabilise the market, or else they erode the volume of sales which in turn puts pressure on the price structure. The complexity of the product may also be so great as to defy definition of quality and reasonable price, as is the case for fats and oils. In oilseeds, for example, some of the product goes to use as oil, in competition with other oils and with butter. Some of the product turns up as oilcake used as feed supplement for animals, in partial competition with feed-grains (and even with wheat used as feed). The variety of oilseeds and the areas of the world in which they grow are far more numerous than even most trade officials realise. In addition, the levels and qualities of crops vary from year to year and from oilseed to oilseed, making any given structure of price differentials relatively meaningless for any length of time.

It is a matter of urgency that both developed and developing countries get on with the search for rationalisation in this area. However, the richer countries in the final analysis have the wealth to sustain inefficient diversion of resources on a massive scale, while the developing countries clearly do not. The relatively poor countries need to allocate their investments in farming in directions which are viable in the long run and which are efficient in terms of short-term resource allocation. They should have, consequently, a far greater incentive to seek long-run structural transformation of world agriculture and harmonisation of national policies than even those developed countries which are large-scale exporters of agricultural products. For the developing countries, it is important to give thought to the longer-run questions in future negotiations, with less emphasis on short-term relief through such ephemeral devices as commodity agreements based solely on price arrangements. And even if commodity arrangements can be worked out which go beyond prices to some understanding on production levels, the developing countries must be wary that they do not become trapped by production ceilings appropriate to the highly distorted conditions of the world market presently prevailing.

As for N.T.B.s, the developing countries should have a far greater incentive to put order into this field than the developed countries. The large exporting firms in the developed countries can often find their way around the N.T.B. problems, sometimes by tailoring their very large-scale production to particular market conditions and rules, sometimes by jumping the barriers by investment in production or assembly facilities in the countries maintaining N.T.B.s. But it is not possible to work out new rules which would result in liberalisation or harmonisation of many N.T.B.s without the developing countries themselves altering their own policies. The use of tariffs for protection of infant industries is one thing; the use of health or safety standards, administrative discretion in customs, licensing and foreign exchange transactions, and similar methods of manipulating trade is another. The developed countries are very unlikely to accept the principle that developing nations should be free to operate completely differently, and still benefit from new codes or rules worked out among the developed countries to simplify, liberalise or harmonise practices. But the developing countries themselves ought to want to change their own practices anyway. Complex procedures characterised by widespread administrative discretion are not efficient instruments of development planning. It would be far better, for the management of development programmes, to convert these complex, non-quantifiable measures which encourage corruption and inefficient decisions to simple, measurable instruments such as tariffs – even if the consequent tariffs must be relatively high.

Indeed, the developing countries which maintain complex mechanisms for controlling or distorting trade are prey to special pressures from within their own countries as well as to criticism from other countries. There is little protection for a minister who does not wish to yield to special pleadings but has no international commitments and no basis for quantifiable explanation at home to use to resist inefficient actions. And in their trade with each other, the developing countries face even more N.T.B.s than in their trade with developing countries (possibly setting aside the use of quantitative import restrictions).

Looking at the problems in this way, the manner of negotiation and the solutions found in the N.T.B. field should be of vital concern to the developing nations. But at the same time they should not only be willing but anxious to develop international rules and procedures which would apply to them as well.

From the point of view of developed countries, there is an emerging consensus that selective trade policies in developing countries, especially import-substitution policies, have gone too far and no longer appear to be as efficient in development terms as once thought. Without diverting space here to the debate between outward-looking and inward-looking development and trade strategies, it can be noted that trade negotiations at this time offer an opportunity for rationalisation of trade policies of the developing countries themselves. It is my own view that this should be brought about by negotiating some new general obligations to which developing countries might agree to adhere in exchange for participation in multilateral trade negotiations and the benefits to be derived from them. In other words, the developed countries need not, and should not, require reciprocity in trade negotiations with developing nations; but they should require the undertaking of those types of obligations which would in the long run encourage more rational development and trade policies, and which would constrain governments from taking trade-distorting actions on behalf of special interests without reference to international rules and procedures.

Such obligations to be undertaken by developing countries might include simplification of their protective mechanisms, and harmonisation of policies relating to standards and classification. They might include rules of equity in the granting of foreign exchange, import licences and other administrative permissions, so that some countries might not be favoured over others except in connection with explicit tariff preference agreements. They might include agreement to participate in consultation and mediation procedures in relation to their own rights and obligations as well as those of other developing (and developed) countries. They might include full adherence to the rules and procedures which might be negotiated in general multilateral negotiations on N.T.B.s. The developing countries might agree to limit themselves to the use of certain types of trade instruments and exclude the use of others.

A requirement that some such obligations should be undertaken is not a matter of imposing onerous new constraints on development. On the contrary, it would be of benefit to the developing countries themselves in the context of the need for greater predictability and orderly adjustment in the world trading system.

The participation of developing countries in the forthcoming multilateral negotiations has been a matter of debate, particularly at the last UNCTAD conference at Santiago. While it should be generally acceptable that as many developing countries as possible do participate, there is a legitimate question to be raised about the nature of their participation if they are not a member of the negotiating body (GATT) and not party to its negotiating rules, rights and obligations.

In order to ensure that negotiations are conducted efficiently and are aimed at fundamental improvements of the system as well as at liberalisation of individual items, the particular positions of countries and their negotiating tactics need to be fitted into the broader framework of multilateral objectives. It seems to me necessary, therefore, to require all negotiating parties, whether large trading countries or small, whether developed or developing, to adhere to common negotiating rules and to undertake at least a minimal number of obligations. The easiest way to achieve this result is to ask of those developing countries not now members of GATT to negotiate 'with the intention of accession to GATT'. If in the end these countries find themselves unsatisfied, and the terms of accession are not agreeable, they have lost nothing but some negotiating time, and are free to withdraw to their previous positions.

Multilateral negotiations should serve three purposes: to liberalise the conditions of access to world markets; to improve the rules and procedures to provide a basis for orderly adjustment over the long run; and to moderate or control the conflicts between national policies which give rise to international frictions and unstable market conditions. The developing countries should bear all these objectives in mind, because only if all three objectives are dealt with can there be a reasonable prospect of achieving a satisfactory restructuring of the world economy which will allow the developing nations to come into their own legitimate position in the international division of labour.

From the point of view of the developed countries, a failure to examine the broader questions raised by this paper will only lead to more problems of disruptive adjustment and more political frustrations in dealings with the developing countries. Specific actions to liberalise access conditions to developed country markets are certainly desirable. The implementation by the United States of a general preference scheme would help. But if these kinds of actions lead to use of other non-tariff measures to offset the liberalisation effects, or to make even more restrictive the conditions of access, then liberalisation in traditional terms becomes meaningless, or even of negative value.

From the economist's point of view, it is the dynamics of structural change and the incentives to bring about change which matter, rather than the conditions of static equilibrium based upon current conditions of comparative advantage. From a public official's point of view, it is the cost of adjustment to market disruption and its duration and scale of impact which matter. It is the process of transition to new circumstances, and the conditions which facilitate or impede progress, which must be uppermost in deciding upon particular areas and forms of liberalisation.

It is true that developed countries have harmed the interests of developing countries through trade policies. But responsible action at this time should not be assumed to be as simple as many diplomats and writers make it out to be. It is not even possible to assume that some developed countries are acting more positively now than others on the basis of recent actions such as implementation of general preferences. The European Community has, for example, been the first to move forward on general preferences. But its scheme in practice has been shown to be of very modest value. And the Community has refused to give up the discriminatory arrangements, with their conditions of reverse preference, which it has negotiated in recent years, to the benefit of some countries and the detriment of others.

And the United States on its side may not have taken many new actions to assist development lately. It may even have introduced some new restrictions. But interestingly enough, the record of United States imports of manufactures remains far better than the record of other countries. Of the total increase in imports of manufactures from the developing countries into the developed countries during the period 1962–9, one-half was accounted for by the United States (while the E.E.C. took about 22 per cent, and Japan only 7 per cent).[6]

New efforts by all the developed countries are needed, on behalf of all developing nations. The developing countries must also make efforts and participate constructively in multilateral negotiations if results beneficial to them are to be achieved. The day of political tirade as an instrument to achieve trade policy changes is drawing to a close. Beggar-thy-neighbour policies based on blame-thy-neighbour arguments can only worsen world market conditions. This concluding thought applies to all countries, whether they are highly developed or in an early stage of economic development. The moment is now close when reforms of the international economic system as a whole are possible, or at least discussable. The opportunity should not be lost in revival of old arguments about circumstances of decades past. Far greater attention will have to be paid to the problems of international economic adjustment in analysing, planning and negotiating a better world economic system. If this is done, not only will trade liberalisation be easier, but the effects of liberalisation will be lasting.

Notes

1. The views expressed in this paper are personal, and should not be interpreted as necessarily representing the official views of any agency of the United States government.

2. *Partners in Development*, Report of the Commission on International Development (New York and London: Praeger, 1969) p. 45.

3. Ibid., p. 80.

4. See Sidney Dell's paper for this Conference, pp. 198–215 below, and Professor Richard Cooper's paper 'The European Community's System of Generalised Tariff Preferences: A Critique', Yale University Economic Growth Center Discussion Paper, no. 132 (Nov. 1971).

5. Other matters could be cleaned up in the negotiation of new rules, such as the present inequities in licensing procedures, quota allocations and classification practices.

6. See 'Review of Trade in Manufactures of the Developing Countries, 1960–1970', UNCTAD document TD/111, 10 Dec. 1971 (prepared for the Third Session, Santiago, Chile, 13 Apr. 1972).

5 Regional Integration between Developing Countries

Regional Integration of Trade Among Less Developed Countries

Felipe Pazos[1]

ECONOMIC ADVISER, INTER-AMERICAN
DEVELOPMENT BANK, WASHINGTON, D.C.

INTRODUCTION

In the last twelve years, several groups of countries in Latin America, the Caribbean and Africa have entered into arrangements to integrate their economies at a more or less rapid pace. Most of the groups include countries at different stages of industrialisation, while some are formed by nations with relatively homogeneous economic structures; some groups have adopted a common external tariff and others not; some have relied mainly on across-the-board tariff reductions and others on product-by-product negotiations; some have attained a relatively close degree of integration and others have had only moderate success in increasing trade among themselves. These different experiences show the evolution of integration among less developed countries under different settings, circumstances and economic policies, offering empirical evidence that permits a factual study of the process. In the case of some important issues, the empirical evidence makes it possible to test the alternative hypotheses that have been debated, and are still debated, in academic circles.

This paper examines the experience of the last twelve years with a view to elucidating the following issues: (1) whether or not integration among less developed countries fosters the rapid expansion of trade within the group; (2) whether the expansion, as far as it occurs, reflects a process of 'trade creation' or of 'trade diversion'; (3) what are the effects of integration on the trade of individual member countries; (4) what are the effects of integration on the growth rate of individual member countries; and (5) what are the main obstacles that hinder integration. The four initial topics are discussed in the first part of the paper under the heading 'Effects of Integration' and the fifth in a second part, under the heading 'Obstacles to Integration and Possible Ways to Overcome them'. The effects of integration are studied mainly on the basis of the groups that have made substantial progress in integrating their economies, especially the Central American Common Market; and the obstacles, of the experience of those groups that have not advanced substantially in that direction, especially the Latin American Free Trade Association.

EFFECTS OF INTEGRATION

Expansion of trade among member countries

Table 1 shows intra-trade figures for six integration groups for which UNCTAD's Secretariat has given data in a recent report.[2] Four of the groups have been in existence for a long enough time to show their effects already, while two were formed in the late 1960s and have had time to influence only the last two years for which figures are given in the table.[3] Of the four 'old' groups, two had a phenomenal rate of intra-trade growth in the eight-year period 1960–8. Intra-trade in the Central American Common Market expanded at a compound rate of 28·8 per cent per year during the eight-year period, having increased more than seven times, from U.S.$33 million in 1960 to U.S.$247 million in 1968. In 1960 exports to other countries of the area represented 7·5 per cent of total exports from Central America and in 1968 they had increased to 26·0 per cent of the total.[4] In the Central African Customs and Economic Union, intra-trade grew at a compound rate of 23·2 per cent per year, from U.S.$3 million in 1960 to U.S.$16 million in 1968. Exports to other members of the group amounted to 1·7 per cent of total exports in 1960 and 4·0 per cent in 1968.

Intra-trade in the other two 'old' groups showed only a moderate rate of growth that was, however, significantly

Integration group	Value of exports to the area (U.S. $ million)				Share of exports to the area in total exports (%)				Annual growth rate of exports to the area (%)		
	1960	1968	1969	1970	1960	1968	1969	1970	1960–8	1969	1970
Latin America											
LAFTA*ᵃ*	564	999	1,206	1,254	8·5	10·7	11·7	10·6	7·4	20·7	3·9
Andean Group*ᵇ*	(40)	(60)	(84)	(109)	(2·5)	(2·2)	(2·9)	(3·3)	(5·2)	(40·0)	(29·8)
C.A.C.M.*ᶜ*	33	247	250	286	7·5	26·0	25·7	26·1	28·8	1·2	14·4
Caribbean											
CARIFTA*ᵃ*	27	52	66	...	5·0	5·9	7·2	...	8·6	26·9	...
Africa											
C.A.C.E.U.*ᵉ*	3	16	21	...	1·7	4·0	4·6	...	23·2	31·2	...
E.A.C.*ᶠ*	63	116	122	142	14·6	17·1	16·8	17·3	7·9	5·2	16·4

ᵃ Latin American Free Trade Association: Argentina, Bolivia, Brazil, Chile, Colombia, Ecuador, Mexico, Paraguay, Peru, Uruguay, Venezuela. Exports of Venezuela to Netherlands, Antilles and Trinidad and Tobago are excluded since they consist essentially of crude petroleum to be refined for subsequent re-export.

ᵇ Andean Group: Bolivia, Chile, Colombia, Ecuador, Peru.

ᶜ Central American Common Market: Costa Rica, El Salvador, Guatemala, Honduras, Nicaragua.

ᵈ Caribbean Free Trade Area: Barbados, Guyana, Jamaica, Trinidad and Tobago, Antigua, British Honduras, Dominica, Grenada, Montserrat, St Kitts–Nevis–Anguilla, St Lucia, St Vincent.

ᵉ Central African Customs and Economic Union: Cameroun, Central African Republic, Congo (Brazzaville), Gabon. Figures for 1960 are not directly comparable with those of 1968–70 owing to improved reporting procedures.

ᶠ East African Community: Kenya, Uganda, United Republic of Tanzania.

Source: UNCTAD, *Trade Expansion, Economic Co-operation and Regional Integration among Developing Countries*, Annex 1, Doc. TD/110, Third Session, Santiago, Chile, Feb. 1972. The document gives the following sources: United Nations, *Monthly Bulletin of Statistics* (June 1971); I.M.F.–I.B.R.D., *Direction of Trade*, various issues; United Nations, *Yearbook of International Trade Statistics* (1968); *El Proceso de Integración en la Asociación de Libre Comercio del Caribe (CARIFTA)* (C/CN. 12/886), 10 Mar. 1971; Office Statistique des Communautés Européennes, *Commerce Extérieur* (1970), vol. II; U.A.R., *Foreign Trade* (Cairo, July 1970); and Statistical Service of Barbados, *Overseas Trade 1969* (Barbados, 1970).

higher than the rate of growth of total trade. Intra-trade in the Latin American Free Trade Association increased at a rate of 7·4 per cent per year during the period, from U.S.$564 million in 1960 to U.S.$999 million in 1968. Since total exports increased at a rate of 4·4 per cent per year, the share of intra-group trade increased from 8·5 per cent of total trade in 1960 to 10·7 per cent in 1968. In the East African Community, exports to member countries increased at a rate of 7·9 per cent per year, from U.S.$63 million in 1960 to U.S.$116 million in 1968. Total exports expanded at a slower rate and the share of intra-trade increased from 14·6 per cent to 17·1 per cent of total trade.

The Caribbean Free Trade Area removed, on 1 May 1968, the customs duties on all trade among its members, except for a reserved list of goods that in the preceding year had a value amounting to 9 per cent of trade in the area. Immediately trade jumped from U.S.$40 million in 1967 to U.S.$52 million in 1968, an increase of 22·8 per cent, which compares with an average annual increase of 5·8 per cent in 1960–7. In 1969 intra-trade surpassed its newly gained high rate of growth, increasing by 26·9 per cent.

The Andean Group also experienced a big jump in the trade among its members in the year in which the group was formed, but the increase in trade cannot be easily attributable to the formation of the group because, although the Cartagena Agreement was signed in May 1969, the first two measures of trade liberalisation were not taken until one year later, in April 1970. From 1960 to 1968 trade among the countries that were to become members of the group increased at an average annual rate of 5·2 per cent, and jumped to 40·0 per cent in 1969 and 29·8 per cent in 1970. The increase in 1970 can be attributed to trade liberalisation, but not the increase in 1969 which, as said before, is not easy to explain.

In the second half of the 1950s, when the Latin American Free Trade Association and the Central American Common Market were in process of negotiation, most economists outside Latin America shared Kindleberger's view that the small amount of commerce among countries of the area indicated the limited possibilities of reallocating production activities in a Latin American union and, hence, the poor prospects for intra-trade expansion.[5] Balassa objected that the argument took as given the structure of the economies and added that the existence of excess capacity in various industries of the area gave promise to the enlargement of trade.[6] The extraordinary rate of expansion of intra-trade in the Central American Common Market and in the Central African Customs and Economic Union fully supports Balassa's reasoning. The lack of rapid expansion of intra-trade in the Latin American Free Trade Association and in the East African Community does not refute the argument, because in neither group has there been a significant degree of trade liberalisation. In LAFTA the agreed programme of tariff reductions was only partially applied, and in the E.A.C. there were departures from the situation of almost free trade existing at the beginning of the period, in the form of authorisations to the two less developed members of the group to protect some specific new industries. Since the countries in these latter two groups have reached a much higher stage of development than the countries belonging to the two former groups, the slow expansion of their intra-trade is clearly due to the maintenance (or intensification) of protective restrictions, and not to their lack of capacity to produce articles with which to trade. Furthermore, the fact that members of the E.A.C. carry almost one-fifth of their total trade within the area proves that they are able to trade among themselves. The extremely quick pace at which trade started to expand in CARIFTA and in the Andean Group, immediately after they were constituted, is further proof of the capacity of less developed countries to trade among themselves.

Table 2 shows that the bulk of the increase in intra-trade in the Central American Common Market was formed by manufactured goods. Of the total expansion in trade during the period, amounting to U.S.$226 million, 74 per cent of the goods traded can be classified as manufactures and only 24 per cent may be considered as agricultural or mineral products. The trade in manufactured products expanded at an annual rate of 38 per cent, and that of primary products at a rate only half as high as that – though also extremely high. Table 3 shows that the fast pace of expansion in intra-trade started from the very beginning of the process, thus indicating that industrial plants had unused capacity available.

Table 2

CENTRAL AMERICAN COMMON MARKET: TRADE AMONG
MEMBERS, CLASSIFIED BY TARIFF SECTIONS, 1960–8
(in U.S. $ million)

	1960	1968	Total increase during period	Annual rate of increase
0. Foodstuffs	15·0	55·8	40·8	18
1. Beverages and tobacco	1·2	2·8	1·6	11
2. Crude materials, inedible	1·6	8·6	7·0	23
3. Fuels and lubricants	0·1	3·9	3·8	55
4. Lard and edible oils	1·6	7·1	5·5	20
(Sections 0 to 4)	(19·5)	(78·2)	(58·7)	(19)
5. Chemical products	2·4	42·6	40·2	43
6. Manufactured goods, classified by material	6·2	80·1	73·9	38
7. Transport equipment	1·5	12·8	11·3	31
8. Miscellaneous manufactures	3·0	44·1	41·1	40
9. Special transactions	0·1	0·5	0·4	23
(Sections 5 to 9)	(13·2)	(180·1)	(166·9)	(38)
Total	32·7	258·3	225·6	29

Source: Instituto para la Integración de América Latina, *El Proceso de
Integración en América Latina, 1968–71* (Buenos Aires, 1972).

Trade creation or trade diversion?

Students of international trade theory may ask whether the
enormous expansion in commercial interchange among members of the C.A.C.M. has been newly 'created' trade transactions, or imports 'diverted' from more efficient producers. The
answer is not easy, owing to multiple reasons. Viner's concepts
of 'trade creation' and 'trade diversion'[7] are difficult to measure
and, given their static character, are not entirely applicable to
rapidly changing economies. Furthermore, economic development involves, almost necessarily, the diversion of trade from
low-cost producers abroad to less efficient infant industries at
home.[8] But without trying to obtain precise answers, we may
inquire if all additional trade within the area comes to substitute lower-cost products from abroad, or if part of it substitutes higher-cost national production. For example, we may
ask if additional imports in Guatemala of shoes produced in

Table 3

CENTRAL AMERICAN COMMON MARKET: TOTAL TRADE AMONG MEMBERS, BY YEARS, 1960–8
(in U.S. $ million)

	1960	1961	1962	1963	1964	1965	1966	1967	1968
Total trade among members	32·7	36·8	50·8	72·1	106·1	135·5	174·7	214·0	258·3
Percentage of total trade	6·4	7·4	9·2	11·0	13·8	15·2	18·6	20·8	24·7
Rate of increase from previous year	16·7	12·6	38·2	41·8	47·3	27·6	29·0	22·4	20·7

Source: As Table 2.

El Salvador are displacing imports from the United States or Guatemalan production. To the extent that this latter is the case, we may further inquire if Guatemala's shoe industry is reducing overall output, or only the production of some types of shoes, e.g. high-quality women's shoes, and expanding other types, e.g. medium-price men's shoes, which are exported to the other Central American countries.

The answer seems to be that additional area trade is partly substituting outside imports and partly substituting national production. Both types of substitution can be inferred from the figures of Table 4. In 1968 imports of non-durable consumer goods from outside the region were only 7 per cent higher than in 1958, while the gross domestic product of the five Central American countries was 71 per cent higher. Since total consumption of non-durable goods probably increased somewhat less – but not much less – than G.D.P., a large part of the potential increase of imports from outside the region was substituted with goods produced in the area. But since total imports of non-durable consumer goods, from outside and inside the area, increased 116 per cent, much more than G.D.P., it is to be presumed that area trade has also displaced consumption of nationally produced goods. Part of the consumption that was formerly supplied with national production has come to be supplied by imports from the region; and part of the production that was consumed nationally is being exported to other countries of the area. This shift explains the enormous increases, shown in Table 5, in the total volume of trade in shoes and textiles, which cannot be attributed to increases in consumption. Table 6 confirms the explanation by showing that there are large amounts of cross-trade in the same products, presumably of different types. The figures indicate that integration has created competition among the producers of the five countries and has probably promoted industrial specialisation by types of products, thus permitting larger production scales and lower costs.

A further indication of 'trade creation' is the small rise in average costs of living. Table 7 shows that costs of living in Central America have increased less than in the United States. Prices in the region have not increased in comparison with those in the country with which Central America mainly trades, in

Table 4

CENTRAL AMERICAN COMMON MARKET: CHANGE IN IMPORTS FROM INSIDE AND OUTSIDE THE AREA, CLASSIFIED BY ECONOMIC TYPE OF GOODS, 1958–68

(in U.S. $ million)

	Imports from area			Imports from outside area			Total imports		
	1958	1968	Annual rate of change (%)	1958	1968	Annual rate of change (%)	1958	1968	Annual rate of change (%)
Non-durable consumer goods	9·0	114·6	29·0	89·2	97·6	0·9	98·2	212·2	8·0
Durable consumer goods	0·7	15·0	36·0	66·8	86·9	2·7	67·5	101·9	4·2
Fuels and lubricants	0·1	3·9	47·0	32·1	16·3	–6·5	32·2	20·2	–3·2
Raw materials	7·1	92·1	29·0	156·3	348·1	8·4	163·4	440·2	10·4
Building materials	1·2	19·0	32·0	31·3	38·6	2·1	32·5	57·6	5·9
Capital goods for agriculture	0·5	2·9	20·0	15·1	22·9	4·3	15·6	25·8	5·1
Capital goods for industry	1·1	3·9	13·5	61·9	136·0	8·2	63·0	139·9	8·3
Capital goods for transport	0·2	0·7	10·9	9·9	45·5	16·5	10·1	46·2	16·4
Miscellaneous	0·2	0·1	–8·8	2·2	2·2	0·0	2·4	2·2	–0·8
Total	20·1	252·2	29·0	464·8	794·1	5·5	484·9	1,046·2	8·0

Source: As Table 2.

Table 5

CENTRAL AMERICAN COMMON MARKET: CHANGES IN IMPORTS OF SHOES AND
TEXTILES FROM INSIDE AND OUTSIDE THE AREA, 1962–5
(in U.S. $ thousand)

	Imports from area			Imports from outside area			Total imports		
	1962	1965	Annual rate of change	1962	1965	Annual rate of change	1962	1965	Annual rate of change
Shoes	1,069	5,381	70	656	380	−42	1,725	5,761	49
Yarn, cloth and clothing	3,931	15,385	58	12,180	12,760	1·6	16,111	28,146	20

Source: Secretaría del Tratado de Integración Económica Centroamericana, *Anuario Estadístico Centroamericano de Comercio Exterior*, several issues.

Table 6

CENTRAL AMERICAN COMMON MARKET: CROSS-TRADE
IN SHOES AND TEXTILES, 1965
(in U.S. $ thousands)

	Guatemala Exports	Imports	El Salvador Exports	Imports	Honduras Exports	Imports	Nicaragua Exports	Imports	Costa Rica Exports	Imports
Shoes	1,511	851	2,181	883	371	1,589	1,133	879	185	1,177
Yarn, cloth and clothing	5,739	4,624	8,848	3,386	104	3,227	287	3,097	408	1,027

Source: as Table 5.

Table 7

CENTRAL AMERICAN COMMON MARKET: ANNUAL PERCENTAGE INCREASE
IN CONSUMER PRICES, 1960–8

	1960	1961	1962	1963	1964	1965	1966	1967	1968
Costa Rica	1	3	3	4	3	0	2	3	3
El Salvador	0	-2	0	1	2	0	-1	3	1
Guatemala	-2	0	2	0	0	-1	3	-1	4
Honduras	-2	2	1	3	5	4	4	-3	5
Nicaragua	-2	0	1	0	4	3	4	1	4
United States	1	1	2	1	1	2	4	3	6

Source: International Monetary Fund, *International Financial Statistics*, several issues.

spite of the higher level of the new Common Tariff[9] and the increased amount of import substitution from outside the area. This is a most interesting phenomenon that deserves study; but in the absence of such a study, the maintenance of price stability seems to indicate that increased competition has not permitted producers to take advantage of the higher customs duties.[10] Another factor that might possibly explain the maintenance of price stability in the presence of higher tariffs is the policy of tax exemptions as incentives to the establishment of new industries. This policy, justly criticised as excessive, has functioned as a subsidy to new industries that may have contributed to keep down their prices. But if this is the reason, it is not clear why the subsidy has worked. When several small industries have been established, competition would explain the subsidy effectiveness: but in the much more frequent case, when only one or two large (in relative terms) industries have been created, the maintenance of prices below the tariff margins is not easy to understand. As stated before, the problem requires study.

Trade, payments balance and rate of growth of member countries

As can be observed in Tables 8 to 11, all Central American countries increased their exports to the area at a very fast rate, and all came to depend on the area market for a large share of their exports. In 1968 the area absorbed 17·1 per cent of Nicaragua's exports, 17·5 per cent of Honduras's, 22·2 per cent of Costa Rica's, 34·9 per cent of Guatemala's and 39·8 per cent of El Salvador's. Correspondingly, all countries increased their imports from the area very rapidly and came to buy in it a large part of their supplies. In 1968 Guatemala bought in the area 19·8 per cent of its imports, Costa Rica 22·8 per cent, Nicaragua 24·9 per cent, Honduras 26·3 per cent and El Salvador 30·4 per cent.

In 1966–8 Guatemala and El Salvador had continuous export balances with the area, Honduras and Nicaragua persistent import balances, and Costa Rica had a small surplus in 1966 and deficits in 1967 and 1968. Guatemala's and El Salvador's trade surpluses with the area permitted them to finance a large part of their trade deficits with the rest of the world; conversely, Honduras financed most of its area deficit with its surplus with

Table 8

CENTRAL AMERICAN COMMON MARKET: AREA TRADE OF MEMBER COUNTRIES, 1960-8
(in U.S. $ million)

	Guatemala			El Salvador			Honduras			Nicaragua			Costa Rica		
	Exp.	Imp.	Bal.	Exp.	Imp.	Bal.	Exp.	Imp.	Bal.	Exp.	Imp.	Bal.	Exp.	Imp.	Bal.
1960	7·3	7·6	-0·3	12·7	13·5	-0·8	7·4	5·3	2·1	3·4	2·8	0·6	1·9	3·5	-1·6
1961	10·3	8·9	1·4	14·4	14·6	-0·2	8·2	6·3	1·9	1·8	2·9	-1·1	2·0	4·0	-2·0
1962	13·4	11·2	2·2	18·5	22·0	-3·5	13·8	8·9	4·9	3·2	5·3	-2·1	1·9	3·3	-1·4
1963	20·8	19·7	1·1	28·7	27·9	0·8	14·0	13·3	0·7	4·2	7·3	-3·1	4·4	3·8	0·6
1964	30·0	26·4	3·6	35·2	39·2	-4·0	18·3	18·0	0·3	6·9	14·3	-7·4	15·8	8·3	7·5
1965	38·4	31·5	6·9	46·2	42·4	3·8	22·2	25·5	-3·3	9·9	21·4	-11·5	18·9	14·7	4·2
1966	55·1	33·8	21·3	57·5	52·0	5·5	21·5	34·0	-12·5	14·9	31·7	-16·8	25·8	23·2	2·6
1967	65·7	42·1	23·6	75·2	54·5	20·7	23·5	40·7	-17·2	18·6	42·4	-23·8	31·0	34·2	-3·2
1968	77·5	49·4	28·1	84·9	65·2	19·7	31·3	48·7	-17·4	26·9	46·2	-19·3	37·7	48·8	-11·1

Source: Instituto para la Integración de América Latina, *El Proceso de Integración en América Latina, 1968–71* (Buenos Aires, 1972).

Table 9

CENTRAL AMERICAN COMMON MARKET: TRADE OF MEMBER COUNTRIES
WITH THE REST OF THE WORLD, 1960–8
(in U.S. $ million)

	Guatemala			El Salvador			Honduras			Nicaragua			Costa Rica		
	Exp.	Imp.	Bal.	Exp.	Imp.	Bal.	Exp.	Imp.	Bal.	Exp.	Imp.	Bal.	Exp.	Imp.	Bal.
1960	110	130	−20	104	108	−4	56	67	−11	53	69	−16	84	106	−22
1961	103	125	−22	104	94	10	65	66	−1	59	71	−12	82	103	−21
1962	105	125	−20	117	103	14	67	71	−4	79	92	−13	91	110	−19
1963	133	151	−18	125	124	1	69	82	−13	96	103	−7	91	120	−29
1964	138	176	−38	143	152	−9	77	92	−15	111	123	−12	97	131	−34
1965	149	198	−49	143	159	−16	105	97	8	134	140	−6	93	163	−70
1966	171	173	−2	132	168	−36	122	115	7	123	150	−27	110	155	−45
1967	132	205	−73	132	170	−38	131	124	7	127	160	−33	113	157	−44
1968	145	200	−55	128	149	−21	148	136	12	130	139	−9	133	165	−32

Source: from Tables 8 and 10.

Table 10

CENTRAL AMERICAN COMMON MARKET: TOTAL TRADE OF MEMBER COUNTRIES, 1960–8
(in U.S. $ million)

	Guatemala			El Salvador			Honduras			Nicaragua			Costa Rica		
	Exp.	Imp.	Bal.	Exp.	Imp.	Bal.	Exp.	Imp.	Bal.	Exp.	Imp.	Bal.	Exp.	Imp.	Bal.
1960	117	138	−21	117	122	−5	63	72	−9	56	72	−16	86	110	−24
1961	113	134	−21	119	109	10	73	72	1	61	74	−13	84	107	−23
1962	118	136	−18	136	125	11	81	80	1	82	97	−15	93	113	−20
1963	154	171	−17	154	152	2	83	95	−12	100	110	−10	95	124	−29
1964	158	202	−44	178	191	−13	95	102	−7	118	137	−19	113	139	−26
1965	187	229	−42	189	201	−12	127	122	5	144	161	−17	112	178	−66
1966	226	207	19	189	220	−31	143	149	−6	138	182	−44	136	178	−42
1967	198	247	−49	207	224	−17	154	165	−11	146	202	−56	144	191	−47
1968	222	249	−27	213	214	−1	179	185	−6	157	185	−28	171	214	−43

Source: International Monetary Fund, *International Financial Statistics*, various issues.

Table 11
CENTRAL AMERICAN COMMON MARKET: PERCENTAGE SHARE
OF AREA TRADE IN TOTAL TRADE OF MEMBERS,
1960 AND 1968

	Share of exports to area in total exports		Share of imports from area in total imports	
	1960	*1968*	*1960*	*1968*
Guatemala	6·2	34·9	5·5	19·8
El Salvador	10·8	39·8	11·1	30·4
Honduras	11·7	17·5	7·3	26·3
Nicaragua	6·1	17·1	3·9	24·9
Costa Rica	2·2	22·2	3·2	22·8
Area	7·5	26·0	6·3	24·7

Source: As Table 8.

third countries; and both Nicaragua and Costa Rica had deficits with the area and with the rest of the world (except for the small Costa Rican surplus with the area in 1966).

The sign and size of intra-trade balances are sometimes considered to be a good measure of the benefits from integration, but they are not. A country may expand its imports from the area more than its exports to it but, thanks to these latter, experience an increase in employment and income and accelerate its rate of growth. The negative element in integration is not the volume of goods imported from the area, but the higher price paid for those goods. The benefits from integration may thus be measured by the increase in national product induced by the expansion in exports to the region,[11] minus the higher payments made for area imports, as compared to their level if the goods had been imported from third countries. Following this criterion, all Central American countries have received considerable net benefits from integration.

Table 12 shows that the five countries of the area had an average annual rate of growth of 6·0 per cent during the period under study. The average rises to 6·9 per cent if we take the period 1962–8, eliminating 1960 and 1961, which were years in which integration had not yet had time to produce effects, and which were also years when exports to the world market were practically stagnant. Individually, Central American countries had relatively close rates of growth that ranged from 5·7 per cent in Guatemala to 6·9 per cent in Costa Rica. Countries

Table 12

CENTRAL AMERICAN COMMON MARKET: RATE OF GROWTH OF GROSS DOMESTIC PRODUCT, 1960–8
(in percentage increase from previous year)

	1960	1961	1962	1963	1964	1965	1966	1967	1968	Average 1960–8	Average 1962–8
Guatemala	3·1	2·7	2·9	10·0	9·2	7·3	5·5	4·1	5·7	5·7	6·4
El Salvador	4·2	2·4	11·8	3·6	12·3	6·9	7·2	5·4	-1·2	5·8	6·6
Honduras	0·5	5·3	7·3	3·0	5·9	10·3	7·6	6·5	7·0	5·9	6·8
Nicaragua	1·1	6·5	10·6	7·2	8·5	9·7	3·1	5·3	4·7	6·3	7·0
Costa Rica	5·5	2·8	10·4	8·6	6·9	8·1	7·3	7·1	5·8	6·9	7·7
Area	3·1	3·3	6·6	9·1	9·1	7·5	6·2	5·3	4·1	6·0	6·9

Source: Inter-American Development Bank, *Socio-Economic Progress in Latin America* (1969).

with an area trade surplus were not those that had higher rates, but rather those that had lower – though not much lower. As may be seen in Table 13, Guatemala and El Salvador expanded their exports to the area at an extremely fast rate, but their exports to the rest of the world increased very slowly,

Table 13

CENTRAL AMERICAN COMMON MARKET: AVERAGE ANNUAL PERCENTAGE RATE OF EXPANSION OF EXPORTS AND G.D.P., BY COUNTRIES, 1960–8

	Exports to area	*Exports outside area*	*Total exports*	*Gross domestic product*
Guatemala	34	3·6	8·4	5·7
El Salvador	27	2·7	7·8	5·8
Honduras	20	12·9	13·9	5·9
Nicaragua	29	11·8	13·7	6·3
Costa Rica	45	5·9	8·9	6·9
Area	29	6·9	10·1	6·0

Source: from Tables 8, 9, 10 and 12.

dampening down the rate of expansion of total trade and restraining somewhat the pace of overall economic growth. It might be argued that the growth of world exports of these countries was hampered by the fast expansion of exports to the area, but this could not be the case because the products exported were different. It is possible, however, that efforts to promote world exports would have been stronger in these two countries if area markets had not been available. In any case, the three deficit countries expanded their world exports with relative rapidity (which explains their ability to import from the area more than they exported to it) and experienced a slightly higher rate of economic growth than the two surplus countries.

Tables 14 and 15 show that all countries developed very rapidly their manufacturing industries, which increased their contribution to the gross domestic product. In no country did the competition of area imports prevent the rapid expansion of domestic industry.

The rapid rate of economic growth of Central American countries in 1960–8 was not brought about by integration only but, as Table 16 shows, was due to a large extent to the boom

Table 14

CENTRAL AMERICAN COMMON MARKET: RATE OF GROWTH OF
VALUE ADDED IN MANUFACTURING, 1960–8

(in percentage increase over previous year)

	1960	1961	1962	1963	1964	1965	1966	1967	1968	Average 1960–8
Guatemala	4·5	5·8	1·0	13·5	12·6	6·7	5·8	6·5	5·1	6·8
El Salvador	11·7	7·7	8·8	9·2	13·1	14·0	13·7	7·0	6·5	10·2
Honduras	5·0	13·1	6·0	2·0	16·3	7·8	11·6	7·8	8·4	8·6
Nicaragua	3·2	7·9	14·5	14·5	12·7	5·6	17·3	6·8	9·6	10·2
Costa Rica	9·5	10·6	10·6	9·6	4·4	7·3	11·8	11·4	7·1	9·1
Area	6·7	8·0	7·8	12·3	12·1	8·0	10·7	7·6	6·7	8·9

Source: Inter-American Development Bank, *Socio-Economic Progress in Latin America* (1969).

Table 15

CENTRAL AMERICAN COMMON MARKET: SHARE OF MANUFACTURES
IN THE GROSS DOMESTIC PRODUCT, 1960–8

(in percentage of G.D.P.)

	1960	1961	1962	1963	1964	1965	1966	1967	1968
Guatemala	12·7	13·2	13·0	13·1	13·8	14·6	14·6	14·9	14·9
El Salvador	15·2	15·5	15·1	15·8	16·4	17·7	18·8	19·1	19·6
Honduras	12·2	12·7	12·6	12·5	14·0	13·9	14·4	14·7	14·9
Nicaragua	12·4	12·3	12·7	13·4	14·2	12·8	14·6	14·8	15·4
Costa Rica	16·1	16·0	16·8	17·5	18·0	17·7	18·3	19·0	19·3

Source: as Table 14.

Table 16

CENTRAL AMERICAN COMMON MARKET: RATES OF EXPANSION
OF EXPORTS AND G.D.P., 1960–8

(in percentage increase from previous year)

	1960	1961	1962	1963	1964	1965	1966	1967	1968
Rate of expansion of exports to area	17·8	12·6	38·2	41·8	47·3	27·6	29·0	22·4	20·7
Rate of expansion of exports to countries outside area	0·8	1·4	11·1	11·7	10·1	10·4	5·9	–3·1	7·9
Rate of expansion of total exports	1·8	2·3	13·3	14·9	14·6	13·2	10·1	2·2	11·1
Rate of expansion of gross domestic product	3·1	3·3	6·6	9·1	9·1	7·5	6·2	5·3	4·1

Source: Instituto para la Integración de América Latina, *El Proceso de Integración en América Latina, 1968–71* (Buenos Aires, 1972); Inter-American Development Bank, *Socio-Economic Progress in Latin America* (1969).

experienced by their world exports in the years 1962 to 1965 (both included), when exports increased at rates above 10 per cent per year. The export boom (experienced also by Guatemala and El Salvador) induced a rapid income expansion in the five countries and softened the resistance of vested interests to integration, greatly facilitating the process. Integration, in its turn, contributed to accelerate income expansion and, when the external boom ceased in 1966, the rapid increase in trade among member countries was able to maintain a high rate of income growth in the area.

OBSTACLES TO INTEGRATION AND POSSIBLE WAYS TO OVERCOME THEM

Fears of liberalising trade

The experience of Central America shows that, under appropriate circumstances, the elimination of restrictions on the trade among a group of developing countries brings about considerable expansion in their commercial interchange, fuller use of industrial capacity, specialisation of production, economies of scale, increased industrialisation and faster economic growth, without any rise in the number of industrial failures or in the amount of unemployment on account of the competition forthcoming from other member countries. But governments of developing nations are not generally confident that the positive results of across-the-board tariff elimination will be as large, or that negative effects will be so small, and are reluctant to risk their protected industries, or to renounce the possibility of creating new ones under protection. The short-term benefits of national protection are present and certain, whereas those of opening new markets in neighbour countries are future and uncertain. In order to forego the short-term benefits of national protection, countries must have a great faith in the future effects of integration, or a strong political motivation, or a firm conviction that they cannot develop within their own borders.

Large developing countries are not, as a rule, strongly motivated towards integration because they believe that their national markets are large enough to support industrial development; and small countries, generally less developed than the large, have strong motivations but are afraid to integrate with their bigger and more developed neighbours. Countries with high tariff walls fear to expose their plants to the competition of less protected industries; and those with low duties consider protective tariffs as a status symbol of political and economic independence. Owing to different reasons, the resistance to liberalising trade, even within a group of neighbours, is strong and widespread.

Deficiencies in joint industrial planning

If integration is defined as the establishment of a rational division of labour among a group of countries, it can be theoretically attained by the co-ordination of economic plans, thus avoiding the risk of industrial failures and increases in unemployment that the general elimination of tariffs may bring about. The theoretical possibility of pursuing integration through joint planning, with tariffs reduced only for planned industries, has permitted governments to conciliate their desire for integration with their reluctance to liberalise trade. But unfortunately, joint industrial planning has not gone much beyond the intention of applying it. In a recent report, UNCTAD's Secretariat expresses the opinion that little significant progress has been made in regional planning, attributing its lack of success to

the great difficulty that even a single country experiences in deciding on a long-term industrial plan involving both political and technical judgements on the feasibility and desirability of any given schedule of priorities and locations for regional industries. The dovetailing of national industrial plans, which are themselves the product of complex internal compromises at the national level, into a coherent regional plan has so far eluded the planning bodies of the regional groupings, composed as they are of representatives of sovereign States, each with a veto right concerning decisions affecting its own industrial development. Moreover, the absence in most regions of sufficient entrepreneurial and financial resources to ensure the implementation of a hypo-thetical regional industrial plan reduces the incentive for striking a compromise, since countries are understandably

unwilling to forego the option of establishing given industries
for which external financial and technical resources might
become available in exchange for the right to establish other
industries for which no such support is assured.[12]

The Andean Group countries are carrying ahead their
integration agreement, partly through automatic trade liberalisation in a large number of items, mainly light manufactures,
and partly through joint sectoral programmes on basic industries – metal working, petrochemicals, steel, aluminium,
automobiles and trucks, electronics, etc. The joint sectoral
industrial programmes are agreements to distribute the location
of production among member countries and to eliminate trade
restrictions on articles originating in the country to which
production is assigned, while maintaining restrictions on those
produced in other member countries and in the rest of the
world. The monopolistic advantages granted by the agreements
are, however, only temporary because trade restrictions within
the group have to be eliminated not later than 1980, except for
some tariffs to protect Bolivian and Ecuadorian industries that
will be maintained until 1985.

In August 1972 the Andean Group countries approved the
sectoral programme on metal-working industries, which is the
first one subscribed. The programme assigns 7 types of products
to Bolivia (e.g. compressors, pneumatic tools, drills); 23 to
Colombia (e.g. harvesters, mills, centrifugal pumps, small
aeroplanes, surgical instruments, toys); 22 to Chile (some
common to those assigned to Colombia and some different,
such as electric generators and motors, railway equipment,
fixed-focus photographic cameras); 11 to Ecuador (machinery
for the dairy industry, measurement and control instruments,
clocks and watches); and 25 to Peru (most of them common to
those assigned to some other country and some exclusive to
Peru, such as packing machinery and machinery for the ceramic
industry). As already mentioned, such assignments involve the
commitment by other member countries to grant immediate
free entry to the products originating in the assigned countries,
while maintaining restrictions on those produced in other member
countries and in the rest of the world. Also as previously
mentioned, the advantage given to the assigned countries is

only temporary. In the case of existing industries the monopolistic position will cover a period of eight years (thirteen years for Bolivia and Ecuador) because tariffs within the group will have to be eliminated not later than 31 December 1980 (31 December 1985 for products assigned to Bolivia and Ecuador) and, in the case of non-existent industries, the advantage will be substantially shorter, since the installation of a manufacturing plant takes a number of years. When countries do not notify their decision to produce the assigned article within two years (three for Bolivia and Ecuador) or do not install the plant within an additional period of three years, the advantage is lost and the product automatically becomes a free-trade item within the group.

Since the Andean sectoral programmes are not fully fledged development plans but only agreements to distribute the location of future industries, the reasons given in former pages to explain the difficulties of negotiating and implementing joint investment plans may not be fully applicable to them. Furthermore, the successful negotiation of the programme on metal-working industries seems to show the feasibility of these agreements. But the task ahead will be very far from easy and the programmes in other sectors will probably face more obstacles than those in the first one. The difficulties of distributing future industries among countries will be greater, the greater the number of industries already operating in the region – which in the metal-working sector are few – and the greater the savings in costs that can be obtained by integrating production in large industrial complexes – which in many metal-working industries do not seem to be large. Future sectoral programmes will therefore present difficult problems that may induce the Andean countries to try new formulas. To this effect, the experience acquired in the preparation and negotiation of the agreements on metal-working industries, successfully completed, and on the petrochemical sector, still under discussion, will prove invaluable.

In theory, integration can be attained through negotiated tariff reductions, but in practice trade liberalisation has to be applied across the board. This does not mean, however, that the schedules of tariff removals should be the same for all member countries, nor that a programme of trade liberalisation should be launched without the necessary preparations, nor that the promotion of new large industries in an integrated group of countries should be left to the free play of the market, any more than it should in individual countries. In developing countries, new large industries are seldom established without the concession of official facilities and the assistance of government financial institutions, which usually analyse their costs and their benefits to the country's economy. In integration groups, both national and regional financial institutions must examine the role that new large industries will play in the region's economy, check that they do not come to duplicate capacity and encourage their location in the relatively less advanced countries.

Differences in development level

When there are considerable differences in development level among members of an integration group, a programme of uniform trade liberalisation would give undue advantage to more developed countries, whose manufactures might invade the market of the less advanced members and stifle their industrial growth. This may not occur, owing to differences in wages and other costs not inversely related to plant size, but less advanced members believe firmly that it will, and are therefore reluctant to join programmes of automatic trade liberalisation, and prone to withdraw when they have joined them. As shown in previous pages, the Central American Common Market accelerated Honduras's industrial growth, but this may not be a good example, because the differences in development levels in the C.A.C.M. are much narrower than in other groups. And even if Honduras's industrial growth was not negatively affected by the Common Market, she had the subjective feeling of not receiving a fair share in the benefits, and such sentiment probably contributed to strengthening her decision to withdraw, which was mainly provoked by the border conflict with El Salvador. Liberalisation programmes should therefore establish delayed schedules of tariff reductions for less advanced members. In this respect, the agreements which organised the Andean Group and the Caribbean Free Trade Area have set excellent examples.

Differences in level and structure of protection

Another two important obstacles which must be overcome, or neutralised, before the removal or significant reduction of intra-trade restrictions, are (*a*) differences in the level and structure of protection, and (*b*) differences in the rate of inflation. Both types of differences are extremely pronounced among LAFTA countries. According to Balassa,[13] the *ad valorem* average rates of nominal protection in Brazil, Chile and Mexico, in the years mentioned, were as follows:

	Brazil (1966)	Chile (1961)	Mexico (1960)
Primary products	59	28	6
Intermediate products	92	53	22
Non-durable consumer goods	140	204	25
Consumer durables	108	84	49
Machinery	87	92	29

Given these great tariff differences, their removal among partners without their unification towards the rest of the world would give an enormous competitive advantage to countries with lower external tariffs.

Free-trade associations are functionally possible among countries with low rates of protection, but not among highly protected countries, where the differences in tariffs to third countries are generally very large and create great divergences between the cost and price structure of member countries. External customs duties have to be unified, or intra-trade tariffs cannot be lowered. LAFTA countries did not even consider unifying external tariffs because unification would have involved – would still involve – gigantic changes in the foreign trade system and in the structure of prices and costs of each member country. But maintenance of the different external tariffs did not permit significant reductions of the restrictions to trade among members. The practical conclusion seems to be that LAFTA countries should work gradually, but steadily, to bring their tariffs to a uniform lower level, which ideally should be that of the lowest effective tariff (i.e. the lowest tariff not supplemented by other types of import restriction). Since the large LAFTA countries are now embarked on a policy to promote the export of manufactures, and such policy makes it necessary (and possible) to diminish protection, the process could be used to narrow the differences in customs duties to third countries, thus preparing the ground for their elimination in intra-LAFTA trade.

Differences in the rate of inflation

In the period 1969–71 price changes in LAFTA countries were as follows:[14]

	1969	1970	1971
Argentina	6	21	39
Bolivia	3	4	5
Brazil	22	18	20
Chile	29	35	22
Columbia	11	4	14
Ecuador	6	8	7
Mexico	3	8	3
Paraguay	3	0	6
Peru	6	5	8
Uruguay	15	21	36
Venezuela	2	3	3

With such differences in the rate of inflation, the total elimination of trade restrictions among these countries would bring utter chaos, except if their rates of exchange varied simultaneously, in the amount necessary to neutralise price rises. Such neutralisation would have been unthinkable a few years ago, but is now perfectly within the realm of possibility. The experience of Chile from 1965 to 1970, of Colombia since 1967 and of Brazil since 1968 shows that a 'crawling peg' is a perfectly feasible exchange system – by far the best for a country with chronic inflation. If all members of integration groups adopted policies of complete exchange-rate flexibility, differences in inflation would cease to be an obstacle to trade liberalisation. This may take a few years, because not all countries with chronic inflation are yet fully convinced of the virtues of con- tinuous exchange-rate adjustments, but the delay will probably not be long. In any case, countries with chronic inflation need to adopt a flexible exchange-rate policy in order to promote exports to the rest of the world, even more than to facilitate economic integration with their neighbours. As in the case of gradual tariff reductions to third countries, measures to facilitate integration coincide entirely with measures to promote exports to the world market.

Concluding remarks

The study of recent integration arrangements among developing countries shows that some groups overcame the fears and obstacles that hinder trade liberalisation and eliminated restrictions to the commerce among them. These groups experienced fast expansion in their trade and substantial acceleration in their rate of growth. Trade expanded at a much faster rate than overall consumption, thus indicating the development of competition among member countries. Integration not only facilitated import substitution from third countries, but fostered competition, specialisation and industrial efficiency.

The study also shows that some groups are not entirely successful in eliminating restrictions to their trade. In addition to the resistance of vested interests, trade liberalisation is being hindered by differences in level of development, level of protection and rate of inflation among member countries. The first obstacle is being met by the application of different schedules of trade liberalisation, with the more advanced countries lowering their barriers at a faster rate. The second is not being met by one of the groups, on account of the great disruptions which would be provoked by a rapid equalisation of tariffs, but could and should be attacked by a co-ordinated gradual reduction of the rate of protection; and the third would be neutralised if all member countries adopted a flexible exchange-rate policy.

Groups that are progressing towards integration are placing themselves in a better position to trade with the rest of the world; and those making less progress would quicken their pace towards integration by following policies which would also serve to promote their world-wide exports. Integration policies and world trade policies do not seem to be in conflict, but to reinforce each other.

Notes

1. This paper has been written in a personal capacity and the opinions expressed in it are the sole responsibility of the author.

2. UNCTAD, *Trade Expansion, Economic Co-operation and Regional Integration among Developing Countries*, Annex 1, Doc. TD/110, Third Session, Santiago, Chile, Feb 1972. In addition to the six groups included in Table 1, the document gives figures for the Maghreb Permanent Consultation Committee (Algeria, Morocco, Tunisia) and for the Regional Co-operation for Development (Iran, Pakistan, Turkey), which may not be properly considered as integration groups. The document does not give figures for the Arab Common Market (Egypt, Iraq, Jordan and Syria).

3. Both LAFTA and C.A.C.M. were formed in 1960. C.A.C.E.U. was formed in 1964 but had been preceded by the Federation of French Equatorial Africa; and the common market among E.A.C. countries has existed since colonial times. CARIFTA was formed in 1968 and the Andean Group in 1969.

4. The eight-year period 1960–8 is chosen instead of 1960–70, for which figures are available, because in mid-1969 a grave frontier conflict between two members induced one of them (Honduras) to withdraw from the Common Market. 1969 and 1970 are not, therefore, comparable with the preceding eight years.

5. Cf. C. P. Kindleberger's testimony before Congress in *Foreign Economic Policy: Hearings before the Subcommittee on Foreign Economic Policy of the Joint Economic Committee on the Economic Report* (84th Congress, 1st session) p. 521.

6. Bela Balassa, *The Theory of Economic Integration* (London: Allen & Unwin, 1962).

7. Jacob Viner, *The Customs Union Issue* (New York: Carnegie Endowment for International Peace, 1950).

8. For a discussion of trade creation and trade diversion in another Latin American integration group, see Carlos F. Díaz-Alejandro, 'The Andean Common Market: Gestation and Outlook', Yale University Economic Growth Center Discussion Paper, no. 85 (May 1970).

9. In a list of 83 tariff sub-items, selected as a representative sample of imports (excluding machinery), the new Common Tariff was found to apply rates of 70 per cent *ad valorem*, or more, to 34 sub-items, whereas an average of the old five national tariffs reached, or surpassed, the 70 per cent level in only 15 sub-items.

10. In maintaining the thesis that integration in Central America has fostered competition, I am closely following the ideas of José A. Guerra, Senior Economist in the South America Department of the International Bank for Reconstruction and Development, who showed me his reports on the subject, and discussed them at length with me.

11. This assumes that the country has unemployment and idle capacity, as is generally the case in less developed nations, and that it cannot readily expand its exports to the world market. The presence of this second condition is not as easy to determine as the first one. It may be argued

that many less developed countries could expand their exports to the world market by following better policies in relation to exchange rates, taxation and level of protection; but better export policies would seldom bring about as quick results as integration. Furthermore, given the margin of excess capacity existing in most countries, integration does not hinder the promotion of exports to the world market. Far from hindering export promotion, it facilitates it by fostering specialisation, economies of scale and lower costs.

12. UNCTAD, op. cit., p. 29. In a footnote to the paragraph quoted, the document cites Brewster, 'Industrial Integration Systems' (TD/B/345) and 'Trade Expansion and Economic Integration among Developing Countries' (TD/B/85/Rev. 1), United Nations publications, Sales No.: 67.II.D.20, chap. v.

13. Bela Balassa and Associates, *The Structure of Protection in Developing Countries* (Baltimore: Johns Hopkins Univ. Press, 1971). For rates of protection in former years, see Santiago Macario, 'Proteccionismo e Industrialización en América Latina', in *Hacia una Tarifa Externa Común en América Latina* (Buenos Aires: INTAL, 1969).

14. International Monetary Fund, *International Financial Statistics*, xxv 8 (Aug 1972).

Regional Integration of Trade: Policies of Less Developed Countries

Bela Balassa

PROFESSOR OF POLITICAL ECONOMY, THE JOHNS
HOPKINS UNIVERSITY, BALTIMORE, AND
CONSULTANT, INTERNATIONAL BANK FOR
RECONSTRUCTION AND DEVELOPMENT,
WASHINGTON, D.C.

I

Questions of economic integration in less developed areas have received much attention in recent years. More often than not, however, these questions have been considered in isolation, without taking account of other policy choices. A different approach is followed in this paper. Regional integration will be regarded as a facet of development strategy, with emphasis given to the choices open to developing countries as regards general trade policies, preferential arrangements and regional integration.

Once an economy has progressed beyond the subsistence stage, export expansion or import substitution customarily provides the engine of growth. Countries such as Australia, Canada and Denmark attained high income levels relying chiefly on the exportation of primary commodities. Most of the less developed countries, however, cannot expect to duplicate their experience, because of resource and/or demand limitations on their primary exports. Indirect benefits obtainable through improvements in the quality of the labour force and the expansion of related industries also favour the development of manufacturing industries.

When industrialisation is a necessary and desirable part of a development strategy, countries may follow various routes in promoting manufacturing activities. The time-honoured way is import substitution, first in non-durable consumer goods and their inputs, and later in intermediate and durable goods. This policy found application during the post-war period in the major Latin American and Asian countries, which embarked on import substitution behind high protective barriers. More recently, several countries, including Korea and Taiwan, took a different route and moved from import substitution in non-durable goods and their inputs to the exportation of these commodities.

Industrialisation based on import substitution is limited by the size of the domestic market. The smaller this market, the more restricted are the possibilities of establishing industries which cater exclusively to domestic demand and the higher are the costs of production. In the manufacturing of intermediate products and durable goods in particular, efficient operations require large-scale production, with costs rising substantially at lower output levels. The size of the domestic market also limits the extent of product specialisation in individual firms and restricts the possibilities of manufacturing parts, components and accessories on an efficient scale. Last but not least, the sheltering of domestic markets reduces the extent of competition and provides little incentive for technological improvements.

These considerations indicate the importance of market size for the success of a policy of import substitution. But how to measure the size of domestic markets? Since economies of scale and competition are of greatest importance in the manufacturing sector, the consumption of manufactured goods may provide an appropriate indicator. It will then be apparent that, compared with the industrial nations, domestic markets are small even in developing countries with a large population. At the same time, thirty developing countries but no developed nations have a population less than 2 million.

No developing country has a market for manufactured goods one-half of that of France, a medium-sized industrial nation; it is between one-fifth and one-half of the size of the French market in four countries (India, Brazil, Mexico and Argentina), and between one-tenth and one-twentieth in another two (the

Philippines and Turkey). The comparisons become even more unfavourable if the value of manufacturing consumption is expressed in world market prices, since in most developing countries protection has raised domestic prices much above prices in the world market.

Notwithstanding the relatively large size of the French market for manufactured goods as compared with developing countries, France has found it necessary to turn towards exporting and to open its market to foreign competition. This policy change has had beneficial effects for the French economy as entry into the European Common Market has contributed to substantial improvements in the manufacturing sector. Similar conclusions apply to Italy which, together with France, had the highest levels of protection among the Common Market countries. Yet levels of protection in developing countries which have followed a policy of import substitution are several times higher than in France or Italy.

II

As the possibilities for economic growth through import substitution are limited by the extent of a country's domestic market, countries of different size will need to have recourse to exports at differing levels of industrialisation in order to ensure the continued expansion of their manufacturing industries. In small African countries where the consumption of manufactured goods does not exceed $100 million a year, the domestic market is not sufficiently large even for the production of relatively simple manufactured goods. At the other end of the scale, India and Brazil established a diversified industrial structure serving domestic needs. However, many of their industries exhibit inefficiencies and high costs, and the two countries attempt to rely increasingly on exports of manufactured goods.

The expansion of manufacturing exports contributes to economic growth in a variety of ways. Exports of manufactures permit the exploitation of economies of scale in one-product plants, lengthening production runs in conjunction with product specialisation in individual plants, and participating in the international division of the production process through the exchange of parts, components and accessories whose manufacturing is subject to substantial scale economies.

The expansion of exports also tends to raise a country's national income by increasing the availability of foreign exchange necessary for economic growth and by improving resource allocation through specialisation according to the country's comparative advantage. Thus export industries utilise the country's abundant resources – generally labour – whereas import substitution increasingly leads to the establishment of capital-intensive industries. Finally, familiarity with foreign markets provides inducements for technological change and improvements in product quality.

Exports of manufactured goods may be orientated towards the markets of countries in the same region, to developing countries in other regions, or to developed nations. Providing incentives to exports would benefit sales in all foreign markets; regional integration would boost exports to partner countries; while preferential schemes extending over several less developed regions would stimulate exports to other developing countries.

It has been suggested that preferential arrangements among developing countries – whether or not on a regional basis – are undesirable, since purchases from other countries would be made at higher than world market prices. According to the proponents of this view, trade liberalisation, combined with the provision of equal incentives to exports and import substitution, would offer a better alternative.

The establishment of the European Common Market and EFTA indicates, however, that even industrial nations see advantages in establishing regional groupings. There are various reasons for this. First of all, a country participating in a regional integration scheme benefits from the elimination of barriers to trade by the partner countries, thereby widening markets for its industry. This is of especial importance for developing countries that encounter high barriers to some of their major export commodities (e.g. textiles, shoes) in developed country markets. Also, if the member countries are at similar levels of development, they will suffer less dislocation than would occur if trade barriers were reduced on imports from countries at higher levels of industrialisation possessing technological advantages or from those at lower levels that have labour-cost advantages. At the same time, economic integration increases the bargaining power of the participants in trade negotiations.

Considerations of risk and uncertainty, also, favour regional integration schemes. Thus there is more information on prices and costs in neighbouring countries than in far-away nations, thereby lessening uncertainty as regards the effects of trade liberalisation on domestic industry. Uncertainty in intra-regional trade is further reduced through the acceptance of commitments to refrain from reimposing restrictions on imports or granting subsidies to exports, which has often happened in the past. And in a regional union it will be easier to reach – and to police – agreements to forego the use of measures which provide indirect benefits to domestic industry at the expense of their competitors in the partner countries.

In the E.E.C. an additional consideration has been to create large markets for highly sophisticated industries, such as air-craft, computers and electronics, where national markets of the member countries are too small for efficient operations, while protecting these industries from U.S. competition. This argu-ment applies *a fortiori* to developing economies which need protection for their infant industries.

In a regional union the cost of infant protection will be lower than in individual countries, since a wider market permits the establishment of larger plants and greater specialisation, as well as more competition. At the same time, the markets of the partner countries can serve as a training-ground for exporting elsewhere. In fact, we can speak of infant export activities that need to learn quality control as well as marketing tech-niques.

The question arises, however, whether reciprocal reductions in trade barriers could not be extended to all developing countries at similar levels of industrialisation, regardless of their geographical location. This possibility should not be excluded, but in practice various considerations militate against its adoption. To begin with, the potential benefits of such a scheme are limited by high transportation costs, while it would involve considerable risk and uncertainty. There is uncertainty as regards the balance of costs and benefits, because of limited information on costs and prices as well as on governmental policies in countries located on different continents.

Also, in the absence of an agreement on policies extending to external tariffs, quotas, licences, export subsidies and indirect incentives, the balance of advantages can easily be upset and trade will be subject to artificial distortions. Yet agreement on these policies is difficult to accomplish, because the loss of sovereignty involved may not be compensated by the prospective benefits. And not only do benefits promise to be larger in intra-regional trade, but countries in a particular region, having similar history, customs and even language, can be expected to possess greater solidarity and common interests necessary for policy co-ordination than nations separated by great distances.

III

The last point leads to the question of how much policy co-ordination is necessary for regional integration schemes. First of all, there is need for agreement on the irreversibility of commitments to eliminate protective measures on intra-regional trade, in order to ensure that countries could reimpose tariffs or quantitative restrictions only under carefully defined and temporary escape clauses. Second, governments should forswear the use of measures, such as tax concessions and credit preferences, which have an indirect effect on trade among the participating countries. Third, protection and exchange-rate policies need to be co-ordinated so as to avoid distortions in competitiveness. In the following, I shall elaborate on the last point.

Differences in tariff–subsidy arrangements will affect competition through inter-country disparities in input protection and in the combination of tariffs, subsidies and exchange rates applied. While the prices of final products are equalised under regional free trade, differences in tariffs on inputs imported from non-member countries will create artificial distortions in competitiveness. Thus, if country A levies a 50 per cent tariff, and country B a 20 per cent duty, on cotton, with cotton accounting for two-fifths of the value of textiles, firms in A will have production costs 12 per cent lower than in B, solely because of differences in input prices. At the same time, the freedom of member countries to modify tariffs and subsidies will create uncertainty as to future changes in competitiveness.

The competitive position of industries in the member countries is further affected by the combination of tariffs, subsidies and exchange rates applied. Take the case when country A applies the basic exchange rate to traditional primary products; it provides a 10 per cent tariff and export subsidy on non-traditional primary exports, and it accords a 32 per cent tariff and export subsidy to manufactured goods. In turn, in country B, the basic exchange rate applies to non-traditional primary commodities; there is a 9 per cent export tax on traditional exports, and a 20 per cent tariff-cum-export subsidy is granted to manufactured goods. The relative incentives provided to the three sectors will be equivalent in the two countries, the ratio of relative prices being identical in both cases.

The elimination of tariffs on intra-regional trade will, however, affect competitiveness in the union. This is because country A will eliminate a 32 per cent and country B a 20 per cent tariff on manufactured goods imported from the other, whereas– intra-regional trade being a relatively small part of the total trade of the member countries – exchange rates will hardly be affected.

The conclusion is strengthened if export subsidies on intra-regional trade are also eliminated, since country B's exporters will now be put in an even more favourable position than exporters in country A. Not only will they enjoy a larger reduction in tariffs in partner country markets, but they will experience a smaller decline in export subsidies. Nor is the conclusion affected if export subsidies were not initially provided; exporters in country B will again be in a more favourable position since they enjoy larger tariff concessions than country A's exporters. Correspondingly, country A will be reluctant to participate in an integration scheme.

Distortions in competitiveness due to inter-country differences in input protection and in tariff, subsidy and exchange-rate arrangements thus create obstacles to regional integration. To remove these obstacles, the system of protection needs to be harmonised. This would involve adopting a common customs tariff on imports from non-member countries, together with agreed-upon rules on export taxes and subsidies. Now if exchange rates are free to adjust, distortions in competitiveness will be eliminated.

But the relative competitiveness of the member countries' industries will vary over time if the rate of inflation differs among countries and devaluations take place only intermittently. Such variations will occur in conjunction with the inflation–devaluation cycle; the deterioration in the competitive position of a country with a higher rate of inflation will give place to a sudden improvement at the time its currency is devalued.

The following example can serve as an illustration. Take the case when prices in countries A and B, respectively, rise 5 and 3 per cent a year faster than average world inflation, and devaluation occurs whenever the cumulative price change reaches 15 per cent. Starting out from an equilibrium situation, country A's competitive position vis-à-vis country B will now deteriorate at a rate of 2 per cent a year over a period of three years, at which time devaluation will provide A with an absolute price advantage of 9 per cent. This advantage will decline in the next two years and, at the end of the fifth year, B's 15 per cent devaluation will result in a price disadvantage of 10 per cent for A. The process will repeat itself as long as higher (or lower) than average rates of inflation are not accompanied by exchange-rate changes.

Variations in exchange rates adjusted for changes in relative prices are equivalent to variations in tariffs and subsidies. As a result, uncertainty is created in regard to both the domestic currency value of foreign exchange proceeds and the sale price of foreign competitors. Apart from giving rise to inefficiencies in intra-regional trade, this uncertainty creates obstacles to regional integration since countries do not wish to be exposed to sudden changes in trade flows with potentially adverse effects on domestic industry. Such effects are accentuated if countries 'over-devalue', i.e. they devalue by more than is warranted by changes in domestic prices and their balance-of-payments position.

These adverse consequences could be avoided if member countries adopted a policy of devaluing *pari passu* with domestic inflation. This is equivalent to maintaining the real exchange rate – the ratio of an index of nominal exchange rates to the domestic price index – constant. In this way, sudden shifts in competitiveness will not occur.

The problems and difficulties described here are far from imaginary. They have plagued the Latin American Free Trade Association and have created obstacles to regional integration in other areas also. In order to eliminate these distortions that hamper the process of regional economic integration, it would thus be necessary for the prospective member countries to adopt a common customs tariff, to renounce the use of tariff and non-tariff barriers on intra-area trade, and to exclude variations in real exchange rates. As long as member countries are at a similar level of industrialisation, these measures would contribute to an equitable distribution of the benefits of integration. However, the treatment of individual industries – old and new – is the subject of much controversy.

IV

Fears have often been expressed as to the possible adverse effects of economic integration on existing industries. These fears reflect the assumption that economic integration would be followed by inter-industry specialisation, so that in each member country some industries would expand and others contract or even disappear. The experience of the European and the Central American common markets has shown, however, that these fears are greatly exaggerated.

In both areas the elimination of barriers to intra-regional trade has been followed not by inter-industry but by intra-industry specialisation, characterised by the increased exchange of products within each industry. Rather than the decline or demise of particular industries, the adjustment to integration has taken the form of changes in product composition as the expansion of trade has led to the exchange of similar products, including, among others, textiles, shoes and machinery.

Product specialisation brings economic benefits by permitting the use of large-scale production methods and longer production runs. Further gains are due to increased competition in an integrated area. Competition provides inducements for product improvements and technological change. At the same time, the disappearance of monopoly profits and the lowering of consumer-goods prices tend to reduce income inequalities.

These potential benefits point to the need for including

existing industries in regional integration schemes. However, the elimination of barriers to trade may be spaced over a relatively long period in order to avoid dislocations. This should be done according to an agreed-upon timetable so that industrialists can prepare themselves for future changes.

As to new industries, it has been suggested that the objective of the equitable distribution of benefits would be served if member countries agreed on their allocation and forswore the establishment of competing firms. These suggestions are, however, open to the objection that the establishment of industries would become the subject of political bargaining at the expense of considerations of efficiency. At the same time, it is difficult to reach agreement on the distribution of industries. This is shown not only by the failure of the Central American Common Market to agree on more than two integration industries, but also by the dearth of specialisation agreements in the Comecon, whose members are the East European communist countries.

In fact, the comparison of the experience of the European Common Market and the Comecon indicates the superiority of market methods over planned allocation. While in the E.E.C. integration has been followed by a rapid expansion of trade, in the Comecon trade has increased at a slow rate, expectations on the co-ordination of economic plans have been disappointed, and participating countries have not even succeeded in establishing a multilateral clearing system which was created in Western Europe two decades ago.

The application of market methods in regard to new industries whose financing needs exceed the availability of funds in the individual countries or are multinational in character would take the form of financing through an Investment Bank on the basis of economic criteria. The Investment Bank could also give preferential treatment to countries at lower levels of industrialisation in a union, but the most appropriate method of dealing with such cases is a temporary tax–subsidy scheme for manufactured products. In this way, the manufacturing sector of countries at lower levels of industrialisation would enjoy temporary benefits on an across-the-board basis without giving special treatment to selected industries.

V

In the introduction, I have noted that regional integration should be considered as part and parcel of a development strategy. Thus regional integration should not become an objective *per se*, as this could lead to the establishment of a sheltered, high-cost area. Rather, regional integration should be undertaken *pari passu* with liberalisation of trade.

Trade liberalisation would take the form of reducing the level of protection, equalising rates of protection among manufacturing industries, with temporary exceptions on infant-industry grounds, and providing similar treatment to import substitution and to the exports of manufactures. The adoption of such measures would provide a stimulus to export, reduce the scope of inefficient import substitution, and forestall the establishment of monopoly positions in new industries.

Possibilities for regional integration may not be open to all developing countries, however. In such cases overall trade liberalisation would have to be the centrepiece of a development strategy, possibly complemented by preferential arrangements with other developing countries at similar levels of industrialisation. But avenues for regional integration should be explored whenever such possibilities exist.

6 The Impact of Regional Integration between Developed Countries on Developing Countries

European Integration: Lessons for the Developing World

Gerard and Victoria Curzon

GERARD CURZON: PROFESSOR OF INTERNATIONAL
ECONOMICS, GRADUATE INSTITUTE OF
INTERNATIONAL STUDIES, UNIVERSITY OF GENEVA
VICTORIA CURZON: LECTURER IN INTERNATIONAL
ECONOMICS, INSTITUT UNIVERSITAIRE D'ÉTUDES
EUROPÉENNES, UNIVERSITY OF GENEVA

Both the European Economic Community and the European
Free Trade Association have succeeded in establishing, the one
a customs union, the other a free-trade area. Both organisations
have also gone beyond the immediate requirements of forming
areas of economic integration, the E.E.C. because its ultimate
objective was economic union, and EFTA because it was
unable to avoid some of the problems raised by the harmonisation issue. Neither the E.E.C. nor EFTA encountered any
real difficulties until they embarked on these secondary forms
of economic integration.

Primary integration in this context may thus be defined as that
which eliminates distortions in the market aimed specifically
against foreign goods, which usually take the form of tariffs
and quotas or discriminatory taxes levied at the frontier. The
market distortions which remain, however, are still sufficiently
large to prevent the reallocation of resources within the area
from even vaguely approaching the underlying pattern of
comparative advantage and optimal allocation. These market
distortions arise from different government action within the
participating domestic economies, and advanced forms of
economic integration have to take account of them. Thus

secondary integration may be defined as that which attempts to co-ordinate government action in such a way that no one country is permitted by its own actions to load the dice too much in its favour. It is concerned with maintaining an equitable balance of advantages within the area of integration and in distributing the gains of integration in a manner which is acceptable to each of its members. Primary integration comes to an end when tariffs and quotas on intra-area trade have been eliminated and when the transitional period is over, while secondary integration problems arise with the first tariff cuts and last the lifetime of the association.

Europe's experience during the 1960s was that primary integration was easy to achieve – indeed, far easier than was originally expected. Two observations lead one to this conclusion: one, that both groups accelerated their tariff-cutting schedules and finished their transitional periods well within the decade they had allowed themselves; two, that difficulties in particular sectors due to tariff disarmament were extremely rare and escape clauses were rarely invoked. At the same time, both groups had a marked effect on the pattern of trade of their respective members. Intra-area trade grew at a much faster pace than trade with the rest of the world,[1] suggesting that industry responded very actively to the new trading conditions created by the two groups. The lack of difficulties cannot therefore be attributed to the lack of effects. On the contrary, the effects of integration were highly visible in both groups, but they were not accompanied by any of the disagreeable side-effects which customs union theory might have led one to expect, in particular the idea that only the fittest industries could survive the creation of a customs union or free-trade area.

This successful and, on the whole, pleasant first experience of economic integration in Europe encourages one to think that there may be some positive lessons to be drawn from it by others, in particular developing countries.

Regional arrangements seem to be appropriate for developing economies, many of which are too small to indulge in the mildest form of economic nationalism and too immature to place their trust in a relatively open economy. Regional economic integration appears to be a neat way out of this dilemma, since it combines elements of greater trade liberalisation with elements of greater protection. Many developing countries reached this conclusion themselves, to judge by the number of regional arrangements which were launched during the 1960s, a process in which the demonstration effect of the E.E.C. was obvious.

Despite numerous attempts to integrate economically by forming either customs unions or free-trade areas, developing countries have not enjoyed much success and many of their schemes remain incomplete, not only because they have some-times failed to carry out the provisions of their treaties, but also because the schemes themselves were tentative and limited in the first place. The question to which this paper addresses itself is whether there is anything in the more encouraging European experience of integration which could serve as a guide for action in the developing world.

In a first section we shall analyse some of the factors which contributed to the relative success of European integration in the 1960s, reaching the conclusion that a conjunction of these factors is not generally to be found in developing areas. In a second section, having concluded that integration in developing areas is likely to be uphill work in the best of circumstances, we discuss the advantages of using the simpler and less exacting method of integration worked out in the European testing station during the 1960s – the free-trade area technique. A final section is devoted to the case of Portugal in EFTA, which suggests that some institutional links between developed and developing countries can be economically beneficial to the latter, provided political bloc-building and 'neo-colonialism' are avoided.

SOME FACTORS CONTRIBUTING TO THE RELATIVE SUCCESS
OF EUROPEAN INTEGRATION

Both the E.E.C. and EFTA embarked on their regional inte-gration schemes after ten years of experience in trade liberalisa-tion under the auspices of the O.E.E.C. and GATT. Although the level of tariff and quota protection in Europe at the end of the 1950s was still considerable, European countries were on the downward slope of the protection curve when they began integrating. This probably helped them to adopt and carry out comprehensive integration schemes, involving the liberalisation of all industrial trade flows. The same cannot be said of developing countries, most of which are still on the upward slope of the protection curve. This means that the general attitude to tariff and quota policy tends to hinder rather than help efforts to achieve regional free trade.[2]

By the mid-1950s most European countries were comparatively industrialised, with small primary sectors, and the bulk of their exports consisted of industrial products. The brunt of the integration effort was therefore borne by a large, diversified and adaptable industrial sector. Integration, in Europe, was a question of increasing the degree of industrial specialisation, not necessarily between countries, but essentially between firms in existing industries. There is no doubt that most firms adapted to the new environment with ease. On the other hand, Europe's attempts to integrate agricultural production and trade have proved disappointing and difficult, perhaps because the agricultural sector, like most primary forms of production, adapts slowly and grudgingly to new circumstances. In developing areas the relationship of primary to secondary sectors is the converse. Industrial production is in an early stage of development and the primary sector dominates the economy to a large extent. In these circumstances it is not surprising that efforts to integrate have met with little success. The European experience suggests that the primary sector is not easily susceptible to integration techniques, while the industrial sector in developing countries is too incomplete to permit regional free trade in industrial products to occur without imbalances appearing within the area.

In Europe, some countries probably gained more from integration than others, but the effects were sufficiently diffuse that no single country could consider that it had actually lost anything in the process, even if some industries found it harder to adjust than others. In many developing countries the fate of the national steel mill or the principal chemical processing plant is of the highest political significance, because so few other industries exist. Any reduction in output due to competition from within an integrating area would be immediately apparent and would meet with strong domestic protest. Thus it would be asking a lot of a developing country to allow regional trade to develop according to comparative advantage. One could only hope, in the medium term, for the planned specialisation of future industry, rather than for the improved efficiency of existing industry, which is all that Europe succeeded in accomplishing. It should be emphasised that the planned specialisation of future industry implies far more team spirit than Europe has yet managed to generate either in the E.E.C. or in EFTA, and that therefore, if developing countries are to succeed in forming economically meaningful integration areas, they must either reach an unheard-of level of international co-operation or wait until their industrial structures fill out. The intermediate solution – that of pursuing national industrialisation policies within the framework of a partial preference arrangement, such as might in due course be negotiated under the 1971 Protocol – is probably the only feasible one in the immediate future.

Europe was also extremely fortunate in that its first attempt at economic integration was carried on the crest of a wave of economic prosperity and relative monetary stability. These conditions made it easy for governments to subject their respective industrial structures to a major change in trade policy. In times of unemployment and payments uncertainties this relaxed attitude to economic integration would have been difficult to maintain. At the first signs of strain, escape clauses would have been invoked, trade barriers reimposed and the whole exercise imperilled.

By contrast, most developing countries suffer not only from chronic balance of payments deficits but also from overt or disguised unemployment. It is therefore not surprising that they should approach economic integration extremely warily.

Thus Europe started off at the end of the 1950s with at least three trump cards in its hand, which developing areas, for the most part, do not yet possess. Since integration in developing areas cannot help being more difficult to achieve than it was in Europe, there seems to be little sense in adding to the difficulties by adopting the more complex technique of integration – the customs union – when an easier model is available – namely the free-trade area.

The free-trade area is generally considered by economists and political scientists alike to be inferior to the customs union as a form of economic integration. A free-trade area does not attempt to harmonise the individual tariffs of member countries and, as a result, is obliged to administer a system of origin rules in order to prevent trade deflection (the process by which goods from third countries would enter the free-trade area where the duty was lowest and proceed, free of duty, to where customs charges were higher). EFTA has satisfactorily demonstrated that there is nothing mysterious or difficult about operating a simple origin system[3] and, in exchange, there are certain practical advantages in being able to integrate economically with a minimal loss to national sovereignty.

In the first place, many developing countries are still in the early stages of nationalism, having not yet suffered any of the disappointments of this type of political philosophy, and indeed looking forward to enjoying its euphoric power. Such countries might be readier to integrate economically with their neighbours if they could be sure of remaining free politically (the functionalist school of European integration, which predicted the existence of a slippery slope leading from economic to political integration, may have done the cause of economic integration in developing countries some harm in this connection). For such sets of countries the EFTA experience is instructive, since a free-trade area is the loosest form of economic integration which remains capable of achieving a meaningful degree of intra-area specialisation.

Secondly, where tariff disparities among developing countries are large, it is logical to think that they would find it correspondingly difficult to adopt a common outer tariff. To the extent that this is so, the EFTA experience is also useful, since it shows that countries do not have to harmonise their tariffs in order to enjoy the benefits of integration. There is no doubt that excessive tariff disparities would cause serious distortions in resource allocation within the area, but a happy medium exists between such excessive tariff disparities and complete tariff harmonisation which some developing countries might well explore. The distortions caused by tariff disparities could even be turned to advantage within a free-trade area which wished to influence the pattern of specialisation in order to redistribute the gains from integration.

Thirdly, to the extent that areas of potential integration contain countries at markedly different levels of economic development, the experience of Portugal in EFTA may also offer some encouragement. Portugal was one of the founding members of EFTA, but was required to reduce its tariffs at a markedly slower rate than the rest of EFTA, because of its low level of economic development. In effect, this arrangement gave competitive Portuguese exports the full benefit of the EFTA preference, but shielded inefficient Portuguese industries from corresponding import competition from the EFTA area, since the transitional period for Portugal was stretched over twenty years instead of ten. This privilege was subject to a self-regulatory mechanism, known as the '15 per cent rule', whereby Portuguese tariffs had to be reduced at the standard EFTA rate if, on a three-year average, exports accounted for 15 per cent of the domestic production of any particular product. The arrangement was undoubtedly beneficial to Portugal, which received considerable capital inflows on the strength of its right of free access to British, Scandinavian and Swiss markets and achieved spectacular increases in its exports to the EFTA area, but it required a rare degree of magnanimity on the part of its partners. Nevertheless, the staggering of transitional periods according to the degree of industrial development is one way of attempting to redistribute the benefits of economic integration in an acceptable fashion. This technique is, of course, not an exclusive feature of free-trade areas *per se;* it simply happens that EFTA offers an unusually generous example of it at work.

Finally, to those developing countries which consider that they cannot afford the administrative superstructure of Brussels-like dimensions, EFTA also demonstrates that economic integration can be an unbureaucratic process. It is a matter of choice.

Leaving aside the possible practical merits of a free-trade area as a vehicle for economic integration in developing areas, the Portuguese experience in EFTA and the Yaoundé experience in the E.E.C. also raise the problematic issue of economic integration between developing and fully developed countries. We have discussed some of these problems elsewhere[4] and will only touch on the subject here. A preference of the relative size enjoyed by Portugal in EFTA is of great benefit to the developing partner, and since it is not obliged to reduce its own tariffs fully, it can enjoy trade expansion without suffering the inconvenience of trade creation or the full potential loss from trade diversion. By the time it is obliged to integrate fully, the presumption is that it will have gathered sufficient strength to take the changes imposed by trade creation in its stride and to bear the losses from trade diversion. In view of the great difficulties encountered in negotiating a generalised scheme of preferences for developing countries, should one advocate discriminatory preference schemes of the Yaoundé type? Leaving aside the inevitable accusations of neo-colonialism that such a policy would entail, regionalism of such dimensions would have disastrous effects on the multilaterialism achieved to date among developed countries. Therefore, even if there were some short-run benefits to be enjoyed by developing countries in integrating with developed ones on the basis of staggered transitional periods, it would be preferable to avoid this short-cut to economic development and integration, and concentrate on the much harder objective of amalgamating the natural integration areas of the developing world.

Notes

1. In the E.E.C., intra-area trade increased by 323 per cent from 1960 to 1970, while trade with the rest of the world rose by only 132 per cent during the same period. A similar, but less marked, trend could be observed in EFTA, where intra-area trade increased by 190 per cent and extra-area trade by 100 per cent over the decade.

2. However, we are in a highly dynamic world. In December 1971, sixteen developing countries – Brazil, Chile, Egypt, Greece, India, Israel, Korea, Mexico, Pakistan, Peru, Philippines, Spain, Tunisia, Turkey, Uruguay and Yugoslavia – agreed on a Protocol Relating to Trade Negotiations among Developing Countries, whereby they themselves have undertaken to liberalise trade between themselves without passing their concessions on to developed countries. (The contracting parties to GATT have consented to a waiver for this preference scheme, which does not fall under Article XXIV, since it reduces (but does not eliminate) barriers to some (and not substantially all) trade.) Concessions under this protocol so far cover 300 tariff positions in the Brussels Nomenclature and concern exports to the value of U.S. $550 million. This preference scheme obviously contains a danger of trade diversion, but quota liberalisation under the auspices of the O.E.E.C. presumably did so too, and in a dynamic situation preference schemes which start off by being trade-diverting could well end up by being trade-creating, especially if they embrace a wide selection of countries. If developing countries continue to liberalise trade among themselves by means of the 1971 Protocol, they may in due course acquire the same type of experience which helped Europe to integrate at the end

of the 1950s. For the time being, however, this type of experience is lacking in the developing world.

3. Indeed many developing countries have long-standing experience with origin systems in connection with former colonial trade preferences.

4. Gerard and Victoria Curzon, 'Neo-Colonialism and the European Economic Community', *Year Book of World Affairs*, xxv (1971) 118–41

Regional Groupings and
Developing Countries

Sidney Dell[1]

BROAD TRENDS

In the E.E.C. and EFTA countries alike, imports from developing countries declined from 1958 to 1969 both as a proportion
of G.N.P. and in relation to total extra-area imports (Table 1).
Much – although probably not all – of this decline was due to
characteristic properties of imports from developing countries,
particularly the low income elasticity of import demand. In the
United States the relative decline was larger, but Japan showed
a noteworthy gain. There was also a sharp relative increase in
imports from the developing world by the member countries
of the Council for Mutual Economic Assistance (C.M.E.A.),
though this has to be viewed in terms of the low starting level,
and in relation to special factors affecting particular components
of this trade, notably with Cuba.[2]

A number of economists have tried to quantify the effects of
the formation of the E.E.C. and EFTA in bringing about trade
creation and trade diversion. The estimates are of varying levels
of statistical sophistication, but no satisfactory methods have
been found of isolating the 'integration' effect from other
effects. The estimation of dynamic effects has also proved
elusive. Such as they are, the available studies appear to suggest
the tentative conclusion that both the E.E.C. and EFTA have
generated much more trade creation than trade diversion.[3] But
not all countries have benefited from the trade creation, and
there are indications that there has been some trade diversion
from a number of developing countries.

Even if it were the case that integration had led to a substantial acceleration in the growth of income of the regional
groupings and hence to a stepping-up of their total demand for

Table 1

SELECTED INDICATORS

(billions of current dollars; percentages)

	E.E.C.		Expanded E.E.C.		EFTA		C.M.E.A.[a]		U.S.A.		Japan	
	1958	1969	1958	1969	1958	1969	1958	1969	1958	1969	1958	1969
1. G.N.P.	169·8	426·8	245·3	563·3	104·0	207·2	203·1	421·3	454·9	947·8	31·9	166·4
2. Extra-area imports	16·2	39·3	23·7	51·9	15·9	32·8	4·3	9·5	13·3	35·9	2·6	12·5
3. Imports from developing countries	6·9	14·7	11·0	20·6	4·9	7·5	0·8	2·6	5·8	9·2	1·1	6·2
4. Ratio of extra-area imports to G.N.P.	9·5	9·2	9·7	9·2	15·3	15·8	2·1	2·3	2·9	3·8	8·3	7·5
5. Ratio of imports from developing countries to G.N.P.	4·0	3·4	4·5	3·6	4·7	3·6	0·4	0·6	1·3	1·0	3·6	3·7
6. Ratio of imports from developing countries to extra-area imports	42·6	37·4	46·4	39·7	30·8	22·9	18·6	27·4	43·6	25·6	42·3	49·6

[a] Member countries of the Council for Mutual Economic Assistance: Bulgaria, Czechoslovakia, German Democratic Republic, Hungary, Mongolia, Poland, Romania and the U.S.S.R.

Source: UNCTAD Secretariat, Document TD/131, Table 1.

imports from developing countries – neither of which is certain –
the expansion of trade with the latter countries was clearly not a
primary objective of integration but rather an incidental result.
It is therefore more interesting to inquire into the deliberate
policies of the regional groupings vis-à-vis the developing
countries than into the involuntary side-effects of their creation.

EFTA

There is little to be said from this standpoint about EFTA.
Since EFTA confined itself to the creation of a free-trade area
in industrial products, maintaining the *status quo* in agriculture,
and did not establish any new forms of association with developing countries, no major policy issues arose, at least up to the
time when certain EFTA members applied for admission to the
E.E.C. Some trade diversion in manufactures may have taken
place but this was probably of limited significance, especially
in view of the continued preferential access by Commonwealth
countries to the United Kingdom market.

C.M.E.A.

More important policy issues arise in connection with the
integration of C.M.E.A. countries. Although the trade of these
countries with the developing world has been growing rapidly,
it is still quite small in absolute terms and the scope for further
expansion is clearly very great. The question is partly a matter
of the extent to which C.M.E.A. countries will be prepared to
increase their intake of tropical beverages and foodstuffs, of
which their present consumption is far lower than that of other
countries at comparable levels of per capita income. But it also
concerns the willingness of C.M.E.A. countries to rely on
developing countries for imports of basic raw materials as well
as finished and semi-finished manufactures.

An elaborate programme of C.M.E.A. co-operation was
worked out in 1971 covering a much longer time-span than
previously (fifteen to twenty years) and aiming at more far-
reaching structural changes. Particular emphasis was placed on
joint planning, and on the co-ordination of long-term plans for
individual branches of industry. Since the degree of inter-country

specialisation within C.M.E.A. is to increase, long-range joint planning of this type has obvious implications for foreign trade, and involves a major effort of foreign trade planning and forecasting.

The plan figures for 1971–5 indicate a growth of intra-C.M.E.A. trade by 10·4 per cent a year, compared with an expansion of just over 8 per cent a year in total C.M.E.A. trade. This would imply that trade with non-C.M.E.A. countries would grow more slowly than in 1966–70. However, past experience suggests that the plan figures tend to reflect the greater certainty of trade agreements among the C.M.E.A. countries than of comparable arrangements with other countries, and in practice trade with the rest of the world has usually expanded faster than had been envisaged in the plan.

A major question for the future, however, is whether the C.M.E.A. countries are prepared to regard the developing countries as reliable sources of supply for raw materials and intermediate goods and components. It seems likely that socialist countries could obtain many such goods more cheaply from developing countries than they could produce them themselves. On the other hand, considerable emphasis is placed by C.M.E.A. planners on stability and security of supplies. In order to achieve this result, socialist countries have entered into particularly close ties with such countries as Egypt and India in order to obtain as much assurance as they can that their overall plans will not be frustrated at critical moments by shortage of key supplies. But it remains to be seen to what extent other developing countries may be prepared to envisage joint arrangements of the same type.

C.M.E.A. countries also see possibilities for expanding the number of industrial co-operation agreements with developing countries. Such agreements provide for specialisation and exchange. C.M.E.A. countries consider, however, that for maximum effectiveness this approach requires an efficient and reliable system of planning in the partner countries as well as an adequately developed public industrial sector. It will be obvious that a large number of developing countries do not meet these requirements, which have political implications. Nevertheless, C.M.E.A. countries show up relatively well, in relation to the developed market economy countries, as regards the size and growth of the share of manufactures in their total imports from developing countries, as may be seen in Table 2.

Table 2

COMPOSITION OF EXPORTS BY DEVELOPING COUNTRIES
TO C.M.E.A. COUNTRIES

	1965 %	1969 %
Food, beverages, tobacco (S.I.T.C. 0 + 1)	43·2	38·4
Crude materials (S.I.T.C. 2 + 4)	32·7	31·8
Mineral fuels and related materials (S.I.T.C. 3)	0·3	1·0
Manufactures (S.I.T.C. 5, 6, 7, 8)	23·8	28·9
Total	100·0	100·0

Source: UNCTAD, Document TD/112/Supp. 1, Table 9.

More generally, the C.M.E.A. countries now view their trade with developing countries as being gradually integrated into a complex system of co-operation, covering several fields – including not only the exchange of goods and services but also economic and technical assistance (accompanied by provision for repayment in kind), transfer of technology, payments arrangements and the creation of a link between the plans and programmes of developing and C.M.E.A. countries in a manner designed to provide for assurance of supplies on both sides, as well as for mutual adjustment of production structures where possible and mutually agreeable. Clearly, the willingness and ability of developing countries to become involved in such complex forms of co-operation vary greatly. A number of developing countries, however, including India and Iran, have become interested in this type of approach and have entered into discussions with the C.M.E.A. countries on the elaboration of long-term plans of co-operation covering a period of a decade or even more.

E.E.C. AND THE COMMON AGRICULTURAL POLICY

In the field of primary commodities, the E.E.C. takes the view that its agricultural price and marketing policies are of considerable benefit to the developing countries. France in particular has been advocating the concept of 'organisation of markets' for many years. Although this concept has never been precisely defined, it would appear to imply planned and controlled production, trade and prices for primary products. Whenever developing countries have sought to obtain from the E.E.C. acceptance of the idea that industrial countries should adjust their agricultural protection in such a way as to ensure greater access to their markets for the exports of developing countries, it has been pointed out in reply that uncontrolled access might benefit other developed countries rather than developing countries. The E.E.C. sees no reason why it should not protect its own relatively poor farmers against the much more affluent farmers of North America and other developed primary-producing areas. For example, greater access to the E.E.C. market for imports of wheat would, it is argued, benefit countries like Australia, Canada and the United States much more than developing countries, which are not major producers of wheat; an exception is Argentina, but that country is on the borderline between the conventionally regarded developed and developing countries. Even in a case like fats and oils, of which developing countries are indeed major producers, uncontrolled access would, it is believed, benefit United States exports of soya-beans rather than exports of competing products from developing countries, because of the price advantage of the former.

In so far as the E.E.C. Common Agricultural Policy does confer advantages on developing countries, the benefits are intended mainly for the associated countries. Moreover, while it may be true that a more liberal and non-discriminatory policy on imports of temperate products would benefit primary producers in other developed countries rather than in developing countries, this does not necessarily imply that the market should be controlled in such a way as to limit imports from developing as well as from developed countries. Developing countries do not at present produce temperate-zone commodities in quantity, but if greater access to the E.E.C. market were available on a preferential bais, such production might well expand not only in the Mediterranean area but also in a number of other countries where agricultural productivity has advanced rapidly in recent years.

Of great concern, moreover, is the severe damage done to exporters from developing countries by heavy direct or indirect subsidies to Community production of competing commodities. It has been estimated that the major developed market economy countries spend $21 to $24 billion annually in support of domestic agriculture, of which the unenlarged E.E.C. alone spends $11 to $13 billion, or about one-half. The margins of agricultural protection in the E.E.C., as measured by the excess of domestic prices over import prices, increased markedly from 1956/57–1958/59 to 1970/71 for several major commodities, including wheat, barley and butter. In the case of sugar, of particular interest to developing countries, the domestic price premium increased from a range of 2 to 45 per cent in the earlier period to 110 per cent for the E.E.C. as a whole in 1970/71 (though there was a sharp reduction in the premium from 1968/69 to 1970/71). The E.E.C. not only produces for itself but ships large quantities of sugar abroad at heavily subsidised prices. Moreover, the Community declined to joint the International Sugar Agreement in 1968 because other countries were unwilling to concede it an export quota of 1·3 million tons a year. It would be difficult to estimate the loss to developing countries that results from this policy – not only in pre-empting export markets but also in forcing down sugar prices in the free market. But if, instead of throwing subsidised sugar on to the world market, the E.E.C. were to limit uneconomic domestic production only to the extent required to make room for imports equivalent to, say, 10 per cent of their current consumption of sugar, the gain to developing countries would probably amount to something of the order of $100 million annually.

Equally damaging is the policy of producing rice for domestic consumption and for subsidised sales abroad. The *ad valorem* tariff equivalent of variable levies on rice in the E.E.C. rose from 18 per cent in 1967/68 to 110 per cent in 1970/71. Italian exporters are currently quoting rice in Singapore at the Rangoon f.o.b. price. Italian costs per ton are a large multiple of this, the difference being made up by a subsidy from the E.E.C. Agricultural Fund. Other products of export interest to developing countries subject to various kinds of protective devices include beef and veal, tobacco, citrus fruit and vegetable oilseeds.

The situation described above would deteriorate further if exporters of sugar were to lose part of their United Kingdom market after the E.E.C. is enlarged. Similarly, Burma stands to lose part or all of its rice market in the United Kingdom. Even if the E.E.C. agreed to a standstill on existing agricultural exports to the United Kingdom from non-associated developing countries, there is a danger that the latter may be asked to forego whatever expansion had previously been in prospect.

E.E.C. POLICIES ON MANUFACTURES: PREFERENCES

The E.E.C. countries were the first to implement the UNCTAD decision concerning the introduction of the generalised system of preferences (G.S.P.) on 1 July 1971. As such, they have a claim to be considered as the most forward-looking of the industrial countries in this respect.

In assessing the practical effect of the E.E.C. system, however, much depends on whether one takes the view that a start has now been made and that improvements can be expected in due course as the Community gets used to the idea, and finds that little or no market disruption ensues; or whether one believes that the scheme, being highly restrictive, will not achieve the basic purposes of G.S.P., and that it will tend to maintain the discrimination between associated and non-associated countries.

The E.E.C. scheme grants duty-free treatment, within certain quota limitations, for imports of all industrial products, as well as duty reductions on a limited number of processed agricultural products. The ceilings on preferential imports are equal to the sum of the value of Community imports in 1968[4] of the products in question from beneficiary countries and territories under the scheme, excluding those already benefiting from various preferential tariff regimes granted by the Community, increased by 5 per cent of the value of imports from other sources, including countries and territories already benefitting from such regimes. Preferential imports of products originating in any of the beneficiary countries cannot as a rule exceed a maximum Community amount corresponding to 50 per cent of the ceiling, and in some cases the proportion may be lower.

The E.E.C.'s total dutiable imports from beneficiary countries in 1967 amounted to $2·7 billion, of which imports of dutiable manufactures and semi-manufactures totalled $668 million. Of the latter amount, 88 per cent ($591 million) is covered by the scheme. Of the trade covered, 25 per cent ($146 million, consisting entirely of textiles) is excluded from preferential treatment because of a narrower listing of beneficiaries. Of the remaining $444 million of imports from eligible beneficiaries, $257 million or 58 per cent are listed as 'sensitive'[5] and are therefore subject to rigid preferential quotas for which administrative machinery has been set up. This leaves $187 million of non-sensitive imports which are still subject to the ceilings referred to above, but which may be administered more liberally.

It should be noted that the associated countries, which enjoy E.E.C. preferences that are generally more favourable than the preferences granted under the G.S.P. scheme, are placed in a separate category, so that generally speaking they do not have to share their preferences with other developing countries. Of the $550 million of the E.E.C.'s dutiable imports from the associated African countries, only 4 per cent ($21 million) is covered by the G.S.P. scheme of the E.E.C.

The limited scope of these arrangements must be viewed in the context of the past record of the E.E.C. countries as markets for imports of manufactures from developing countries. In 1969 developing countries supplied only 3·8 per cent of the total imports of manufactures by the E.E.C., compared with 8·6 per cent for the United Kingdom and 11·4 per cent for the United States. Between 1962 and 1969 developing countries improved their share in the import markets for manufactures of the United States, Japan and a group of miscellaneous developed countries (notably Australia, Canada and New Zealand); but their share declined in the E.E.C. and EFTA countries, as shown in Table 3.

Care is necessary in interpreting the above trends, since the imports of the E.E.C. and EFTA groups include their rapidly growing intra-trade. By analogy, inter-state trade in manufactures within the United States may likewise have recorded a more rapid increase during the period than imports of manufactures from developing countries.

It should, however, be borne in mind that E.E.C. imports of manufactures from developing countries (other than those

Table 3
DISTRIBUTION OF THE INCREASE IN O.E.C.D. COUNTRY
IMPORTS OF MANUFACTURES FROM DEVELOPING COUNTRIES,
1962 to 1969

	Percentage share of the increase in total O.E.C.D. imports of manufactures from developing countries	*Developing countries' 1969 share in O.E.C.D. imports divided by the 1962 share*
U.S.A.	50·1	1·16
E.E.C.	22·3	0·83
EFTA	14·1	0·94
Japan	6·9	2·22
Others	6·6	1·15
Total	100·0	1·08

Source: Statistical Office of the United Nations and UNCTAD Secretariat, Document TD/111, Table 5.

from associated countries) were subject to both tariff and non-tariff barriers that did not apply to intra-trade. The non-tariff barriers appear to have been particularly effective in keeping out certain types of imports from the E.E.C. countries. French and Italian imports of textiles and clothing from developing countries in 1969 were very low both in absolute terms and in relation to total imports in these categories, as shown in Table 4; and the share of cotton textiles, imported from developing countries, in domestic consumption in France (as in Japan) was very low.

Another limitation on the E.E.C. system of preferences has been pointed out by Professor Richard Cooper. The E.E.C. method of determining import ceilings for the G.S.P. scheme involves the use of data covering a period of two years earlier than the year to which the ceiling applies. Professor Cooper has shown that the normal growth in exports is likely to overtake – and in many cases has already overtaken – the duty-free quota, so that additional exports will have to pay the full duty.[6] Where actual exports do exceed quota ceilings, no new incentive to exports or to investment in export-orientated industries is supplied at the margin.

A further issue is raised by the allocation of Community preferential tariff quotas among member countries as follows: Federal Republic of Germany, 37·5 per cent; Benelux, 15·1 per

Table 4

IMPORTS OF TEXTILES AND CLOTHING FROM DEVELOPING
COUNTRIES[a], 1969

(millions of dollars; percentages)

	Value of imports from developing countries	Share of imports from developing countries in total imports of textiles and clothing	Imports from developing countries as a percentage of consumption of cotton textiles
O.E.C.D. countries	2,013	17·9	...
E.E.C. countries	453	8·9	13·2
Federal Republic of Germany	309	14·6	18·5
France	45	5·0	6·5
Italy	33	8·6	10·6
EFTA countries	439	14·9	31·0[b]
United Kingdom	287	32·9	37·3[b]
Canada	105	17·4	13·1[b]
Japan	68	34·0	6·3[b]
U.S.A.	934	44·0	8·1

[a] Textiles relate to S.I.T.C. 65, clothing to S.I.T.C. 84; the third column relates to cotton textiles only.

[b] 1970.

Source: O.E.C.D., *Trade by Commodities* (Jan-Dec 1969); third column based on GATT sources.

cent; France, 27·1 per cent; Italy, 20·3 per cent.[7] It is not yet clear what would happen in the event that the quota share of any one member were not fully taken up. Unless deliberate arrangements were made for the transfer of unused portions of quotas, the practical effect would be to reduce the aggregate quota for the Community as a whole. Similar considerations apply as regards the allocation of quotas to importers within each country. Moreover, the allocation of quotas in this way creates a possibility that competition among exporters would transfer part or all of the gains from duty-free quotas to the importers, thereby reducing or eliminating the additional financial incentive to exporters. Importers would, of course, in that case have a special incentive to seek out products qualifying for duty-free treatment, but the G.S.P. has hitherto been envisaged as a means of stimulating new investment in export-orientated industries in developing countries.

Thus despite the Community's early adoption of a scheme of G.S.P., it is not yet clear whether the scheme offers important advantages to the developing countries. The large number of sensitive products, the complicated array of restrictions of uncertain impact, and the preservation of the special relationship of the associated countries already suggest certain doubts. In addition, the method of calculation of the system of ceilings implies that tariff-free quotas will be largest where the existing share of the market in the hands of developing countries is smallest (such as motor vehicles and aeroplanes) and smallest where the developing countries are already significant suppliers (so that the 5 per cent of shipments from developed countries, which determines the supplementary quota, would also be small). Moreover, the context in which the new system is being applied is characterised by a low base level resulting from tariff and especially non-tariff barriers.

E.E.C. officials suggest that the ceilings on non-sensitive items may never be invoked as long as market disruption does not occur. The difficulty here is that the system, as it stands, does not provide the kind of long-term assurance that an investor needs before he can afford to commit large funds to a particular project requiring substantial export markets. Thus, unless liberalised, the E.E.C. system of G.S.P. may fail to provide adequate incentives to investors to tackle the E.E.C. market, simply because of the fear that the more successful a firm is in gaining a share of the market, the more likely would it be that protective measures would be taken against it sooner or later.

With the enlargement of the Community, the United Kingdom system of preferences will presumably be adjusted to that of the E.E.C. It is not yet clear what the overall effect of this might be, but there is a potential danger that the effect might on balance be more restrictive than the present arrangements, because of the application of the E.E.C. quota system to the United Kingdom as a safeguard mechanism, instead of the more general escape clause applicable to the present United Kingdom scheme. Certain textiles are excluded from the present United Kingdom scheme of preferences, whereas they are included in the E.E.C. scheme except for certain beneficiaries. Despite this, the overall effect of the enlargement of the Community on imports of textiles is quite uncertain, though there may well be pressure from textile manufacturers in the United Kingdom for the adoption of the more restrictive policies towards imports characteristic of the E.E.C. countries.

Notwithstanding the reservations mentioned above, it is important to bear in mind that the system of generalised preferences is in its infancy, that it was, perhaps, natural that the early approaches should be quite cautious, and that the E.E.C. scheme might well be extended and liberalised as experience is gained. Certainly, there are strong forces within the Community itself that would welcome liberalisation of the scheme. The fact that the United States has not yet made good its commitment to introduce its own scheme is also an important element in the picture, since it was always understood that the effectiveness of the system as a whole depended on the willingness of all the leading developed countries to accept their fair share of the obligations. Thus the ability and willingness of the Community to liberalise its scheme will undoubtedly depend in part on the action taken by the United States. The character of action by the United States will, however, in turn depend on the evolution of the relationship between the E.E.C. and the developing countries, especially of Africa.

SPECIAL RELATIONSHIP WITH AFRICA

E.E.C. spokesmen consider that the relationship that has been developed between the Community and Africa is entirely for the benefit of the associated countries, which are free to discontinue it at any time they please. If the E.E.C. insists on reverse preferences, it is only because these are essential to comply with the free-trade area provisions of GATT. Moreover, the divisive effect of the separation into anglophone and francophone countries may be greatly mitigated when Britain enters the E.E.C.

The difficulty, however, is that it is far from clear that the Eurafrican relationship really benefits African development. The fact that the associated countries are free to end the relationship does not mean that the relationship is a beneficial one: continued association may reflect the inertia of tradition and the political realities of Africa rather than a balance of advantage.

It can be argued that the whole assumption of the association agreements is that the natural function of the African countries is to concentrate on supplying Western Europe with primary products in exchange for finished manufactures. However much it is contended that African countries are free under the Treaty of Rome and the Yaoundé Convention to protect their own industries, the fact remains that little use has been made of this right; on the contrary, it is taken for granted that the preferences on the export of primary commodities enjoyed by African countries in the E.E.C. must be paid for by the reverse preferences that E.E.C. countries have retained in associated Africa.

The associated countries are perfectly well aware that the reverse preferences granted to the E.E.C. depress their terms of trade and inhibit the growth of their own industries. Yet they are unwilling to seek the abolition of the reverse preferences, because they recognise them as part of an interdependent set of arrangements. They are one element, but still a key element, in the total structure. Unless one has decided that one is ready to demolish the structure as a whole, one hesitates before trying to get rid of one particular part of it.

It was no doubt considerations of this sort that prompted Dr H. Hendus, Director-General of the Development Aid Commission of the E.E.C., to say: 'There is no doubt whatever that the association of African States and Madagascar with the member states of the E.E.C. . . . has created exclusive relations, and as such constitutes a form of belated colonialism.'[8] Dr Hendus believed that the Common Market countries had exercised great restraint in this association with Africa. But, he continued:

> This does not mean that the E.E.C. countries do not wish to use the position they have obtained under the Convention as a means of safeguarding the black African area against anti-European influences, just as our African associates for their part have an interest in a policy aimed at maintaining and even strengthening still further their economic, financial, technical and cultural co-operation with the European Communities.[9]

The E.E.C. considers that the trade and aid features of the Yaoundé Convention have benefitted the African countries concerned – which also happen to be among the poorest of the developing countries – while not harming any other countries. In fact, from 1958 to 1969 the average annual rate of growth of E.E.C. imports from associated countries was 6·0 per cent, compared with 7·1 per cent for imports from other developing countries. Consequently, Dr Dieter Friedrichs of the E.E.C. Commission staff feels able to conclude that 'The expected effect of exclusivity . . . has been nil.'[10]

Here, Dr Friedrichs is perhaps claiming too much. If association has had no effect, why maintain it?

Moreover, the argument that association agreements were necessary because the countries involved were among the least developed loses some of its force as one examines the tremendous proliferation of various types of association – some of the countries involved being the relatively more advanced countries of the Mediterranean basin.

The Arusha agreement with the East African countries, which came into force at the beginning of 1971, provides for a free-trade area among the participating countries, but not for financial and technical aid as the Yaoundé Convention does. The East African countries acquired access to the E.E.C. similar to that of the African associates, except that quantitative ceilings were retained for certain tropical products (coffee, cloves and pineapple). Reverse preferences were granted by the East African countries on sixty products, the margins ranging from 2 per cent to 9 per cent. A similar arrangement with Nigeria never came into force because two E.E.C. members did not ratify it; and indications at UNCTAD III were that Nigeria is not anxious to pursue an arrangement of this type.

Similar arrangements have been made with Malta, Morocco and Tunisia, while negotiations are in progress or envisaged with Algeria, Cyprus, Egypt and Lebanon. A preferential trade agreement is in force with Israel and a most-favoured-nation agreement with Yugoslavia. Transitional periods of mutual tariff reduction are in force with Spain and Turkey and limited arrangements govern relations with Greece.

Three alternatives have been offered to the African members of the Commonwealth after the enlargement of the E.E.C. They may joint the Yaoundé Convention; they may form a new association consisting mainly of mutual trade obligations; or they may conclude a trade agreement with the Community.

Altogether over thirty countries are already involved in special association relationships with the E.E.C. The view has been expressed that the whole of Africa and the Mediterranean countries ought eventually to be brought into relationship with the E.E.C. But why should this matter stop there? Having established a pattern of this kind, why should the E.E.C. not extend it?

Moreover, new tendencies may develop, particularly after the enlargement of the Community. It may be true, as claimed by Friedrichs in the comment mentioned above, that association policy has not thus far prevented other developing countries from increasing their exports to the E.E.C. faster than the associated countries have. But the larger the number of countries achieving associate status, the greater will be the danger of damage to the interests of non-associated developing countries, and the greater the possible erosion of the privileged position of the original associates.

There was already a tendency to reduce preferential trade advantages for the associated countries in the second Yaoundé Convention. The extent of discrimination in favour of the associated countries was reduced both generally, through the Kennedy Round, and specifically for coffee, cocoa beans and palm oil. Financial aid for price support in excess of world markets levels was also lowered. Compensation was provided in the form of preferential treatment for imports of certain farm products from the associated countries. Aid channelled through Community institutions also increased from $800 million to $1,000 million. However, the latter benefits did not remove the feeling of the original associates that their position was highly precarious. The result has been that instead of moving in the direction of greater independence and self-reliance, the original associates appear to be more vulnerable, if anything, at the present time than they were ten years ago; and the fear of what might happen when the Community is enlarged has served to strengthen the discipline of the associated countries within the E.E.C. framework, their feeling of commitment to it, and their reluctance to support any ideas or proposals regarded as unacceptable to the E.E.C. countries.

The political implications of the spreading network of E.E.C. relationships were pointed out by George Ball, formerly United States Under-Secretary of State, testifying as a private individual before the United States Congress. As Ball put it:

> Should we not insist, in other words, that arrangements for commercial preferences carry with them substantial obligations on the part of the industrialised partner? Thus, for example, if the European Economic Community continues to expand its system of preferences for Africa should not we make it clear that we will look to the nations of the Community to carry the burden of economic assistance and, where necessary, political tutelage for those African countries that enjoy such preferences?[11]

The implication seems to be that a consolidation of Eurafrica would result in counterpart United States economic assistance and political tutelage for Latin American countries, which would be given countervailing preferences in the United States. This hardly seems to be a framework of thinking that could commend itself to a world which has moved a long way from pre-war concepts of spheres of influence within colonial or neo-colonial systems. Whatever the developed countries might have to say about this, there is little evidence to suggest that developing countries would in the long run fare better in a world of discriminatory political and economic compartments.

Notes

1. The views expressed in this paper are those of the author, and are not necessarily those of the UNCTAD Secretariat of which he is a member.

2. Cuba accounted for 21 per cent of the exports of developing countries to the C.M.E.A. countries in 1968. Cuba joined the C.M.E.A. in 1972, but is not included as a C.M.E.A. member in the present paper.

3. See, for example, M. E. Kreinin, 'Effects of the E.E.C. on Imports of Manufactures', *Economic Journal* (Sep 1972).

4. The basic quota is fixed for a number of years; the supplementary quota will be recalculated annually but may not be reduced.

5. 'Sensitive' products include certain petroleum products, fertilisers, certain rubber, leather, wood, paper and glass products, some copper and zinc semi-manufactures, sewing-machines, certain electric machinery, motors and apparatus, transistors, bicycles, furniture, dolls, and certain textiles, iron and steel and footwear products.

6. Richard N. Cooper, 'The European Community's System of Generalised Tariff Preferences: A Critique', *Journal of Development Studies*, VIII 4 (July 1972).

7. For further details of present arrangements, see UNCTAD Secretariat, *The Generalised System of Preferences*, documents TD/124 and TD/124/Add.1.

8. *Inter Economics* (Hamburg), Dec 1968, p. 359.

9. Ibid.

10. Ibid., Mar 1972, p. 84.

11. *The Future of U.S. Foreign Trade Policy*, Hearings before the Subcommittee on Foreign Economic Policy of the Joint Economic Committee, 90th Congress, 1st session, vol. I, p. 277.

The Impact of European Integration on Trade with Developing Countries: Empirical Evidence and Policy Implications

Seev Hirsch

DEAN, LEON RECANATI GRADUATE SCHOOL OF
BUSINESS ADMINISTRATION, UNIVERSITY OF
TEL-AVIV

I. SUMMARY AND CONCLUSION

This paper seeks to establish whether, and to what extent, non-members and especially developing countries were affected by trade-diversion effects of economic integration in Western Europe.

Section II defines the terms *inward and outward trade diversion* as related to international trade flows and outlines a method for identifying these effects. The method is tested on empirical data pertaining to trade between the two European trading blocs and the rest of the world. The findings point to substantial inward trade diversion between members of the two blocs and significant outward trade diversion between bloc members and outsiders. Developing countries in Latin America, Asia, but not in Africa, are clearly affected by outward trade diversion. The effects of European integration on trade with some of the leading industrialised countries are less clear-cut.

In section III a micro-economic view of inward and outward trade diversion is discussed. It is postulated that the adverse effects of exclusion from a trading bloc on large firms are weaker than on small firms, and the validity of this hypothesis is demonstrated on a sample of Dutch and Danish firms. The section goes on to draw conclusions from these findings for the trading prospects of the developing countries, whose industries are characterised by a high proportion of small firms.

In section IV, some policy implications of the above are dealt with. The potential contribution of multinational corporations to exports is examined and the superior export performance of the multinationals in comparison with domestic corporations is demonstrated. The section concludes with a brief discussion of questions pertaining to ownership and control of multinational corporations. It is suggested that the breaking-up of multinational corporations makes only limited economic sense and that a feasible alternative is for the developing countries to establish their own multinationals or to gain control of existing ones.

II. INWARD AND OUTWARD TRADE DIVERSION: A MACRO-ECONOMIC VIEW

Economic literature distinguishes between the trade-creating and trade-diverting effects of customs unions or free-trade areas (F.T.A.s). Trade creation takes place as a result of trade barriers coming down between members of the F.T.A. Dutch exporters to France obviously benefit from the establishment of the European Economic Community because their exports compete on more equal terms with French manufacturers, who before the establishment of the E.E.C. were protected by tariffs.

United States exporters to France, on the other hand, are worse off after the establishment of the E.E.C. Before, they competed with Dutch exporters on equal terms in France; after the establishment of the E.E.C. they are discriminated against vis-à-vis both French and Dutch competitors. It is the outsiders who suffer from trade diversion and the insiders who gain from trade creation. While the establishment of an F.T.A. may be highly beneficial to the efficiency and economic well-being of the insiders, those who remain outside its borders invariably suffer from worse conditions of entry.

It is important to bear in mind in this context that the lowering of average tariffs which were negotiated during the

1960s, following the establishment of the E.E.C. and EFTA, does not fundamentally affect the conclusions following from the above analysis. A fifty per cent tariff reduction obviously improves the competitive position of foreign suppliers. It does not, however, alter their basic disadvantage vis-à-vis those who enjoy a 100 per cent tariff reduction because of their location within the F.T.A.

The E.E.C. and EFTA are, as their names imply, European organisations whose benefits have until recently been extended to their European members and to some ex-colonies, located mainly in Africa. The majority of the developing countries (D.C.s), along with the rest of the world, had to put up with the added competitive disadvantage which exclusion from the E.E.C. and EFTA brought about.

To assess empirically the trade-creating and diverting effect of the E.E.C. and EFTA on the D.C.s, information on the supply and demand elasticities of the F.T.A.s and D.C.s – in respect to both price and income – is needed. It is extremely difficult to estimate these parameters on the basis of available statistics, as is indicated by the dearth of empirical inquiries into these problems.

Balassa measured trade creation and trade diversion of the E.E.C. by comparing income elasticity of demand for 'total imports', 'intra-area imports' and 'extra-area imports' in two periods, 1953–9 and 1959–65. He reasoned that changes in income elasticity of demand in the second period reflect the effect of the Common Market which was established in 1958:

> Under the assumption that income elasticities of import demand would have remained unchanged in the absence to integration, a rise in the income elasticity of demand for intra-area imports would indicate gross trade creation, while an increase in the income elasticity of demand for imports from all sources of supply, would give expression to trade creation proper. In turn, a fall in the income elasticity of demand for extra-area imports would provide evidence of the trade-diverting effect of the union.[1]

Using these measures on overall imports to the E.E.C., Balassa found that income elasticity of demand for intra-area rose more than for extra-area imports. However, since income elasticity of demand for imports from both areas increased, he concluded that no import diversion took place.[2]

To be valid, Balassa's measures must be corrected for price changes.[3] Moreover, they are based on the implicit assumption that the composition of demand for different imports does not change over time and that the supply functions for these goods in the exporting countries are perfectly elastic. Under these assumptions, changes in income elasticity of demand for imports reflect the trade-creating and trade-diverting effect of the F.T.A.

Balassa stipulates that income elasticity of demand should increase for trade creation to take place. When it declines, trade diversion is indicated. It is, however, possible that *ex-ante* income elasticity of demand for imports from a given country rises and that the demand cannot be fulfilled because of the country's inadequate supply capacity. Balassa's measure fails to take this possibility into account. The measures defined below, which distinguish between inward and outward trade diversion, are more sensitive to such possibilities.

Consider country A's relations with a certain F.T.A. Now define:

x_1, x_0 = country A's total exports in periods 0 and 1

y_1, y_0 = country A's total exports to the F.T.A. in periods 0 and 1

z_1, z_0 = F.T.A.'s total imports in periods 0 and 1.

Now let: $\alpha = \left(\dfrac{y_1}{x_1}\right) - \left(\dfrac{y_0}{x_0}\right)$ = change in the F.T.A.'s share in A's exports

$\beta = \left(\dfrac{y_1}{z_1}\right) - \left(\dfrac{y_0}{z_0}\right)$ = change in A's share in the F.T.A.'s imports

$\gamma = \left(\dfrac{x_1}{z_1}\right) - \left(\dfrac{x_0}{z_0}\right)$ = change in the ratio of A's exports to the F.T.A.'s imports.

Inward trade diversion take place when $\alpha > 0$ *and* $\beta > 0$, i.e. when the F.T.A.'s share in A's exports increases *and* when A's share in the F.T.A.'s imports increases.

Outward trade diversion takes place when $\alpha < 0$ *and* $\beta < 0$, i.e. when the F.T.A.'s share in A's exports decreases *and* when A's share in the F.T.A.'s imports decreases.

Distinction is made between ordinary and strong inward diversion on the one hand and ordinary and strong outward diversion on the other. *Strong inward diversion* takes place when $\alpha > 0$, $\beta > 0$ *and* $\gamma < 0$, i.e. when A's exports grow at a lower rate than the F.T.A.'s imports. In this case A increases its share of the F.T.A.'s market by diverting exports from other markets. *Strong outward diversion* takes place when $\alpha < 0$, $\beta < 0$ *and* $\gamma > 0$, i.e. when A's exports increase at a higher rate than the F.T.A.'s imports. A is definitely capable of supplying the F.T.A.'s demand, but is presumably prevented from doing so by the F.T.A.'s discrimination against extra-area suppliers.

The situation is indeterminate when $\alpha < 0$ and $\beta > 0$, i.e. when the F.T.A.'s share in A's exports declines while A's share in the F.T.A.'s imports rises. The situation is also indeterminate when $\beta < 0$ and $\alpha > 0$.

The six possibilities are summed up in Table 1 below.[4]

Table 1

CONDITIONS FOR INWARD AND OUTWARD DIVERSION

	$\gamma > 0$		$\gamma < 0$	
	$\alpha > 0$	$\alpha < 0$	$\alpha > 0$	$\alpha < 0$
$\beta > 0$	Inward diversion (I.D.)	Indeterminate (I)	Strong inward diversion (I.D. +)	Infeasible
$\beta < 0$	Infeasible	Strong outward diversion (O.D. +)	Indeterminate (I)	Outward diversion (O.D.)

The terms 'inward and outward diversion' are used here to avoid confusion with the traditional 'trade creation' and 'trade diversion'. Trade creation and trade diversion, as defined by Balassa, are manifested by changes in the income elasticity of demand for imports. Our measure is related to changes in the distribution of market shares, following institutional modifications in the terms of foreign entry.

Our definitions dispense with the need to correct for price changes which are required to identify changes in income elasticity of imports. The F.T.A.'s share in A's exports could rise as a result of price inflation in the former rather than as a result of increases in the F.T.A.'s real share. If, however, this were the reason for the increase in the F.T.A.'s share in A's exports, A's share in the F.T.A.'s imports would not rise since the value of other countries' exports to the F.T.A. would also be affected by inflation.

These definitions have another merit: they take into account supply as well as demand conditions. *Ex-post* decline in the F.T.A.'s income elasticity of imports from A, interpreted by Balassa as trade diversion, could, as was noted already, be due to A's failure to respond to increased demand. Our definitions take care of this problem by specifying that $\alpha < 0$ *and* $\beta < 0$ for diversion to be indicated.

If B's suppliers fail to keep up with demand, this will presumably be reflected by the volume of total exports and not by the change in the F.T.A.'s share of A's exports.

And a final point: for our definitions to make economic sense, two conditions must hold: $x_1 > x_0$ and $z_1 > z_0$.

If exports of A and imports of the F.T.A. do not increase over the period under consideration, inward and outward trade diversion cannot be indicated. If $x_1 < x_0$, A's failure to increase its market share in the F.T.A. could be due to its inability to meet the latter's demand and not to discrimination against A's exports. If $z_1 < z_0$, then A's share in the F.T.A.'s imports could increase too, while the volume of A's exports to the F.T.A. fails to rise. This is clearly not a case where outward trade diversion takes place.

Table 2 shows the evidence regarding inward and outward trade diversion of the two European free-trade areas, the E.E.C. and EFTA. The table is based on trade figures pertaining to the 1960–8 period. The E.E.C. was established in 1958 and EFTA early in 1960. However, trade liberalisation took place only gradually and intra-bloc tariffs were brought down to zero only in 1968. The period is therefore appropriate for observing the effect of intra-bloc trade liberalisation on bloc members and on outsiders.

Trade figures are divided into several groups: E.E.C., EFTA, Latin America (excluding Venezuela), Asia (excluding the Middle East, Japan, China and North Korea), Africa and a selected sample of large international traders. Oil-producing areas were excluded from the sample.

The table demonstrates the inward-looking effects of the two blocs' trading policies. E.E.C. members, as expected, enjoyed

inward trade diversion in the intra-bloc trade. The only area
outside the E.E.C. which experienced inward trade-diverting
effects was Japan, whose exports to the E.E.C. increased by
394 per cent between 1960 and 1968. However, in relative terms,
Japan's exports to the E.E.C. were clearly negligible – 4 per cent
of total exports in 1964 and 5 per cent of total exports in 1965.

Table 2

PERCENTAGE CHANGES IN TRADE OF E.E.C. AND
EFTA, 1960–8

Change in exports
(1960 = 100)

Exports to	E.E.C. Y	EFTA Y	World X	E.E.C.	EFTA
E.E.C.	282	172	216	I.D.	I
EFTA	178	212	170	I	I.D.
excluding U.K.	168	230	197	O.D.	I.D.+
U.K.	197	174	149	I	I.D.+
Other developed countries					
U.S.A.	176	185	168	I	I.D.+
Canada	157	123	229	O.D.+	O.D.+
Japan	394	331	320	I.D.+	I.D.+
Latin America[a]	152	114	160	O.D.+	O.D.+
Asia[b]	119	95	122	O.D.	O.D.
Africa excluding E.E.C. associates	132	124	117	I	I
E.E.C. associates	206	459	215	I	I.D.+
All extra-area trade	162	154	161	I	O.D.+

[a] Excluding Venezuela.
[b] Excluding Middle East, Japan, China, North Korea.

Source: I.M.F., _Direction of Trade, 1971_.

Even in 1968 the E.E.C. was just beginning to open up its
markets to Japan. The D.C.s of Latin America and Asia experienced outward trade diversion in their trade with the E.E.C.,
and on African countries not associated,
and on African E.E.C. associates, were indeterminate.

The inward trade-diverting effects of EFTA are somewhat
more widespread. Areas which benefit from that effect include
(aside from EFTA members), the United States, Japan and,

rather surprisingly, African E.E.C. associates. Like the E.E.C., EFTA's trade with Latin America and Asia was characterised by outward diversion and the effect on trade with non-E.E.C., affiliated African countries was indeterminate.

Calculations of the trading effects of the two blocs with all non-members show EFTA to be characterised by overall outward trade diversion, while the E.E.C.'s effect is indeterminate.

The picture which emerges from the analysis is fairly clear: the inward trade-diverting benefits which the two European free-trade areas have produced during the first period of their existence were, with few exceptions, reserved for their own members. The E.E.C. increased its imports by over 100 per cent during the period. It is only to be expected that this impressive increase in trade of the world's largest trading area will be shared to some extent with non-members, including the developing countries. The fact, however, remains that despite the high rate of increase in imports of the E.E.C., its share in the exports of very few outsiders increased. EFTA, whose imports increased by a comparatively low rate (57 per cent), presents even more depressing prospects to outsiders who are forced to seek outlets for their export products elsewhere.[5]

III. TRADE CREATION AND TRADE DIVERSION: A MICRO-ECONOMIC VIEW

Thus far the discussion has focused on large economic units – on countries. Exports, however, are not made by countries; they happen as a result of actions taken by individual firms which respond to opportunities they perceive in the market. Do firms located in the D.C.s respond differently to these opportunities from firms located in the industrialised countries? We have no direct evidence about such differences. The evidence we have pertains to variations among firms of different size groups whose response pattern to the creation of F.T.A.s varies markedly. Assuming that most firms located in the D.C.s are small by European and U.S. standards, then our evidence has important implications for these countries. Before exploring the implications, let us review the evidence.

Table 3 shows the distribution of exports of a sample of Danish and Dutch firms in six industries to EFTA and the

E.E.C. respectively, in 1968. The sample, which is divided into
large and small firms, clearly shows the differences which exist
between the two groups. With the exception of food and
textiles manufacturers, small firms market, as a rule, a higher
proportion of their total exports in the F.T.A.s than large
firms.

Table 3

SHARE OF F.T.A.S IN THE EXPORTS OF DANISH AND DUTCH
FIRMS GROUPED BY SIZE, 1968

Industry	Share of EFTA in exports of Danish sample			Share of E.E.C. in exports of Dutch sample		
	Small %	Large %	n	Small %	Large %	n
Food	36	37	19	41	61	20
Chemicals	53	37	28	53	51	22
Textiles	76	80	25	77	78	21
Machinery	49	36	29	63	46	36
Electrical	60	42	28	84	45	13
Electronics	56	40	26	96	72	8
Entire sample	55	54	155	64	57	120

Source: Data collected by the author and his colleagues for the study
*The Export Performance of Six Manufacturing Industries: A
Comparative Study of Denmark, Holland and Israel* (New York:
Praeger, 1971). Division into small and large firms based on the
median in each group.

Attitudes towards risk and considerations of scale economies
explain this pattern. Changes in exchange rates, currency
regulations, tariff levels and other trading rules combine to
make export a riskier business than domestic marketing.
Communication problems, and the need to maintain stocks and
service organisations in foreign markets, which as a rule buy a
relatively small portion of individual firms' output, similarly
raise export above domestic marketing costs.[6] Large firms are
better equipped to assume these risks because the absolute cost
of entering a specific market may be high and the volume of
their total resources enables them to take failure of individual
projects in their stride. Failures of similar magnitude, which
may be irreducible owing to high fixed costs, can completely
ruin small firms, which consequently prefer not to engage in
risky projects, even if their expected returns are higher than less
risky ones. The pattern of small firms' preference for the

relatively protected markets of the F.T.A.s is thus explained in terms of the 'risk aversion' of those who cannot afford to gamble for high stakes.

The implications of the above for the D.C.s should by now be obvious. The creation of F.T.A.s from which they are excluded penalises the D.C.s twice: in the first place, they suffer because goods shipped by competitors which were admitted to the area pay no customs duties, while their goods do. In addition, they suffer because of their industrial structure. Small firms, located in the F.T.A.s, are able to increase their exports because of the reduction in the element of risk involved in intra-area marketing. Small firms located outside the area do not benefit from risk reduction. If our assumption that D.C.s are characterised by a higher proportion of small firms than industrialised countries is correct, we must conclude that the penalty paid by the D.C.s, owing to their exclusion from the E.E.C. and EFTA, is compounded.

The establishment of a tariff-quota system, which allows limited quantities of duty-free imports from the D.C.s into the markets of the industrialised countries, should go a certain way towards cancelling the disadvantages facing the former, following the establishment of F.T.A.s in Europe. The extent of the improvement will depend on the size of the quotas, on the degree of confidence which exporters in the D.C.s will have in the stability of the system, and on the chances they have of benefitting from the tariff-free quota. The higher the confidence, the larger the number of small firms which the new policy will help to turn from potential into actual exporters.

IV. COUNTERING OUTWARD TRADE DIVERSION

What can the D.C.s do to improve the export performance of their firms and thus counter the trade-diverting effects of the free-trade areas? It is possible to make a long list of administrative, fiscal and monetary measures which governments can adopt to make exports less risky and more profitable. Here we propose to deal only with those measures which are suggested by the discussion of the previous sections.

The first and obvious conclusion is to create conditions which will encourage large firms to come into being. Large firms are, as we have seen, better equipped to assume the risks and high costs involved in export marketing. Steps should therefore be taken to encourage mergers and take-overs and, when possible, to establish firms whose initial size is sufficiently large to enable them to enter foreign markets as soon as possible after they commence operations.

In their search for organisations which are best adapted to promote exports, governments will be well advised to give close attention to the multinational producing enterprise (M.P.E.). Discussing the M.P.E.'s characteristics, P. Streeten has stated:

> Attention has recently shifted from the contribution that it makes through the transfer of capital to the contribution it makes through its ability to draw on a fund of not freely available knowledge, subject to economies of size, or a network of information, or managerial and technical skills, including those of marketing the product (again subject to scale economies) and on the institutionally built-in propensity to adapt and innovate.[7]

These characteristics give the M.P.E. a significant edge over purely domestic corporations in exports, especially in exports of skill-intensive products: their physical presence in several markets simplifies the marketing process and reduces the costs involved in obtaining market information, communicating with customers, as well as shipping, stock-keeping, etc. The costs involved in providing these services may be quite high and, more important, some of them are fixed in the sense that they do not vary with sales volume. The fixed portion of these costs has already been incurred by the M.P.E. in those markets where it operates. It already has a marketing organisation, stocking facilities, agents, sales offices, etc. Its marketing costs are, under these circumstances, lower than those of the domestic firm which wishes to enter foreign markets.

The M.P.E., moreover, has advantages over the domestic firm even in markets where it has no subsidiaries. Its organisation is geared to international operations, and it is likely to maintain departments which deal with control of foreign operations, international finance, international marketing, international law, etc. These services can easily be extended to support exports to countries where the M.P.E. has no operating subsidiaries.

The edge of the M.P.E.s over domestic firms in exports has been dramatically demonstrated by R. Vernon, who quotes a U.S. Department of Commerce study covering some 264 U.S. parents and their subsidiaries. The study indicates that the 264 U.S. parents and their foreign subsidiaries were responsible, whether as buyers or as sellers, for about half of all U.S. exports of manufactured goods.[8]

C. Tugendhat estimates that 'On the basis of present trends, it seems quite possible that by 1980, 40 per cent of Britain's manufactured exports could be provided by U.S.-controlled companies and a further 10 per cent by foreign-owned concerns.'[9] The relevance of these estimates may be challenged on the ground that they pertain to giant companies operating in large, industrialised, high-income countries. Even if the M.P.E.s establish subsidiaries in D.C.s, they are unlikely to be large (by developed countries' standards) except in the petroleum and other extractive industries where their output has a captive market.

If Vernon's findings and Tugendhat's predictions have general validity, they ought to be demonstrable on non-U.S. firms and on firms which operate in all countries. Moreover, they ought to be demonstrated on domestically controlled M.P.E.s, as well as on foreign-controlled ones.

Table 4 provides such evidence. It shows the export performance of a sample of nearly 500 firms from Denmark, Holland and Israel – three small countries whose economies are highly dependent on international trade.[10] The sample, unlike that of Vernon, is drawn from a universe consisting of *all* firms in a particular industry. It was divided two ways: domestic firms vis-à-vis M.P.E.s (defined as firms with manufacturing plants in more than one country[11]), and high vis-à-vis low skill-intensive industries (food products, textiles, clothing and footwear were defined as low skill-intensive; chemicals, machinery, electrical and electronics were defined as high skill-intensive). M.P.E.s include both locally and foreign-controlled firms. Comparative export performance figures are shown in Table 4.

The table demonstrates the superior performance of the M.P.E.s in all three countries in the high skill-intensive group and in two countries in the low skill-intensive group. Though the figures are not statistically significant, they suggest that when governments calculate the costs and benefits of M.P.E.s, they should not neglect to take into account their potential contribution to their country's exports.

Table 4

SHARE OF OUTPUT EXPORTED BY M.P.E.S AND DOMESTIC FIRMS[a]

Country	Denmark		Holland		Israel	
Corporation	Domestic	M.P.E.	Domestic	M.P.E.	Domestic	M.P.E.
Low skill-intensive	0·37	0·41	0·26	0·35	0·35	(0·28)
High skill-intensive	0·49	0·59	0·25	0·45	0·13	0·22

( )=sample of 1.
[a] With the exception of the Dutch high skill-intensive group, differences are not statistically significant.

Finally, a word about ownership and control of M.P.E.s. Impressed by the economic advantages of the M.P.E.s, C. P. Kindleberger predicted that they will dominate the world economy in the foreseeable future.[12] E. Penrose vigorously attacked this prediction, claiming that disintegration is just as likely to take place. She mentions the petroleum industry as an example and predicts that governments of oil-producing countries will tend to gain control over oil production and will negotiate with the distributing firms the allocation of profits between production, refining and distribution. She concludes that 'Arguments that integrated control by a few big Western firms is essential for efficient operation of the industry are little more than assertions based on very flimsy assumptions.'[13]

My own view is that Penrose's predictions regarding the oil industry are correct and that her conclusions have general validity for mature industries whose production process is stable, easily transferrable across national boundaries and separable into distinct stages. Specifications of products manufactured by these industries are easily available; demand for them is highly price-elastic and marketing can easily be separated from the production stage. What about skill-intensive products, however? It is difficult to envisage the production and marketing process of computers, pharmaceuticals and cars broken down into neat, separable stages, facilitating arm's-length negotiations between designers, manufacturers and marketers.

Developing countries which are content with manufacturing and marketing products belonging to the first category can indeed pursue a policy of disintegration without too much economic loss. If, however, they wish their export basket to include high-technology products, disintegration may be impossible.

If the D.C.s do not wish their industries to be controlled by foreign M.P.E.s, they should perhaps consider establishing their own. Japan has been following this policy in recent years. There is no reason why countries such as India, Venezuela, Brazil, Argentina and Iran, which have passed the threshold of industrialisation, should not follow in Japan's footsteps.

True, establishment of M.P.E.s by the D.C.s will usually require capital exports in the short run. This will surely represent a light burden for most of the oil-producing countries, whose huge foreign exchange reserves are mainly invested in low-yielding government securities. Even in countries which lack foreign reserves, governments should bear in mind that capital outflows associated with establishment of their own M.P.E.s may represent a small price when measured against the benefits inherent in the acquisition of high-technology, export-orientated industries.

Notes

1. B. Balassa, 'Trade Creation and Trade Diversion in the European Common Market', *Economic Journal* (Mar 1967) p. 5.
2. When the figures are disaggregated by major industry group, extra-area imports are shown to have a declining income elasticity of demand in food, raw materials, and chemicals and other manufactured goods. Intra-area imports suffer from such a decline only in food. Ibid., p. 8.
Another computation which compares actual with hypothetical imports based on the pre-E.E.C. import growth rate shows that actual imports from the D.C.s in 1965 were less than expected imports. Ibid., p. 12.
3. This is indeed what he has done.
4. Note that the table contains two infeasible situations:
(1) $\alpha > 0$ and $\beta < 0$ when $\gamma > 0$;
(2) $\alpha < 0$ and $\beta > 0$ when $\gamma < 0$.

The highly improbable case when α = 1, β = 1, γ = 1 is omitted. In the case of such an occurrence, the situation should be properly regarded as indeterminate.

5. These conclusions are confirmed by other studies published in recent years. The U.N. *Trade in Manufactures of Developing Countries, 1970 Review* (New York, 1971) reported the following changes in the share of several trading areas in the exports of developing countries:

	1962	1969
E.E.C.	4·6	3·8
EFTA	4·5	4·4
D.M.E.C.*	5·0	5·5
U.S.A.	9·8	11·4
Japan	3·7	8·2

* Developed market economy countries.

See also M. K. Carney, 'Developments in Trading Patterns in the Common Market and EFTA', *Journal of the American Statistical Association* (Dec 1970) pp. 1455–9. Carney, who used a different model to measure trade creation and diversion, concluded that trade of both the E.E.C. and EFTA with outsiders was characterised by diversion.

6. For a more detailed discussion of these issues, see S. Hirsch, *Location of Industry and International Competitiveness* (Oxford: Clarendon Press, 1967) chap. 4, and S. Hirsch, *The Export Performance of Six Manufacturing Industries: A Comparative Study of Denmark, Holland and Israel* (New York: Praeger, 1971) chap. 4.

7. P. Streeten, 'Costs and Benefits of Multinational Enterprises in Less Developed Countries', in J. H. Dunning (ed.), *The Multinational Enterprise* (London: Allen & Unwin, 1971) p. 240.

8. R. Vernon, *Sovereignty at Bay* (London: Longman, 1971) p. 16.

9. C. Tugendhat, *The Multinationals* (London: Eyre & Spottiswoode, 1971) p. 112.

10. Export performance is measured by the share of sales exported by the firms during the 1964–8 period. The share was weighted by the year 1964 getting a weight of 1, 1965 2, etc. The data were collected by interviews for a comparative study of export industries. See Hirsch, *The Export Performance of Six Manufacturing Industries.*

11. Vernon's M.P.E. must have manufacturing operations in six or more countries.

12. C. P. Kindleberger, *American Business Abroad: Six Lectures on Direct Investment* (New Haven: Yale Univ. Press, 1969). See also S. Hymer 'The Multinational Corporation and the Law of Uneven Development', in J. N. Bhagwati (ed.), *Economics and World Order* (New York: World Law Fund, 1970).

13. E. Penrose, 'The State and Multinational Enterprises in Less Developed Countries', in Dunning, op. cit., p. 236.

7 Trade and Technology

Frances Stewart[1]

SENIOR RESEARCH OFFICER, INSTITUTE OF
COMMONWEALTH STUDIES, UNIVERSITY OF OXFORD

'Necessity is the mother of invention' (old English proverb)
'Invention is the mother of necessity' (Veblen)

One of the major achievements of economics as a discipline has
been to establish propositions and policies that appear counter
to common sense, and that might for this reason have been
overlooked in the absence of economists. The futurists have
formalised and popularised this achievement as the 'counter-
intuitive character of social systems'.[2] On closer examination of
the most famous examples of counter-intuition the phenomenon
tends to disappear. In some cases the initial common-sense
reaction, or intuition, turns out not to be *tabula rasa* common
sense at all, but the product of some earlier, false theory, as
with the ideas preceding the Keynesian revolution. In others the
initial reaction is simply a failure to think things through in a
rather obvious way, while elsewhere the counter-intuition itself
turns out to be false.

However, the theory of international trade has some claim
to represent a substantial counter-intuitive achievement. Since
Ricardo first developed the theory of comparative advantage,
each generation has had to learn anew, and each time experienced the almost incredible triumph of reason over belief,
in discovering that indeed both England *and* Portugal gain from
free trade, despite England's supposed absolute superiority in
the production of both corn and cloth. International trade
theory has of course come quite a long way since Ricardo, but
the basic policy prescriptions remain: both rich and poor
nations would gain from free trade despite the absolute advantages of the rich nations; that the misguided attempts of the

poor countries to vindicate their (protective) intuitions against the (free trade) theory have been in large part responsible for poor performance. Far from attempting to protect their high-cost and relatively inefficient industries, the developing countries should open all gates to unmitigated competition from the developed countries, and then they too will experience *in practice* the gains from trade that so many students have experienced *in theory*.

FREE TRADE PHILOSOPHY

At its simplest, the case for free trade for all can be readily demonstrated. Let us assume that a single country can produce alternative combinations of two goods, say bicycles and food, as shown along *PP* in Fig. 7.1 below, and that the country's welfare can be described by a series of social indifference curves, *S'*, *S''*, *S'''*, with *S'''* representing a higher level of welfare than *S''* and *S''* than *S'*. With no trade, the country's 'best' position – i.e. highest welfare – will be reached by 'producing at *X*. Now

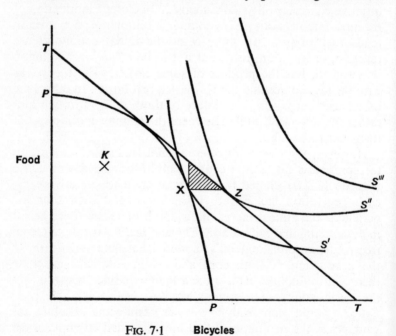

Fig. 7·1   **Bicycles**

suppose international trade is possible at an exchange rate represented by the slope of *TT;* then by producing at *Y* and exchanging food for bicycles until position *Z* is reached, the country will arrive at a higher level of welfare (*S″*) than in the previous position (*S′*).

As is shown in the diagram, the case for free trade does not rest on the (controversial) assumption of the existence and meaningfulness of community indifference curves. Trade enables a community to have more of *both goods*, so that some people can be made richer without anyone being made poorer.[3] With trade, and production at *Y*, the community can consume any combination of goods represented by *TT*. Except at *Y* itself, *TT* lies above *PP* which represents consumption possible without trade. For any point on the no-trade possibility curve, *PP* (apart from *Y*), there is some point on the trade possibility curve, *TT*, which involves more of both food and bicycles. The shaded area in the diagram shows all the combinations made possible by trade which involve more of both goods than the no-trade equilibrium point, *X*. The composition of trade, who exports what, who imports what, and the potential gains for each country will depend on the production possibilities open to each country – the alternative combinations of food and bicycles – and international prices for the commodities, themselves a function of international supply and demand. The well known Heckscher–Ohlin theory of international trade states that such trade will be conducted in accordance with international factor endowment, so that countries with relatively abundant supplies of capital will export capital-intensive goods, while countries with relatively abundant supplies of labour will export labour-intensive commodities and import capital-intensive commodities. This arises because the capital-abundant countries will be able to produce capital-intensive commodities relatively cheaply while the labour-abundant countries will be able to produce labour-intensive commodities relatively cheaply. Thus the theory would suggest that developing countries – labour-abundant – would specialise in labour-intensive goods, while the developed countries would concentrate on capital-intensive goods, and *both sets of countries would gain* by the exchange by specialising in what they are relatively efficient at, and exchanging these goods for what they are relatively inefficient at: for example, the Indians would acquire more investment goods by specialising on the production of textiles, and exchanging these for investment goods, than they would if they set out to produce the investment goods for themselves.

The Heckscher–Ohlin theory had to be modified when Leontief discovered that the United States – clearly capital-abundant in relation to all other countries – actually exported labour-intensive goods and imported capital-intensive goods.[4] Other cases that run counter to Heckscher–Ohlin predictions have also been identified: for example, Japan was revealed to export capital-intensive and import labour-intensive goods in the 1950s[5] while Canada similarly exported capital-intensive goods, despite the fact that her main trading partner was the capital-abundant United States.[6] Among the many theories put forward to explain this phenomenon,[7] the most widely accepted explanation, and that most in accordance with the empirical evidence,[8] is that the Leontief paradox neglected human capital: the U.S. 'apparently labour-intensive exports' are in fact highly skilled-labour intensive.

Both in terms of positive economics – or the description and prediction of the nature of international trade flows – and in terms of normative or welfare economics, the approach to international trade that has been very sketchily described above rests on an extremely stringent set of assumptions.[9] Among the necessary assumptions are the absence of economies of scale,[10] the presence of perfect competition, nationally and internationally, full employment of resources in both countries, identity (or very close similarity) of production functions (and therefore also of technical knowledge) and patterns of tastes in all countries concerned, and the absence of tariffs and other barriers to trade. The theory is, in addition, *static:* the main parameters, for example tastes and technology, are assumed unchanging over time.

The obvious invalidity of many (possibly all) of these assumptions does not necessarily invalidate the approach. As H. G. Johnson summarises the position: 'These assumptions are, like the assumptions of all theorising, abstractions from the complexity of reality capable of refutation as universally valid assumptions by an appeal to the facts of observation: the scientific issue however is whether observed deviations of facts from assumptions are empirically significant enough to destroy the validity of the conclusions of the theory.'[11] Relaxation of some of the assumptions can be fairly readily incorporated into the theory: thus the presence of monopolistic conditions in international trade has led to the justification, from a purely national point of view, of an optimal tariff. But others are less easily dealt with, either for positive or normative analysis, or both. For example, given the obvious actual widespread use of all sorts of barriers to trade, natural and artificial, whether efficient or not, these must obviously be taken into account if one is trying to predict the likely nature of trade. If the Indian government, for example, prohibits the import of certain types of machinery, or the governments of many of the rich countries restrict the import of textiles, a theory which denies the existence of such restrictions will come up with inaccurate descriptions and prediction, and wrongly derived policy conclusions.[12] Persistent inability to achieve full employment of resources in one country (so that production is not on the frontier as in Fig. 7.1, but some way below it, as for example at K) may also challenge the foundations of the theory.

Despite the unrealism of many of the assumptions, the majority of economists probably concur in believing that free – or at least freer – trade between developed and developing countries should be promoted to the benefit of all. The economic justification for intervention in free trade is taken to be confined to the arguments for an optimum tariff, in those cases where a country has monopoly power, and to 'infant industry' considerations rather narrowly interpreted. This view is to be found in numerous places.[13] Two recent examples may be cited. Little, Scitovsky and Scott in their O.E.C.D. study[14] make a powerful case, and plead for virtually[15] free trade on grounds of classical comparative advantage and learning[16] while condemning the past experience of many developing countries in pursuing import substitution at the expense of efficiency. Similar arguments for free trade are to be found in *Trade Strategy for Rich and Poor Countries*,[17] in which Johnson concludes: 'The ideal solution in principle would be to eliminate the discriminatory protectionist barriers to free international trade, and to seek to promote world economic development on a basis of dynamic comparative advantage.'[18]

This paper is concerned solely with technology and its relation to international trade. Among the assumptions of the trade models discussed above were three that specifically concerned technology: first, 'production functions and factors are assumed to be identical in all countries'; second, 'on the consumption side [it is assumed that] tastes . . . are given', third '. . . on the 'production side technology and the supply of factors of production are given'.[19] In other words, it is the assumption of the model that technology is the same for different countries and that tastes and technology are *unchanging* over time. The question is whether modification of these assumptions, inevitable once technology is introduced, might modify some of the conclusions reached.

Technology, like so many things, is easier to discuss than to define. Many definitions have been suggested, some extending to the entire range of methods of production in use in an economy. This is the type of definition used here. Technology is taken to mean the ways in which commodities are produced, and the nature of the commodities being produced. Four important characteristics of technology relevant to this discussion are:

(i) Technology changes over time, as new methods of production and new products are developed. Such changes are the product of deliberate expenditure to promote them, through research and development, and also of improvements that occur through learning, education, etc. Changes in technology are now so much part of the economic system of developed countries that it is absurd to assume an unchanging technology.[20] At any one time, in any one country, different goods, and different qualities of goods, are being produced in a variety of ways, some of which date back a considerable time, and others which represent the latest ways of doing things. Knowledge of how to produce extends even further – both backward in time to methods once used but now abandoned, and forward to developments which for economic or other reasons have not yet been introduced. Thus if we refer to the technology of a particular country at a particular date, we may be referring to the whole range of knowledge, to the whole range of methods in use, or to those (generally the most recently introduced) currently being installed. In what follows I shall mean the technology embodied in current investment decisions in referring to the technology of a country.

(ii) Second, just as technology needs to be dated because it changes over time, it also needs to be placed because, in all possible definitions of technology, it differs according to the place in question. Thus, U.S. 1971 technology differs from U.S. 1961 technology but also from U.K. 1971 technology which in turn differs from Indian 1971 technology. There are causal links over time and place. Through patents, licences and imitation, U.S. technology of 1971 is communicated to the rest of the world, more or less perfectly and with more or less of a time-lag so that some, if not all, of the U.S. 1971 technology may be available for use in the rest of the world in the 1970s. U.S. 1971 technology has more or less perfect access to U.S. 1961 technology; to a lesser extent the U.K. or India also have access to U.S. 1971 technology, but this time filtered through the transfer of technology mechanisms[21] as well as through time. The process of innovation allows a temporary monopoly to the innovator:[22] the length of time before the innovation can be adopted in other countries depends on a number of factors, including standards of technical know-how, the nature of the innovation, available methods for technology transfer, and similarity of economic conditions between innovatory and recipient country. During this time-lag there will inevitably be a difference – which has been termed a technological gap – between technology in the innovatory country and technology elsewhere.[23] Because innovations occur continuously and not once and for all, continuous differences persist: as soon as one gap is closed another opens. Generally, the differences in technology between countries are likely to be greatest the greater the differences in economic conditions and scientific and technical standards.[24] Thus the assumption of identity of technology between countries is wrong; the greater the economic difference between countries, the more technologies will differ. It is a particularly inappropriate assumption in analysing trade between developed and developing countries. Technology between these groups is likely to differ partly because research and development expenditures, scientific and technical skills and know-how, and subsequent innovations are heavily concentrated in the developed countries.[25] Hence the developed countries have earlier and easier access to the innovations that occur, and because of the continuous nature of innovations, this gives them a permanently more 'advanced' technology. Secondly, the technology developed in the advanced countries is inappropriate to the conditions of the developing countries (to be discussed in more detail below) so that it may never be introduced there, thus accentuating differences in technology.

(iii) A third important characteristic of technology is that it involves a particular set of factor requirements. A technology consists in a series of specific methods of production, requiring certain inputs to get certain outputs. In economic terms the inputs may be classified as unskilled labour, skilled labour and capital. Given a particular method of production, a certain amount of each of these inputs is required to achieve the product in question. Engineers may, theoretically, be able to combine inputs in a variety of ways; in practice at any time only the economically efficient methods will be developed. What is economically efficient depends on the ruling factor prices in the country in which the method is being developed. Given the level of real wages in the United States, only methods which lead to a level of labour productivity that permits the payment of such real wages will be worth developing. Indeed, given the almost unavoidable yearly rise in real wages, this too must be allowed for in developing new methods of production. Thus products and processes developed in the United States will tend to be relatively capital-intensive, involving high rates of capital expenditure per man, and relatively labour-saving, in the sense of involving relatively low rates of labour use per unit of output, or high rates of labour productivity. As the United States is, relatively, a skilled-labour-abundant economy, new methods may also involve high ratios of skilled labour to unskilled labour. The factor-use characteristics of a technology will therefore depend on the economic conditions, in terms of factor prices and availability, of the country in which the technology is developed, at the date at which it is developed. So if we specify the date and place of a technology we shall also specify, broadly speaking, the factor use involved in that technology.[26] The transfer of technology from one country to another also involves, within limits, the transfer of a particular factor use. One cannot transfer a new technique in plastics, for example, without also transferring the machines involved, and requiring similar employment of skilled and unskilled labour. Of course, one may be able to add to the unskilled labour used, but one can rarely deduct from it, or deduct from the other inputs involved. Transformation of methods so that a different factor mix is possible amounts to the development of a new technology and requires the same sort of resources, of scientific and technical know-how, expenditure on research and development, etc., that went to the initial technological development. Given this, the phenomenon would no longer be a question of technology transfer but of technology development. This characteristic of technology, of involving a particular factor mix, means that technologies tend to be appropriate to the economic (and climatic, social and political, but this is a different story[27]) conditions of the country in which they are developed, but not to other countries with different economic characteristics. The further apart countries are in terms of factor endowment and socially correct factor prices, the less appropriate will each country's technology be for the other. This does not mean that it will not be introduced, as we shall see, but it does mean that if introduced it will be inappropriate in the sense of using a country's factors of production in a profligate way in relation to available resources.

(iv) Each technology is associated with a unique range of products in terms of type and quality. While human needs, in the broadest sense, are common to most men and unchanging over time, the ways in which these needs are fulfilled – the particular products consumed – change with changes in technology, and differ between countries and within a country over time. It is customary to classify technology into methods of production, or processes, and products. In general, more attention has been devoted to the process-improvement aspects of technological developments (e.g. whether changes that occur are 'neutral', capital- or labour-saving) than to product developments. This is a result of the serious conceptual difficulties raised by product changes. Once we allow for product changes, quantities produced become ambiguous depending on the way in which new products are valued compared with the old. Whatever the reason, the neglect of product developments has been seriously misleading: in the first place, research on the relative importance of process and product improvements has suggested that product developments substantially outweigh process improvements. In the second place, which in a way makes nonsense of the first assertion, conceptually and practically it is very often impossible to distinguish between process and product developments. The difficulties arise because a new method of production or a new process will involve a new product in two ways. First, it will often, if not always, involve a new or radically improved machine or other input for the process, and since machines and other inputs are the product of other industries, it will therefore involve a new product. Second, a change in the method of production nearly always affects the quality of the product in some way. It may be a relatively minor change, for example mechanisation leading to standardisation of quality as compared with hand methods; it may consist of the substitution of one material for another; or it may affect the speed of operating and consequently, for those products for which this is relevant, the quality of the final product. At the other extreme, changes may be made that amount, in normal parlance, to a completely new product. Thus products change with process changes. There are also deliberate product changes, which themselves require process changes to achieve. The evidence is that a very large proportion of research and development expenditure is designed to secure major product innovations or developments. One inquiry in the United States[28] found that for 48 per cent of manufacturing firms the main aim of their research programme was new products, for 11 per cent new processes, and for 41 per cent improvements of existing products. Thus about 90 per cent of the firms' programmes were mainly concerned with new products or product developments; a large proportion of the remainder, mainly devoted to new processes, would probably also affect product quality in the way discussed. Other studies[29] have found that three-quarters of applied research and development in the United States is devoted to product as against process innovations. Bloom also suggests that 'it is probably the rule rather than the exception that improved processes which reduce costs also yield improved products'. In one of the few attempts to measure quality changes in what normally counts as the 'same' product, Adelman and Griliches estimate that a very large proportion of price rises in automobiles in fact reflected quality improvements: they conclude that 'It is not at all improbable that correctly measured there has been no real rise in the general price level since 1952.'[30]

Product developments[31] thus play a very important part in technological development. If we allow for changes in product characteristics and quality as well as completely new products, the technology of successive periods will be very largely composed of changed products. Two aspects of product development are particularly relevant to questions of international trade.

First, the nature of products – in type, characteristics and quality – is in part a function of the type and wealth of consumers for whom they are intended. Any particular product can be regarded as a bundle of characteristics that fulfil, more or less efficiently, a number of different needs of consumers. For example, a shirt may provide warmth, protection from the sun, look attractive or indicate the social standing of the wearer, eliminate the need for ironing, etc. Any consumer good can be categorised similarly, into the needs which it fulfils. As products change, the needs which they fulfil and the efficiency with which they fulfil various needs also change. The change itself may fulfil a need – to avoid monotony. As consumers get richer they do not simply consume the same products as before and more of them. Engel pointed out that the proportion of income allocated to broad groups of expenditure changed as incomes rose – that expenditure on food fell and other items rose as a proportion of income. The changes that occur are not just a question of proportions: the nature of the products consumed to fulfil man's basic needs, the other needs which are fulfilled, and the extent and way in which they are fulfilled also change. Meat replaces maize; the Bahamas, Margate. Products fulfilling the same need are refined, developed and replaced. Thirst that may be satisfied by water may for rich consumers be quenched by Coca-Cola, Tab or Scotch. These other products not only fill the original basic need but also others. A standard piece of cloth that provides essential clothing for the poor is replaced by an endless concatenation of materials, styles and fashions. The nature of a product thus reflects the wealth and demands of consumers for whom it was intended when developed. This means that products first introduced into rich countries will tend to be inappropriate for poor countries, possessing characteristics that overkill in relation to their needs, i.e. which provide for more than the appropriate (to their incomes) needs. This may be seen in excessive standards, e.g. of roads, houses, hygiene, or excessive product sophistication, e.g. electric toothbrushes, colour television, Mercedes cars. Ultimately, it is, of course, the aim that standards in developing countries should be as high as (though this does not mean identical with) those the rich enjoy. But it is the nature of being poorer as a society that the same standard of living as the average in richer countries cannot be afforded for all. If developing countries provide the rich countries' products for part of the population, it will mean neglecting the needs of many of the people. It follows then that if developing countries do consume rich countries' products, it will mean overkill in relation to some needs (and/or some consumers) while neglecting other more important needs. For example, Coca-Cola for all, or for some, may mean inadequate protein for all, or for some. Applying developed countries' building methods may lead to a few comfortable high-standard buildings, while the mass of housing is left in a primitive state. The type of products appropriate to the needs of poorer societies differs from that appropriate to rich societies.[32]

The second relevant characteristic of product developments is that the changes in products and the changes in taste that go with them tend to be *irreversible*. As the goods produced in an economy change, the goods consumed also change. Tastes keep pace with technology partly because the changes in product and technology are themselves one aspect of increases in income, as discussed above, partly through promotional expenditure, and partly because consumers can only consume what is available. Once consumers' tastes have changed, such changes are largely irreversible. For one reason invention is the mother of necessity, as Veblen pointed out. Radio and black-and-white television, trains, ballpoint pens, matchbox cars and powdered instant coffee started as luxuries, soon became necessities and are now, for many, inferior goods replaced in their luxury (indeed even in their normal) goods status by colour television, cars and planes, felt pens, hot wheels and crystallised coffee.[33] Today's luxuries are tomorrow's necessities. The irreversibility of consumers' tastes is reinforced by the relationship between products and income levels, discussed above, so that at higher income levels consumers require high-income products. A very large proportion of goods sold are intermediate goods, not for final consumption. Changes in such goods tend to be irreversible not only because of the irreversibility of the consumer goods for which they are ultimately used – derived irreversibility – but also because of links between productive processes such that each stage of the productive process tends to be designed for particular inputs, and will not operate successfully with other quality inputs. The more automated processes become, the stronger the links between different stages of production. Hence technological development is such that consumers will not and producers cannot be satisfied with the products of a previous era. The significance of the irreversibility of consumption patterns comes when we combine it with the previously discussed characteristic of technology – that the factor mix of a technology is determined by the factor availability and factor prices of the country when and where it was introduced. It means that the technological requirements, in terms of factor use, of each product will depend on the factor availability of its time and place of introduction. Products innovated and first introduced into the developed countries will be capital-intensive in relation to the factor resources of the developing countries. As time proceeds, techniques of production in the developed countries get increasingly capital-intensive, as incomes and therefore savings and investment per head rise. This is illustrated for a few developed countries in Table 1. Thus, the later products are first introduced into developed countries, the more capital-intensive their technology is likely to be. The production structure of the developed countries also becomes increasingly human-capital-intensive, or skill-intensive, as the relative supply of skilled manpower increases. Table 2 shows how the educated manpower has increased, as a proportion of the total, in the United States during the twentieth century. Again, this means that the skill-intensity of a product is likely to be greater the later its date of introduction. The scale of production units has also increased with time in the developed countries, as Table 3 indicates for the United Kingdom.[34,35] Thus the later products are introduced, the larger in scale production units tend to be.

Table 1
CHANGES IN CAPITAL PER MAN, U.K., U.S.A. AND NORWAY

Fixed capital per man in U.K. manufacturing

	£ (1963 prices)	(1920 = 100)
1920	1,540	100
1930	1,930	125·1
1938	1,770	115·0
1948	1,990	129·1
1958	2,415	156·8
1968	3,140	210·0

U.S.A.

	H.P. per man in manufacturing		Reproducible capital per member of the labour force ($'000, 1929 values)
1899	1·63	1879	2·32
1909	2·35	1889	2·77
1919	2·65	1899	3·56
1929	3·85	1909	4·17
1939	4·85	1919	5·19
1962	9·05	1929	5·87
		1939	5·12
		1944	5·70

Norway: Real capital per man year
(1900 = 100)

1900	100
1920	134
1939	184
1950	190
1955	243

Sources: *The British Economy: Key Statistics 1900-1970*, Tables E and I; *Statistical Abstract of the United States, 1969*, Table 1108; S. Kuznets (ed.), *Income and Wealth Series*, II (Cambridge, 1952) Table 11; Goldsmith and Saunders (eds.), *Income and Wealth Series*, VIII (Cambridge, 1959) Table IV, p. 97.

As argued above, new products (in type and quality) tend to displace old products both as consumption goods and as intermediate goods. This means that the composition of goods gets yearly more capital-intensive and larger-scale, not just in the sense that actual methods used in the developed countries are *de facto* more capital-intensive and skill-intensive, but that

Table 2
COMPOSITION OF THE U.S. LABOUR FORCE

(as percentage of total)

	1910	1920	1930	1940	1950	1960	1968
Professional and technical	4·4	5·0	6·1	6·5	7·5	11·2	11·2
Proprietors	23·0	22·3	19·9	17·8	10·8	10·6	9·9
Clerks and kindred workers	10·2	13·8	16·3	17·2	19·2	21·3	22·0
Skilled and foremen	11·7	13·5	12·9	11·7	12·9	12·8	13·2
Semi-skilled	14·7	16·1	16·4	21·0	20·4	17·9	18·4
Unskilled	36·0	29·4	28·4	25·9	29·2	26·2	25·3

Sources: *Statistical Abstract of the United States, 1943*, Table 132; ibid., *1969*, Table 322.

Table 3
TRENDS IN INDUSTRIAL CONCENTRATION IN THE U.K.

Industry	Size of largest plant	% of total employees employed in the largest plant		
		1935	1951	1958
Food, drink and tobacco	1,500+	18	33	22
Chemicals	1,500+	18	25	32
Metal industries	1,500+	13	23	30
Engineering and shipbuilding	1,500+	29	36	38
Motors	1,500+	52	56	62
Aircraft	1,500+	52	67	73
Textiles	750+	19	16	15
Clothing	500+	19	16	18
Footwear	1,000+	15	11	7
Bricks	1,000+	10	18	21
Timber	400+	10	12	12
Rubber	1,500+	44	41	34
Paper manufacturing	1,000+	11	16	21
Printing	1,000+	19	20	23
All manufacturing	1,500+	15	24	27

Source: A. Armstrong and A. Silberston, 'Size of Plant, Size of Enterprise and Concentration in British Manufacturing Industry, 1935-58', *Journal of the Royal Statistical Society*, Series A, CXXVIII (1965) Table A.

the only methods ever developed for these products are capital-intensive because of the date, place and circumstances when they were first introduced into production.

The above argument is true only of innovations that take place in the developed countries. The evidence, both of research and development expenditure and of analysis of innovations, is that at present virtually all innovations do take place in the developed countries.[36] Hence the composition of production and consumption patterns gets annually more capital-intensive, with the earlier, more labour-intensive products being displaced by later goods, while the irreversibility of consumption patterns means that these patterns cannot be reversed. Development of more appropriate (i.e. labour-intensive and small-scale) techniques for producing products of the same characteristics not only requires expenditure on research and development, but may also fail because of the near one-to-one relation between product characteristics and techniques of production. Even where successful, success is likely to be only temporary as new research in the developed countries, and higher incomes, bring about further product developments making the old products obsolete.

TRADE AND DEVELOPING COUNTRIES

The technological developments described affect the developing countries in two ways: directly through trade, and indirectly through determining the kind of technology available to them from developed countries.[37] Here I am primarily concerned with trade. It is clear that the introduction of technology into the discussion makes nonsense of some of the assumptions made in international trade theory, as described above: in particular, one cannot assume that the technology available to developed and developing countries is the same, nor can one assume it (or tastes) to be unchanging over time. Technological considerations may explain a good deal of the inefficiencies of past programmes of import substitution, and shed serious doubt on the export promotion strategy that has been proposed as an alternative.

Import Substitution

The most natural first step in industrialisation is to examine the pattern of goods being consumed and see how far home production may be substituted for imports. The markets are securely established and with protection this seems the least risky alternative. The infant-industry argument is readily at hand if theoretical justification is required. A major drawback of this course lies in its technological implications. The actual pattern of consumption established in a country before industrialisation is determined in the light of its income distribution and the availability and relative prices of goods from the developed countries. But the goods available and their prices reflect the technology currently employed, and the factor availabilities, of the developed countries. Any import substitution programme which aims to substitute exactly[38] for previously imported goods will necessarily lead to over capital-intensive methods of production: to produce identical or near identical goods to those which were previously imported requires identical or near identical technology. Choice of product determines choice of technology. The chosen instrument of many import substitution programmes – the foreign firm that once exported and subsequently produces locally behind tariff and quota barriers – possibly made the outcome, identity of product and technology with the developed country's counterpart, more certain. But the foreign firms cannot be blamed. Any firm, local or foreign, that aimed to produce the same goods as those previously imported would have to use the technology available for the production of those goods, the technology designed for the developed countries where it was initiated,[39] though international firms have their own reason for promoting a policy in which they will be the obvious instrument, and also an interest in maintaining identical product standards and technology throughout the world. Hence they tend to be both initiators and effective agents of the policy. The policy of import substitution thus inevitably led to capital-intensive techniques in the modern sector such that only a small proportion of the work-force could be employed; those that were employed enjoyed relatively high rates of labour productivity and wages, leading to substantial disparities between this sector and the rest of the economy with the consequence of a growing employment and political problem. Some of those consequences are illustrated in Tables 4 and 5.

The many problems arose not so much from distorted prices of factors of production, overvalued exchange rates or evil-minded international managers who preferred machines to men, but from technological considerations. If the same pattern of goods were to be produced locally as those previously imported, capital-intensive technology was inevitable. In a trivial but illuminating way the process was illustrated in Kenya when imported soft drinks were replaced by local bottling. Black-currants were imported from England so that the Kenyans could continue to receive their vitamin C in the way they had previously – a way, of course, that reflected British weather which made blackcurrant production possible but not oranges.[40]

The immediate impact of import substitution may be to produce mirror-image (though smaller-scale or at a lower level of capacity utilisation) production to that carried out abroad. But as time proceeds, new technology, and with it new products, will be developed overseas. If these are allowed to compete freely they may displace the locally produced products, or make it necessary to adapt them so as to compete. Such innovations are likely to be in a further capital-intensive direction. The consequences that flowed from the import substitution pro-grammes adopted – the capital-intensity of production and the consequent employment problem – have been used by many economists to discredit the whole idea of development initiated from import substitution. But, as argued above, these conse-quences did not stem from import substitution as such but from the form of import substitution adopted. If the locally produced substitutes were to be identical in all but place of assembly with the previous imports, the consequences were inevitable. By the same token, capital-intensity of production will increase, the optimum scale of production (and hence deviations from it necessary for a small market) will increase and labour produc-tivity and real wages will also increase if attempts are made to update import substitution to keep locally produced products abreast of developments in the developed countries. A policy of import substitution based on producing identical goods to those previously imported is also liable to have an adverse

Table 4

PERCENTAGE INCREASE IN INSTALLED CAPACITY[a] PER PERSON EMPLOYED

Industry	Argentina 1939-53	Brazil 1950-60	Chile 1938-58	Colombia 1953-8	Mexico 1937-44	U.A.R. 1948-58
Non-metallic minerals	26	89	120	60	163	62
Fabricated metal products	101	6		1		4
Electrical machinery		54				
Transport equipment		20				
Furniture		22				
Paper and paper products	58	47		-8		287
Rubber	10	17		17		
Leather	71	51		1		150
Chemicals	99	28		152		189
Textiles	52	48	18	16	116	120
Clothing and shoes	52	33	129	11		
Food products }		58	33			
Drinks	36	62	47	33	55	150
Tobacco		4				
Printing and publishing	107	26		7		
Basic metals	156		160	87	-32	491
Wood products	90	39		43		
Miscellaneous	74	13		30		
Total	62		109	38	56	167

[a] Defined as H.P. per person.

Source: W. Baer and M. Herve, 'Employment and Industrialisation in Developing Countries', *Quarterly Journal of Economics*, LXXX (1966) Table II.

Table 5

RATES OF GROWTH OF OUTPUT AND EMPLOYMENT IN INDUSTRY, 1955-65

Industry group	All developing countries		Latin America		East and South-east Asia	
	Output	Employment	Output	Employment	Output	Employment
Food, drink, tobacco	5·1	3·3	4·5	4·1	6·1	2·9
Textiles	4·0	2·1	2·4	– 1·0	4·4	2·3
Paper and products	9·7	5·0	7·7	2·6	11·0	7·4
Chemicals	8·0	5·2	7·3	3·4	8·6	6·2
Non-metallic minerals	7·6	4·6	5·6	2·6	10·1	6·1
Basic metals	10·0	7·3	8·0	5·1	11·2	9·3
Metal products	10·9	6·8	9·6	—	12·8	8·4
Light manufactures	5·4	3·8	4·0	2·0	6·7	4·2
Heavy manufactures	9·3	6·1	7·9	3·6	10·9	7·7
All manufacturing	7·1	4·4	5·8	2·5	8·1	5·0
Industry as a whole	7·4	4·0	5·9	2·3	8·5	4·8

Source: D. Turnham, *The Employment Problem in Less Developed Countries: A Review of the Evidence* (Paris: O.E.C.D., 1970) Table 1, p. 131.

effect on the local distribution of income. This follows partly from the technology employed: with high labour productivity it is difficult to avoid passing on some of this productivity in real wages. But it is also a question of market creation. As argued earlier, the imported goods from the developed countries tend to be inappropriate for the developing countries: if local markets for such goods are to be maintained, and expanded, unequal purchasing power may be an unavoidable requirement. If all consumers had the incomes of the average, markets for the rich man's goods would be severely curtailed. However, a policy of import substitution based on the production of different and more appropriate products could have quite different implications for factor requirements and income distribution.

Export promotion

The alternative suggested to the import substitution policy strategy is to adopt an export orientated strategy in accordance with comparative advantage.[41] Developing countries should specialise on relatively labour-intensive goods, and also relatively labour-intensive processes,[42] and allow imports to enter freely. Apart from the feasibility of such a policy, which is in grave doubt given the restrictions on imports from developing countries imposed by developed countries, the policy has technological implications. The fact that technology is not static but changes over time means that the products in which developing countries have a comparative advantage also change over time. As Bruno puts it, 'in the static Ricardian model we saw that one could unambiguously rank activities by factor productivity alone. In a dynamic world this is no longer possible. Ranking involves both goods and time.'[43] Bruno illustrates this empirically, showing that ranking of industries according to their dynamic comparative advantage varies substantially with time. This means, in the first place, that developing countries will continually be faced with the necessity to change their production structure to keep up with dynamic comparative advantage. The export strategy will therefore involve considerable adjustment costs which will offset some of the gains from trade.

Both Hufbauer and Vernon have put foward models of how dynamic comparative advantage may operate. Hufbauer[44] suggests that the developed countries will innovate, and because of their technological superiority will export the products of the innovation: this is 'technological gap' trade. But once the technological gap is closed in a particular product, i.e. the technology has been transferred, the low wages of developing countries will give them a comparative advantage: they will be responsible for 'low wage' trade, which they will exchange for 'technological gap' goods. Vernon's product cycle[45] involves a similar though somewhat more complicated process. Again the developed country innovates, but when production is standardised and the product has reached 'maturity', production may be transferred to less developed countries with low wages. In both theories developing countries acquire dynamic comparative advantage in goods for which research and development and innovation occur in the developed countries. But this means, as argued earlier, that the technology of these goods will reflect the factor availability of the developed countries, and the products will be designed with the needs and standards of the developed countries in mind. Hence the process of production – in terms of capital per head, scale for which it is designed, and type of production produced – will be appropriate for the developed countries, not the developing countries. It is true that developing countries' dynamic comparative advantage will always lie with the relatively most labour-intensive products (ignoring skill requirements); but as technological developments occur, products, and processes, will be changed, almost always in a capital-intensive direction.[46] Markets for the products in which the developing countries once had an advantage will disappear, and the developing countries will either have to adapt their product characteristics and processes in line with such developments, or switch their specialisation. Generally, these switches will lead to increasing capital-intensity of production. The kind of continuous adaptation required is indicated by an analysis of the composition of countries' manufacturing exports in 1965, which looked at the first date at which each traded product had been included as a special category in the S.I.T.C. No country had an average first date of earlier than 1944. The analysis only allowed for products sufficiently different from

existing products to qualify for a category of their own in the
S.I.T.C. It thus excluded changes in product characteristics
which, if included, would give a more recent date.[47] The requirements that international trade imposes were illustrated in a
minor way in a recent investigation of foreign investment in
India. The manager of one subsidiary argued that foreign
ownership was essential in the manufacture of chocolate
because this was the only way a firm could be guaranteed
continuous access to the latest technological developments in
chocolate. When asked why it was essential to have such access,
the manager replied that this was the only way to maintain
exports to other developing countries, where they faced competition with chocolates from the developed countries.[48] On the
export side the free trade strategy, while initially probably
leading to more labour-intensive production techniques than
the type of import reproduction strategy adopted in the past,
will subsequently require continual modification in a capital-
intensive direction, so long as innovations continue to come
primarily from the developed countries. Thus the relatively
labour-intensive products will be displaced by more capital-
intensive products and the exports and production of the
developing countries will have to adapt accordingly. Technological dependence on the developed countries will be maintained, since without the technological transfer from the
developed countries the developing countries will not be able to
compete in international trade. Modification of techniques in a
labour-intensive direction will rarely be possible because this
would lead to modification of product unacceptable to the
developed countries who, by hypothesis, provide the main
markets. Equally, sticking to the labour-intensive techniques
will not be possible because the products so produced will
become unsaleable.

Export of labour-intensive processes

So far the discussion has concentrated on the consequences of
export orientation based on exporting labour-intensive products.
Different considerations arise from exporting labour-intensive
processes:[49] they too are likely to be subject to change as the
products, of which they form a part, change. But such change

need not involve more capital-intensity – in so far as the existence of relatively cheap labour is taken into account by the multinational corporations when they develop new products. Thus, such an export strategy need not involve the dynamic technological implications (and disadvantages) of the products policy. But, as compared with a products policy, a process policy has its own disadvantages which may limit its adoption, both within and between countries. In the first place, such a policy implies specialisation according to factor endowment in a particularly simple form: the developing country provides the unskilled labour, the developed country any management skills and materials required. Although there may be incidental linkages and externalities these are likely to be minimal, and a continued policy encouraging such developments involves continued specialisation on unskilled labour – which by some would be defined as a continued process of underdevelopment. A products specialisation policy is much more likely to generate linkages both backwards and forwards and develop local skills of various kinds. Secondly, such a policy has continued dependence built in. The labour-intensive process is just one part of the operation of a multinational company. This one part, therefore, is dependent on the parent company for supplies of inputs, for outlets for outputs, and for all decisions about the continuation and scale of operations. The country has a very limited bargaining position since without the co-operation of the parent company they will probably be unable to secure inputs or sell output. In contrast, the worst that can happen to the company is that the country stops co-operating and it can then switch to other countries – which, since the investment required is small,[50] will not be costly. For reasons such as these (and because of the growing opposition among developed countries' unions) it seems unlikely that process specialisation will be accepted on a sufficient scale to make the discussion of product specialisation irrelevant.

Free trade and inputs

The free trade strategy will also ensure that a considerable proportion of consumer goods in developing countries are imported. This has implications for consumption patterns. As argued earlier, products produced in, and primarily for, developed countries will often be inappropriate for poorer countries. Free trade will ensure that developing countries have continuous access to the latest product developments in the developed countries. The result is likely to be that those who have income will spend it on such products, creating dissatisfaction among those who have less income, and leading to the neglect of any attempt to develop appropriate products that might be consumed on a mass scale. In Argentina they are now debating whether to introduce colour television, despite the subsistence standards of one-third of the population. A recent *Times* Survey[51] contrasted consumption patterns in mainland China and Taiwan: 'Correspondents remarked on mainland streets empty of vehicles except for bicycles and called attention to the universal, sexless costume of tunic and trousers. Taiwan has traffic jams and fashion shows. The mainland is estimated to have 100,000 television sets. Taiwan has 1,000,000 and three networks reaching all the heavily populated parts of the island.'

So long as developing countries are following a free trade strategy with the developed countries, their technology, and their own consumption patterns, will be largely dictated by product and taste developments in the developed countries. Dynamic comparative advantage, as outlined by Hufbauer and Vernon, involves continuous technological dependence on the developed countries. Any attempt to devote resources to their own innovations, to product and factor proportions appropriate to their own circumstances, is likely to be thwarted by the far greater resources of the developed countries, so that the new technologies developed may be unable to compete with those of the developed countries. So far the belief appears to be that the sincerest form of competition is imitation. Even industries producing capital goods have departed little from the technology of the developed countries.[52] Developing countries do not have the resources to initiate new products and new patterns of consumption in the developed countries; hence they are for ever followers, never leaders. The technological dependence that such policies tend to maintain involves substantial costs for the technologically dependent countries, not simply in terms of lack of independence, or psychic costs, but in terms of bargaining position vis-à-vis the initiators of the foreign technology, and consequent payments for technology and inputs.[53] Recent estimates[54] show that in 1968 open payments for technology transfer amounted to 5 per cent of export earnings, and these are likely to rise to about 15 per cent by the late 1970s. But these estimates exclude the more hidden methods by which some payments are made, e.g. overpricing of inputs.[55] The few cases[56] in which these payments have been identified suggest that they may be far larger than the overt payments.

CONCLUSION

Products are the link between production and consumption, technology and tastes. Products designed in and for the developed countries are doubly inappropriate for developing countries: inappropriate for production because their technology reflects the capital- and skill-intensive and large-scale conditions of their country of origin; inappropriate for consumption because their characteristics are those appropriate for the much richer consumers in developed countries. Hence it follows that it is inappropriate for developing countries to consume those goods that developed countries produce, and inappropriate for developing countries to produce those goods that developed countries consume. Free trade which encourages production for and consumption from developed countries is likewise under suspicion. But the failure of the past programme of import substitution does not suggest that this is a desirable alternative. This failure, it was argued above, was due to the wrong type of import substitution: an attempt to produce identical products to those previously available from the developed countries. What is needed is the development of appropriate products based on an appropriate technology – one developed in the light of conditions and factor availability in the developing countries. Necessity is the mother of invention. So long as needs are met by developed countries, product developments in the developing countries will be limited, while so long as competition with developed countries takes place in other developing countries, each country may be forced to adopt the latest technology. If the Philippines prohibited chocolates or chocolate technology from the advanced countries, India would not need to adopt the latest Western technology to compete there, and a simpler and more appropriate technology and product could be maintained.

Of course, there are many difficulties to the course advocated, and many gains from trade not discussed here. To stop the sale of primary goods and hence the valuable acquisition of foreign exchange would be self-defeating. In any case, the arguments do not apply to most primary products since production and technical innovation is concentrated in developing countries. This accounts, in large part, for the continued labour-intensity of processes such as tea and coffee picking and processing. The rapidly growing phenomenon of process specialisation may also be exempt from the increasing capital-intensity of methods resulting from technical change, to which product specialisation is subject. However, this development has its own drawbacks. Some products from the developed countries are essential, e.g. some drugs. Others are much cheaper than the alternatives despite their other disadvantages, and may remain cheaper despite research. The policy is only a possibility if the developing countries have resources to devote to the development of appropriate technology and products. For this reason it is not a possibility for any single country, but is a policy for developing countries jointly to pursue. What is being argued here is not no trade, but controlled trade and a substantial reorientation towards *inter-developing* countries' patterns of trade.

This paper has been concerned with some of the implications of changing technology combined with free trade. Little emphasis has been placed on the costs of adjustment to changing technology. Such costs were brilliantly illuminated in D. H. Robertsons' well-known parable – originally developed with reference to U.S.–U.K. trade:

The simple fellow who, to the advantage of both, has been earning a living by cooking the dinner for a busy and prosperous scientist wakes up one day to find that his master has invented a completely automatic cooker, and that if he wants to remain a member of the household he must turn shoeblack. He acquires a kit and learns the techniques, only to find that his master has invented a dust-repelling shoe, but would nevertheless be graciously willing for him to remain on and empty the trash-bins. Would he not do better to remove himself from the orbit of the great man and cultivate his own back garden? And if he can find some other simple fellows in the same boat with whom to gang up and practise the division of labour on a less bewildering basis, so much the better for him.[57]

Notes

1. I have benefitted from comments on an earlier draft from N. Norman, H. Singer, G. Helleiner, S. J. Patel and P. P. Streeten.

2. See *The Futurist*, v (1971) no. 4, p. 153.

3. This, of course, is the widely accepted Pareto criterion of an increase in economic welfare. It need not represent an actual increase in welfare if in fact, as a result of the change, the distribution of income worsens and those who lose are not compensated by those who gain. It need not represent a potential increase in economic welfare if external diseconomies of consumption are such that there is no distribution of the additional goods in which the benefits conferred by consumption of the extra goods outweigh the costs imposed by the jealousies, etc., engendered by seeing others get more goods or, in de Graaff's terms, external effects in consumption are 'excessive'. See J. de V. Graaff, *Theoretical Welfare Economics* (Cambridge Univ. Press, 1957) p. 51.

4. W. W. Leontief, 'Domestic Production and Foreign Trade: The American Capital Position Re-examined', *Proceedings of the American Philosophical Society*, xcvii (1953) 332–49.

5. See M. Tatemoto and S. Ichimura, 'Factor Proportions and Foreign Trade: The Case of Japan', *Review of Economics and Statistics*, xli (1959).

6. D. F. Wahl, 'Capital and Labour Requirements for Canada's Foreign Trade', *Canadian Journal of Economics and Political Science*, xxvii (Aug 1961).

7. Other explanations had to do with resource-intensity, factor-intensity reversals and the structure of tariffs for the United States. For other countries the downward/upward breakdown of trade patterns explained part of the paradox.

8. See H. B. Lary, *Imports of Manufactures from Less Developed Countries* (New York: National Bureau of Economic Research, 1968).

9. These are rigorously described in J. Bhagwati, 'The Pure Theory of International Trade: A Survey', *Economic Journal* (1964), reprinted in *Surveys of Economic Theory*, 2 (London: Macmillan, 1965), and in H. G. Johnson, *International Trade and Economic Growth* (London: Allen & Unwin, 1958) p. 18.

10. For the Heckscher–Ohlin theory to provide a unique solution, rising marginal costs must be assumed. The assumption of perfect competition itself requires rising costs, so strictly these are not separate. See

P. Scaffa, 'The Laws of Returns under Competitive Conditions', *Economic Journal* (1926).

11. H. G. Johnson, *Comparative Cost and Commercial Policy Theory for a Developing World Economy* (Wicksell Lectures, 1968) pp. 9–10.

12. That this is so is of course accepted in the development of the theory of the second best.

13. For an earlier theoretical justification of the view vis-à-vis development, see H. G. Johnson, 'Tariffs and Economic Development: Some Theoretical Issues', *Journal of Development Studies*, I 1 (Oct 1964).

14. Ian Little, Tibor Scitovsky and Maurice Scott, *Industry and Trade in Some Developing Countries* (Oxford Univ. Press, 1970).

15. They argue for an average rate of promotion to manufacturing industry among the less developed countries of 5 per cent (ibid., p. 158); among the 'wealthier developing countries . . . very little by way of subsidisation (or protection) can be justified at all'.

16. The dynamic advantages of trade were perhaps best put by John Stuart Mill: 'A people may be in a quiescent, indolent, uncultivated state, with all their tastes either fully satisfied or entirely undeveloped, and they may fail to put forth the whole of their productive energies for want of any sufficient object of desire. The opening of foreign trade, by making them acquainted with new objects, or tempting them by the easier acquisition of things which they had not previously thought attainable, sometimes works a sort of industrial revolution in a country whose resources were previously undeveloped for want of energy and ambition in the people: inducing those who were satisfied with scanty comforts and little work, to work harder for the gratification of their new tastes, and even to save, and accumulate capital, for the still more complete satisfaction of those tastes at a future time.' J. S. Mill, *Principles of Political Economy*, vol. II, bk iii, chap. xvii, sec. 5, quoted in G. M. Meier, *The International Economics of Development* (New York: Harper & Row, 1968). It is interesting to compare Mill's demonstration effect, which operates on production as well as consumption, inducing work and savings to satisfy the aspirations to different standards which develop through contact, with the modern (Nurkse) demonstration effect which is confined to consumption and not production, and hence tends to bring about unrealisable demands.

17. H. G. Johnson (ed.), *Trade Strategy for Rich and Poor Countries* (London: Allen & Unwin, 1971).

18. Ibid., p. 14.

19. Quotations from Johnson, *International Trade and Economic Growth*.

20. L. U. Wagner found that post-1945 innovations resulting from applied research and development were obsolete after nine years, according to a survey he conducted: 'Problems in Estimating R. and D. Investment and Stock', *Proceedings of the American Statistical Association, Business and Economic Section* (1968) pp. 189–97.

21. See 'The Channels for the Transfer of Technology from Developed to Developing Countries', for a comprehensive discussion of the different

mechanisms involved, prepared by C. Cooper with F. Sercovitch, UNCTAD document, TD/B/AC 11/5 (1971).

22. This of course is Schumpeter's view of innovation.

23. The implicit assumption that within a country at each point of time for each industry there is a single technology is very misleading. There are (sometimes considerable) internal lags between the adoption of a new technique by one firm and its widespread diffusion within the same country. These internal lags apply both within the innovating country and within the recipient country. Internal lags between innovation and diffusion have been explored by W. E. G. Salter in *Productivity and Technical Change*, 2nd ed. (Cambridge Univ. Press, 1969).

24. M. V. Posner, 'International Trade and Technical Change', *Oxford Economic Papers* (Oct 1961) argued that the gap between innovation and imitation provided an important source of international trade: for similar reasons G. Hufbauer, *Synthetics and International Trade* (1966) classifies trade arising from innovations in one country as 'technological gap' trade, and provides examples of such trade in synthetics. C. Freeman, 'The Plastics Industry: A Comparative Study of Research and Development', *N.I.E.S.R.*, no. 26 (Nov 1963) provides evidence of the way in which research and development may lead to innovations and subsequently to international trade.

25. 98 per cent of all research and development expenditure that takes place in the world is located in the developed countries, according to the 'Draft Introductory Statement for the World Plan of Action for the Application of Science and Technology to Development, prepared by the "Sussex Group" '.

26. J. Schmookler, *Invention and Economic Growth* (Cambridge, Mass.: Harvard Univ. Press, 1966) shows that economic considerations dominate even at the *invention* stage: the number of capital goods patents issued is a function of the level of investment in the industry, i.e. the economic potential of the invention. At the development stage profitability considerations, which subsume questions of factor prices, are bound to be even more important.

27. Though a relevant one: differences in such factors can outweigh differences in purely 'economic' factors in determining the most appropriate choice of technique. For example, Hirschman believes that the machine-paced/operator-paced distinction combined with social conditions justifies the use of capital-intensive techniques in developing countries. See A. O. Hirschman, *The Strategy of Economic Development* (New Haven: Yale Univ. Press, 1958).

28. See W. E. Gustafson, 'Research and Development, New Products and Productivity Change', *American Economic Review, Papers and Proceedings*, LII (1962).

29. See G. F. Bloom, 'Union Wage Pressure and Technological Discovery', *American Economic Review* (Sep 1951), and Wagner, op. cit.

30. I. Adelman and Z. Griliches, 'On an Index of Quality Change', *Journal of the American Statistical Association* (Sep 1961).

31. Schmookler, op. cit., illustrates how apparently stable products are

continuously improved over time in the case of horseshoes: during the latter half of the nineteenth century more than fifty new patents were granted annually for horseshoes and horseshoe calks. The rate of patent issue fell to virtually nothing as the twentieth century proceeded, reflecting the declining use of literal horse-power in the United States, and illustrating the importance of economic conditions in the country of origin on the type of product developments that occur. See ibid., Fig. 8 and Table A-3.

32. For a fuller discussion of the relation between products and needs, see F. Stewart, 'Choice of Techniques in Developing Countries', *Journal of Development Studies* (Oct 1972).

33. Just as there are internal lags between innovation and diffusion in techniques (discussed above), there are also product lags – lags between the initial introduction of a new product and its internal diffusion. The two types of lag are interrelated. Product lags are in part responsible for technique lags and vice versa; hence the factors which account for one type of lag help account for the other. But primary explanations of the lags differ. On the product side, consumer reaction, promotional expenditure, income levels, rate of growth and distribution are important; on the technique side, changes in factor prices.

34. S. Marglin has recently suggested in an unpublished paper, 'What Do Bosses Do? The Origins and Functions of Hierarchy in Capitalist Production', that the initial – early capitalist – pattern of production on the basis of relatively large units was, technically, a relatively arbitrary matter, and represented social rather than technical forces. Historically this may have been so, but once the pattern was established, technological developments fell in line with it so that large-scale production became an essential feature of production even though it may have started as an unnecessary one.

35. M. C. Sawyer, 'Concentration in British Manufacturing Industry', *Oxford Economic Papers*, XXIII 3 (Nov 1971) provides evidence of a further increase in concentration between 1958 and 1963.

36. Figures for innovations, e.g. those for synthetic materials in Hufbauer, op. cit., and for pharmaceuticals in L. H. Wortzel, *Technology Transfer in the Pharmaceutical Industry*, UNITAR Research Report, no. 14, confirm the almost complete hegemony of the developed countries in innovations. According to Wortzel: 'Innovation, in general, is more likely to be brought about by firms operating in markets which are large, rather than small, and which have high income rather than low income.' These are all organised modern-sector innovations. There are product innovations in the informal sector of many developing countries, e.g. the development of sandals made out of old car tyres.

37. For a detailed discussion of the implications for available techniques, see Stewart, 'Choice of Techniques'.

38. Keith Marsden has used the term *import reproduction* to describe the type of import substitution in which exact replication takes place. A policy of import substitution need not imply a policy of import reproduction – since import substitution may occur where imports are replaced (in terms of need fulfilment) by the local production of a different set of

goods. The technical definitions of import substitution used by those who are attempting to measure it, described in P. Desai, 'Alternative Measures of Import Substitution', *Oxford Economic Papers*, XXI (Nov 1971), vary, but probably that most commonly used is that of Hollis Chenery who defines import substitution as 'the difference between growth in output with no change in the import-ratio and the actual growth' ('Patterns of Industrial Growth', *American Economic Review*, (Sep 1960). Whether this definition requires import reproduction or not depends on the way in which output and imports are defined. If the definition is applied to the whole economy, it is clearly possible for import substitution to take place without import reproduction; but if production and imports are related to the same industry, narrowly defined, then import substitution requires import reproduction.

39. R. Hal Mason, *The Transfer of Technology and the Factor Proportions Problem: The Philippines and Mexico*, UNITAR Research Report, no. 10, found very little difference in factor proportions adopted, between U.S. firms and local firms producing the same product.

40. Celso Furtado made essentially this point about the technological implications of an import substitution strategy: 'The industrial nucleus linked with the domestic market develops through a process of displacing importation of manufactured goods . . . . The greatest concern of the local industrialist is therefore to provide an article similar to the one imported. Thus the technological innovations which appear most advantageous are those making it possible to approach the cost and price structure of the developed countries.' *Development and Underdevelopment* (Berkeley: Univ. of California Press, 1964) p. 139.

41. See Johnson, *Trade Strategy for Rich and Poor Countries*, and Little, Scitovsky and Scott, op. cit.

42. The best-known examples of such process specialisation are those of electronic parts that are shipped semi-processed from Japan and the United States to Taiwan, where further labour-intensive activities are carried out and the parts are then shipped back for further processing, and the case of the Swiss watches flown to Mauritius for holes to be drilled and then returned to Switzerland for finishing.

43. M. Bruno, 'Policy for Dynamic Comparative Advantage', in R. Vernon (ed.), *The Technology Factor in International Trade* (New York: N.B.E.R., 1970).

44. In *Synthetics and International Trade*.

45. See R. Vernon, 'International Investment and International Trade in the Product Cycle', *Quarterly Journal of Economics* (May 1966).

46. A similar argument is developed in T. Balogh, *Unequal Partners* (Oxford: Blackwell, 1963) pp. 169–73.

47. Shown in G. Hufbauer, 'Hypotheses and Tests of Trade Patterns', in Vernon (ed.), *The Technology Factor in International Trade*.

48. Information supplied by S. Lall.

The following information is to be found on the packets of K.P., 'Britain's No. 1 NUT': 'The Nuts in this pack are roasted to nut perfection by a special process developed over many years by skilled K.P.

Nut Roasters. They are carefully salted down to the last pinch. They are then packed in the most modern *materials* in Europe's largest and *most up-to-date* Nut Processing Factory, which produces more nuts than are sold by any other brand in the United Kingdom. That is why they taste **fresher, better,** and of course why they are **Britain's No. 1 Nut.**' (Bold type indicates their underlining, italics mine.) For developing countries to compete successfully in this business will require similar methods of production – the 'most up to date', the most 'modern materials' – and consequently almost certainly a large and capital-intensive factory.

49. See G. K. Helleiner, 'Manufactured Exports from Less Developed Countries and Multinational Firms', *Economic Journal*, LXXXIII (March 1973) no. 329, and 'Manufactured Exports and Multinational Firms: Their Impact upon Economic Development' (mimeographed, 1972) for discussion of some of the implications of such specialisation.

50. Figures for the Kaohsiung export-processing zone in Taiwan show capital per employee at the remarkably low level of £520; see Asian Development Bank, *South East Asia's Economy in the 1970s* (London: Longman, 1971). The low figure shows how labour-intensive such processes are – though since the capital comes from the foreign companies, it cannot be said to economise in the country's scarce capital.

51. 8 Oct 1971.

52. See, e.g., W. A. Johnson, *The Steel Industry of India* (Cambridge, Mass.: Harvard Univ. Press, 1966), and N. H. Leff, *The Brazilian Capital Goods Industry, 1929–1964* (Cambridge, Mass.: Harvard Univ. Press, 1968).

53. See C. Vaitsos, 'Transfer of Resources and Preservation of Monopoly Rents', Development Advisory Service, Economic Development Report, no. 168 (mimeographed, 1970), who estimates that foreign firms in pharmaceuticals in Colombia are earning effective rates of return of well over 100 per cent, largely owing to the technological dependence and consequent weak bargaining position of Colombia.

54. 'Transfer of Technology', UNCTAD, Doc. TD/106, chap. ii (mimeographed, 1971).

55. The other methods are outlined in para. 24 of UNCTAD, Doc. TD/ 106.

56. Notably by Vaitsos, op. cit.

57. In D. H. Robertson, *Britain in the World Economy* (Allen & Unwin, 1954) pp. 58–9.

8 Domestic Farm Policies and International Trade in Agricultural Goods

Tim Josling

READER IN ECONOMICS, LONDON SCHOOL OF
ECONOMICS AND POLITICAL SCIENCE

The benefits of specialisation and trade among countries are like motherhood and apple pie; who could possibly be against them? And yet the recent history of trade in agricultural goods is of deliberate distortion of trade patterns, and international discussions of trade liberalisation rapidly reach stalemate. Will agriculture continue outside the liberal trading system developed in the post-war period, or are we merely witnessing a lag as the farming sector becomes reconciled to competition with imports, just as labour unions have in the past come to modify their attitudes towards trade? This paper deals with some of the issues shaping the development of agricultural trade, in particular the importance of national farm policies. The tone is cautiously optimistic; the degree of sophistication with which countries approach agricultural problems is increasing, albeit from a low level. It is not impossible that within the present decade major changes in attitudes and policies will have occurred. But first a brief review of the present situation.

I. STATE OF WORLD TRADE IN FARM GOODS

Agricultural trade increases steadily despite the multitude of restrictions and the development of even more comprehensive forms of protection. Total trade rose by about 5 per cent per year over the last decade. This rate is somewhat slower than that of trade in manufactures, but it exceeds the growth in production and consumption. Schmidt, in a recent paper, has outlined some of the main developments during the 1960s. These include the following:[1]

(i) continued instability and 'surpluses' in many products;
(ii) the continued dominance of developed countries in trade both as a source of exports (55 per cent) and as a destination for imports (71 per cent of trade value);
(iii) the decrease in the share of agricultural trade from developing countries and their continued reliance on developed countries for their food imports;
(iv) the growing dependence of centrally planned economies on imports, in particular from developed countries.

But within these major trends, the situation for individual commodities can be very different. In particular, the market for grain in the Pacific area has expanded, largely owing to the changing attitude of the Japanese government towards agricultural imports. On the other hand, the demand for grain in some parts of Asia has been static or declining as their own agricultural potential is enhanced. The U.K. market for grain and other products has been static for over a decade, as successive governments made room for the fruits of technical change in domestic agriculture by tightening import restrictions. In the E.E.C. a buoyant market for feed-grain during the 1960s concealed the trade-diverting effect of Community preference from American exporters. Trade patterns changed dramatically as the E.E.C. used export subsidies aggressively, in some cases forcing other countries to restrict production to maintain prices. In view of the relatively small amount of world agricultural production that enters trade, the growth noted in the 1960s was quite modest. Suppose, for example, trade represents 10 per cent of production and importing and exporting areas are of comparable size. A 10 per cent increase in production in exporting countries and a corresponding increase in demand in importing countries would imply a 50 per cent increase in trade. That no such changes occur suggests that specialisation is not an increasing influence on agricultural trade. Output and demand increase in both importing and exporting countries and trade increases *pari passu*.

The 'statistical future' is not encouraging from the point of view of the development of trade. F.A.O. projections, based on a continuation of past trade policies and on constant prices, suggest major imbalances as output increases more rapidly than demand for cereals, oilseeds and cakes, fats and oils, and some tropical products.[2] Livestock products in general are expected to experience demand increases sufficient to offset technical change. In an ambitious study brought out as part of the projections exercise, the F.A.O. in collaboration with UNCTAD have relaxed their constant-price assumptions to suggest market-clearing world prices and quantities.[3] Wheat and coarse grain prices might have to decrease by 15 per cent to allow the market to clear in 1980. Similar price declines are suggested for pigmeat. Only for mutton and lamb is the price expected to rise significantly. In other words, governments must accommodate themselves to a steady decrease in the price ratio of grains to livestock products, or use other methods to shift production and consumption patterns. This relative price shift is only to be expected, both as demand for proteins grows faster than for starchy foods and as the generally labour-intensive livestock products are affected more by inflation and are less susceptible to rapid improvements in technology and husbandry. Changes in the rural structure, if isolated from price shifts, also favour extensive cereal production. But in national policy, the grain sector is often a strong political influence and the protection for this sector is seen as the cornerstone of the whole policy. Until governments grapple with this problem, the prospects for an orderly expansion of trade are bleak.

Do we have the institutions that might preside over the better development of world agricultural trade? Certainly, GATT, when established, envisaged that such trade would benefit from the regulation and reduction of protectionist policies. The principles of GATT recognise that agricultural trade based on international division of labour is to the potential advantage of both importing and exporting countries. But countries have found it expedient both to ask for derogations from GATT rules and to be less rigorous in the enforcement of such rules even when exceptions have not been granted. GATT did give exceptional treatment to quantitative import restrictions where allied to domestic supply control.[4] This proviso was inserted on the insistence of the United States, and was designed to cover existing farm programmes. Further support to domestic farm policies was given under the 1951 amendment to Section 22 of the U.S. Agricultural Adjustment Act, which required quotas to be imposed on imports threatening to interfere with domestic farm programmes irrespective of any international obligations. This led to a GATT waiver in 1955 which effectively undermined the U.S. position when asking other countries to adhere to the Articles with regard to agriculture.

The E.E.C. did not need such elaborate legislative machinery: the variable levy common to the major imported products acts as a highly effective quota, only allowing in that quantity of imports which will sell at the price designated as the domestic 'target'. The European countries had in general used the GATT 'balance of payments exceptions'[5] in the post-war period to justify the development of protective devices for agriculture. Quotas, levies and state trading abounded, even for trade within Europe. Attempts to liberalise intra-European trade predated the Treaty of Rome, but needed the imperative of the E.E.C. to bear fruit. Such trade developed rapidly with the removal of restrictions and intra-E.E.C. specialisation flourished at the expense of third countries. One major question for the future is the extent to which developments in agricultural trade liberalisation can take place within GATT, with its chequered history in this field, or whether bilateral or other multilateral institutions will have to be developed.

The history of international commodity agreements has not been inspiring, mainly owing to the inability of governments to develop ways of sharing the costs and distributing the gains from such schemes. The potential benefit of international action has been lost. Producers have rarely been able to achieve the discipline needed to raise prices, and where successful they have often lost markets to non-signatories and to substitute goods. Consumers have no incentive to enter agreements unless price rises are expected – in which case no agreements are suggested. The scope for such action is discussed later, but agreements on a world-wide scale have not been a notable feature of agricultural trade over the last decade. The demise of the Wheat Trade Convention of the International Grains Arrangement stands as a memorial to the commodity agreement solution.

II. NATIONAL POLICIES AND TRADE

Trade liberalisation and expansion in agricultural goods has been hampered by the considerable complexity of national agricultural policies. Many of these policies operate through tariffs and levies on trade, others through quotas and licences, yet more through domestic subsidies and taxes and various rural development and adjustment schemes. Among the more subtle are phytosanitary and animal health regulations, domestic content ratios, marketing organisations, export-credit schemes and tax concessions. All influence trade, and a high proportion of such policies are specifically designed to change trade patterns away from those which would prevail under a liberal trading regime. But not all farm policies reduce the level of trade. A classification of farm policies which has some merit is illustrating this is as follows:

(1) *Policies which alter the demand for farm-owned resources:*

   (*a*) Policies affecting the demand conditions (or the price) of the products.
   (*b*) Policies affecting the supply conditions (or the price) of non-farm inputs, or imported farm inputs.
   (*c*) Policies which influence the market conditions (i.e. the character of the demand relationship) for farm-owned resources.
   (*d*) Policies which change the productivity of farm resources through technical developments or constraints.

(2) *Policies which alter the supply of farm-owned resources:*

   (*a*) Control over the supply of, say, land.
   (*b*) Policies changing the opportunity cost to the farm sector of, say, labour.
   (*c*) Policies influencing the quality of resources, or the effective supply.

Clearly, while many policies under 1(*a*) and (*c*) increase output (and restrict consumption), those under 1(*b*) and 2(*a*) and (*b*) often decrease production in the domestic farm sector. The effect on trade volume is often incidental to the main aims of the policies.[6]

It would be as wrong to condemn all methods of farm support as being trade-distorting as it would to condone these policies as being a purely internal matter of no concern to other countries. Nations insist on the right to control the distribution of both population and income within their territories, even if they have very imperfect control over the levels of these variables. A farm policy which blends elements of rural education, of farm opportunities and of technical change in agriculture can hardly be criticised on the grounds that it influences the level of wheat imports of that country. It might be as well to define overtly protective measures in a more narrow sense to include specifically those policies which fall under categories 1(*a*) and (*b*) above. In this list, examples of these policy measures are given on the left-hand side; on the right are some policy instruments which might be thought of as non- (or only indirectly) protective.

Protective	*Non-protective*
Import restrictions	Farm wage legislation
Export subsidies	Income subsidies
Direct payments	Pensions and social security
Input subsidies	Education schemes
State trading	Research and extension
Market discrimination	Land-improvement schemes
Mixing regulations	Amalgamation grants
Multiple exchange rates etc.	Acreage control etc.

The main advantage of such a classification is that it clarifies both the major issues in agricultural trade-policy discussions by ruling many of the most complex of rural policies to be purely domestic matters, and also the problem of the measurement of protection by concentrating on instruments more capable of quantification. Such a measure of protection is needed at the present time.[7] It could perhaps be undertaken by an international organisation with considerable statistical resources, such as the F.A.O. in conjunction with the GATT, O.E.C.D. and UNCTAD secretariats.

Much of the dissatisfaction with protection measures has come about through the use of concepts inappropriate to the question at hand. Two concepts would seem to be useful in the discussion of national farm policies at the international level:

the *marginal* degree of protection, referring to the effect of small changes by one country in its policy for a particular good; and the *average* degree of protection, when that country removes its policy altogether or replaces it by another. The latter requires knowledge of the effect on the terms of trade and on the relevant parameters of supply and demand response. The same division is appropriate for considering action by groups of countries together.

The marginal degree of protection is useful for a country in deciding on its farm policy.[8] Studies which compare domestic and foreign supply price are implicitly using this concept. Estimates of the effects of removal of policies are rare. One recent F.A.O. study[9] has attempted to gauge the impact of the removal of all protection on prices, output, consumption and income relative to the projected 1980 equilibrium values of these variables if present policies were maintained. Some of the results are reproduced in Tables 1, 2 and 3. The implications are clear, even if there is room for doubt about individual figures. Protection severely restricts total demand for cereals, sugar, beef and butter (Table 1). It is no coincidence that (except for beef) these are 'problem commodities' in world

Table 1

CHANGES IN NATIONAL PRICES, SUPPLY AND DEMAND
VOLUMES IMPLIED BY REMOVAL OF AGRICULTURAL
PROTECTION IN ALL COUNTRIES, RELATIVE TO 1980
EQUILIBRIUM
(percentage changes)

	Developed countries			Developing countries		
Commodity	Price	Supply	Demand	Price	Supply	Demand
Wheat	−16·9	−1·8	1·6	0·0	−1·1	4·9
Rice	−68·1	−22·1	12·7	22·8	6·1	−1·5
Coarse grains	4·5	3·2	10·4	3·9	0·6	1·2
Sugar	−12·4	−14·2	6·4	28·7	14·1	1·2
Vegetable oils	1·7	1·9	3·2	9·1	3·2	−0·4
Beef	−5·8	−5·1	4·8	13·0	8·9	−2·9
Pigmeat	0·3	39·0	−1·6	9·6	−0·3	−4·3
Poultry	−15·5	13·3	−2·6	−1·7	1·1	7·3
Cheese	−2·3	2·5	2·5	23·9	−12·0	−12·0
Butter	−22·6	−4·8	13·9	−12·9	−20·9	16·7

Source: F.A.O., *Agricultural Commodity Projections, 1970-1980*, vol. I, CCP 71/20 (Rome, 1971).

trade. Protection has overpriced wheat relative to feed-grains in developed countries by perhaps 20 per cent. Coarse grains, vegetable oils, pigmeat, poultry and cheese have enjoyed negative effective protection in that their supply would increase with its removal. The same is true for most commodities in developing countries. But marginal rates of protection considerably overstate the average rates for developed countries: world prices (Table 2) would rise for each commodity with the

Table 2

INCREASES IN WORLD PRICE AND VOLUME IMPLIED BY REMOVAL OF AGRICULTURAL PROTECTION
(percentage increase over 1980 equilibrium)

Commodity	Price	Volume	Commodity	Price	Volume
Wheat	28·3	0·8	Beef	20·1	2·2
Rice	64·4	1·6	Pigmeat	9·9	1·3
Coarse grain	23·9	2·5	Poultry	27·8	0·9
Sugar	53·8	3·1	Cheese	30·8	-2·6
Vegetable oils	11·1	2·0	Butter	30·8	5·0

Source: as Table 1.

removal of protection, as would the volume of world production and use in most cases. Some individual industrial countries would find that removal of protection along with that in other nations would increase farm prices. Value added in agriculture (Table 3) would increase substantially as protection was

Table 3

ECONOMIC GAINS FROM A REMOVAL OF AGRICULTURAL PROTECTION

	Total ($ billion)	Per capita ($)
Value added in agriculture:		
Developed countries	19·0	176
Developing countries	27·7	19
Central Plan economies	18·7	27
World	65·4	28
Gross domestic product:[a]		
Developed countries	26·4	27
Developing countries	37·6	16
Central Plan economies	20·3	16
World	84·3	18

[a] Includes value of resource transfer to non-farm sector and development benefits from increased export earnings.

Source: as Table 1.

removed. An increase in per capita income of $18 may not appear to be significant; for the developing countries it represents about 6 per cent of per capita income. However well justified each individual protective device appears to be at the level of domestic farm politics, it is clear that the overall system of agricultural protection is satisfactory to no one.

III. FUTURE DEVELOPMENTS IN AGRICULTURAL TRADE POLICY

To return to the present situation: though studies of the kind described above are essential to indicate the international implications of domestic protective policies, progress towards freer trade will come only gradually and with great difficulty. The arguments for autarky will become increasingly more sophisticated as farm policy 'objectives' are redefined to justify particular policies. Particular farming patterns, themselves a product of *ad hoc* policy decisions, will be sanctified on environmental or social grounds. Spurious quality differences, undetected by consumers, can be used to exclude foreign food. The temptation to resist change by increasing protection will persist, even at the risk of repercussions in other sectors. But in an increasingly interdependent world, countries will eventually find ways of relating domestic to trade policy in a way that neither inhibits their internal development nor causes friction internationally. Only the time-scale is uncertain.

The case for autarky need not be rehearsed. It is not fashionable in international circles, and it is not easy for an economist to do it justice. But it can be easily detected; the use of self-sufficiency ratios in discussions about trade betray the widespread attachment to autarky. The mercantilist concept of trade dominates much of the present controversy. There is a powerful mercantilist argument for trade expansion which is in the nature of an advertising campaign. 'Low-cost suppliers' chide importing countries for restricting markets. One attempts to get 'access' into markets and has as evidence traditional trading patterns and market shares. For an exporter faced with a static home market, diplomatic activity abroad may well be the only way of securing an expansion of demand necessary to justify new investment. But such expansion is often very limited; if exports are but a small part of total sales, a very large increase in trade is needed to expand total demand. Governments too are not averse to salesmanship. A cynic might regard the desire for multilateral agreements as ways of (*a*) establishing some control over the policy of others, and (*b*) avoiding the need for adjustment policies at home. This would appear to be the justification for many actual and proposed commodity agreements. In importing countries, mercantilism is manifest in demands to give home producers preference; imports are seen as debilitating the national economy.

The liberal case for removing trade restrictions rests principally on three contentions:

(i) Interference with trade is an inefficient way of achieving domestic objectives. Except in the case of an 'optimum tariff', such objectives can be better secured by other means: direct subsidies if the aim is to increase production, or income transfer unrelated to output if the aim is income support. Tariffs involve a side-effect, distortion of consumption patterns, which is in general not an aim of the policy.

(ii) Countries have, for reasons of internal political pressure, followed trade policies against their best interests. To persuade governments to relax trade restrictions is to get them to improve their own policies.[10]

(iii) Countries may be able to dismantle tariffs which were put up in retaliation against those of others; although individual action is limited, a multilateral approach may benefit all concerned. It is certainly true that one nation's tariff posture must be decided in the knowledge of that of others. Therefore, a tariff negotiation holds out more promise than a series of unilateral actions.

On the somewhat optimistic assumption that countries do over time develop policies which conflict less with trade – by removing unwanted consumption distortions – and do revise their notions about the desirable level of agricultural protection, one is left to consider the third rationale for trade-liberalisation discussions. Possibilities for action here fall into at least three categories:

(*a*) The chance of negotiating protective barriers which have themselves been premised on the existence of such barriers in other countries. An obvious example is the limitation of export subsidies which in effect procure markets for the country with the largest and most generous treasury. Countries which are the recipients of such generosity often complain that their own farm policies are made more costly. There is some limited scope for agreement on export subsidies on a multilateral basis, even though each individual exporter would suffer a heavy loss in export sales if he were to act alone.

(*b*) The chance of exchanging 'concessions' both within agriculture and also in the markets for other products. Nations would, in essence, be arranging for a transfer of employment among sectors in their own economies by means of adjusting trade barriers. This may in fact be more convenient than using domestic sectoral policies for the same ends. One problem that immediately arises here is that farm policy is in most cases the jealously guarded province of a special ministry. That department commonly identifies its own success with the growth of output of the domestic farm sector. If automobile tariffs were negotiated by the Department of Domestic Automobile Production, and so on with other industries, one would be surprised if the GATT system could have worked. Again one may expect change, but this will require a significant domestic transfer of authority in many countries.

(*c*) The chance of mutual action to benefit a specific country or group of countries. In particular, it might be possible to provide better access to developing country exports under a multilateral deal, whereas individual countries would be unable to act alone. This again depends largely on a political initiative from outside the context of domestic agricultural policy.

One's views on the future development of international agricultural trade diplomacy depend to a large extent on the emphasis given to the arguments above. Much of the conflict between the United States and the E.E.C. regarding the development of the Common Agricultural Policy has centred on the mechanism of the variable levy, the hallmark of the C.A.P. The variable levy is to agricultural policy what the flexible exchange rate is to monetary policy: a device to allow domestic objectives to be pursued without being 'blown off course' by other countries' actions and sudden developments in the rest of the world. Unlike flexible exchange rates, it is an expensive way of buying autonomy. To grant the same degree of income guarantee to producers by more direct means would 'at a stroke' reduce the internal costs, both real and financial, to the Community. Such a change will occur gradually, but it is not easy to see whether diplomatic pressure from other countries will speed up this process or produce a defensive reaction.

The proliferation of variable levies and export subsidies – not only in the E.E.C. – has undoubtedly increased instability on the world market. When goods are exported from a country with a variable export subsidy to one with a variable levy, no 'equilibrium' price exists. Indeed, one might conceive of a 'policy-induced surplus' as existing for those commodities where requirements of importers and exporters do not coincide. Consider some volume of foreign supplies which an importing country will welcome in that it does not depress the price to domestic producers below an acceptable level. Similarly, in an exporting country there will be some volume of production available for export, induced by an acceptable producer price in that country. If the importer will accept less than the exporter has to sell, then a surplus exists. Price changes cannot clear the market, since producers (and consumers) are isolated from such changes. In the absence of domestic policy changes, the world market becomes unstable and the isolationist policies are apparently vindicated. Releasing consumers from the constraints of such policies would improve the functioning of the international market. One may expect increasing pressure on governments to modify the method of farm support both on domestic and also on commercial policy grounds, but one must assume that attempts to improve the stability of farm incomes will continue. The E.E.C. will, for instance, undoubtedly move more towards income support by direct methods and towards lowering the cost of grain and of dairy products to the user or consumer. In this respect the United States is in advance of the

E.E.C. Enlargement of the Community will add to these pressures as the impact of the C.A.P. begins to be felt.

Modifications in the level of protection, as opposed to its method, are more amenable to direct bargaining among governments. Possible approaches to the overall measurement of protection were mentioned in the previous section. Armed with such information, there may be scope for negotiation. Perhaps a binding of the level of support for key commodities is a necessary first step. But it is much more likely that governments will choose to modify the protection they grant to farmers for internal reasons. It is not apparent that the political visibility of farm groups declines with their numbers. It is, however, the case that there is a growing disenchantment with the costs of agricultural protection and in particular with the distribution of these costs and the related benefits.[11] Prices have been reduced, payments to farmers limited, supply controlled and taxes on output levied in the past. It is not the case that all governments are caught on the treadmill of higher farm protection. But the pace by which such adjustments can be made depends on developments in the non-farm economy; it may not be fast enough to prevent the increase of international tension.[12]

Multilateral efforts at reducing trade distortions are at present under discussion. The advanced countries committed themselves, as part of the Smithsonian agreement of December 1971, to a new trade initiative. It is inevitable that this must include agriculture, though it is unlikely that countries will insist on symmetrical progress in this area. In any case, discussions have to take place under the cover of Article XXIV(6) of GATT on possible compensation for injury caused by enlargement of the E.E.C. The products concerned will include temperate-zone foodstuffs. As part of an initiative predating somewhat the Smithsonian talks, the O.E.C.D. established a High Level Trade Group comprising independent members chosen by the governments concerned. Under the chairmanship of Jean Rey, they considered, among other things, the future of trade policy in the agricultural sector.[13] The report exemplifies the divergence of opinion on agricultural trade matters, but it does suggest a list of proposals for improvement 'in the short and medium terms'. Paraphrased from the bland committee prose, these are:

(*a*) to change price ratios among farm products to encourage production to meet anticipated demand and to have periodic (international?) price reviews;

(*b*) to freeze the present level of support;

(*c*) to remove unused protection from trade policies;

(*d*) to review standards, licences, health regulations and other non-tariff trade barriers;

(*e*) to regulate export aids and subsidies;

(*f*) to co-ordinate stockholding policies;

(*g*) to reduce the domestic prices of goods which are sold with an export subsidy;

(*h*) to control supply 'in extreme cases';

(*i*) to give adjustment assistance to producers affected by trade liberalisation;

(*j*) to consider international commodity agreements for certain products;

(*k*) to improve access for developing country exports, by restricting production and reducing protection;

(*l*) to co-ordinate food aid between countries;

(*m*) to increase technical and financial assistance for agricultural development;

(*n*) to establish a framework for consultation and information on agricultural trade problems.

All this was, however, to be done within 'the framework of existing agricultural policies', a restriction which some would view as overly restrictive. The group acknowledge that a measure of progress would be needed such as the *montant de soutien* or the self-sufficiency ratio.

Statements of this kind from governmental and international bodies are not rare. But there does appear to be a consensus emerging on the agenda. Governments may, in the not too distant future, be able to commit themselves to a set of pragmatic measures which, while not extending GATT, make more specific its intentions for agriculture. Coupled with domestic policy developments, this would lead to a considerable improvement in economic and political relationships.

Notes

1. See Stephen C. Schmidt, 'An Enlarged European Community and Agricultural Trade Policy Choices for Third Countries', presented to the Agricultural Economics Society, Oxford, July 1972.

2. F.A.O., *Agricultural Commodity Projections, 1970–1980*, vol. I, CCP 71/20 (Rome, 1971).

3. F.A.O., *A World Price Equilibrium Model*, CCP71/WP3 (Rome, 1971).

4. Article XI(2)(c) of the General Agreement on Tariffs and Trade.

5. Article XII(3)(b).

6. The prime objective in most farm policies is to increase the income of people in farming. Presumably the returns to resources in the farm sector can in the short run be increased by some mixture of policies to increase the demand and to reduce the supply of such resources. Unfortunately, it is much more difficult to maintain an artificially high level of resource returns in a competitive industry where entry is not controlled. Rents accrue to those with specialised skills and to those who own resources not freely available from the non-farm sector. The farm sector commonly adjusts in size to the level of support it receives through government programmes; the new entrant and the marginal unit of investment earn little more than they would in the absence of such policies. The important corollary of this is that removal of farm support harms many in the short run but after adjustment leaves the marginal resource returns relatively unaffected.

7. A measure of protection is, however, only the first stage in the classification of the interaction of national policies on the world market. It would be necessary to extend this to a measure of the production and consumption effects of the protective devices. The production effect will rest on the increase in domestic profitability occasioned by the policy, and there will be a consumption effect depending on the impact on users of the product. These should be measured separately, though the net trade effect will be the sum of the two.

8. See T. Josling, 'A Formal Approach to Agricultural Policy', *Journal of Agricultural Economics* (May 1971).

9. F.A.O., *Agricultural Commodity Projections, 1970–1980*.

10. Liberal and mercantilist arguments are often juxtaposed; a country may be exhorted to open its markets to imports so that it may gain from cheaper supplies while the exporter gains from higher sales.

11. For a recent study of these effects, see T. Josling *et al.*, *Burdens and Benefits of Farm Support Policies*, Agricultural Trade Paper, no. 1 (London: Trade Policy Research Centre, 1972).

12. The desirability of domestic change for its own sake is emphasised in F. McFadzean *et al.*, *Towards an Open World Economy* (London: Macmillan, for the Trade Policy Research Centre, 1972). See also J. Schnittker, *Problems of International Agricultural Trade*, Conference Paper, no. 3 (Newcastle-upon-Tyne: Agricultural Adjustment Unit, 1972).

13. O.E.C.D., *Policy Perspectives for International Trade and Economic Relations: Report by the High Level Group on Trade* (Paris, 1972).

9 Trade negotiations in the Field of Manufactures

Jan Tumlir[1]

DIRECTOR, TRADE INTELLIGENCE DIVISION,
GENERAL AGREEMENT ON TARIFFS AND TRADE,
GENEVA

INTRODUCTION

Since the end of the Kennedy Round, commercial policy problems have been accumulating among the main trading countries, some arising from basic trends of international trade, some created by policy conduct of individual countries and trading entities. It is tempting to make a distinction between real problems and policy irritants, but the distinction would not be an easy one to make, and in practice the latter weigh no less heavily than the former in the contemporary climate of international economic and political relations. The collapse of the monetary system to which the conduct of trade had become attuned provided an occasion to come to grips with these problems.

There is a chance that the negotiation to which all the major trading countries are now committed will establish a new system to rule the conduct of international trade for the next quarter-century. For this chance to be realised the negotiators will need a perspective. In a protracted negotiation such as the one in prospect, the ephemeral irritants can be allayed, or may simply pass away; but the resulting system can be durable only to the extent that it accommodates the basic, the long-term and secular economic needs already manifest in international trade. From this perspective, this paper will concentrate on two main problems to be faced in the negotiation.

The assigned topic being 'negotiation on trade in manufactures', this is the point at which to emphasise the crucial importance of the simultaneous negotiation about agricultural trade. The pattern of trade interests within and between the main trading countries is such that little could be agreed on with respect to trade in manufactures unless a reconciliation of views on, and of interests in, agricultural trade is achieved. The assumption that this is possible underlies the whole subsequent argument.

LONG-TERM TRENDS IN TRADE PATTERNS

The rate of global economic growth achieved in the 1960s was distinctly above that of the preceding decade. The composition of that growth also became more satisfactory, for whereas in the 1950s the growth of total production was more rapid in the industrial than in the less developed areas, in the course of the following decade this difference was reversed. Statistics of international trade show an average annual expansion rate of 7·0 per cent for the 1950s,[2] rising to 9·3 per cent in the following decade. Here too the acceleration was more pronounced in the trade of less developed areas, although the trade of the developed areas continued to grow more rapidly. The proportion of manufactured products[3] in total trade has risen from 45 per cent in 1953 and 50 per cent in 1957 to 62 per cent in 1971. Table 1 summarises the development of these exports, by large product categories and by origin, in the last decade.

The rapid growth of manufactured exports by less developed countries, at an average annual rate almost four percentage points higher than that of exports by industrial countries, deserves attention. It cannot be explained away by reference to the small absolute base, since an analysis by sub-periods shows a continuous acceleration, both in the absolute sense and in relation to world trade in these products.[4] The statistic is in fact the best vindication of the decades of development effort: the compound element of this growth reflects the fact that a *growing* number of less developed countries are reaching that stage of industrial organisation at which production at competitive prices is possible over a *widening* range of manufactures.

Engineering products, including road motor vehicles, constitute more than one-half of manufactured exports originating in industrial countries, and textiles and clothing, together with

Table 1
MAIN FLOWS OF WORLD TRADE IN MANUFACTURES[a]

Exports to: → Exports from: ↓	Industrial areas[b] 1970 ($ billion)	Growth rate 1961-70 %	1961-71 %	Developing areas 1970 ($ billion)	Growth rate 1961-70 %	1961-71 %	Eastern trading area 1970 ($ billion)	Growth rate 1961-70 %	1961-71 %	World[c] 1970 ($ billion)	Growth rate 1961-70 %	1961-71 %
INDUSTRIAL AREAS[b]												
Total manufactures of which:	114·77	13·5	13·6	31·38	7·3	7·9	6·25	13·2	12·8	158·82	11·8	12·0
Iron and steel	9·93	12·2		2·59	6·4		1·03	9·1		13·83	10·6	10·1
Chemicals	12·94	13·5		4·44	8·4		1·09	17·3		19·17	12·1	12·0
Engineering products, incl. road motor vehicles	59·31	14·8		17·37	7·8		2·81	12·5		83·37	12·7	13·0
(Road motor vehicles)	(15·98)	(20·5)		(3·21)	(6·9)		(0·19)	(38·7)		(20·43)	(16·7)	(17·4)
Textiles and clothing	10·05	11·6		2·41	3·8		0·56	24·1		13·56	9·6	10·2
Other manufactures	22·54	11·9		4·57	7·2		0·76	12·7		28·89	10·9	11·1
DEVELOPING AREAS												
Total manufactures of which:	5·96	19·2	19·5	3·19	11·4	12·4	0·42	22·0	22·7	9·80	15·8	16·5
Iron and steel	0·27	18·2		0·25	19·6		0·03	..		0·55	19·6	18·3
Chemicals	0·41	10·3		0·39	14·0		0·05	19·6		0·87	11·4	12·5
Engineering products, incl. road motor vehicles	0·83	33·9		0·77	19·1		0·03	(..)		1·65	24·5	25·0
(Road motor vehicles)	(0·01)	(..)		(0·04)	(..)		(—)	(..)		(0·05)	(..)	(..)
Textiles and clothing	2·04	16·2		0·83	6·5		0·23	25·6		3·23	12·6	14·0
Other manufactures	2·41	21·7		0·95	9·8		0·08	11·5		3·50	17·2	17·3

[a] S.I.T.C. Sections 5–8, excl. division 68 (non-ferrous metals).

[b] United Kingdom figures include all re-exports, and exports of pearls and precious stones. Exports of ships to be registered in Liberia and Panama have been allocated to industrial areas. Exports which are not specified by destination have been distributed proportionately to the value of established exports to the three regions distinguished.

[c] Including Australia, New Zealand and South Africa.

Note: 1971 figures are preliminary estimates only.

Source: GATT, *International Trade 1971*, and previous issues.

other manufactures, more than two-thirds of manufactured exports originating in less developed countries. The narrow spread of category growth rates in the exports of industrial countries, from 10·2 per cent per annum for textiles and clothing to 13·0 per cent per annum for engineering products, can be partly explained by differences in the level of economic development within the group, the relatively less advanced ones among the countries classified in it having been or become dynamic exporters of textiles and other labour-intensive manufactures. One might nevertheless have expected the growth of textile and clothing exports by industrial countries to be less rapid, and that of the same exports by less developed countries to be more so.

The classical labour-intensive[5] products are concentrated in the categories of textiles and clothing, and other manufactures. In the former, both industrial and less developed countries export largely similar products. The latter, on the other hand, contains a variety of products among which two large groups can be distinguished: other labour-intensive consumer manufactures (footwear, travel and sports goods, toys, etc.), prominent in the exports of other manufactures originating in less developed countries, and certain basic semi-manufactures (metal manufactures, pulp and paper, wood panels, etc.) which account for the bulk of industrial countries' exports in this category.

Since the comparative advantage of less developed countries should be at least as pronounced in textiles and clothing as it appears to be in other manufactures, the striking difference in the growth of these two categories of their exports can only be explained by commercial policies of industrial countries. In addition to high tariffs, the protection of their textile industries relies to a large extent on quantitative restrictions and is in several respects of a discriminatory character. The labour-intensive goods included in other manufactures encounter higher-than-average tariffs in all industrial counties, but have so far not been subject to quantitative restrictions to the same extent as trade in textiles and clothing.

Bound tariffs cannot protect against *changes* in comparative advantage. It is important to have a notion of the magnitude of the change likely to occur in this respect between the less developed and the industrial countries in the coming decades. The demographic estimates presented by Mr Robert McNamara to the 1971 annual meeting of the I.B.R.D. provide a succinct indication.

Assuming that intensive birth-control efforts succeed in attaining a net reproduction rate of one (an average of two children per couple) in the less developed areas by the year 2040 and in the developed areas by 2020, the population of the less developed areas would stabilise at 13·9 billion, implying an annual growth rate of 2·42; that of the developed areas would grow by 0·71 per cent per annum to stabilise at 1·8 billion.[6]

For the next fifteen years the growth of total labour force in the two areas is already determined by the age structure of the existing population. The size of the manufacturing labour force in industrial areas can be expected to begin to stagnate or decline in the next thirty years, whereas the urban labour force of less developed areas will be growing at rates from 5 per cent per annum upwards. The relatively labour-intensive industries in the industrial areas lag behind manufacturing as a whole in the growth of labour productivity, while their wages rise in step with the manufacturing wage level, whereas in the less developed areas the same industries, growing rapidly, can achieve significant productivity increases merely through organisational improvements, i.e. with less investment per unit of output, while their real wages are pressed down by continuing unemployment.

The influence of economic policy must also be considered. The sharp acceleration of manufactured exports from less developed areas occurred in a decade in which the import-substitution development strategies, though already waning, still held considerable sway. The visible success of the alternative export-based strategies, pursued so far by only a limited number of less developed countries, can be expected to make converts in the 1970s, especially if the announced trade negotiations succeed in establishing effective safeguards for a continued access of manufactured exports from less developed to industrial countries.

All these prospective developments add up to a strong tendency for most of the classical labour-intensive manufacturing, as well as other manufacturing sectors with relatively stable technology, to move from industrial countries towards the main concentrations of easily available labour.

The categories of chemicals and engineering products contain most of the relatively modern, research-and-development-intensive industrial goods moving in world trade. Highly concentrated among industrial countries, trade in these goods has been expanding very rapidly. In general, it encounters only low tariffs and is practically free of restrictions. Its expansion has been strikingly smooth and free from protectionist agitation.

In the industries included in these two categories, each industrial country is an exporter as well as an importer and the growth of trade among them has been distributed fairly evenly. The fact that trade expansion in this area has assumed the form of intra- rather than inter-industry specialisation cannot, however, fully explain its speed and smoothness. An important but not exactly ascertainable part of these exchanges takes place between firms belonging to the same international concerns, exchanging manufactures at different stages of completion; here, obviously, the import-adjustment problem is minimal.[7] Nonetheless, the larger part of imports, particularly of engineering products, consists of finished products exported by independent firms. A progress towards specialisation enforced through competition among independent producers would have been more gradual and would have given rise to much more protest by import-competing firms than was actually heard. The difference between specialisation issuing from such a protracted competitive struggle, and the decisive, large-scale conversion which seems in fact to have been the rule, must be assumed to have been made by inter-firm agreements. Specialisation agreements or directives can be automatically assumed in the case of multinational firms. The purely or mainly national firms in these industries, at least in Europe, are being forced by the competition of the multinationals into co-operative agreements with their counterparts across the border. These agreements usually provide for joint research, marketing, components production or subcontracting and, ultimately, for product differentiation and specialisation. Fostered by such devices, production specialisation proceeded so rapidly that in many European countries and industries, e.g.

industrial machinery, scientific apparatus, etc., a substantial proportion of imports is no longer directly competitive with domestic output.[8]

Engineering products are also the most rapidly expanding export flow from less developed countries. Its growth seems to stem from two characteristics which could be only imperfectly documented at present. It appears that in less developed countries, multinational firms supply a considerably higher proportion of engineering exports than they do in the industrial countries.[9] Second, and in part related to the preceding, a higher proportion of engineering exports by less developed countries consists of components and of re-exports of products brought in for 'contract processing'.[10] Jointly, these two conditions make it possible for the less developed countries to participate in the most rapidly expanding area of world trade on the basis of their comparative advantage based on abundance of labour and, even more important, to do so in a way which minimises the export-marketing and import-adjustment problems.

Only a broad qualitative assessment of the prospects for science-based or technological-gap trade is possible in view of the difficulties of statistical measurement in this area. It seems on the whole reasonable to expect that the rapid development observed in the past decade will continue and may even accelerate further. At the present level of research and development effort, the scope for organisational improvements is enormous. Communication systems are being improved at a rate which dwarfs all other productivity increases. Technology is increasingly fluid internationally, and in basic science a perfectly internationalised system exists within which knowledge and talent move at minimum cost. While these conditions facilitate specialisation in research, the growing importance of research expenditures in total cost of production enforces it. The frequent resort to formal agreements on pooling or co-ordination of research by European firms has already been mentioned. Those firms which for various reasons have to keep their research internal characteristically devote a significant, probably also growing, part of it to finding out what their competitors are doing; and on balance, this information must also tend to reduce the area of directly competitive research.

The general intensification and better organisation of both scientific and applied research must also be expected to lead to the emergence of new science-based industries, some growing up spontaneously at the frontiers of knowledge, some created by deliberate concentration of effort in certain areas. The amounts of government funds spent on research in such industries as aerospace, electronics and nuclear engineering suggest that, within very broad limits, any industry could become science-based if given sufficient priority in public research budgets. Social demand for new technologies in such areas as environment protection, energy generation, transport, education, medical care, etc., is growing rapidly, and while in the defence industries public-financed research will continue to be essentially competitive, in these areas it is more likely to be co-ordinated, i.e. specialised, internationally, with predictable effects on national industries.

These two trends thus point to an increasingly 'fine-mesh' international specialisation in the advanced-technology industries and a growing intensity of trade. In the progress of this specialisation, the possibility of any one country dominating trade in several of the most advanced industries would steadily diminish.

These are, in sum, the main facts with which international economic organisation will have to cope. The dynamism evident in contemporary world economy has been shown to derive from three sources: divergent population trends between the less developed and the industrial areas; increasingly specialised and effective application of science to production; and the growing ease with which capital and technology can be transferred internationally. These basic tendencies explain the remarkable acceleration of the flow of international trade since 1960, in the course of which other important changes have taken place. Industries in all countries, but especially the advanced-technology industries of the most developed ones, have become much more trade-dependent than before. A number of less developed countries have acquired substantial stakes in the export of manufactures, and others have begun to revise their economic policies with a view to deriving from the expansion of this trade new impulses for their own development. While differential rates of trade expansion have brought about a redistribution of commercial power among the United

States, the E.E.C. and Japan, the combined trade of this group of three[11] continued to grow more rapidly than world trade.

The difficulty of adjustment to this manifold change was the main cause of the growing tension in the international economic system which finally erupted in the monetary and commercial crisis of 1971.

NEGOTIATIONS

The post-war payments system – the I.M.F. and GATT – was designed with the tasks of reconstruction uppermost in the minds of its engineers. In the perspective just outlined, the paramount function of the system to emerge from the forthcoming monetary and trade negotiations will be twofold. It should promote the growth of the production capacity of less developed areas by integrating it more efficiently with that of the more advanced regions, while allowing the industrially advanced countries to control the accelerating transformation of their own economies, societies, and even physical environment, without impairing the economically vital features of their interdependence.

These two objectives require not so much a power balance as an active and intensive co-operation among the largest trading units. To formulate an international trade policy capable of securing that co-operation, the announced trade negotiation will have to agree on new rules of conduct in those matters in which most political tension has been generated in the recent past. With respect to trade in manufactures, there are two: preferential trading agreements (GATT Article XXIV) and emergency trade restraints imposed in disregard of existing rules (Articles XII[12] and XIX).

The trade negotiation will be facilitated by the parallel reform of the international monetary system. Three distinct issues are involved in this reform, of which two – the supply of reserve liquidity, including its link with economic assistance, and the composition of reserves, including the problems of dollar convertibility and of the 'overhang' – are not directly related to conditions of trade and can be negotiated separately. The third, however – the adjustment mechanism – has an immediate bearing on the conduct of commercial policy.

What made trade negotiations so difficult in the past was the need of each party to obtain reciprocal concessions as an offset to the balance of payments and employment effects of its own tariff cuts, combined with the fact that in the precise form in which reciprocity was needed, that is, in the form of concessions so arranged as to match the volumes of *incremental* imports and exports, it could not be exactly determined in advance. A monetary system allowing a higher degree of exchange-rate flexibility, automatic and/or discretionary, would provide offsets to the deflationary effects of tariff changes. It would thus not only reduce the technical difficulty of trade negotiation by lessening the importance of reciprocity, but also alter the balance of domestic interests impinging on the negotiator by giving the export sector a reason to press for even unilateral reductions in the national tariff.

TARIFFS

The tariff has been shown to be increasingly ineffective as a means of protection. In the classical labour-intensive industries, the comparative advantage of the less developed countries has already become too large to be frustrated by a customs tariff at any politically tolerable level. Here the preferred means of protection are quantitative import restrictions and 'voluntary' export restraints which are capable of insulating the protected industry from adverse *changes* in comparative advantage without making the cost of protecting it too visible. The same insufficiency of tariff protection exists in those more modern sectors of manufacturing, particularly engineering, in which production processes can be subdivided according to their factor-intensity and located accordingly.

In the capital- and research-intensive sectors of manufacturing, specialisation is making tariffs increasingly unnecessary, in some cases even unwanted. In these industries, the domain of the large, oligopolistic, internationally mobile firm, the effects of the tariff on the profitability of the national firms have become questionable. Where the tariff might constitute a significant advantage to those behind it, it attracts direct investment;[13] and as a local producer, the foreign firm will be a more formidable competitor than it was as a distant exporter.

National firms are therefore increasingly looking towards subsidies, government purchasing practices and non-tariff means of a similar nature for assistance in competition against multinational firms; and the governments, for their part, are becoming aware of the wastefulness of international investment motivated solely by obstacles to trade.

In the shrinking middle ground between these two extremes, tariffs continue to play their traditional role, the protection they provide being particularly important for industries supplying certain basic semi-manufactures, the production of which in industrial countries is largely dependent on imports of significantly weight-losing primary materials. The nominal protection granted to these industries in the industrial countries is only moderate, but since the value added by them generally represents a relatively small fraction of gross product value, the effective protection they have been enjoying has been considerable.

The available alternatives as to tariff-negotiating techniques have already been described, analysed and assessed in some detail by such writers as H. G. Johnson, H. Corbet[14] and the Curzons. The following brief review of these alternatives will attempt to stress those aspects which may not have received adequate attention before.

There is an agreement among the above-mentioned writers to the effect that the *Kennedy Round formula* of linear reductions – both as a method and as an objective – is unpromising, given its inherent arduousness in relation to its maximum possible achievement. An additional disadvantage is the difficulty of including in this type of negotiation the labour-intensive industries of immediate export interest to less developed countries – a problem which it was possible, to some extent, to defer in the 1960s but which could no longer be deferred this time.

The notion of *tariff harmonisation* as a possible negotiating method does not seem to have much chance of being adopted, not merely because there is little attractiveness in the idea of having harmonious tariffs, but mainly because the basic premise of the approach, namely that the most protective element of a tariff is to be found in the last few percentage points, seems contradictory to economic reasoning and experience. The opposite assumption, that the early cuts will generate more additional trade than cuts eliminating the last few percentage points of a formerly high tariff,[15] is much more plausible. The elasticity of import demand with respect to price (or tariff) change should be the higher, the smaller the share of imports in domestic consumption of the product in question; and to the extent that tariffs protect, the higher the tariff, the lower in general would be the share of imports in domestic consumption.

The *sectoral approach*, favoured by some countries, is to an extent inevitable: any negotiation will, at a certain stage and in certain areas, have to proceed by broadly defined sectors, given the large number of sector-specific problems. A negotiation which would aim at different degrees of liberalisation in different sectors would, however, already at the outset encounter the serious difficulty of exactly defining the sectors. The repercussions of a given degree of liberalisation in one sector on other sectors would differ from country to country, and each would consequently need a different definition.

These three techniques were either used or contemplated and discussed in previous negotiations. This time, governments of the main trading countries are also exploring a new and much more radical approach, namely the possibility of an agreement on a complete elimination of tariffs and of all except temporary non-tariff restrictions[16] on trade in industrial products over ten to twenty years, to be extended on a most-favoured-nation basis to less developed countries. A recognition of the growing inadequacy of tariffs as a means of protection, and of the misallocation of international investment they cause, has no doubt helped this proposition to be considered a realistic possibility at the official level. However, the main condition which makes a negotiation aimed at tariff-free industrial trade both possible and urgent has ripened only in the past year.

The crisis of the autumn of 1971 has revealed the full extent of the tensions created in the fabric of international relations by the proliferation of preferential trading arrangements in the last fifteen years.[17] Coinciding with the crisis, the establishment of a free-trade area comprising virtually the whole of Europe represents a major watershed. The enlarged European market is bound to attract a new wave of foreign investment and a new host of applicants for special association arrangements which, in view of precedents, it might be difficult to refuse. Should the continued existence of tariffs be taken for granted, counter-moves would follow almost of necessity, inducing a development the ultimate outcome of which could be the disintegration of an open economic system into trading blocs and contested spheres of influence. The only constructive alternative to this course is a transition to free trade in industrial products among all industrial countries, guaranteed by a formal agreement.

The novel element of this approach, let us note, is the agreement, not the transition. The objective of free trade in ten to twenty years does not imply annual tariff reductions any larger than those effected, on annual average, in the last twenty-five years. More specifically, the transition is equivalent to holding two more Kennedy Rounds, resulting in tariff cuts of the same absolute extent as the first one, at, say, six-year intervals. The comparison of these two alternatives may be enlightening.

The experience of the Kennedy Round has shown that the technical difficulties intrinsic to reciprocal tariff bargaining tend to fill the negotiation period, leaving little time for non-tariff barriers and such amendments of the basic rules as changing conditions may require. The relevant political aspect of this technique is that it proceeds towards an agreement, precarious until the end, by a series of national confrontations in which the common interest disappears from sight; the conclusion of each negotiation thus opens a period of uncertainty during which the protectionist elements can rally.

The main advantage of the free-trade agreement, in contrast, is that it gives certainty over a long period, to the trading community as to the future policies of each country, and to each national industry as to the competitive situation it will be facing. Import-competing industries naturally prefer protection to adjustment and, when there is a chance of obtaining the former, will devote much effort and ingenuity to political campaigns; when faced with a firm schedule of tariff reductions, the effort and ingenuity will go into adjustment. Technically, this approach is more appropriate to a negotiation the objective of which is not merely tariff reductions but a reform of the trading system: the negotiation would start from an agreement and be about modalities, schedules of liberalisation and rules of conduct.

With the phasing-out of tariffs, less developed countries

would lose the advantage they now possess under the various generalised schemes of preference. They would, it is true, continue to receive special tariff treatment beyond the period for which it was originally granted, and the scope of the treatment could be extended in the transition to tariff-free industrial trade. None the less, the preferential margins would be diminishing. In planning their negotiating strategy, less developed countries should take three points into account.

First, while it is admitted that preferences constitute an advantage, for theoretical as well as practical reasons the value of this advantage cannot be determined with any degree of precision. The existing schemes are complex and in constant revision, the extent of preferential access they allow remaining uncertain. It will be impossible to distinguish imports that are competitive by virtue of the preference from those competitive across the most-favoured-nation tariff; indeed, where limits are enforced, even a statistical distinction between preferential and m.f.n. imports from the same country may be impossible.

Second, the progressive elimination of tariffs would give a further stimulus to the expansion of trade among industrial countries precisely in those areas in which it has been growing rapidly and has already attained a high degree of intensity, that is to say, in the relatively modern or technologically advanced industries such as chemicals, industrial, transport and scientific equipment, and in those manufactured consumer goods which are traded mainly on the strength of their quality and design. Since these countries continue, with only minor interruptions, to experience relatively very high levels of employment, this expansion of trade and of the export-producing industries would bring about a more rapid withdrawal of resources, particularly labour, from those of the import-competing industries in the industrial areas which are of immediate export interest to less developed countries. In other words, the tariff-free situation would promote a more rapid progress towards a new global division of labour than has been experienced in the past.

Third, and most important, the expansion of less developed countries' exports in the past decade, indicating their export potential, suggests the appropriate form of compensation to be demanded for the gradual disappearance of preferences. As their export industries grow in scale and efficiency, the issue of security of their access to markets abroad grows in importance. To safeguard their unrestricted access to the large markets and to obtain more liberal access for those exports which are already under restraint, less developed countries need additional commitments and strengthened international procedures of enforcement. It is in the negotiation of such safeguards that less developed countries could obtain most valuable concessions.

SAFEGUARDS AND QUANTITATIVE RESTRICTIONS

To be able to commit themselves to a schedule of tariff cuts extending over a number of years, governments need safeguards, that is, agreed rules according to which tariff cuts might be postponed, or quantitative restrictions imposed, on imports whose unrestrained growth exceeded the adjustment capacity of the corresponding domestic industries, or threatened other unacceptable damage. A number of countries feel strongly that the formulation of such rules should be an integral part of the forthcoming general trade negotiation.

GATT already contains at least nine different safeguard clauses,[18] the most general of them in Article XIX on emergency action on certain imports, yet they have been invoked less and less frequently. Article XIX authorises emergency import-restricting measures on the conditions that (*a*) actual or threatened injury to domestic industries is shown, (*b*) the countries concerned consult each other and (*c*) the import restraints are non-discriminatory. However, most of the numerous import restraints imposed in this period for the purpose for which Article XIX had originally been intended were imposed either under the much more permissive Long-Term Arrangement on Trade in Cotton Textiles, or without any GATT sanction at all. Faced by this reluctance of trading countries to use the existing safeguard clauses, apparently because the obligations which they impose on the import-restraining country are considered too onerous, are we not to fear that the new clause to emerge from the new negotiation could be so loose as to empty the tariff agreement of meaning? In this situation, Corbet's conclusion that 'GATT needs not so much to be reformulated as reasserted' seems hard common sense.

Yet it is, on reflection, rather wistful. It is hard to believe that

GATT could be reasserted by a simple collective agreement to return to a situation *quo ante*, an Eden before the fall where rules had been observed, without some old rules being rewritten and some additional principles and rules being formally accepted. The economic changes and prospects described earlier make Article XIX even less satisfactory today, to even more countries, than it was a decade ago. The Article is at the same time too exacting, in that the country invoking it risks retaliation or paying too much for taking emergency action, and too lenient, in allowing emergency protection to become permanent.

Should the consultation required by Article XIX not satisfy a country whose export interest was adversely affected, it could retaliate against the country taking action by withdrawing from it, in a discriminatory fashion, past concessions of substantially equal value. To avoid retaliation, countries invoking Article XIX offered in certain cases compensation in the form of most-favoured-nation concessions on selected products exported by the complaining country. It is clear, however, that cases amenable to settlement by a withdrawal or offer of *equivalent* concessions must be exceedingly rare. Since the emergency action itself must conform to the most-favoured-nation rule, it may adversely affect a number of exporting countries each of which may demand or withdraw a concession on a different product. In most instances, it can be seen beforehand that it will be impossible to reach a mutually satisfactory settlement on the basis of reciprocity and the country in emergency does not invoke the Article.

On the other hand, Article XIX authorises protective action against imports which 'cause or threaten serious injury' for 'such time as may be necessary to prevent *or* [italics mine] remedy such injury'. No remedial action being prescribed, protection is in effect sanctioned for as long as the threatening export capacities continue to exist abroad. The consultative procedures developed in practice actually give Article XIX a bias towards making the emergency protection permanent. A retaliatory withdrawal or a compensatory offer settles the account once and for all; and if an exporting country which was not offered compensation decides against retaliation in the first consultation, Article XIX prohibits such action to be taken after three months.

If these shortcomings are serious enough from the viewpoint of any current emergency, they make Article XIX a wholly inadequate instrument for – indeed, a positive obstacle to – any joint effort to liberalise and dismantle the existing non-tariff restrictions. One of the main difficulties in this respect has been the somewhat specious distinction made between legal and illegal restrictions,[19] combined with the strongly held view of certain countries that legal restrictions could be liberalised through reciprocal bargaining, whereas the illegal ones must be either liberalised unilaterally or legalised, i.e. submitted to consultation under Article XIX.

It can be seen, now, that a major deterrent to the use of Article XIX has been the requirement that specific injury be shown combined with the principle of reciprocity which, however useful and necessary in tariff bargaining, has, in its narrow sense, no legitimate function in the regulation of emergency protection. Reciprocity also means mutual dependence, mutual responsibility and co-operation. It is surely destructive of the spirit of reciprocity in this sense for a country in an emergency to be obliged to pay for taking bona fide temporary action, negotiate such a payment, and risk retaliation if it does not settle. The main problem here is how to ensure that an alternative procedure would remain limited to real emergencies. It would change very little in the present practice if it were to be agreed that in cases of 'justified need' no compensation was required or retaliation allowed, the justification to be decided in each case by consultation.

If, on the other hand, a procedure were developed which would recognise the right of a country to emergency protection, the right would have to be balanced by a commitment and a procedure giving its trading partners an assurance of a continuously growing access and of foreseeable removal of the emergency measures. The main problem on this side is one of enforcement.

The balance between a right and an obligation would be achieved in a safeguard clause under which a country experiencing difficulty would be authorised to take protective action on three conditions: (*a*) the emergency protective action must be degressive on a finite time-scale to be negotiated but in no case longer than x years; (*b*) it should be accompanied by a demonstrable adjustment effort on the part of the government taking emergency action; and (c) it must be open to multilateral surveillance from inception to termination.

The acceptance of these principles would resolve the first of the problems mentioned above: the emergency procedure would be protected against abuse. Protectionist pressure on governments would lessen as industries would be less likely to organise costly campaigns for temporary protection only; at the same time, the adjustment obligation would be sufficiently heavy for governments to resist invoking the safeguard clause except in cases of clear need.

Would the governments be willing to accept these obligations instead of those implied in Article XIX which they so often find unacceptable? It is possible to be optimistic in this respect. For a government taking emergency action, the procedure of Article XIX implies domestic political difficulty: it is difficult indeed to explain to the legislature, and to the public at large, why compensation should be given for what cannot but appear to them a rightful action. The principles of the alternative procedure are easier to defend politically. In public debate, they would tend to isolate the protectionist interest.

The problem of enforcement must be admitted to remain at best only half resolved. It may thus be objected against the suggested procedure that it requires countries to give up their right to compensation and retaliation. It would not, however, be a definitive sacrifice. It would indeed be the essence of this approach that no government which accepted the principle of degressive finite protection and the obligation to assist adjustment could be asked for compensation on imposing the emergency measures. If it arrested the phasing-out process after a few years, or if its adjustment effort, on which it would have to report annually, were found inadequate, countries adversely affected could then demand compensation or retaliate in a discriminatory fashion. This right might remain only theoretical, however, in which case the countries concerned would have no more practical means than the drawn-out process of attrition in annual multilateral consultations. But at least they would have the multilateral consultations which are lacking on all occasions of emergency protection except when resort is made to Article XIX.

Once these principles were accepted for emergency action, there would also be a basis for an attack on all existing import restrictions. Also, the danger of cartelisation implied in the spreading practice of limiting imports by exporters' self-restraint would be considerably reduced. Since the new principles of emergency protection would at the same time facilitate adjustment in the importing country and strengthen the legal and political position of the exporter, exporters' self-restraints would become less necessary and more difficult to negotiate.

It is only through an acceptance of principles of this kind that the most powerful economies can make an adequate contribution to the functioning of a world economic system in which the less powerful would feel safe.

OUTLOOK

The two challenging objectives of the coming negotiations on trade in manufactures are an agreement on a transition to free trade, combined with strengthened emergency procedures which would safeguard the importing countries against market disruption exceeding reasonable adjustment capacity but not against the need for adjustment, while also safeguarding not only a continued access but a continued expansion of exports to that market. With these adaptations, the multilateral trading system would facilitate the economic and social transformations foreseeable in the remaining decades of the century.

In the mature industrial societies, social preference for industry in general is becoming qualitatively differentiated into a preference for the more skill-intensive industries and is giving way to preference for tertiary occupations. In the guaranteed income era, on the threshold of which these societies now stand, the change in occupational preferences will accelerate. These changes, creating the necessary conditions for continued growth, respond to the concern with the 'quality of life', the economic elements of which are an interesting occupation and increased security.

Complementary to this process of change is the growth of productive capacity in less developed countries. If it is to be commensurate with the growth of their population, these countries will need – and will be able – to supply an increasing part of the consumption of standard manufactures in the industrial societies, in exchange for investment goods.

Among the many factors threatening to inhibit, misdirect and disrupt this complex development, the two most significant will continue to be inflation domestically and economic-political friction internationally. The new rules of trade would strengthen our defences in both respects.

Notes

1. The opinions expressed in this paper are those of the author, and are not to be interpreted as reflecting the views of the organisation of which he is a member.

2. 1953–60.

3. Excluding non-ferrous metals.

4. Growth rates of the two flows of manufactured exports (defined in the same way as in Table 1) in three sub-periods have been calculated by UNCTAD:

Average Annual Growth Rates of Exports of Manufactures

	1955–60	1960–67	1967–69
Industrial countries	8·8	9·4	16·4
Less developed countries	6·6	12·3	21·2

Source: UNCTAD, *1972 Handbook of International Trade and Development Statistics*, p. 193.

5. To be distinguished from labour-intensive exports in more modern industries such as engineering.

6. I.B.R.D., 1971 Annual Meeting of the Board of Governors, *Summary Proceedings*, p. 11.

7. Indeed, the expansion of these exchanges is welcomed by European labour organisations. In conditions of a general labour shortage, workers made redundant by imports are not dismissed but retrained, which generally means upgrading, within the enterprise.

8. Already in the mid-1960s, surveys made in the Federal Republic of Germany and the United Kingdom established that more than a half of imports of industrial machinery and equipment were of types not produced at home. See *I.F.O. Schnelldienst* (Munich), no. 27, 8 July 1966, pp. 4–12; National Economic Council, *Imported Manufactures: An Enquiry in Competitiveness* (London, 1965) p. 18.

9. In certain Latin American countries, four-fifths and more of national exports in this category are said to be supplied by multinational firms.

10. Only the latter type can be reliably followed in statistics, since re-imports of 'contract-processed' goods are admitted under special tariff headings. In all industrial countries, these imports have been growing at rates twice to three times the growth rate of all manufactured imports

in the last decade, with imports from developing countries increasing particularly rapidly. Trade in components, which cannot be separated statistically, can be assumed to have grown at least as rapidly as that in 'contract-processed' goods.

11. The share of the group in world exports increased from 41 per cent in 1960 to 49 per cent in 1971; with the enlarged Community of nine, the group will account for some 57 per cent of world exports on present reckoning.

12. Problems relating to Article XII, authorising trade restrictions to safeguard the balance of payments, will not be discussed in this paper.

13. Thomas Horst has found a significant positive correlation ($R^2 = 0.70$ with nominal, and $R^2 = 0.71$ with effective protection) between the level of a national tariff protecting a given industry and the relative volume of production and sales by foreign-owned firms behind it. See his 'The Industrial Composition of U.S. Exports and Subsidiary Sales to the Canadian Market', *American Economic Review* (March 1972) pp. 37–45.

14. See, for example, H. G. Johnson and H. Corbet, 'Optional Negotiating Techniques on Industrial Tariffs', in *Towards an Open Economy* (London: Trade Policy Research Centre, 1972).

15. By 'high', meaning a tariff of up to 50 per cent, which may be prohibitive for specific products classified under that position but across which there is, nonetheless, a significant flow of imports.

16. A concept narrower than that of non-tariff barriers or distortions, which also include measures whose trade effects are only incidental.

17. It is easy to see why such arrangements, even when indisputable under the existing trade rules and economically beneficial not merely to the participants but to the trading community at large, have historically been one of the most potent international irritants. In the policy-making process of countries which are outsiders to such agreements, the export interests affected by trade diversion feel the effect immediately, whereas those which are eventually to benefit from trade creation cannot anticipate the effect, and when it materialises are not likely to connect it with the original cause. National policy will soon reflect this imbalance, just as it usually reflects the imbalance between the concentrated producer interest and diffuse consumer interest.

18. Articles VI, XI(2)(c), XII, XVIII(2), XIX-XXI, XXV, XXVIII.

19. i.e. those maintained with multilateral consent and those imposed without multilateral consultation – the majority of the existing restrictions in the field of manufactures being of the latter type.

10 Multinational Enterprises and Trade Flows of Developing Countries

John H. Dunning

PROFESSOR OF ECONOMICS, UNIVERSITY OF
READING

I

As a diagnostic or prescriptive device, any economic theory is only as useful as the relevance and validity of the postulates on which it is based. Evaluated on these criteria, the principle of static comparative advantage falls short, either as an explanation of the level and composition of trade between nations, or as a guide to the best pattern of resource allocation within a nation. Applied to the current situation of the less developed countries (L.D.C.s), with their sights set on increasing real output per head in a world of imperfect markets, trade barriers and rapid technological change, its assumptions of identical (or largely identical) production functions, completely free movement of goods but immobility of factor inputs, constant returns to scale and homogeneous tastes seem far removed from the facts as they really are.

An obvious rejoinder to this observation is that while acknowledging the inadequacies of the theory as an explanatory tool, its normative value remains unimpaired; and that rather than asking economists to produce second-best theories of trade to fit third- or fourth-best situations, policy-makers would do better to eliminate the obstacles which weaken the validity of first-best theories. This is true, but in a dynamic context the simplistic premises of a static model cannot apply. In particular, the presumption of similar production functions is totally unrealistic where technology is produced and sold in imperfect markets; and as soon as this is recognised, the possibility of a whole new set of international economic relationships, and in particular those which arise from the operations of multi-national enterprises[1] emerge.

In this paper, we shall take as axiomatic the efforts of the L.D.C.s to formulate policies suited to improving their dynamic comparative advantage. We shall ignore political objectives and constraints, although we accept that these, and particularly the desire for sovereignty in decision-making, may be of overriding importance.

In considering the dynamics of trade and development, two aspects might be considered: first, the extent to which trade, through permitting increased specialisation, enables the production frontiers of participating countries to be extended; second, the extent to which the exogenous growth of resources affects the comparative advantage of countries, and hence their trade and development. Using a comparative static model, classical theory had something to say about both these aspects, but its main emphasis lay in explaining changes in resource allocation due to changes in the quantity or price of factor inputs. This was because it assumed that advances in technology by one country were instantaneously and freely available to others. Information was treated as a free good rather than a scarce input. In these circumstances, there were no obstacles to a country attaining its potential comparative advantage.

Such an approach is no longer acceptable. In the world of the second half of the twentieth century, not only are advances in productive knowledge a much more important vehicle of economic development than they once were; it is also clearly demonstrable that such knowledge is neither immediately nor freely transferred across national boundaries. From this three things follow: first, production functions may differ between countries – at least temporarily; second, countries may not always be able to exploit their potential comparative advantage; third, that because productive knowledge is often the specific property of enterprises, the possibility of these enterprises exploiting their advantages by producing outside their own boundaries becomes a reality (see below, Section III).

Some modern theories of trade flows (Hufbauer, 1970) have

attempted to incorporate changes in technology into their analysis. Both the *technological gap* and *product cycle* theories, which implicitly assume knowledge is costly and that there is a lag in its transmission between countries, examine some of the ways in which products and processes innovated in one country may subsequently become more efficiently produced in others. However, they neither provide comprehensive explanations of trade flows; nor do they help us to understand the root causes of trade. They are, in no sense (nor do they claim to be), normative theories, and hence take us very little way in evolving an appropriate trade strategy for a developing world. Partly, as we shall see, this is because they do not sufficiently take account of the foreign direct investment of enterprises, an understanding of which, perhaps, lies more in the theory of industrial organisation (Kindleberger, 1969; Caves, 1971).

It is clear, then, that in imperfect competitive conditions there is no hidden hand which ensures that all countries will optimise their dynamic comparative advantage, or gain an equitable distribution of the benefits of trade. This being so, it is understandable that countries which believe themselves to be losers from the economics of interdependence should wish to take action to protect their interests. For the purposes of this present discussion, it may be helpful to think of the L.D.C.s pursuing policies in an attempt to overcome barriers to entry (or expansion) into lines of economic activity where they believe their comparative advantage would lie if there were no constraints on the transference of technology and if international factor and product markets were perfect. We believe that these obstacles are normally greater for L.D.C.s than for developed countries, although there is no necessary relationship between the height of the obstacles and the policies which should be undertaken. *Inter alia* these will depend on the cost of overcoming the barriers, of resource allocation.

Generally speaking, most L.D.C.s see their best chance for prosperity in industrialisation; they also view their greatest obstacles in this direction. These barriers are put down to imperfections in world market structures and political constraints; far from reflecting the principle of comparative dynamic advantage, the existing system of trade militates against it. To overcome these disadvantages, some protection or aid to industrialisation is believed necessary, geared either to the import replacement of manufactured goods or to the encouragement of manufacturing exports. In the short run, assuming full employment and balance of payments equilibrium, the structure of both manufacturing imports and exports might be out of balance, as well as the level of trade. Without knowledge of the actual situation, there is no *a priori* reason to suppose policy will increase or reduce the share of foreign trade in the national output. In the long run, with the aim of increasing the growth of industrial output, there is a strong presumption that the share of both exports and imports will rise. Most industrialisation policies of L.D.C.s aim either to complement export earnings or to replace part of those derived from primary production.

In purely resource-allocative terms, the argument for import replacement is that the importing country is paying too high a price for its import of goods, in the sense that if the resources now used to earn the necessary foreign exchange were used to produce the goods internally, they could, *in the long run at least*, do so at lower cost. The case for export promotion is the converse of this; it asserts that the exporting country could earn foreign exchange from exports which would enable it to import a greater quantity of goods than the resources now allocated to exports could have produced in other activities.

Once one drops the full-employment assumption, then a new situation emerges. Here it is argued that the income or growth potential of L.D.C.s is retarded because they cannot improve their production functions; in Keynesian terms, both supply and demand functions are constrained by an under-utilisation of resources caused by an inability to exploit dynamic comparative advantage. If this is so, then anything which promotes demand for unused resources or removes bottlenecks in obtaining foreign resources will have both the normal multiplier effect and, through the improvement of production functions and external economies, a technological spillover effect as well (Quinn, 1968). In other words, growth will occur through a better use of existing resources and the employment of unemployed resources, although the origin of such growth will be brought about by improved resource allocation.

In practice, of course, neither import substitution nor export promotion will necessarily lead to an improvement in allocative efficiency or growth, particularly where policy is geared to political goals, or is implemented inefficiently by an indiscriminate use of import controls. In the short run, again, such devices might be acceptable – and the L.D.C.s are not alone in the implementation of such policies (it is doubtful if the restrictionist policies of the U.K. or U.S. governments towards outward investment in the late 1960s could be justified in terms of resource-allocative efficiency). For our purposes, however, we shall assume that the primary objective is economic development, and that policy towards trade is geared to this end and evaluated solely by its contribution to it.

II

There are some obstacles to economic development which can only be overcome by appropriate domestic policies of the L.D.C.s and/or by changing attitudes and motivations of economic agents. Others, of which agricultural protectionism is the most obvious example, reflect the policies of the developed countries. Similarly, there are some constraints about which it might be impossible to do anything, simply because of the supply inelasticity of resources. Here, we are concerned with obstacles to development of the L.D.C.s which arise because they are not being able to take advantage of the resources they do possess, owing to difficulties in obtaining either complementary resources (supply-orientated barriers) or the markets necessary to make production worth while (demand-orientated barriers). It is further assumed that these barriers are the result of forces hindering the efficient allocation of resources: in other words, the price which L.D.C.s have to pay to obtain these resources or entry to markets is in some sense too high.

The *supply-orientated* barriers can be conveniently discussed in terms of one factor input, viz. capital, defining capital in the Fisherian sense of anything which is capable of generating an income stream. Harry Johnson (1969) has distinguished between three kinds of income-generating assets, viz. *material capital*, e.g. plant, equipment and buildings, etc.; *human capital*, essentially the stock of manpower from which the services of labour flow – the quality of which is a function, *inter alia*, of innate ability, education, training and motivation; and *productive knowledge* which, given the factor inputs as defined in the traditional sense, will determine the form of the production function, i.e. the technical efficiency of firms. Now as far as the first two varieties of capital are concerned, the L.D.C.s may be able to hire these at a price which (discounted for risk) is, by and large, the reflection of competitive forces.[2] Most certainly, some price discrimination may exist against the L.D.C.s (in the same way as small firms may be discriminated against); and some monopolistic pricing does occur. But assuming that the inputs can be used productively, there is no real barrier to acquiring them.

The situation is somewhat different in respect of the stock of productive knowledge for two main reasons. First, part of this asset is, in practice, neither produced nor distributed under the principles governing the allocation of resources in a private-enterprise economy. This obviously applies to most knowledge to do with the defence industry, for which the State is often producer and consumer; the criteria for evaluating such knowledge differ, and the normal rules do not apply, except, perhaps, to the efficiency of the actual production process. Second, and more relevant in the present context, within the private sector, the production of commercially viable knowledge is, in most cases, only thought worth while if the results of such knowledge remain, at least for some time, the exclusive possession of the producing firm.

The reason for this highlights a characteristic of productive knowledge: it is costly to produce, but once produced and incorporated in a marketable product or process, it can be very easily assimilated by other firms. Hence, society has introduced the patent system, the purpose of which is to ensure that investment in the creation of knowledge (which is later embodied in marketable products or processes) can earn a return at least equivalent to that on any other expendable asset. But such protection inescapably creates a barrier on the free transference of knowledge or to its acquisition by other firms.

Of course, not all knowledge, once created, is costly to acquire. Many of the findings of fundamental research are published in the scientific and professional journals. Often firms are prepared to sell information to other producers, e.g. through licensing, though there may be restrictive conditions attached to this. Technology may be embodied in goods; in other cases it may be easily imitated. The extent to which any enterprise can acquire and benefit from knowledge to improve its competitive position will depend on (*a*) whether the knowledge is saleable, (*b*) the conditions of sale and (*c*) whether the firm can make use of (or effectively absorb) such knowledge (which is dependent on its other resources, including human capital). To give an obvious example, the knowledge of how to produce motor-cars using fully automated methods is of little use to a specialist producer of racing cars. Likewise, the extent to which a *country* can obtain and benefit from knowledge produced by another will be influenced by similar criteria; cf. the Japanese and German ways of acquiring foreign know-how. We have suggested that the argument of the L.D.C.s is that the price they have to pay for productive knowledge is too high or they are inhibited in obtaining it. But without some form of external help, it cannot be domestically produced either. At first sight this is a variant of the infant-industry argument; in fact it is more akin to the optimal tariff argument against monopolistic pricing.

We have illustrated one important supply-orientated barrier. There are, of course, others. Firms in L.D.C.s may not have access to raw materials or other inputs bought from firms outside their boundaries, or, where they do, they may have to pay more than the competitive price for them: this could put them at a disadvantage vis-à-vis their larger foreign competitors. Once again, we have an example of monopolistic pricing in the first case and the economies of size and integration in the second. This latter might be construed as an advantage which, *in practice*, occurs only in an imperfectly competitive situation (where such economies are only profitable within an oligopolistic market structure); the difficulty is that part of the production process might best be undertaken by firms in L.D.C.s but this is not economic because of high setting-up costs. Nor may it be convenient for the integrated firms to subcontract or license local producers. But, in so far as size of established producers impedes the development of potentially more efficient competitors, then, again, some kind of protection against foreign competition might be needed, particularly where barriers to entry are high.

The L.D.C.s might also be faced with *demand-orientated* barriers. Once again, the principle of comparative advantage assumes the absence of such barriers. Nevertheless, they apply within industries within countries, and for obvious reasons are greater across national boundaries. Again, an independent firm seeking outlets in an industry controlled by integrated competitors might find these difficult to acquire. Obvious cases in the United Kingdom include new outlets in the petroleum and brewing industries. This is another variant of imperfect competition and is a genuine barrier, as too is the case where there are high costs of market entry.

Summarising, countries, like firms, may have to face barriers to entry into new lines of economic activity. Where these reflect the result of competitive forces, there may be little justification for a protectionist policy. Where they are not, the argument for an optimum tariff (or its equivalent) may hold. All these arise either because of the monopolistic behaviour on the part of individual firms or groups of firms, or even countries, or because of the size of established producers and/or the indivisibility of production processes. Examples of the obstacles include the difficulties in obtaining enterprise-specific knowledge, or other inputs, or markets held by firms to which access can be denied. The latter type of barrier arises from the size and integration of existing producers; the argument is not against size as such, but that, in some of the processes undertaken by large firms, which cannot be separated from the rest of their operations, it is possible that L.D.C.s might have the advantage. But they cannot take this because firms are not willing to release control over processes. Integration is an enterprise-specific advantage.

III

Part of the difficulty of the L.D.C.s wishing to establish new activities or patterns of trade lies in the simple fact that the established producers of the goods in the developed countries, operating largely within a private-enterprise framework, have a certain control over the availability and/or conditions of sale of inputs and markets, which is accepted (and in some cases fostered) by the system in which they operate. The reason why it is accepted is due largely to the protection which consumers in countries have from the competition *between* large firms. This is not the case with potential competitors in the L.D.C.s. It follows that if there was some way of embracing the L.D.C.s into the operational network of the established producers of developed countries, many of these barriers might be overcome. It has been suggested that this is precisely where the multi-national enterprise comes into the picture.

How far can the multinational enterprise break down barriers now facing the L.D.C.s and help them achieve their goal of maximising comparative dynamic advantage? And what are the costs of so doing? Of the theories purporting to explain the growth of the production of firms outside their national boundaries, perhaps the most helpful is that which emphasises the necessary prerequisites for such production. These are, first, that such firms must have a distinctive advantage over indigenous companies in the countries in which they are producing, or contemplating production – including advantages of not having to overcome barriers; and second, that local production is the best way to exploit these advantages rather than alternative means, e.g. exports or licensing. These conditions can only exist where there are market imperfections: in the first case, of factor movements, particularly of productive knowledge; and in the second, of goods and services. In other words, if all firms producing similar products had the same production functions and were faced with the same price-taking situation, the resource allocation predicated by the principle of static comparative advantage would hold good.

Once one introduces imperfections, either as regards the transfer of goods or resources to produce goods, the situation changes. The multinational company is a product of such imperfections, and, within any prospective profit or growth situation, operates most vigorously in those areas where the obstacles to exploiting the market by other means, or by competitors, are greatest. The obstacles are of two kinds. The first are those imposed by countries, which are potentially hosts to foreign investment, on imported goods, which may cause firms in exporting countries to exploit the market by setting up local production units in it rather than exporting to it; much of *defensive* foreign direct investment originates in this way. The other type of barrier takes the form of enterprise-specific advantages which firms in investing countries possess over firms in host countries, and which enable them to produce in these latter countries under the equivalent of a tariff barrier. Of these advantages, we have suggested that access to productive knowledge, to markets and to the economies of integration of an enterprise-specific character are among the most important. With this protection, which is sometimes temporary, firms are able to earn profits sufficient to overcome the disadvantages of producing in foreign markets.

An examination of the industrial structure of the leading multinational companies confirms that they tend to be concentrated in industries in which the barriers of entry to *new* producers are among the highest, and the share of the local output in the industries of host countries reflects their comparative advantages of overcoming these barriers vis-à-vis indigenous firms. Moreover, even within the countries where they operate, multinational companies may choose to be selective in the products they produce or the processes they engage in; in this respect, a foreign affiliate is like any other branch plant of an enterprise whose main activities are located elsewhere. To compete effectively, competitors may have to set up a completely new organisation; in other words, the barriers to entry are measured not by the activities of the branch plant but by those of the entire organisation of which it is part.

This, indeed, is a most substantial advantage which an established knowledge-intensive firm has over its potential competitors in new markets. The setting-up of a new range of manufacturing facilities by such a firm may require little investment in productive knowledge or central administration; the marginal costs of these items will be considerably lower than their average total cost to newly established firms. (This *inter alia* explains why administrative costs to sales ratio of foreign subsidiaries in countries often tends to be lower than that of their indigenous competitors (Dunning, 1966)). In other words, wherever capital costs external to any particular operation of a firm, but internal to the firm are high, the barriers to entry to new producers are that much greater, and hence, too, is the profitability of international production. This is a further reason why international investment tends to be concentrated in research-intensive industries (Gruber, Mehta and Vernon, 1967). Put another way, where the economies of size of firm are most marked, then the more multinational firms will stand to gain, partly because they are large, but also because of their comparative advantages over domestic firms mentioned earlier.

Technological and market forces in advanced countries are causing output to be more concentrated and making it more difficult for completely new firms to enter the market. This might not matter too much in countries where there are several large existing firms already competing with each other. But in countries seeking to develop a new industry from scratch, it may impose insuperable barriers (of the kind described) for indigenous entrants and thus freeze the comparative advantage of existing producers built on these barriers. In this situation, it is the very firms responsible for the barriers which, in part, help to overcome them by establishing local manufacturing facilities. In so doing, however, they enhance their own economic power, as once they are producing in the L.D.C.s they make entry of local competitors more difficult.

Having suggested the origin of direct manufacturing investment in the L.D.C.s, one now has to look at its possible consequences on resource allocation. For our purposes, we are interested in identifying characteristics of affiliates of foreign companies which make their impact on trade flows different from that which might be expected from indigenous firms. It is generally agreed that the unique contribution of inward direct investment over other forms of resource importation is the multiplicity of barriers which it can overcome for the recipient country. At one and the same time, it can offer a package deal of a superior production technology, managerial skills and marketing methods; of access to markets in inputs and outputs which it has accumulated over the years; and of being part of an organisation which may be benefitting from economies of scale and integration. Some of these benefits will remain specific only to the affiliates; others, in various ways, will permeate the economy, i.e. there will be external economies. The character of these has been fully investigated in the literature (Watkins, 1968). Many of these advantages could have been obtained by other means, i.e. by buying the ingredients of the package separately (Penrose, 1973). Here, one is suggesting that the value of the package is greater when the ingredients are not only provided, but put together, by the same source and that inward direct investment is an instrument which, in one swoop, can overcome many of the obstacles to the L.D.C.s in improving their comparative advantage.

The unique problem of inward direct investment cannot easily be separated from its advantages.[3] Partly these arise because the goals of multinational enterprises are different from those of the L.D.C.s and, because of this, their contribution to development is bound to be partial and uneven; and partly because the control exerted over the behaviour of an affiliate by the enterprise which owns it, and over the sharing of the benefits which arise from it, may not be in the best interests of the host countries. Not always will *particular* decisions taken by Detroit or London or Amsterdam be of benefit to individual L.D.C.s, or as much benefit as they would like; it would be surprising if they were. For just as a multinational company can open markets to L.D.C.s, it can shut them off or inhibit their growth. It can control (or attempt to control) the sourcing of its inputs in a way which the host country might not approve; it can control (or attempt to control) the type of output (including the production of knowledge) and the terms on which goods and services are exchanged between members of the group; it can control (or attempt to control) dividend policies and the pattern and rate of growth of new investment; it can control (or attempt to control) the extent to which it moves funds across national boundaries, and so on. All these may affect resource allocation and impinge upon national economic management.

The extent to which these unique features of inward direct investment are demonstrated is dependent on a host of factors, not least on the economic policies of the host country. But the net outcome of the activities of foreign affiliates will be a sharing of costs and benefits between the host country and the rest of the enterprise, depending *inter alia* on the bargaining strength of the two parties. This in itself raises a whole set of interesting issues which are not new in principle, but which pose a variety of new problems. Compare, for example, the operations of a multinational company with those of a multiregional national company. The behaviour of the latter will have distributive effects throughout the regions in which it produces, such that some regions may gain and others may lose. But in the last resort it is the national government which has responsibility for the welfare of the regions under its authority, and it can take compensatory action (through fiscal policy or direct controls) to protect the well-being of any region adversely affected by economic events. In other words, it is a supra-regional authority, responsible for ensuring that private economic agents do not cause an inequitable sharing of costs and benefits among regions. A moment's reflection shows that there is no corresponding international mechanism to ensure that actions of multinational companies do not result in inequitable sharing of costs and benefits. And the weaker the nations participating, the less likely they are to get a fair share. In the absence of any supranational authority, individual nation-states take unilateral action.

It will be observed that, in so far as decisions of multinational companies conform to principles of dynamic comparative advantage, then all countries stand to gain – including the L.D.C.s. The question, then, is entirely one of the distribution of the gains. But the trouble is that the development process generated by multinational companies is not only motivated differently from the goals of the L.D.C.s in which they operate (Johnson, 1971), but it is very often in response to an imperfect competitive environment. Obvious examples of imperfections are differences in tax rates and fixed exchange rates; both, while not affecting the behaviour of indigenous firms, may greatly affect the conduct of multinational companies, and not always in the ways in which host countries might like. Moreover, in some ways a multinational enterprise may act like a country. It has fixed assets in different parts of the world and wishes to protect the interests of these assets. The extent to which a Brazilian subsidiary is permitted to export to other parts of Latin America may depend upon the proportion of capacity utilised in the Mexican plant. A purely domestic firm would not be faced with this kind of 'protectionism'.

IV

As a practical exercise, it is difficult to evaluate the effects of multinational enterprises on the trade flows of particular L.D.C.s This is because, first, one has to make some hypothesis about what would have happened had they not made the investment – and this is largely dependent on assumptions made about governments' ability to effect resource allocation; and second, because, given the presence of affiliates of multinational enterprises, their impact will depend on the domestic economic policies pursued. But given these assumptions, it seems reasonable to postulate that the greater the barriers to the exploitation of dynamic comparative advantage, the greater the potential contribution of inward direct investment may be. And the more these barriers can only be overcome by the package deal unique to inward direct investment, and the more the signals to the behaviour of such firms provided by governments reflect these goals of economic development, the more the potential may become an actual contribution.

The ways in which trade flows may be affected by multinational enterprises are many and varied: *a priori*, as we have seen, they may either raise or reduce the level of trade in the short run; in the long run they will almost certainly raise the level. But as far as *individual* investments are concerned (as compared with the effects of all investment), foreign affiliates may enable a country to reduce imports (import-substituting investment); to make possible exports which might otherwise not have occurred (export-generating investment); to replace exports, where a company previously exporting is taken over by a foreign concern and exports re-routed through other parts of the organisation (export-substituting investment); or to increase imports, where a subsidiary is established to advance the exports of the parent company (import-generating investment). In other instances, inward direct investment might change the pattern of imports or exports, or the terms on which they are bought and sold.

We have said that some dynamic theories of trade composition have offered an explanation for the ways in which international companies affect trade. Vernon's product-cycle theory suggests that investment will first be of an import-substitution kind to the recipient country, but subsequently may turn out to be export-creating as well, which both strengthens the balance of payments and aids development. His approach, like that of Hufbauer, is less convincing in explaining the kind of trade which arises from a global strategy of established multinational companies, which is based largely on the product or process specialisation within the companies. These strategies may vary between the firms. Some will engage in *horizontal* specialisation of products, e.g. the Philips company which manufactures separate domestic electrical appliances in different factories in Europe and supplies the entire European market from these. Others practise *vertical* specialisation – making different processes in different countries of the world and producing the final product in only one or two centres; I.B.M. is a classic case. Clearly, such strategies tend to accord with the principle of comparative advantage (in so far as the price structure of inputs and outputs is realistic). By contrast, other strategies within the multinational enterprise may inhibit the fullest benefits of dynamic comparative advantage, e.g. an ethnocentric policy towards the location of research and development facilities. Any positive theory of trade must take into account the implications of ownership of firms which arise due to the factors we have mentioned, and accept that some forms of functional specialisation will be enterprise-specific, which cannot easily be undertaken outside the firm. Likewise, any normative theory must assess not only the effects of the operations of multinational enterprises in terms of the opportunity cost of their contribution on trade flows, but also on the ways in which the costs and benefits of these operations are shared between the countries in which they operate and the rest of the organisation of which they are part.

V

The empirical studies so far undertaken on the effects of multinationals on trade flows in the countries in which they operate have been summarised in a paper recently prepared for UNCTAD by the author and two colleagues (Dunning, Robertson and Pearce, 1971). Of these, those of INTAL (1972), de La Torre (1971), May (1971), Vaitsos (1972), Streeten and Lall (1973) and

Cohen (1973) may be especially mentioned. The paper also includes a scheme for new research on the impact of U.K. companies on the trade flows of a group of L.D.C.s. It is suggested that the activities of such multinationals might be conveniently classified into five main groups, viz.:

(1) those producing products or services chiefly for the domestic market which are not normally traded across national boundaries;
(2) those producing products or services primarily for local consumption which otherwise might have been imported;
(3) those producing products and services both for local consumption and for export, but primarily to other L.D.C.s;
(4) those producing basic resources (minerals, raw materials, foodstuffs) mainly for export to developed countries;
(5) those producing semi-manufactured or finished goods mainly for export to developed countries.

The activities of some affiliates will, of course, straddle across these groups. Equally, it may be desirable to subdivide the groups by other criteria: the extent to which import substitution is likely to be different for a firm producing finished goods, e.g. typewriters, than for one producing intermediate products, e.g. tin cans; the trading pattern of a firm engaged in processing operations, e.g. rubber tyres, detergents, etc., may not be the same as that of one engaged in fabricating activities, e.g. agricultural tractors. A lot also may depend on the size and age profile of the affiliate; cf. the operations of British Leyland in India which are largely self-sufficient of imports, with those in Turkey or Iran which are much smaller and more recent in origin, and rely very heavily on imports.

Subsidiaries and associates in each group engage in four main types of (external) trade. Imports include purchases of:

I(i) capital equipment;
I(ii) inputs of materials and semi-processed goods;
I(iii) finished goods for resale;
I(iv) services, e.g. insurance, technical know-how, contributions to overheads of parent company, etc.

Exports consist of two main items:

E(i) output of all kinds of goods, e.g. raw materials, capital equipment, semi-processed goods and finished goods;

E(ii) services, e.g. technical know-how.

Each of these kinds of trade may take place *within* the enterprise or system of which the affiliate in the L.D.C. is part, or *between* the affiliate and an independent buyer or seller. It is important to distinguish between these two groups of trade.

Using the classifications outlined above, it is, in theory, possible to construct a variety of trading matrices both for affiliates of U.K. multinationals in L.D.C.s, classified, for example, by industry, size, financial structure, organisational patterns and so on, and for particular L.D.C.s, again variously classified, e.g. by policies adopted towards foreign direct investment, imports, export promotion, etc., population, income levels and so on. To do this is clearly beyond the scope of this paper, but our reading of the literature and our own researches would suggest that a number of very general propositions can be made. These are set out in Table 1. Here, all we are doing is to suggest, in the most qualitative way possible, the trading patterns most likely to be associated with different types of U.K. multinationals operating in L.D.C.s. We list just four possible impacts on visible imports and exports, viz: negligible (or none), some, substantial and variable. These, it must be emphasised, neither evaluate the *effect* of the operations of these affiliates on the trade of L.D.C.s (to do this, some calculations of what might have occurred in the absence of their operations has to be made), nor do they take account of the spillover or multiplier effects which result from their presence. These might move in either direction and completely swamp the patterns suggested in the table.

When one comes to explaining the data, it would seem useful to pay particular attention to three main causes:

(i) Structural factors, e.g. type of products produced, markets served, age and size profile of affiliates, ownership patterns, etc.

(ii) The logistics or strategy of the multinational enterprise towards its foreign affiliates, and especially the extent to which it sees these as part of an integrated network of world-wide or regional activities.[4]

Table 1

MOST PROBABLE TRADING PATTERNS OF AFFILIATES OF U.K. FIRMS IN LESS DEVELOPED COUNTRIES[a]

	Group 1		Group 2		Group 3		Group 4		Group 5	
	A	B	A	B	A	B	A	B	A	B
Imports										
I(i)	N[b]	Some	N	Some	N	Some	N	Some	N	Some
I(ii)	N	N	V	V	V	V	V	V	V	V
I(iii)	N	N[c]	V	N	V	N	N	N	N	N
I(iv)	Some	N	Some	N	Some	N	N	N	N	N
Exports										
E(i)	N	N	N	N	Some	Some	Some	S	S	Some
E(ii)	V	N	V	N	V	N	V	N	V	N

A = Intra-group trade   B = Independent trade
(excluding when either the buyer or the seller acts as an agent for another company or group of companies)
N = Negligible   S = Substantial   V = Variable.

[a] For classification of groups, see p. 315f.
[b] Except where the enterprise, of which the subsidiary is part, itself produces capital equipment.
[c] Except where parent company also produces traded goods.

(iii) The economic and political environment in which the affiliates (or the enterprises of which they are part) operate; in particular, government policies in the L.D.C.s towards foreign direct investment, industrialisation, regional integration and so on.

Clearly, these factors are interrelated; an enterprise's strategy towards a particular affiliate's operations will be influenced by the policies pursued by the host government, both as they are specifically designed to affect its behaviour, e.g. by tax incentives import licensing, etc., and by more general economic measures. Similarly, such measures may be affected by the activities of foreign affiliates, e.g. the way in which their trading patterns are geared towards the interest of the system of which they are part, rather than those of the country in which they operate.

In our study we shall be looking into each of these variables. Conceptually, the first and third are fairly straightforward and some empirical work has been done on both. By contrast, the impact of different strategies of the multinational enterprise on trade flows has not received systematic investigation, although it is known to be important. We have already suggested ways in which influence might be exerted, notably through control over the products produced and the markets served by affiliates. But our knowledge is very incomplete, both of causes and results of different strategies of multinational enterprises on resource allocation in the L.D.C.s, and it is hoped that our study will provide the data which might make possible a more enlightened assessment.

Notes

1. Simply defined as enterprises which operate or control production units in more than one country.
2. Although it is accepted that the *supply* of human capital may be influenced by non-market forces, e.g. the educational policy of governments.
3. For a more detailed analysis of both advantages and disadvantages, see Streeten (1973).
4. For a discussion of the way in which corporate strategy affects the export activities of multinational enterprises, see de La Torre (1971).

Selected References

BALDWIN, R. E. (1970). 'International Trade in Inputs and Outputs', *American Economic Review*, LX 2.

CAVES, R. E. (1971). 'International Corporations: The Industrial Economics of Foreign Investment', *Economica*, XXXVIII (Feb).

CHENERY, H. B. (1961). 'Comparative Advantage and Development Policy', *American Economic Review*, LI 1.

COHEN, B. I. (1973). 'Comparative Behaviour of Foreign and Domestic Export Firms in a Developing Economy', *Review of Economics and Statistics*, LX (May).

DE LA TORRE, J. R. (1971). 'Exports of Manufactured Goods from Developing Countries: Marketing Factors and the Role of Foreign Enterprise', *Journal of International Business Studies* (spring).

DENNISON, E. (1967). *Why Growth Rates Differ* (Washington, D.C.: Brookings Institution).

DUNNING, J. H. (1966). 'U.S. Subsidiaries in Britain and their U.K. Competitors', *Business Ratios* (autumn).

——, ROBERTSON, D. H. and PEARCE, R. D. (1971). 'Multinational Enterprises and their Impact on the Trade Flows of Less Developed Countries' (unpublished report for UNCTAD).

GRUBER, W., MEHTA, D., and VERNON, R. (1967). 'The R and D Factor in International Trade and International Investment of United States Industries', *Journal of Political Economy*, LXXV (Feb).

HEALEY, D. T. (1972). 'Foreign Capital and Exports in Economic Development', Institute for International Economic Studies, University of Stockholm, Seminar Paper, no. 15.

HELLEINER, G. K. (1973). 'Manufactured Exports from Less Developed Countries and Multinational Firms', *Economic Journal*, LXXXIII (Mar).

HUFBAUER, G. C. (1970). 'The Impact of National Characteristics and Technology on the Commodity Composition of Trade in Manufactured Goods', in R. Vernon (ed.), *The Technology Factor in International Trade* (New York: Columbia Univ. Press, for National Bureau of Economic Research).

INTAL (1971). *The Industrial Enterprise in the Integration of Latin America: An Empirical Study* (Buenos Aires: Institute for Latin American Integration).

JOHNSON, H. G. (1969). *Comparative Cost and Commercial Policy for a Developing World Economy* (Wicksell Lectures).

—— (1971). 'The Multinational Corporation as an Agency of Economic Development: Some Exploratory Observations', in Ward, B., d'Anjou, L., and Runnals, J. D., eds, *The Widening Gap: Development in the 1970s* (Columbia University Press).

KINDLEBERGER, C. P. (1969). *American Business Abroad* (Yale University Press).

MAY, H. K. (1971). *The Effects of United States and Other Foreign Investment in Latin America* (Washington, D.C.: Council of the Americas).

MYINT, H. (1958). 'The Classical Theory of International Trade and the Underdeveloped Countries', *Economic Journal*, LXVIII (June).

PENROSE, E. (1973). 'The Growth of International Corporations and their Changing Role in Less Developed Countries' (mimeo).

QUINN, J. B. (1968). 'Scientific and Technical Strategy at the National and Major Enterprise Level', paper for UNESCO Symposium on *The Role of Science and Technology in Economic Development* (Paris).

STREETEN, P. P. (1973). 'The Multinational Enterprise and the Theory of Development Policy', in J. H. Dunning (ed.), *Economic Analysis and the Multinational Enterprise* (London: Allen & Unwin).

—— and LALL, S. (1973). *Evaluation of methods and basic findings of UNCTAD study of Private Overseas Investment in Selected Less Developed Countries*, UN TD/B/C. 3/111.

UNCTAD (1972). 'Restrictive Business Practices: The Operations of Multinational Enterprises in Developing Countries', UN TD/B/399.

VAITSOS, C. V. (1972). 'Interaffiliate Charges by Transnational Corporations and Inter-Country Income Distribution', submitted in partial requirements for a D.Phil. degree at Harvard University (June).

VERNON, R. (1966). 'International Investment and International Trade in the Product Cycle', *Quarterly Journal of Economics*, LXXX (May).

—— (1972). *Sovereignty at Bay* (New York: Basic Books).

WATKINS, M. (1968). *Foreign Ownership and the Structure of Canadian Industry*, report of the Task Force on the Structure of Canadian Industry (Ottawa).

11 International Trade: A Background Paper

A collation of facts and figures, and a brief introduction to the main issues, prepared by the Economic Planning Staff, Overseas Development Administration, Foreign and Commonwealth Office.

This paper is intended as a general background document to the Conference. It presents some of the basic facts and figures and identifies the main problems, but does not attempt to provide solutions. The early part contains a few salient facts and figures on trade flows, terms of trade, etc.

PATTERNS OF WORLD TRADE

The most remarkable feature of international trading patterns to emerge in the past decade has been the considerable growth of intra-developed country trade. This is brought out in the following tables:
In terms of rates of growth, this increase in intra-developed country trade is only paralleled by the growth in trade between the centrally planned economies and the rest of the world (see Table 2).

On the other hand, intra-L.D.C. trade has grown least rapidly. The rate of growth of L.D.C. imports has marginally exceeded the rate of growth of L.D.C. exports, leading to an increase in those countries' payments deficits with the rest of the world. A noticeable feature of L.D.C. trade has been the growth of trade with the centrally planned economies, albeit from a small base.

Table 1
WORLD TRADE, 1961 AND 1971
($ billion)

	1961 Imports (f.o.b.) into				1971 Imports (f.o.b.) into			
From:	Developed countries	L.D.C.s	Centrally planned economies	Total[a]	Developed countries	L.D.C.s	Centrally planned economies	Total[a]
Developed countries	63·0	21·7	3·2	89·9	192·0	47·4	9·0	249·2
L.D.C.s	19·8	6·1	1·5	27·6	44·2	11·8	3·2	59·7
Centrally planned economies	3·0	1·7	10·7	15·4	9·1	5·4	21·9	36·4
Total	85·8	29·5	15·4	132·9	245·4	64·6	34·1	345·3

[a] Includes trade which it is not possible to allocate by group.
Source: U.N. *Yearbook of International Trade Statistics*, and U.N. *Monthly Bulletin of Statistics*.

Table 2

AVERAGE ANNUAL PERCENTAGE RATES OF GROWTH OF TRADE,
1961-71

	Developed countries	*L.D.C.s*	*Imports (f.o.b.) into Centrally planned economies*	*Total*
From:				
Developed countries	11·8	8·1	10·9	10·7
L.D.C.s	8·4	6·8	7·8	8·0
Centrally planned economies	11·7	12·2	7·4	9·0
Total	11·1	8·2	8·3	10·0

Source: from Table 1.

Table 3 shows a breakdown of world trade by S.I.T.C. categories. Clearly, the growth areas are in manufactured products, even in intra-L.D.C. trade, although total volume is still very small. This situation seems likely to persist, especially with the inauguration of the Generalised Preference Scheme. On the primary commodity side, it is interesting to note that the F.A.O. *Agricultural Commodity Projections, 1970–1980*, expect growth in world agricultural trade to be about 2·5 per cent per annum in constant prices. This is marginally higher than in the past decade. In addition, the F.A.O. forecasts that 'the tendency for developing countries to provide a declining share of world exports would cease and might even be reversed'.

In an effort to prevent erosion of the L.D.C.s' position, a number of international agreements have been concluded, covering trade in some relatively homogeneous products. These include coffee, sugar, wheat, olive oil and tin. The short-term Tea Agreement has, for the time being, ceased to operate. It is very difficult to estimate whether these agreements have resulted in increased export earnings of L.D.C.s; however, the suggestion has been made that the Coffee Agreement in particular may be worth as much as $600 million a year to the L.D.C.s in increased earnings. Certainly, agreements have contributed to the orderly marketing of commodities and hence to a reduction in price fluctuations. However, a frequent problem has been the accumulation of stocks which has so far not been resolved other than through fortuitous circumstances (e.g. disease and drought in the case of Brazilian coffee, and unusually large

Table 3

PATTERNS OF WORLD TRADE BY STANDARD INTERNATIONAL
TRADE CLASSIFICATIONS

S.I.T.C. categories	Total 0–9	Food, etc 0 + 1	Raw materials, excl. fuels 2 + 4	Fuels, etc 3	Chemicals 5	Machinery 7	Other manufactures 6 + 8
(a) Exports from developed areas to developed areas ($ billion):							
1960	58·75	8·48	9·76	2·66	4·17	14·44	18·75
1970	172·47	18·73	16·75	6·45	13·57	58·06	56·32
Average annual rate of growth (%)	11·4	8·3	5·6	9·2	12·5	14·9	11·6
(b) Exports from developed areas to developing areas ($ billion):							
1960	21·19	2·96	0·95	0·55	2·02	7·59	6·75
1970	41·93	4·54	1·95	0·62	4·54	17·27	11·74
Average annual rate of growth (%)	7·1	4·4	7·6	1·2	8·4	8·6	5·7
(c) Exports from developing areas to developed areas ($ billion):							
1960	19·78	6·23	5·75	5·16	0·18	0·05	2·34
1970	39·93	9·60	7·33	13·90	0·37	0·74	7·85
Average annual rate of growth (%)	7·3	4·4	2·4	10·4	7·5	30·9	12·8
(d) Exports from developing areas to developing areas ($ billion):							
1960	6·02	1·46	1·10	2·27	0·10	0·14	0·90
1970	10·60	2·14	1·38	3·81	0·38	0·57	2·28
Average annual rate of growth (%)	5·8	3·9	2·3	5·3	14·3	15·1	9·7

Source: U.N. *Monthly Bulletin of Statistics.*

purchases by the U.S.S.R. and China in the case of North American wheat). It seems likely, none the less, that commodity agreements will continue in being; indeed, additional products which may be the subject of future agreements include cocoa and vegetable oils.

Commodity agreements have sometimes been intended not only to smooth out fluctuations but also to prevent or arrest a long-term decline in the price of the product covered. A very recent development is the attempt of coffee producers (following the success of the petroleum exporters) to combine as exporters in an attempt to raise coffee prices. It remains to be seen what success they will have. Countries dependent upon one or two particular commodity exports are very vulnerable and can suffer severely in the face of rising import prices; the example frequently quoted is that of Ghana, where it now requires the export of 5 tons of cocoa to purchase a tractor, whereas five years ago 2 tons were sufficient. However, taking L.D.C.s as a whole, the statistics published by the United Nations and reproduced in Table 4 below indicate that the period of the 1960s has been one of relatively stable terms of trade. If the oil-exporting countries are excluded, there has been some mild improvement in the recent past.

The aggregate figures presented in Table 4 conceal considerable differences between individual L.D.C.s. Some countries, dependent for a large part of their foreign exchange on commodities which have suffered from declining price levels, are in a much worse position than others. Sri Lanka (tea and rubber), for example, has faced substantial deterioration in its terms of trade, while India and other countries such as Peru and Cyprus have benefitted from improvements in their terms of trade.

RECENT MOVES TOWARDS TRADE LIBERALISATION

Since the Second World War there has been a steady trend towards trade liberalisation, both globally and between groups of countries. The background to this was the pre-war Great Depression, which was aggravated by the competitive escalation of tariffs, and the momentum of liberalisation has been maintained by fear of the unemployment and fall in output which

Table 4

TERMS OF TRADE

(1963 = 100)

Year	Developing areas[a]	Developing areas (less fuels)/ Developed areas[b]	Primary/ Manu- factured[c]	India	Sri Lanka	Ghana
1958	106	103	105	92	119	168
1959	103	102	104	99	124	145
1960	103	103	101	106	122	123
1961	100	99	98	103	108	101
1962	98	100	100	104	107	95
1963	100	100	100	100	100	100
1964	100	104	101	100	97	104
1965	99	101	98	101	88	81
1966	100	103	97	103	85	89
1967	99	101	95	115	78	100
1968	99	102	96	109	72	131
1969	102	104	96	113	68	146*
1970	100	105	94	106	67	134*

* Estimate.

[a] Unit-value index of exports from developing areas divided by unit-value index of exports to developing areas.

[b] Unit-value index of exports (excl. S.I.T.C. section 3) from developing to developed areas divided by unit-value index of exports from developed to developing areas.

[c] Unit-value index of world exports of S.I.T.C. sections 0-4 divided by unit-value index of world exports of S.I.T.C. sections 5-8.

Sources: U.N. *Monthly Bulletin of Statistics;* U.N. *Yearbook of Trade Statistics;* I.M.F., *International Financial Statistics.*

would result from a movement back to high-tariff protectionism. This trend has been eased and strengthened by the international institutions set up after the war, in particular the I.M.F. and GATT: the former by providing financial facilities which reduce the need for short-term protectionist measures in the face of balance of payments problems; the latter by acting as a negotiating forum and as a pressure group for liberalisation. In particular, the central GATT principle of the 'most favoured nation' (m.f.n.) has done much to prevent the proliferation of preferential bilateral trading agreements. (The m.f.n. principle requires that liberalisation measures accorded by one contracting party to another must be extended to all other contracting parties, except where the concession forms part of the creation of a common market or a free-trade area.) Since 1964 the United Nations Conference on Trade and Development (UNCTAD) has provided a further forum on trade matters, primarily those concerning trade between developed and developing countries.

GATT

Since 1947 there have been six 'rounds' of GATT negotiations. Of these, the most important in terms of the volume of trade covered were the first (at Geneva in 1947) which covered some U.S.$10,000 million of trade, and the recent 'Kennedy Round' (1964–7) which covered some U.S.$40,000 million of trade. Cuts under the Kennedy Round were completed at the beginning of 1972. According to Professor Balassa, the average tariff on imports of manufactures into the industrialised members of GATT fell from 10·9 per cent to 6·5 per cent as a result of the Kennedy Round negotiations. As far as the developing countries are concerned, however, the average duty on their manufactured exports to the developed market economy countries fell from 17·1 per cent to 11·8 per cent. Proportionally, this was a bigger cut than the average, but the continued higher-than-average level of the tariff that developing countries have to face on their exports is attributable to the concentration of their exports in relatively few goods – textiles, footwear, etc. – in which production in developed countries is declining (and often geographically concentrated), and the fear of social problems has resulted in the retention of higher-than-average tariffs.

Despite its very real positive successes, perhaps GATT's major achievement to date has been the avoidance of the breaking-up of world trade into large but isolated blocs, which has seemed a serious possibility from time to time. There have been periodic outbreaks of protectionist pressure in the United States – most recently, in the months preceding the currency realignment of 1971 – and it could be argued that the institutional framework provided by GATT has helped to restrain these pressures. Part of the Americans' problem has stemmed from the decline of domestic industry in the face of 'low-cost foreign competition', which is reflected in the negotiation of voluntary restraint agreements on the export of non-cotton textiles to the United States from Asian suppliers. Another important element in the 1960s has been American concern at the trade policies of the E.E.C., in particular the impact of the Common Agricultural Policy of the Community on American farm exports, and also the preferences accorded to the E.E.C. by the growing number of developing countries associated with the Community. There have, of course, been problems on the other side: the American Selling Price system (which acts as a variable levy on exports of chemicals to the United States) is one example. But the major problem has been in the field of agriculture, where the structural problems tend to be more intractable than in the case of manu- factured goods. It is likely that all these various problems will continue to threaten the continuation of the trend towards trade liberalisation. They will be the object of a detailed study by GATT during 1973 which the United States in particular has requested.

UNCTAD

The major achievement of UNCTAD to date has been the promotion of the Generalised Preference Scheme (or rather 'schemes', since it has proved impossible for the developed countries to agree on a common scheme, with the result that all the schemes vary in both the range of products covered and in the extent of the concessions made). In principle, the schemes were to allow unrestricted duty-free entry to all manufactured exports and reduced rates of duty on a range of processed agricultural products coming from developing countries. In practice, duty-free entry has not been accorded to all manu- factures. For example, for both the E.E.C. and the United Kingdom it is estimated that the result of the Generalised Preference Scheme, and already existing duty-free entry, will be that some 70 per cent of developing countries' manufactured exports will enjoy duty-free entry without limitation. For many of the products in which the developing countries are successful exporters, tariff (or, in the case of the E.E.C., duty-free quota) restrictions are applied. The schemes are thus less generous than was originally hoped, but the G.P.S. has none the less been a major achievement, which has introduced a new principle into international trading relations – that of non-reciprocal trading preferences for developing countries only.

Measures of protection

Several policy measures are available – and have been used – to protect domestic industry from foreign competition. Of these, the most important has been the tariff, although its relative importance has declined as a result of the trade-liberalisation measures described above. Before looking at the evidence on the levels of tariffs, it is useful to consider their effects. (Other, non-tariff, barriers to trade are considered in a later section.)

Tariffs are of two types. An *ad valorem* tariff is a charge which is based on the *value* of the imported good. Thus an *ad valorem* tariff of 15 per cent simply means that a duty of 15 per cent of its value is levied on imports of a good. A *specific duty* is a duty levied on the *quantity* of a good, e.g. a specific duty of £3·25 per lb. on tobacco. *Nominal* tariff rates are the percentage increase in the price of an import sold in the domestic market which results from the imposition of the tariff. Obviously, where an *ad valorem* tariff is concerned, the nominal rate is the same as the *ad valorem* rate. A specific duty is easily converted to an *ad valorem* equivalent, and thus to a nominal rate. For example, if 1 lb. of the tobacco mentioned above is worth £2·50, the specific duty of £3·25 per lb. is equivalent to a nominal tariff of 130 per cent.

Since it measures the increase in the price of a good which results from the tariff, the nominal tariff rate (or, as it is often called, the *nominal rate of protection*) is a measure of the increased cost that the tariff structure imposes on the consumer in the protected market. The nominal rate is not, however, a satisfactory measure of the effects that a tariff structure has on the allocation of resources (and production) between industries within a country, or internationally. For this, a measure is needed (the *effective rate of protection*) which indicates the protection given by tariffs and other trade measures to in-dividual processes in the production of goods.

The following example illustrates the concept of effective protection. Suppose that the production of shoes involves only two stages of processing – the production of leather, and the making of shoes from the leather. Let us suppose further that in the absence of any tariffs it would cost £1·20 to produce enough leather to make a pair of shoes, and that converting the leather into shoes costs a further £0·80. Thus the final selling price of shoes in this free-trade situation would be £2.

Now suppose that a tariff of 20 per cent is imposed on the import of shoes, but that imports of leather continue to be duty-free. The price of shoes will rise to £2·40 in the domestic market as a result of the 20 per cent tariff, and this is a loss to the consumer. The protective benefit of the tariff accrues to the domestic shoemaker, since the domestic leather producer must continue to sell leather at £1·20, otherwise leather will be imported for the same price. Thus, the result of the tariff is that the shoemaker now receives £1·20 for the production of shoes from leather (£2·40 minus £1·20 – the cost of the leather): an increase of 50 per cent. Thus, while the nominal rate of protection on shoes is 20 per cent, the *effective* rate of protection on shoemaking is 50 per cent, since this is the price rise which the tariff structure allows to the shoemaker.

Now suppose that there is a change in tariff policy, and that the 20 per cent tariff on shoes is maintained, but in addition a 10 per cent tariff is imposed on the import of leather for shoe production. This has no effect on the nominal tariff on shoes, and implies no additional cost for the consumer – shoes still sell for £2·40 – but the shoemaker must now pay £1·32 rather than £1·20 for his leather. He now receives £1·08 for processing leather into shoes, so under this new tariff structure the effective rate of protection on shoemaking is 35 per cent, compared with 50 per cent when there was no tariff on leather. The rate of effective protection for domestic leather producers (who do not import any of their inputs) is now 10 per cent, the same as the nominal rate.

It is possible for a tariff structure to protect inputs to such an extent that the protection on a subsequent stage of processing is cancelled out, or even made negative. In our shoes and leather example, suppose that a tariff of 33⅓ per cent is levied on imports of leather for shoemaking. Domestic leather producers can now raise their price to £1·60, and with the final selling price of shoes still at £2·40 because of the 20 per cent tariff on shoes, the shoemaker receives £0·80 for making shoes (£2·40 less £1·60 for leather). Since this is no more than the shoemaker would receive if there were no tariffs at all, the effective rate of protection on shoemaking is zero, despite the existence of a 20 per cent tariff on the import of shoes. Indeed, if the tariff on leather were greater than 33⅓ per cent, the effective protection on shoemaking would be *negative*, that is, the tariff structure would work in such a way as to tax the domestic shoemaker compared with his foreign competitor, although the presence of the 20 per cent tariff on shoes might at first suggest the opposite.

Obviously, in real life the calculation of effective rates of protection is a more difficult exercise than in the simplified example given above. One of the hardest problems is in deciding what the cost of certain stages of processing would be in the absence of tariffs, and for this reason the data which follow should be viewed as giving only an approximation to effective rates of protection. None the less, there are two general rules which can act as a rough guide: (*a*) for a given tariff structure, effective protection on a particular process is higher, the smaller the share of that process in final output; (*b*) for any one process, the effective protection is higher, the higher the nominal rate of protection on the process's output, and the lower the nominal rates of protection on the process's inputs.

In the tables which follow, the nominal rates are to be taken as a measure of the consumer cost of tariffs, the effective rates as measures of the protection given to domestic production against imports. Table 5 shows that although both developed and developing countries benefitted from the Kennedy Round negotiations, the latter continue to face higher-than-average protection on their manufactured exports to developed countries (their absolute gain from the round was, however, higher than average).

Table 6 gives *pre*-Kennedy Round figures on average effective rates of protection for the United Kingdom, the United States, the E.E.C. and Japan, and Table 7 average rates of effective protection for manufactured products of particular interest to the developing countries. While the Kennedy Round has resulted in some reduction in these rates (see Table 5), the pattern is unlikely to have altered much. Table 8 gives some post-Kennedy Round data for the United Kingdom and the

Table 5[a]
AVERAGE[b] OF NOMINAL AND EFFECTIVE TARIFFS ON
INDUSTRIAL COUNTRIES' IMPORTS OF MANUFACTURES,
BEFORE AND AFTER THE KENNEDY ROUND
(percentages)

	Nominal Imports from:		Effective Imports from:	
	All sources	Developing countries	All sources	Developing countries
Pre-Kennedy (1967)	10·9	17·1	19·2	33·4
Post-Kennedy (1972)	6·5	11·8	11·1	22·6

[a] Figures for effective protection in this and following tables should be taken as indicating orders of magnitude rather than precise measures.

[b] The weights used in calculating these average tariffs were non-preferential imports. The height of the tariffs is somewhat overestimated because of this.

Source: Bela Balassa, *The Structure of Protection in Industrial Countries*, I.B.R.D. Report No. EC-152a, quoted in Little, Scitovsky and Scott, *Industry and Trade in Some Developing Countries* (O.E.C.D., 1970).

Table 6
AVERAGE LEVELS OF EFFECTIVE RATES OF PROTECTION,
PRE-KENNEDY ROUND
(percentages)

	All commodities	Intermediate products I	II	Consumer goods	Investment goods
E.E.C.	18·6	12·0	28·3	30·9	15·0
U.S.A.	20·0	17·6	28·6	25·9	20·0
U.K.	27·8	23·1	34·3	40·4	15·5
Japan	29·5	23·8	34·5	50·5	29·5

Source: Balassa, *Journal of Political Economy* (Dec 1965), quoted in John Pincus, *Trade, Aid and Development* (1967).

United States. Table 8 includes estimates of the effects of non-tariff measures; these are discussed below.

On the face of it, the tables paint an unexpected picture of the relative protectionism of the major industrial countries. If anything, the E.E.C. emerges as the most liberal, and Japan would not appear to be markedly more restrictive than the United Kingdom. It should be noted, however, that these

Table 7
ESTIMATED EFFECTIVE RATES OF PROTECTION FOR CERTAIN
MANUFACTURED PRODUCTS IN 1962
(percentages)

	U.S.A.	U.K.	E.E.C.	Japan
Textiles	50·6	42·2	44·4	48·8
Hosiery	48·7	49·7	41·3	60·8
Clothing	35·9	40·5	25·1	42·4
Other textile articles	22·7	42·4	38·8	13·0
Shoes	25·3	36·2	33·0	45·1
Leather	25·7	34·3	18·3	59·0
Rubber goods	16·1	43·9	33·6	23·6
Plastic articles	27·0	30·1	30·0	35·5
Bicycles	26·1	39·2	39·7	45·0
Sports goods, toys, etc.	41·8	35·6	26·6	31·2

Source: as Table 6.

Table 8
NOMINAL AND EFFECTIVE RATES OF PROTECTION IN THE
U.S.A. AND THE U.K. BY COMMODITY GROUP, 1972:
POST-KENNEDY ROUND
(percentages)

	Nominal rates	Effective rates	
	Tariffs only	Tariff and non-tariff measures	Non-tariff measures only
U.S.A.:			
Primary commodities	7	17	8
Intermediate and consumer goods	7	18	7
Capital goods	6	7	-1
Average	6	15	5
U.K.:			
Primary commodities	2	18	n.a.
Intermediate and consumer goods	3	11	n.a.
Capital goods	8	17	n.a.
Average	3	13	n.a.

Source: R. E. Baldwin, *Non-Tariff Distortions to International Trade* (1971) Tables 5 and 7.

averages have been calculated on the basis of m.f.n. tariff rates. The estimates for the United Kingdom (and to a much lesser extent the E.E.C.) are thus inflated, since they do not take account of the large volume of trade under preferential arrangements. In the case of the United Kingdom the existence of the Commonwealth Preference system is not taken account of, nor that of EFTA. In 1969 the former accounted for 26·8 per cent of all U.K. imports, and EFTA for 15·1 per cent.

Non-tariff barriers

Tariffs are not, of course, the only obstacles to international trade, and as liberalisation of tariff barriers has proceeded, the relative importance of other, non-tariff barriers has increased. Non-tariff barriers (or N.T.B.s) may be defined as legal or administrative acts and procedures which reduce the flow of trade, and which increase the cost of a good in the domestic market (although in the case of some N.T.B.s, such as production subsidies, the increased cost of the good is reflected in a greater tax burden rather than in an increased price for the good itself). An exhaustive list of N.T.B.s is probably impossible, but the following covers the major ones:

(*a*) *Quantitative restrictions.* The most familiar example is the *quota* on the import of a particular good – import of the good is prohibited beyond a certain amount. Examples of quotas are those operated by most of the developed countries on imports of cotton textiles from developing countries, under the GATT Long-Term Arrangement on Cotton Textiles. (The L.T.A. provides for a 5 per cent annual growth rate in the quotas on imports of cotton textiles from developing countries.)

A similar example of quantitative restriction is the *import-licensing* system, under which all imports, or imports of certain goods, can only be undertaken against a licence granted by the licensing authority. While licensing is more flexible than a quota (the latter is usually set for one year, the former can be varied by increasing or decreasing the rate at which licences are issued), this system can involve considerable administrative delays and costs to the importer, as well as the costs of running the licensing authority. Import licensing can also be used to discriminate between sources of supply, on criteria other than the quality or price of goods. Import licensing is common in developing countries.

Less common is *export licensing*, which simply involves prohibition of the export of goods, except under licence.

Another variant is the *voluntary restraint agreement*, by which an exporter, usually under the threat of other action, agrees to limit the volume of his exports to the domestic market. Usually such agreements allow for a steady (though often modest) increase in the volume of trade each year. An example is the recent agreement negotiated between the United States and the major Asian suppliers of non-cotton textiles.

The effect of quantitative restrictions is to insulate part of the market from the competition of imports. Unless quotas are very large in relation to market size, or licences are issued freely, the effect is to reserve a portion of the domestic market for domestic producers, and inevitably higher prices result. While tariffs modify comparative advantage, quantitative restrictions nullify it, except within the permitted volume of imports.

(*b*) *Variable levies*. The variable levies operated in the E.E.C.'s Common Agricultural Policy are a well-known example of this device. The variable levy works by imposing a customs duty (or levy) which brings the price of the import up to a target price set for the good in the domestic market. Domestic producers are thus assured of a price in the domestic market at which they can sell without the fear of being undercut by imports. The effect of a variable levy is, once again, to raise the price which a consumer has to pay for a good. Like quantitative restrictions, a variable levy also has the effect of destroying the comparative advantage of foreign exporters, as far as the domestic market is concerned: as long as the foreign supplier can export at or below the target price in the domestic market, it makes no difference whether other foreign suppliers can produce more cheaply; the competitive difference is wiped out by the variable levy.

(*c*) *Subsidies to domestic production*. This is an alternative to protecting domestic production by raising the domestic price: domestic producers receive a subsidy (e.g. an increased price from a marketing board; exceptionally high depreciation allowances; relief from normal taxation; improvement grants;

subsidies on services to the industry, such as agricultural extension services, etc.) which allows them to compete with imports in the home market and/or to increase their ability to export. Such measures are particularly common in the agricultural sectors; but they have also been applied to other industries, e.g. shipbuilding. The effect of these measures is to make some of the cost of production external to the industry, so that this part of the cost is borne out of general taxation, rather than by making consumers pay a higher price for the product.

(*d*) *Exchange controls and export credit.* These measures are grouped together, since they apply to goods as a whole, rather than specific products.

(i) *Exchange controls* limit the amount of foreign exchange which is made available to importers for the purchase of foreign goods. While general in application, they are often administered in a way which specifies which goods are eligible for foreign exchange. For this purpose, import licensing is usually combined with, and in fact becomes the instrument of, exchange control (see above).

(ii) *Export credit* measures can be used to subsidise the rates of credit which exporters offer to importers of their goods. In the 1960s there was a rapid softening of credit terms, and this has led to agreements on the maximum levels of credit to be permitted on some exports – notably ships and aircraft. Strictly, of course, measures which encourage exports are not *non-tariff* barriers – just the reverse; but they are included here for the sake of completeness.

(*e*) *Export pricing.* As indicated above, governmental intervention can act to alter the prices of exports. Two other common measures are (i) *export-marketing boards*, common in the field of primary agricultural commodities. Where these have the effect of raising export prices, they are acting as a non-tariff barrier to trade, although from the supplier's rather than from the importer's end of the trade transaction. (ii) *Export taxes* (the reverse of export subsidies) again raise the price in the importing market above the free-trade level.

(*f*) *Administrative practices.* There are many variations on this theme. Among the most important are:

(i) Discriminatory government *procurement practices*, by which governmental agencies are directed to purchase domestic goods to meet their requirements, even though an acceptable foreign good could be imported at a lower price.

(ii) *Health regulations*, which can add to the cost of imports, and cause delay in trade.

(iii) Discriminatory *customs treatment*, which it has been claimed certain countries practise, by which goods of a favoured trading partner are accorded speedier customs clearance than the goods of others.

The major difficulty with the non-tariff barriers, such as those outlined above, is that their effects are difficult, sometimes impossible, to quantify. In theory, it is possible to measure their effects by converting them to a tariff equivalent, that is, the minimum tariff rate which would have to be levied to have the same effect on the price of the good in the domestic market, and/or to restrict the share of imports in the domestic market, to the level that the non-tariff barrier effects. But in practice, assessment of the effects of N.T.B.s in these terms may be impossible for lack of the necessary data, and this is no doubt one of the reasons why progress on liberalising N.T.B.s has been very slow, in comparison with tariff barriers. N.T.B.s, like tariffs, are often justified in terms of objectives other than trading ones. For example, health regulations on meat products will often exist purely to protect domestic consumers and domestic livestock from disease; export taxes are a means of increasing saving in an economy, and will often serve the purpose of maintaining export revenue from a good for which the demand is price-inelastic; the choice of farm subsidies, rather than variable levies, may be in pursuit of the objective of a 'better' domestic distribution of income, as well as easing a decline in agricultural production and employment.

As might be expected, there is little quantitative evidence on non-tariff barriers in general. However, in his book *Non-Tariff Distortions to International Trade*, Professor Baldwin provides estimates of the tariff equivalent of some non-tariff barriers in the United Kingdom and the United States. These are reproduced in Table 8 above. Professor Baldwin's estimates suggest that N.T.B.s are now of an equal order of magnitude to the tariff barriers which remain after the effects of the Kennedy Round.

PROS AND CONS OF IMPORT SUBSTITUTION

'Inward-looking' v. 'outward-looking' policies in developing countries

Until recently, many developing countries have adopted an inward-looking strategy for their industrial development. In part, this was a reaction to the extent of their dependence on international trade for supplies of manufactured goods, and to the instability of international trade during the Second World War. However, the major influences would seem to have been (*a*) the infant-industry argument, but applied broadly to the whole of the industrial sector; (*b*) the role of tariff revenue in raising the rate of savings and the finance available to the government, where other means of taxation have proved difficult; and (*c*) expectation of saving of foreign exchange by cutting the import bill.

It is generally accepted that most industries, when newly set up, need some protection from foreign competition during the period in which the process of 'learning by doing' comes into effect, and efficiency improves. The appropriate level of protection for a new industry, and the length of time for which protection needs to be given to it, will vary from industry to industry, and judgement on these matters is a matter of some skill. Given that the ultimate objective is that the industry should be as efficient as possible, however, there can be un-desired effects if the level of protection is set too high, or is maintained for too long. Where the tariffs or N.T.B.s are high enough to secure all or part of the domestic market for the new industry, industrial growth can be expected to be rapid while substitution for imports take place. However, there is a growing body of evidence which has led some authors to suggest that where the level of protection begins at too high a level, and remains so, competitive pressure – of which imports are an important source – will be lacking, and the long-term goal of efficiency may not be attained. On this, view an excessive level of protection is likely to result in the creation of an inefficient industry, dependent on a high level of protection for its continued operation, and unable to compete in international markets. Little, Scitovsky and Scott have suggested that labour subsidies are preferable to high tariffs as protection for infant industries.

The relevant 'level of protection' in this context is the *effective* rate of protection, for it is this measure, rather than the nominal rate, which measures the protection given to an individual industrial process. As tariff structures become more complex, it becomes more difficult to assess what level of protection is being accorded to industries; no doubt this explains how it happens that investigation has discovered surely unintended instances both of effective protection rates of over 1,000 per cent and of negative effective protection in some industries in developing countries.

Trade measures also have implications for the rest of the economy, and these effects are reinforced when the industrial sector is given preferential treatment in access to scarce (capital) resources. High protection leads to high profits and wages in the industrial sector, and as a result the allocation of domestic resources is biased in the industrial sector's favour, even though the *real* returns in other sectors, such as agriculture, may be higher. Finally, where imports are restrained, the currency will tend to be overvalued, which reduces the competitiveness of the exports of both the protected and the unprotected sectors.

Not all developing countries have pursued such policies (e.g. Hong Kong), and an increasing number of those which have done so in the past are now trying to reverse their policies. The leaders in this change have been Taiwan, South Korea and Mexico, and there have recently been indications that India is becoming increasingly concerned with the problem of en- couraging more 'export-orientated' manufacturing industry. More countries may be expected to move in this direction, with the growing realisation that the high rates of growth which import substitution allows in its early years (a rate of growth inflated by the artificially high price of the protected products in the domestic market) cannot be sustained once the limits of the domestic market are reached. But the longer a policy of import substitution has been pursued, the more difficult it becomes to reverse the policy, owing to the increasing dependence of the industrial sector on protection, and the resultant vested interests in its continuation.

Table 9 gives estimates of effective rates of protection in seven developing countries, broken down by commodity group. The

Table 9

LEVELS OF EFFECTIVE PROTECTION IN SOME DEVELOPING COUNTRIES, BY COMMODITY GROUP

(percentages)

	Year	Consumption goods	Inter-mediates	Capital goods	All manu-factures
Argentina	1958	164	167	133	162
Brazil	1966	230	68	31	118
Mexico	1960	22	34	55	27
India	1961	n.a.	n.a.	n.a.	313[a]
Pakistan	1963-4	883	88	155	271
Philippines	1965	94	65	80	49
Taiwan	1965	n.a.	n.a.	n.a.	33

[a] Figure is for one-sixth of large-scale manufacturing industry.

Source: Little, Scitovsky and Scott, *Industry and Trade in Some Developing Countries*, Table 5.2, p. 174.

figures in Table 9 should be treated cautiously, as indicating orders of magnitude rather than accurate levels of the rates of effective protection. As Little, Scitovsky and Scott point out, the purpose of the protection has often been to save foreign exchange, rather than solely to protect domestic industry. The success of such policies in saving foreign exchange is coming increasingly to be questioned, however: often the protected industry may contribute little value added; inputs need to be imported; and the net foreign exchange saving may be small and can indeed be negative in extreme cases. This is particularly important when the investment is financed from foreign borrowing or foreign private investment. Inasmuch as foreign exchange is being 'saved' for developmental reasons, there would appear to be a vicious circle here: saving foreign exchange leads to investment but it is of little developmental value, owing to the market conditions which the method of foreign exchange saving creates for industry.

Inward-looking policies in developed countries

In the developed countries, levels of both nominal and effective protection are generally much lower than in developing countries (compare Tables 5 and 9). Where high levels of protection persist, there is rarely any foreign exchange or infant-industry argument involved; rather it is a question of retarding the decline of industries whose comparative advantage has gone. Obvious examples are the cotton textiles and footwear industries in most developed countries, and peasant agriculture in the E.E.C. Agriculture in particular poses its own special problems. There are social and strategic arguments in favour of maintaining a sizeable agricultural sector, even at the economic costs reflected in higher prices to consumers and/or in taxation for subsidies. The effects of these policies are similar in kind to those described above for developing countries, but the effects on resource allocation have been much less serious than in the latter case, not least because the levels of protection and their scope compared with the size of the whole economy has been so much less.

None the less, the levels of protection involved in the various protective measures are high and the absolute costs involved are substantial. Relatively little progress has been made in liberalisation of those agricultural products of which both developed and developing countries are producers (these products account for about three-quarters of developing countries' exports of non-petroleum primary products).

Data on agricultural protection in developed countries

The E.E.C. The E.E.C. provides price support and a variable levy system for the major commodities which it produces and which are threatened by import competition. Thus variable levies exist on cereals, dairy products, pigmeat, eggs and poultry meat. In *Non-Tariff Distortions to International Trade*, Baldwin quotes the following rates of effective protection as resulting from the operation of the variable levy system, in the period July–Spetember 1967: soft wheat, 77·1 per cent; barley, 45 per cent; maize, 51·3 per cent; pigmeat, 40·1 per cent; poultry, 21·2 per cent. Rates of protection on butter in the same period varied between 276·4 per cent (Italy) and 355·3 per cent (Belgium), while effective protection on live cattle varied between 28·4 per cent (Italy) and 53·6 per cent (Germany).

In addition, the high price support and government-sponsored technical innovation in agriculture is producing a situation in which imports take a declining share of the market, and surpluses are 'dumped' in overseas markets.

The United Kingdom. Traditional U.K. agricultural policy was to allow foodstuff imports to enter freely, and to pay farmers the difference between the market-determined price and an agreed producer price. In addition, subsidies on the use of fertilisers and on farm improvements, etc., were paid, and amounted to about 6 per cent of the total domestic value added in the agricultural sector in 1967–8. Recently, however, there has been a change towards import-reducing policies, such as the minimum import-price system for grains and bacon, and entry to the E.E.C. will entail the adoption of the E.E.C.'s Common Agricultural Policy. Baldwin (op. cit.) has estimated that the effective rate of protection on 'agriculture, forestry and fishing' in the United Kingdom before the recent policy changes was of the order of 27 per cent, and on cereal foodstuffs of the order of 42 per cent. These figures make provision for the effects of export rebates and subsidies.

The United States. One of the major indirect aids to U.S. agriculture is the government finance of research and development (U.S.$525 million in 1966). Low-interest government loans are also provided for the rural sector. More direct measures consist of price support, including quotas and export subsidies. The latter cost U.S.$507 million in 1965–6, when the export subsidy on wheat was 18 per cent, on milled rice 40 per cent, on cotton 19 per cent and on peanuts 60 per cent (all as percentage of final price). Baldwin estimated the effective rate of protection on livestock and livestock products at only 2 per cent for 1972, but 21 per cent on other agricultural products. Food and kindred products attracted an effective rate of protection of 23 per cent.

Adjustment assistance

Declining industries in developed countries (other than agriculture) are often concentrated in areas in which they provide a major source of employment. Frequently their decline has not been compensated by the appearance of new industries to absorb the surplus labour, and labour immobility has strengthened the pressure for the imposition of high rates of protection. It is often suggested that much of the inefficiency thus created could be avoided were governments to provide adjustment assistance to both labour and employers. Few developed countries have coherent policy programmes of adjustment assistance. The E.E.C. has a social fund which finances the retraining and relocation of labour; the United States has statutory provision for adjustment assistance, but this has so far been little used; Japan has recently set up an adjustment fund, to deal with any disruption which may result from the implementation of the Generalised Preference Scheme. In the United Kingdom, measures have been taken from time to time to ease the problems arising from the contraction of particular industries. In addition, since many of the adjustment problems have been concentrated in particular regions, there has been a long history of attempts to deal with these problems in the context of regional policy. Attention has been particularly directed towards incentives for new investment and a variety of techniques has been adopted. There have also been limited programmes for worker retraining and programmes for assisting farmers to retire and smallholdings to be amalgamated. The fact that after many years of attempts to tackle adjustment problems in general and regional problems in particular, regional disparities are still a matter for concern in Britian, is an illustration of the intractable nature of the problems which can arise.

In a number of developed countries the rate of economic growth has slackened in recent years. In some cases this has made more acute the need for adjustment assistance for particular industries. At the same time, slow growth has made it difficult both to generate the resources for such assistance and to apply them effectively.

REGIONAL TRADING BLOCS

Previous sections have discussed some of the implications of liberalising trade on a global scale. This section looks at the implications for L.D.C.s of liberalising trade on a smaller scale, by the creation of regional blocs. Regional integration is of importance to L.D.C.s in three ways: (*a*) they are affected by regional integration within developed countries in so far as this alters trade relationships between developed and developing countries; (*b*) they are affected by regional integration schemes containing both developed and developing countries; and (*c*) most importantly, regional integration schemes between developing countries have great significance for development.

Regional integration schemes vary in the intensity of the links which they strive to create. At one extreme, Commonwealth Preference aims only at a limited degree of integration, while at the other extreme, the Belgium-Luxembourg economic union envisages a virtually total economic integration. The familiar classification of regional integration schemes in terms of the closeness of the union is as follows (from Kahnert *et al.*, 1969)[1]:

(*a*) The *free-trade area*, which implies the removal of quantitative restrictions and customs tariffs.

(*b*) The *customs union*, which unifies the tariff of the countries within the area against outsiders.

(*c*) The *common market*, where all restrictions on factor movements within the area are abolished.

(*d*) The *economic union*, where economic, monetary, fiscal and social and counter-cyclical policies are to some extent harmonised.

(*e*) The *supranational union*, where the respective governments abandon completely their sovereignty over the policies listed above and a supranational authority issues binding decisions.

One might add to the list, as a still looser bond than the free-trade area, the *preferential trading area*, which raises in essence the same economic issues of trade creation and trade diversion.

These economic issues have been gradually clarified over the last twenty years, thanks mainly to the contributions of Viner (1950)[2] and Balassa (1967)[3]. Of the three fields in which economic integration affects the individual economy – efficient allocation of resources, dynamic consideration, distribution of income – it is the first that has been most thoroughly investigated. In this area, Viner's concepts of *trade creation* and *trade diversion* still provide the simplest exposition of the basic issues (though Balassa's 'positive and negative trade effects' are more rigorous).

Trade creation is said to occur when the removal of trade barriers within the integration area leads to greater utilisation of comparative advantage. If country A has a comparative advantage in the production of motor-cars, and country B has a comparative advantage in textiles, but A maintains an inefficient textile industry behind protective barriers while B has an inefficient protected automotive industry, then it can be expected that economic integration between the two countries will lead to resources being transferred from textile to automotive production in country A, and from automotive to textile production in country B. Everyone will benefit from this process of trade creation.

On the other hand, it may be the case that country A was previously importing textiles from a third country which is not to form part of the proposed integration scheme and which is a lower-cost producer than country B. If country A has a non-discriminatory tariff structure, it will of course purchase from the cheaper source, which we call country C. But as a result of regional integration, tariff and quantitative restrictions are removed for country B's exports, while being maintained for country C's exports. This may lead to an increase in imports of textiles from the high-cost industry in country B, and a reduction in imports of textiles from the low-cost industry in country C. This is what Viner calls *trade diversion*, and it represents a loss for all these countries in terms of efficient allocation of resources (though there may be dynamic benefits to country B). The loss will be most evident to country A, which is paying a higher foreign exchange cost for its imports, and to country C, which has lost an export market. But country B is also being led to specialise in a type of production in which it has no comparative advantage, and unless it has chronic unemployment or shortage of foreign exchange, it too does not benefit from trade diversion.

The assessment of economic integration schemes in 'static' terms is based on whether they give rise predominantly to trade creation or trade diversion. More important in the long run than these effects, however, is the effect that economic integration may have on the rate of growth in the area. The existence of a larger market may facilitate industrialisation or (to take the view of Kahnert *et al.*), if industrialisation is to occur in any case for political reasons, its cost will be lower if the market is larger.

The remaining dimension to be considered in analysing regional integration is its effect on income distribution. It will affect income distribution *within* countries and also *between* countries. Little of general validity can be said about the effects on *internal* income distribution; but on the second issue the point needs to be made that trade diversion may be beneficial if trade is diverted towards less developed countries. A general agreement on this point has been the basis for the various generalised preference schemes that have been, or will be, introduced.

Having sketched out the economic issues, it may be useful to distinguish three different types of regional integration schemes according to the level of development of the participant countries. Each can be briefly examined in terms of its effects on less developed countries:

(*a*) Regional integration among developed countries, e.g. the European Economic Community.
(*b*) Regional integration including both developed and less developed countries, e.g. association with the E.E.C.
(*c*) Regional integration among less developed countries, e.g. the Latin American Free Trade Association.

Naturally, in all schemes there will be some differences in the degree of development of the participants, but this does not detract from the value of the classification.

Regional integration among developed countries

This section is concerned with the effects on less developed countries of regional integration among developed countries. The matter is usually discussed under the headings of 'outward-looking' and 'inward-looking' policies. A particular concern of topical interest is the effect on less developed countries of the United Kingdom's accession to the E.E.C.

What statistics allow one to make some assessment of the likely restrictive effect of the enlargement of the E.E.C.? Firstly, comparative levels of effective tariff protection may be examined;

Tables 6 and 7 above give some indication of the comparison between U.K. and E.E.C. levels. However, as mentioned earlier, the use of most-favoured-nation rates is misleading since much of the trade between the United Kingdom, the E.E.C. and less developed countries is carried on with preferential tariffs. Imports under Commonwealth Preference into the United Kingdom are particularly important; less so, in relative terms, are the E.E.C.'s imports from its associates.

Secondly, one may examine the actual performance of the United Kingdom and the E.E.C. in importing from less developed countries. This is summarised in Table 10.

It can be seen that imports from L.D.C.s per head were about 15 per cent higher in the United Kingdom than in the E.E.C. This is not a great difference, though it should be borne in mind that income per head was 5 per cent lower in the United Kingdom. Of the difference of $11·50 per head, $4 was accounted for by food and $5 by manufactured goods. (It is true that S.I.T.C. 6 contains a number of goods, such as unwrought nonferrous metals, which it is rather misleading to classify as manufactured; however, it is not these goods which accounted for the difference).

This is not the place for a thorough analysis of the effects on L.D.C.s of the United Kingdom's accession. The adoption of the Common External Tariff by the United Kingdom will, as has been shown, improve the access of L.D.C.s which were not accorded Commonwealth Preference. Of the countries which were receiving Commonwealth Preference, those in Africa, the Caribbean, the Indian Ocean and the Pacific will be offered the option of associating with the E.E.C., and so have the chance to retain most of their existing tariff advantages. Problems may, however, arise for some countries among the Asian members of the Commonwealth, though it is to be hoped that they will be solved in the spirit of the Joint Declaration of Intent annexed to the Treaty of Brussels.

Regional integration between developed and less developed countries

Far-reaching schemes for economic integration between countries at very different levels of economic development are

Table 10

PATTERN OF IMPORTS FROM L.D.C.s INTO THE U.K. AND THE E.E.C., 1969

S.I.T.C. No.	Description	Total imports ($m.)	L.D.C. imports ($m.)	L.D.C. imports as % of total (%)	L.D.C. imports per head of population ($)	Total imports ($m.)	L.D.C. imports ($m.)	L.D.C. imports as % of total (%)	L.D.C. imports per head of population ($)
0	Food, live animals	4,201	1,115	26·5	20·1	10,511	3,051	29·1	16·3
1	Beverages, tobacco	441	68	15·4	1·2	978	205	21·0	1·1
2	Crude materials, inedible	2,835	733	25·9	13·2	9,848	2,810	28·6	15·0
3	Fuels	2,185	1,708	78·0	30·8	7,952	5,616	70·6	30·0
4	Oils and Fats	176	78	44·3	1·4	622	248	39·9	1·3
5	Chemicals	1,111	72	6·5	1·3	5,526	145	2·6	0·8
6	Manufactures, classified by material	4,416	943	21·3	17·0	17,435	2,234	12·8	11·9
7	Machinery, transport equipment	3,166	80	2·5	1·4	15,593	97	0·6	0·5
8	Other manufactures	1,232	256	20·8	4·6	6,052	339	5·6	1·8
9	Other transactions	194	23	11·8	0·4	1,059	37	3·5	0·2
10	Total	19,957	5,076	25·4	91·4	75,576	14,782	19·6	78·9

seldom found, since they suffer from serious drawbacks. If one country is mainly a primary producer and the other an industrial producer, there is not likely to be scope for trade creation; any increase in trade following integration would largely be based on trade diversion.

A second drawback would be the difficulty of starting industries in the less developed partner state, as long as the more developed one has duty-free access. While the infant-industry argument is undoubtedly overworked, it does have some validity. For these reasons, agreements between groups of developed and less developed countries nowadays permit the L.D.C.s to impose barriers against imports from the more industrialised partners.

The schemes involving both developed and less developed countries are so loose that it is doubtful whether they fall within the framework of 'regional integration'. The two main schemes are association with the E.E.C. and Commonwealth Preference (the latter will, for the most part, be absorbed into the former as a result of the United Kingdom's accession to the E.E.C.). While it is not intended to quantify the costs and benefits of such schemes, the issues can be categorised in the following way:

(a) *Imports by industrialised partners:*

(i) *Primary products.* If the less developed producers are competitive producers, regional integration will have no effect on trade patterns. If they are not competitive, and if the regional integration or preferential agreement leads to trade diversion, this would not be consistent with the efficient international division of labour, although it might benefit the least developed participants.

(ii) *Manufactures.* If regional integration or preferential trade agreements lead to trade creation in manufactures which increase the exports of L.D.C.s – as has been the case with textiles from India and Pakistan under Commonwealth Preference – this could lead to the more efficient international division of labour, income benefits to L.D.C.s and a higher growth potential, although the redeployment of resources in the developed partner may raise problems. If trade diversion in manufactured goods results, then the damage to efficient division of labour is to be weighed against the distributional and growth benefits to L.D.C.s.

(*b*) *Imports by less developed partners.* The benefits of trade creation will in many cases be outweighed by the setbacks to growth which it may imply; the L.D.C. will usually find it difficult to redeploy its resources. Trade diversion could lead to a higher foreign exchange cost of imports not offset by any distributional or dynamic gain.

Regional integration among L.D.C.s

In recent years many L.D.C.s have recognised the advantages of regional integration schemes, particularly in overcoming the obstacles to growth imposed by small market size. As a result, a number of important integration schemes are in progress in the Third World. The most important among these are as follows:

(i) *The East African Community*, comprising Kenya, Uganda and Tanzania, which was set up in its present form in 1967, though it draws on a long history of regional co-operation. It is a common market with a common external tariff, though some internal duties (known as 'transfer taxes') are permitted, and factor movement is restricted. Intra-trade increased by 16 per cent between 1967 and 1970, but total trade increased by roughly the same proportion so that intra-trade remained at about 10 per cent.

(ii) *The Central African Customs and Economic Union*, comprising Gabon, Congo (Brazzaville), the Central African Republic and Cameroun, which dates in its present form from 1966, though with a somewhat changed membership. It is a fairly loose grouping, and intra-trade is not great, though it is of some importance as far as Congo is concerned.

(iii) *The Latin American Free Trade Association*, comprising Argentina, Brazil, Chile, Colombia, Bolivia, Ecuador, Mexico, Paraguay, Peru, Uruguay and Venezuela. This, the largest regional integration scheme in the Third

World, with a population of 220 million, was set up in 1960 (Bolivia and Venezuela joined in 1968); a rapid increase in intra-trade has taken place, the volume doubling in the first five years of its existence, although the rate of growth has slowed down since 1965.

(iv) *The Caribbean Free Trade Area*, embracing Jamaica, Barbados, Trinidad and Tobago, Guyana, Antigua, Montserrat, St Kitts, Dominica, St Lucia, Grenada and St Vincent, which was set up in 1968. British Honduras acceded in 1971. A significant increase in the proportion of intra-trade seems to have occurred, especially as far as the more developed partners are concerned. Their exports within CARIFTA increased by 29 per cent in 1969 over 1967, while their exports outside CARIFTA increased by only 11 per cent.

(v) *The Central American Common Market*, comprising Costa Rica, El Salvador, Guatemala and Nicaragua. This dates from 1958, and by 1966 considerable progress had been made both in liberalising internal trade and in harmonising the external tariff. In recent years, however, progress has been slowed by political difficulties and these led to the withdrawal of Honduras in 1971.

Evaluation of these schemes, in particular or in general, would be too lengthy a subject. But in terms of the considerations mentioned earlier, it should be borne in mind that for less developed countries, trade diversion and trade creation may well be relatively unimportant issues in comparison with the dynamic effects of larger markets.

Notes

1. F. Kahnert, P. Richards, E. Stoutjesdijk & P. Thomopoulos *Economic Integration among Developing Countries* (O.E.C.D., Paris, 1969).

2. B. Balassa, *The Theory of Economic Integration* (George Allen & Unwin, London, 1962).

3. J. Viner, *The Customs Union Issue* (Carnegie Endowment for International Peace, New York, 1950).

APPENDIX I

Cambridge University Overseas Studies Committee

Professor E. R. Leach, M.A., Ph.D. (Chairman)	Provost of King's College, and Reader in Social Anthropology
Miss P. M. Deane, M.A.	Newnham College, and University Lecturer in Economics
Mr B. H. Farmer, M.A.	St John's College, Reader in South Asian Geography and Director of the South Asian Studies Centre
Dr J. R. Goody, M. A., Ph.D.	St John's College, and University Lecturer in Social Anthropology
Mr A. T. Grove, M.A.	Downing College, and University Lecturer in Geography
Mr S. G. Harries, M.A.	St Edmund's House, and University Lecturer in Education
Dr P. P. Howell, C.M.G., O.B.E., M.A., D.Phil. (Secretary)	Wolfson College, Director of the Cambridge Course on Development
Professor Sir Joseph Hutchinson, C.M.G, Sc.D., M.A., F.R.S.	St John's College, and Emeritus Drapers Professor of Agriculture
Mr E. Lauterpacht, Q.C., M.A.	Trinity College, and University Lecturer in Law

Dr P. H. Lowings, M.A., Ph.D.	Wolfson College, and University Lecturer in Plant Pathology
Dr A. M. M. McFarquhar, M.A., Ph.D.	Downing College, and University Lecturer in Land Economy
Mr J. S. Morrison, M.A.	President of Wolfson College
Professor E. T. Stokes, M.A., Ph.D.	St Catharine's College, and Smuts Professor of the History of the British Commonwealth
Dr B. van Arkadie, M.A., Ph.D.	Queen's College, and Assistant Director of Development Studies (Economics)
Dr H. W. West, M.A., Ph.D.	Wolfson College, and Assistant Director of Research in Land Economy

APPENDIX II

Conference Officers

Conference Chairman: P. P. Streeten, M.A.; (M.A. *Aberd.*)
Warden of Queen Elizabeth House,
Oxford

Conference Secretary: B. W. Wickham, M.A.

Group Chairmen	*Secretary/Rapporteurs*
H.E. the Hon. H. B. Malmgren	G. A. Hughes
Prof. G. Ohlin	M. G. Kuczinski
Dr F. Pazos	D. Newbery
H.E. the Hon. A. I. Phiri	N. R. Norman
Prof. H. W. Singer	Mrs S. E. Paine
R. N. Wood	M. J. Sharpston

House Secretary
Miss Y. K. Onsorge

Secretariat
Mrs N. Belcham
E. W. Goodered
D. H. Lonsdale
Miss A. Moir

Social Secretaries
Jonathan Lewis
Mrs J. Bartosik
Miss E. Chillingworth
Mrs E. Cowan
Mrs S. Goldman
Mrs B. Hardman
Mrs P. Loftus

APPENDIX III

Conference Members

Australia
K. J. Horton-Stephens — Counsellor, Australian Delegation to O.E.C.D., Paris

Barbados
H. E. Williams — Ministry of Trade, Industry and Commerce

Belgium
J. M. Poswick — Counsellor, Permanent Delegation for International Economic Conferences

G. Tilkin — Minister, Economic Development and World Trade Division, Ministry of Foreign Affairs

Botswana
K. G. Bareki — Ministry of Commerce, Industry and Water Affairs

Canada
R. W. McLaren — Canadian International Development Agency, Ottawa

Commonwealth Secretariat
B. J. L. Fernon — Assistant Director, Economic Division

I. R. Thomas — Chief Research Officer, Economic Division

Egypt
A. Agwah — University of Strathclyde, Glasgow

Appendix III

European Economic Community
J.-L. Lacroix

Principal Administrator, Development Policy and Studies Division

France
Prof. I. Sachs

École Pratique des Hautes Études, University of Paris

General Agreement on Tariffs and Trade
M. G. Mathur

Assistant Director-General, Department of Trade and Development

Dr J. Tumlir

Director, Trade Intelligence Division

Ghana
H. P. Nelson

Principal Secretary, Ministry of Finance and Economic Planning

Hong Kong
P. E. Hutson

General Manager, Hongkong and Shanghai Banking Corporation

India
Dr I. G. Patel

Secretary, Department of Economic Affairs, Ministry of Finance

Inter-American Development Bank
Dr F. Pazos

Economic Adviser

International Bank for Reconstruction and Development
Prof. B. Balassa

Professor of Political Economy Johns Hopkins University Baltimore, Md., and Consultant, Economics Department, I.B.R.D.

Israel
Prof. S. Hirsch

Dean, Leon Recanati Graduate School of Business Administration, University of Tel-Aviv

Japan
Dr H. Fukami

Assistant Professor of Economics, Keio University, Tokyo

M. Yanagisawa

Chief, Research Plans and Co-ordination Office, Institute of Developing Economics Tokyo

Kuwait
A. M. Ali

Director, Kuwait Institute of Economic and Social Planning

Dr M. W. Khouja

Kuwait Fund for Arab Economic Development

Netherlands
Prof. J. F. Glastra van Loon

Rector, Institute of Social Studies, The Hague

Prof. Dr F. van Dam

Head of Policy Planning Bureau for Development Aid, Ministry of Foreign Affairs

Nigeria
Prof. O. Aboyade

Head of Economics Department, University of Ibadan

E. A. Nyon

Chief Planning Officer, Services Division, Federal Ministry of Economic Development and Reconstruction

Dr J. A. Oyelabi

Nigerian Institute of Social and Economic Research, University of Ibadan

Organisation for Economic Co-operation and Development

F. G. Wells — Head of Economic Development Division, Development Assistance Directorate

Pakistan

Z. Azar — Additional Secretary, Ministry of Commerce

Philippines

F. Sarmiento — Commerical Attaché, Philippines Embassy, London

Sri Lanka

L. S. Fernando — Assistant Director, Ministry of Planning and Development

Sudan

F. I. Elmagboul — Assistant Under-Secretary, Ministry of Economics and Trade

Sweden

Prof. S. B. Linder — Stockholm School of Economics

Prof. G. Ohlin — National Institute of Economics, University of Uppsala

Switzerland

Prof. G. Curzon — Professor of International Economics, Graduate Institute of International Studies, Geneva

Dr V. Curzon — Institut Universitaire d'Études Européennes, University of Geneva

F. R. Staehelin — Head of Development Service, Commerce Division of the Federal Department of Public Economy, Berne

Trinidad and Tobago

T. Spencer — Trinidad and Tobago High Commission, London

United Kingdom

Miss P. Ady	St Anne's College, Oxford
The Rt Hon. Lord Balogh	Balliol College, Oxford
R. A. Browning	Head of United Nations Department, Overseas Development Administration, Foreign and Commonwealth Office
Sir Edwin Chapman-Andrews	Director, Massey-Ferguson (Exports) Ltd, London
A. L. Coleby	Bank of England
H. Corbet	Director, Trade Policy Research Centre, London
Prof. J. H. Dunning	Department of Economics, University of Reading
C. Edwards	University of East Anglia
E. Eshag	Wadham College, Oxford
F. A. Haight	Trade Policy Research Centre, London
S. G. Harries	St Edmund's House, Cambridge
Dr J. M. Healey	Director, International Economics Division, Overseas Development Administration, Foreign and Commonwealth Office
H. A. Holley	Lloyds & Bolsa International Bank, London
Dr P. P. Howell	Wolfson College, Cambridge
G. A. Hughes	Christ's College, Cambridge
Prof. Sir Joseph Hutchinson	St John College's, Cambridge
J. B. Ingram	Department of Trade and Industry
T. S. Jenkinson	Imperial Chemical Industries Ltd, London

Prof. H. G. Johnson	Department of Economics, London School of Economics and Political Science, University of London, and University of Chicago; Director of Studies, Trade Policy Research Centre, London
P. H. Johnston	Social Affairs Department, Overseas Development Administration, Foreign and Commonwealth Office
Dr A. R. Jolly	Director, Institute of Development Studies, University of Sussex
Dr T. E. Josling	Department of Economics, London School of Economics and Political Science, University of London
Prof. N. Kaldor	King's College, Cambridge
P. King	Director (Public Relations), Massey-Ferguson (U.K.) Ltd, London
M. Kuczinski	Pembroke College, Cambridge
M. P. Lam	Under-Secretary, Department of Trade and Industry
A. Latham-Koenig	McKinsey & Co. Inc., London
Dr E. R. Leach	Provost, King's College, Cambridge
Miss L. G. Lewis	Barclays Bank International Ltd, London
Dr A. M. M. McFarquhar	Department of Land Economy University of Cambridge

J. Mark	Under-Secretary, Overseas Development Administration, Foreign and Commonwealth Office
P. H. R. Marshall	Head of Financial Policy and Aid Department, Foreign and Commonwealth Office
F. Martin	Unilever Ltd, London
R. T. G. Miles	Head of Information Department, Overseas Development Administration, Foreign and Commonwealth Office
D. Newbery	Churchill College, Cambridge
N. R. Norman	Pembroke College, Cambridge
Mrs S. H. Paine	Girton College, Cambridge
Prof. J. V. Robinson	Newnham College, Cambridge
Prof. R. E. Robinson	Balliol College, Oxford
M. F. G. Scott	Nuffield College, Oxford
M. J. Sharpston	Queen Elizabeth House, Oxford
Prof. H. W. Singer	Institute of Development Studies, University of Sussex
Mrs F. Stewart	Queen Elizabeth House, Oxford
P. Tulloch	Overseas Development Institute, London
Dr B. van Arkadie	Queen's College, Cambridge
P. B. Wells	Commonwealth Development Corporation, London
R. N. Wood	Director of Studies, Overseas Development Institute, London
J. K. Wright	Deputy Director-General, Economic Planning Staff, Overseas Development Administration, Foreign and Commonwealth Office

| C. E. Young | Economic Planning Staff, Overseas Development Administration, Foreign and Commonwealth Office |

United Nations

| Dr S. Aziz | Director, Commodities and Trade Division, F.A.O., Rome |
| S. Dell | Director, New York Office of UNCTAD |

United States of America

G. F. Erb	Overseas Development Council, Washington
H.E. the Hon. H. B. Malmgren	President Nixon's Deputy Special Representative for Trade Negotiations
Prof. G. M. Meier	Department of International Economics, Stanford University
C. Michalopoulos	Agency for International Development
R. Muscat	Agency for International Development

West Germany

| Dr A. Lemper | Director, German Overseas Institute, University of Hamburg |

Zambia

| H.E. the Hon. A. I. Phiri | High Commissioner, London |

APPENDIX IV

Conference Programme

Tuesday, 19 September

12.30–2.00 p.m.	Buffet lunch in the Dining Hall
2.30 p.m.	Opening of the Conference in the School of Pythagoras, St John's College, by the Vice-Chancellor of the University of Cambridge, Prof. W. A. Deer, M.A., Ph.D., F.R.S., Master of Trinity Hall
	Introductory remarks by the Conference Chairman, Mr P. P. Streeten
	Short addresses by Prof. Harry G. Johnson and Dr I. G. Patel
	Short introductions by authors of their papers
4.00 p.m.	Tea break
4.20 p.m.	Introductions continued
6.30 p.m.	Sherry in The Cloisters, Chapel Court, St John's College

7.30 p.m.	Opening dinner. The Chairman of the Cambridge University Overseas Studies Committee, Dr E. R. Leach, M.A., Ph.D., Provost of King's College, welcomes all Conference members on behalf of the Committee

Wednesday, 20 September

9.30–10.45 a.m. ⎫ 11.00 a.m.–12.30 p.m. ⎬ 2.15–5.00 p.m. ⎭	Group discussions
6.00–7.15 p.m.	Reception in the Provost's Lodge, King's College. Dr E. R. Leach receives guests on behalf of the Cambridge University Overseas Studies Committee.
7.30 p.m.	Dinner
8.30 p.m.	Group discussions

Thursday, 21 September

9.30–10.45 a.m. ⎫ 11.00 a.m.–12.30 p.m. ⎬	Group discussions
2.15–5.15 p.m.	Mid-Conference Plenary Session to assess progress
7.30 p.m.	Dinner
8.30 p.m.	Group discussions

Friday, 22 September

9.30–10.45 a.m. ⎫ 11.00 a.m.–12.30 p.m. ⎬ 2.15–5.15 p.m. ⎭	Group discussions

7.30 p.m.	Dinner
8.30 p.m.	Group discussions
Saturday, 23 September 9.30–10.45 a.m. ⎫ 11.00 a.m.–12.30 p.m. ⎭	Group discussions–final sessions
p.m.	Free. Guided tour of Cambridge, *or* visit to Fitzwilliam Museum, *or* visit to Ely.
7.30 p.m.	Dinner
	Social evening
Sunday, 24 September	Day free. Tours to Woburn Abbey, *or* to Audley End, *or* to Norfolk
7.30 p.m.	Dinner
Monday, 25 September 9.30–10.30 a.m.	Free for the study of papers
10.30 a.m.	Coffee in the Under Croft
10.45 a.m.–12.30 p.m.	Final Plenary Session in the School of Pythagoras
2.30–3.45 p.m.	Final Plenary Session continues
3.45 p.m.	Tea in the Under Croft
4.00–5.00 p.m.	Final Plenary Session continues
7.30 p.m.	Dinner

Tuesday, 26 September

10.30 a.m.	Coffee in the Under Croft
10.45 a.m.–12.30 p.m.	Final Plenary Session continues
2.30–3.45 p.m.	Final Plenary Session continues
3.45 p.m.	Tea in the Under Croft
4.00–5.00 p.m.	Final Plenary Session and Conference Chairman's final assessment
6.00–7.15 p.m.	Government reception in the Combination Room, The Old Schools. Host: The Baroness Tweedsmuir of Belhelvie, Minister of State at the Foreign and Commonwealth Office
7.30 p.m.	Closing dinner

Wednesday, 27 September

a.m.	Conference disperses

Index of Persons

Index of Subjects

population, heavy pressure of in poor
countries, 16, 89
Portugal's special experience, 194–6
poverty curtain, 11, 101
poverty, relief of, 28
power, inequality of, 8
preferences, general system of, 205–10
preferential trade area defined, 344
Preferential Trading Agreements, 287
price increases, expected (in 1980), 271
Principles of Political Economy (Mill),
23
printing money, 41
private ownership, 100
processes, components and assembly,
19
product cycle theory, 302
production, structure of, 40
products, demand of, 18
protection: arguments for, 12–13;
differences in structure of, 171–2;
in developed countries, 32, 341–2;
measures in international trade,
329–34; rate, effective, 339–40

quality of life, as an economic commodity, 51–2
quantitative restrictions in manufacture negotiations, 292–6, 334–5
quota systems, 181

regional groupings and developing
countries, 198–214
regional markets over large areas, 97
regional trading blocs in international
trade, 343–51
*Remaking the International Monetary
System* (Machlup), 22
research-intensive sector of manufacturing, 288, 310
rice, subsidised sales of, 204
Rio Agreement, 117
rural poverty in underdeveloped
countries, 33, 71, 108

safeguards in manufacture negotiations, 292–6
savings: and investment, 91; development's effect on, 39, 41; gap, 55
second-generation problems in development, 14–17, 106
sectoral approach to tariffs, 290
Singapore, 6, 63

skills, human, concentrated in luxury
goods sector, 54
Smithsonian Declaration, 127, 276
Special Drawing Rights (S.D.R.s),
117
Standard International Trade Classifications (S.I.T.C.), 252–3, 323–4
standard of living, different life-
styles, 13, 100, 262–3
sub-regional trading areas, 97, 99
subsidies, 134, 182–3; and developing
countries, 204; for exports, 181; to
domestic production, 335–6
supply, changes expected (in 1980),
270
supply-orientated barriers, 304
supranational union defined, 344

Taiwan-Korea strategy, 18, 263
tariff: cuts, 292–3; harmonisation,
notion of, 289; on agricultural
products, 109; on industrial products, 31; structure, 4, 80–1, 86–7,
94, 125, 145, 181–3, 205–10, 282,
288–92, 329–31
technological gap theory, 302
technology: and trade, 231–58; definition of, 236–41; force of, 9
tourism, an alternative to exporting
goods, 47
trade: and developing countries, 246–
256; and development, 36, 101; and
national policies, 268–72; and
technology, 231–58; as an engine
of growth, 36–7, 51, 68; terms of,
326; *see also* international trade;
world trade
trade barriers, 29
trade creation, 145–6, 150–6, 223–5,
344–5
trade diversion, 217–23, 225–9, 344–5
trade expansion, 146–50
trade figures for regional integration
(1960–70), 147
trade flows in the developing countries, 300–18
trade growth (1961–71), 323
trade integration, 145–73, 216–29
trade liberalisation, 14–15, 43–8, 128,
325–7, 329
trade negotiations (manufacturers),
279–97
trade outlook (1970s), 21–2